WOMEN AS WARTIME RAPISTS

PERSPECTIVES ON POLITICAL VIOLENCE

General Editors: Laura Sjoberg and Cameron G. Thies

Women as Wartime Rapists: Beyond Sensation and Stereotyping
Laura Sjoberg

Women as Wartime Rapists

Beyond Sensation and Stereotyping

Laura Sjoberg

NEW YORK UNIVERSITY PRESS
New York

NEW YORK UNIVERSITY PRESS
New York
www.nyupress.org

References to Internet websites (URLs) were accurate at the time of writing. Neither the author nor New York University Press is responsible for URLs that may have expired or changed since the manuscript was prepared.

ISBN: 978-0-8147-2927-4 (hardback)
ISBN: 978-0-8147-7140-2 (paperback)

For Library of Congress Cataloging-in-Publication data, please contact the Library of Congress.

New York University Press books are printed on acid-free paper, and their binding materials are chosen for strength and durability. We strive to use environmentally responsible suppliers and materials to the greatest extent possible in publishing our books.

Manufactured in the United States of America

10 9 8 7 6 5 4 3 2 1

Also available as an ebook

For Caron Gentry

who makes this endeavor worth it to me

CONTENTS

ACKNOWLEDGMENTS

This book was an impulsive idea that took a long time to produce. In its production, I relied heavily on the institutional support of the University of Florida, including but not limited to a Humanities Scholarship Enhancement grant that helped me find the time and the resources to do its empirical research. I was lucky enough to have the opportunity to present parts of this book at the annual meetings of the American Political Science Association, the International Studies Association, the International Studies Association-Northeast, and the International Studies Association-West. These audiences, as well as audiences at invited talks at the United States Institute of Peace, Lancaster University, Virginia State University, and the University of Southern California, helped formulate the ideas in this book. Some of my thinking about gendered orders in global politics could not have been clarified without my co-participants in the Hierarchy workshop at the University of California, San Diego, in May 2014. Colleagues' feedback on parts of and early drafts of this project helped to give it direction, empirically and theoretically.

In addition, a number of people have provided significant research support for this project. Ruchan Kaya did some of the early news research. Alex Dehelean's thorough empirical work is reflected in a number of places throughout the final text. Michelle Ascunsion's careful reading of the first draft of this book was helpful, and caught a number of errors. Ilene Kalish and Caelyn Cobb, my editors (for the book and for the series in which it has found its home), have been patient and supportive over the (way too many) years. More than a decade later, I still rely heavily on the sage advice and careful reading of my former dissertation advisor, Ann Tickner. This project was inspired by, and continues to be in dialogue with, my work with Caron Gentry. Caron's correspondence, co-authorship, and friendship over the years has been not only an intellectual stimulus, but one of the most fulfilling parts of this career for me.

I am also grateful to a number of scholars who gave selflessly of their time in order to read parts of this book—Lauren Wilcox, Jennifer Lobasz, Sandra McEvoy, Spike Peterson, Joyce Kaufmann, Kristen Williams, Cynthia Enloe, and Dara Kay Cohen. My students—graduate and undergraduate—helped me work through some of the more difficult theoretical issues in this book. Several of my graduate and undergraduate students helped at various points where I was stuck in the analysis of this book, including but not limited to Jon Whooley, Anna Weissman, Catherine Jean, and Christian Chessman. Rachel Feldman read and edited the first full draft of this book like a pro. On a flight between Amsterdam and Atlanta, then-University of Alabama student Christina Kozuh expanded my thinking about the book's subject matter. Both of my parents actually read a full draft of this book cover to cover and provided feedback—I do not have words to express my gratitude for that. As I was reading the proofs of this book, I lost my father. I will always treasure his involvement with this book. One of the reviewers of the manuscript carefully marked up a full copy with suggestions and queries. It was amazing, and I am humbled and grateful.

Much of this book was written sitting next to (and with the support of) my Chihuahuas. Gizmo struggled with heart problems as I read and wrote heart-wrenching stories. April's refusal to get excited *about anything* was a steady contrast to my moodiness as I wrote. Max's combined cuddliness and viciousness constantly reminded me that no story is as simple as it seems. Together, they make my work possible, peaceful, and enjoyable.

In most of the book acknowledgements I have written, I have told a story about how someone treating me or what I do poorly has inspired the work on a book project. There has certainly been a fair amount of that in the six years this book has been an idea and in progress. Still, as I finished revising it, it was the support of the people who believe in me and what I do that was most important to me. I am forever indebted to friends in the field and outside who care deeply, tolerate imperfection, and assume the best rather than the worst (or, preferably, do not assume at all).

Introduction

The Importance of Women Wartime Rapists

Very few women are wartime rapists. Very few women issue commands to commit sexual violence. Very few women play a role in making war plans that feature intentional sexual violation of other women. Very few women sexually violate other women as they supervise prisons, staff refugee camps, participate in military conflicts, serve on military police forces, or participate in insurgent violence. Very few women advocate strategies of forced impregnation as a method of ethnic cleansing. Very few women force other women to have abortions or miscarriages as they torture them. Very few women skin other women alive and use their tattoos to decorate furniture. Very few women sell women prisoners of war into sexual slavery. Very few women are genocidal rapists. This book is about those very few women—their crimes, their meanings, and the political and legal ramifications of their actions.

It is difficult to write a book about those very few women, though, given that they are frequently invisible, or, when visible, are often sensationalized. Take, for example, the Wikipedia entry on "war rape."[1] All eight uses of the word "female" are characterizations of rape *victims*, even though one describes female combatants as victims. One hundred twenty-nine of the 130 uses of the word "women" in the text refer to them as the victims of wartime and genocidal rape. While this entry recognizes that war rape sometimes has male victims, the primary role of men in the Wikipedia article is as perpetrators. Phrases that describe war rape as "the spiritual bonding of men at arms" and suggest that "men who rape are ordinary Joes," and define the act as "committed by men against women" are repeated throughout the article, and suggest that war rape is an act where men are the perpetrators, whoever the victims are. The Wikipedia article on genocidal rape replicates these assumptions.[2]

I do not mean to hold Wikipedia up as an example of the most in-depth knowledge on the subject of who wartime and genocidal rapists are, or what wartime or genocidal rape is. Instead, I mean to point out that a general description often used for popular consumption *editable by literally everyone* which has many of the key details of the definition of, occurrence of, and history of wartime rape makes no mention of the existence or possibility of female perpetrators. This omission occurs in the great majority of newspaper articles, websites, human rights reports, policy briefs, and scholarly articles that address sexual violence in war and genocide.

Discussions of wartime sexual violence that do mention women perpetrators are few and far between, and many of them sensationalize those women. For example, Ilse Koch was married to Nazi commandant Karl Koch, who headed Buchenwald concentration camp during World War II. Ilse became a guard at Buchenwald. The available evidence suggests that Koch participated in acts of torture and terror in her time at Buchenwald. Compared to other women alleged to have committed wartime sexual violence, Ilse Koch's actions are mentioned in a relatively high number of histories and analyses. Tales of her most well-known transgressions recount her collecting the tattooed skin of women prisoners as home decorations, crafting lampshades and other household goods from the skin of Buchenwald's victims.[3] Even without that accusation (which has been contested), Koch was known around Buchenwald as cruel and sadistic in her behavior towards prisoners. She is alleged to have been both physically and secxually abusive towards them.[4] Her involvement in the torture of female prisoners was part of the reason that she was sentenced to life imprisonment at the end of the war.

Often characterized as a "nymphomaniac," Ilse Koch has been held responsible for the deaths of more than forty prisoners based on her collection of tattooed human skin.[5] Her story was widely reported because "it symbolized the fundamental humiliation of the individual in the concentration camps—particularly when the instigator was a woman."[6] Accounts of Koch call her "the bitch of Buchenwald" and contend that she "sexually tortured" inmates in the concentration camp to keep her husband in "sexual dependence."[7] There were rumors both that she had sexual affairs with officers and that she sexually abused prisoners.. Though early accounts focused on her collection of human skin, later stories paid more attention to her sexuality and to her participation in abuse. Her trial "cited an image of women or female perpetrators that placed the commandant's wife outside human society," as an "animal" or "dehumanized creature"—a "diabolical female" with "unbridled sexuality."[8] As historian Alexandra Przyrembel explains:

> From the case of Ilse Koch there emerged an image of a female National Socialist perpetrator who was criminal, acted out of her own (also sexual) motives, and—unlike the majority of National Socialist perpetrators— could not claim that she had only been acting under superior orders. . . . Perhaps the power of the "image of Ilse Koch" is responsible for the tendency . . . to view female perpetrators in the concentration camps as at most a "remarkably brutal and power obsessed" minority among women.[9]

While this book is about women like Ilse Koch, it looks to avoid what Przyrembel calls the "image of Ilse Koch"—the differentiation and sensationalization of (sexually) violent women into stereotypes of the dangers of femininity gone awry.[10] These two moves, I argue, police gender lines and sustain societal structures of gender inequality.

Coverage like "the image of Ilse Koch" and discussions that omit the possibility and existence of women perpetrators of sexual violence in war and conflict share a number of misconceptions about the nature of women, of gender, and the nature of sexual violence. This introduction discusses those common misconceptions, and how together they render women perpetrators either invisible or sensationalized.

Common Misconceptions about (the Study of) Sexually Violent Women in Global Politics

Misconception #1: The Category of "Woman" Is Easily Discernible, and It Is Possible to Definitively Tell Who Is in That Category and Who Is Outside of It

One element that descriptions of wartime rape that see only men as the perpetrators and descriptions that sensationalize women perpetrators share is the idea that there are people who are men and people who are women, and all people fit into those categories neatly. This is one of the oldest dichotomies in human history. Though obvious exceptions exist, from Dionysus in Greek mythology[11] to India's *hijras*,[12] binary gender categories have been remarkably consistent across time, place, and culture in human social and political relations. The idea that people are either male or female can be found in almost every legal structure in present-day global politics: one must check a "gender" box on immigration forms passing through airports most places in the world; court records identify victims, perpetrators, and witnesses by their "biological sex" and date of birth; combatants are classified as either male or female by militaries, paramilitaries, and terrorist organizations alike.[13] All of these uses of "biological sex" categories assume that all people fall into one of those two categories. In fact, until very recently, doctors who delivered babies who did not fit neatly into one of the two categories often told parents that their babies had "cosmetic" defects in their genital areas that were "corrected" in post-delivery cleanup, rather than identifying those babies as the genetically accurate "intersex."[14] There are a number of different combinations of "sex" chromosomes that produce people of a number of different "biological sexes"—not two, but many.[15] In fact, about one in a thousand people is some form of "intersex" in terms of chromosomal configuration and the physical manifestations of that chromosomal configuration.[16]

So, in common language, what does that mean? It means that the categories of "women" and "men" cannot be understood as mapped onto the (assumed) two common sex chromosomal configurations without regard to the variations that do not match those two dominant categories. At the very least, "biological sex" is a spectrum rather than a dichotomy.[17] More likely, the dichotomized notion of "biological sex" with "male" at one extreme and "female" at another extreme is incoherent—rippled by not only intersex people, but by trans* or genderqueer people, who identify as either/or and/or neither/nor.[18] Therefore, the line between people who are women and people who are men is not as clear as inherited accounts make it seem, and the idea that perpetrators are "men" and victims are "women" is oversimplified by definition. This oversimplification would endure even were it clear that people have essential characteristics in common based on their membership in sex categories. That assumption, though, referred to in the feminist literature as "gender essentialism," is the second misconception necessary to the contemporary invisibility, or sensationalism, of women who commit sex-based crimes in war and conflict.[19]

Misconception #2: Assuming It Is Possible to Parse the Category of "Woman," the People in It Necessarily Have More in Common than Simple Membership in the Category

If many accounts of sexual violence in war and conflict rely on the stability of the categories of "male" and "female," that reliance is based on the assumption that those distinctions are meaningful not only in a biological sense but in a social one. A significant amount of scholarship on sex and gender (generally and in the study of global politics) calls that understanding into question, however.[20] It suggests that "sex" and "gender" refer to different things that are often lumped into one. The simplest form of the sex/gender distinctions refer to "sex" as the biological and/or chromosomal characteristics that people have which give them the sex organs and chemical compositions to be understood as biologically male, female, either/or, or neither/nor.[21] In this understanding, gender is related, but distinguishable. "Gender" is the set of social expectations associated with the perceived biological sex of a person— where people understood to be "men" are expected to display traits associated with masculinity, and people understood to be "women" are expected to display traits associated with femininity. In other words, gender is the imputation of essential characteristics to people because they are (perceived to be) of a particular biological sex.[22]

Gendered expectations of people who are understood to be male include toughness, autonomy, aggression, rationality, confidence, and (hetero)sexuality.[23] These traits are understood by many if not most people to be a part of "masculinity."[24] Gender expectations of people understood to be women include sensitivity, (inter)dependence, passivity, emotionality, quietness, innocence, grace, caring, and purity.[25] These traits are often understood as part of "femininity." Because men are expected to be masculine and women are expected to be feminine, some stereotypical assumptions are frequently made about people on the basis of their biological sex. Some of these expectations are present in everyday social and political discourses. For example, in contemporary

Western culture, men are often expected to like sports, where women are expected to be interested in and well suited for care labor, including but not limited to motherhood. In the same circles, aggressive and/or dominant men are often understood to be fulfilling expectations about who they are and who they ought to be, while aggressive and/or dominant women are understood to be falling outside of normal behavior for women.[26] Women are often seen as in need of protection or even special treatment (e.g., the common suggestion that it is problematic for men and boys to "hit a girl"), where men are seen as responsible for providing that protection.[27]

These day-to-day stereotypes of what "men" and "women" are capable of and/or expected to do sometimes translate into a less public but still well-understood conventional wisdom about men's and women's places in interstate relations and global politics.[28] For example, soldiering is traditionally understood to be men's labor, and the security arena understood to be the purview of men and masculinity.[29] Even militaries that come to include women often do so expecting them both to maintain their femininity and to meet or exceed the standards of masculinity that are set for men in militaries.[30] Men are expected to be responsible for heavy labor in job markets (like construction) and women are expected to do care (like housekeeping) or home-based (like sewing) labor.[31] These expectations come to divide where men are expected to be in global politics, and where women are expected to be. Cynthia Enloe suggests, adding on to the traditional feminist criticism that finds it problematic that women are expected to be in the private sphere and men are expected to be in the public sphere, that this public/private dichotomy also manifests in global politics.[32] She provides evidence that, in global politics, men are expected to be in the international sphere (as soldiers, politicians, diplomats, and businessmen) and women are expected to remain in the private sphere (as care workers, wives, mothers, and house workers).[33]

These assumptions, however, do not bear themselves out in the practice of everyday social and political life, much less in the global sphere. People understood to be women often have characteristics associated with masculinity, and people understood to be men often have characteristics associated with femininity.[34] Many people combine traits associated with masculinity and femininity, and many versions and degrees of masculinities and femininities exist in the world. This hybridity is not the result of some merging or combination of manhood and womanhood, but rather a signifier of the false nature of the dichotomy from the start. Rather than maleness and femaleness translating into masculinity and femininity "naturally" or as a result of biology, gender can be understood as a social construction.[35] By that, I mean that men/masculinity and women/femininity are related by discourse, social expectation, social constraint, and social power rather than by something fundamental and essential that they have in common. This means that the association of men and women with essential traits related to those categories is fundamentally problematic.

This association can be seen as gendering—associating sex and gender. Though there is not one universal "gendering," genderings—sets "of discourses which can set, change, enforce, and represent meaning"[36]—can be found in almost every part of global politics. These socially constituted differences are intersubjective, and constantly evolve with intentional manipulation, changing social norms, and cultural context. In this way, gender relations are not power relations that just happen between men and women (or even between men and men or women and women). They are, instead, a complicated matrix of power relations, often (falsely) reduced to expectations about what men do and what women do.

This book argues that the suggestion that men are the (only) perpetrators of sexual violence in war and conflict and that women are (exclusively) the victims of such violence is yet another essentialist dividing line—where there is something that men have in common as a class (that they do not share with women) that makes them capable of the perpetration of such violence, and there is something that women have in common as a class (that they do not share with men) that makes them both incapable of the perpetration of such violence and likely to be its victims. When women are recognized as having perpetrated such violence, both those women and their violence, like that of Ilse Koch discussed above, are often framed as outside of the normal purview of femininity—there is something *wrong* not only with those women but with their femininity.[37] I argue that this is related to the third common misconception necessary to construct current media, scholarly, and legal frames about sexual violence in war and conflict—that women are more peaceful than men.

Misconception #3: Women Are More Peaceful than Men, and Do Not Commit (Political and Sexual) Violence

The assumption that women are more peaceful than men is almost as old as, and almost as prevalent as, the assumption that the categories of "man" and "woman" are both valid and socially meaningful. For example, the words "woman," "women," or "female" can be found in Thucydides's *A History of the Peloponnesian War* in fifteen different places.[38] In those appearances, the most common role for women is, with children, being taken captive by the victor when they are seen as belonging to the vanquished. Other roles that women play are supportive: they provide men with the supplies to fight, encourage them to be brave, and take care of them when they are injured. Women's care labor earns them men's protection, and it is clearly not acceptable for men to attack women and children.[39]

The story in *A History of the Peloponnesian War* is unique, but the role that women play in it is far from unique. In accounts of war from Thucydides to Grotius, and from Sun Tzu to George W. Bush, women are wars' innocent, peaceful constitutive others—men fight wars to protect women, who are innocent of the cause and the fighting of the wars. Nearly thirty years ago, Jean Elshtain chronicled the ways that both women and men are often pigeonholed by gender ideal-typical expectations about the ways that people of their sex behave in war and conflict.[40] She saw that the stereotype of "just warriors" is often applied to men, under which they are expected on the basis of their manliness to fulfill a duty to protect women and defend righteous causes. Women, on the other hand, are often expected to behave as "beautiful souls," in need of protection and justifying the defense of the state or nation. Still, even women who fulfill expectations of being gender-stereotyped "beautiful souls" to some degree or another often do not receive the promised protection or safety from war—instead, they are often endangered by it. For this reason, feminist scholars have talked about gender-stereotyped roles in war and conflict as a part of a "protection racket"[41] where the chivalric pretension to protection of women underpins war-justifying logic but is not actualized in war fighting.

It is not only a long history of war narratives that suggest women are more peaceful than men, but sometimes women (and even feminists) themselves. In fact, in International Relations (IR) scholarship, a significant amount of the first generation of work on gender and global politics emphasized women's place as outside of war and conflict, peaceful themselves and in opposition to men's wars.[42] This scholarship reflected a number of women's peace movements in the global political arena, including but not limited to the Greenham Women's Common, the Women's International League for Peace and Freedom, and Women in Black.[43]

People who see women as more peaceful than men suggest different reasons why, but all of their reasons are based on the idea that women have something essential in common. Some accounts trace women's peacefulness to women's physical weakness—because women are smaller and daintier than men, they are less able to protect themselves.[44] Women's inability to protect themselves made them conflict averse by default, which evolved into a personal and political commitment to peace.[45] Other accounts relate women's peacefulness to their innocence—women are perceived as more pure than men, without the need to get their proverbial hands dirty in the business of politics and war.[46] In these stories, women have the privileged position of not having to deal with war, and can therefore preserve their purity while men fight for, and over, them and their protection.[47] Still other accounts relate women's peacefulness to motherhood, suggesting that the natural bond between women and their children makes women more nurturing, which leads them to be more peaceful.[48] In this view, women see how fragile and vulnerable children are, and come to love and care for their children.[49] They then see other people (whether friend or enemy) as someone else's children, and have a sense of compassion that only motherhood can bring.[50]

All of these stories, however flattering to women, share the preceding misconception: that there is something essential about women *as women* that they have in common. The women whose stories line the pages of this book, though, are a stunning counterexample to the particular gender essentialism that women are more peaceful than men. Women who perpetrate, participate in, command, and support sexual violence in war and conflict are anything but the passive, innocent stereotype of a woman that the descriptions of women as more peaceful than men support. It is possible to suggest (as many do) that the few women who commit sex crimes during war and con-flict are anomalies—nonfeminine women, abused women, or exam-ples of femininity gone wrong, while most "real" or "regular" women fit (more or less) into the traditional notion of femininity.[51] Recent work, however, suggests that this account is trying to put the square peg of "women" into the round hole of "femininity," where they do not actually fit.[52] This work suggests that women are *as capable as men*, not only in areas where positive personal, educational, or ca-reer opportunity are involved, but also in the areas of negative, vio-lent, and/or criminal behavior. Those "women" (like "men") live in a gendered world, with gendered expectations, gendered opportunity structures, and gendered power—so they (like "men") find them-selves constrained by gender in their choices and opportunities.[53] These constraints, though, are social, rather than natural, biological, or fundamental.

To say that gendered expectations are social constructions and so-cial constraints is *not to say* that they are easy to change, to get around, or to destroy. Gendered expectations, especially gendered expectations about men's violence and women's non-violence, are long-standing and sticky. Social constructions are no less a part of everyday life because they are socially constructed. At the same time, exceptions to and transgressions against the gendered social expectation that women are peaceful demonstrate both that women are not more peaceful than men, and that the social norm that says they are is a problematic over-simplification. It is an oversimplification, however, that is necessary to the illusion that women cannot, and do not, commit sex-based war crimes, and that the women who do are anomalous. As Lori Girshick explains, referring to the LGBTQ community in the United States, "woman-to-woman sexual violence is an invisible form of sexual vio-lation because of our denial that women are sexual perpetrators."[54] In this context, while some "take comfort in statistics showing how rare woman-on-woman assault is,"[55] others see it as important to un-derstand, even though it is rare. However, attempts to understand women's sexual violence in war and conflict often make the same es-sentialist mistakes of accounts of wartime sexual violence that ignore women perpetrators—understanding women's behavior as somehow fundamentally different than men's.

Misconception #4: When Women Commit (Political and Sexual)
Violence, They Do So for Different Reasons than Men Do, and Those
Differences Are Theoretically and Empirically Interesting to Study

Even when news sources, blogs, scholarly articles, and policy analyses do acknowledge that women commit sexual violence in war and conflict, they often start with the assumption that women who commit violence are motivated by different forces than men, and that their violence is somehow quantitatively and qualitatively different from similar acts of violence committed by male counterparts. In *Mothers, Monsters, Whores*,[56] Caron Gentry and I argued that that women's violence in global politics is often dealt with in the media in ways that are sex-specific to women perpetrators. We called these the mother, monster, and whore narratives.[57] The mother narratives characterize women being mothers as fundamental to how they come to participate in violence, either as violent mothers who nurture violent men or as they seek revenge for the loss of their families and maternal identities. The second set of narratives we identified are the monster narratives. These stories of women's motivations for engaging in violence frame female perpetrators as psychologically disturbed persons, harder to control and more monstrous than men who might commit similar acts or be involved in similar organizations. In these accounts, the monstrosity of politically violent women is unique because its source is the sort of irrational anger that only women are seen to be capable of, or the insanity that failing at other aspects of femininity can inspire. The third set of narratives are the whore narratives. In the whore narratives, women's violence is either caused by erotomania/sexual obsession or erotic dysfunction/the inability to satisfy men. Other work has followed up on, complicated, and critiqued this typology, but recognized the existence of each of the narratives.[58]

These three narratives tell different stories but share several things. First, they separate the question of why women commit political violence from the question of why men do so (or even why people generally do so). Second, they distinguish "broken" women who might commit political violence from a stereotypical real or normal woman, who continues to be, as women have always been assumed to be, more peaceful and less physically and emotionally capable of violence than her male counterparts. Third, despite the strong association between normal women and peacefulness, these stories associate violent women's violence with excess, fracture, or frustration specific to femininities.

This is all the more true in the cases of violence among women in this book. If women's perpetration of political violence generally is framed as unnatural, then women's perpetration of sexual violence, especially against other women, seems basically impossible to imagine. It is assumed that, however little all women share, they do (or at least ought) share an understanding of how sexual violence is a key to gender subordination, and therefore resist perpetrating it. If war rape is "an assault against the female gender, violating her body and its reproductive capabilities as a 'weapon of war,'"[59] then it must be men who are violating "the female gender" as a whole.[60] This is compounded by women's presumed interest in women's emancipation. In other words, if rape is gender subordination, female rapists are people who are *both* negatively impacted by gender subordination *and* perpetuating it. This is not unprecedented— for example, some Jews were complicit in the Holocaust, and some Tutsis killed in the Rwandan genocide.[61] Still, for some reason, many people are more unsettled when the oppression in which the oppressed are complicit is sexual violence. Many assume that women *would not* and *cannot* rape, much less commit those crimes in war and/or genocide.

It may be for these reasons that the conventional wisdom fails to group women perpetrators of sexual violence with their male counterparts. With Wight and Myers, I see that a violent woman's gender is "the primary explanation or mitigating factor offered up in any attempt to understand her crime."[62] People with a political interest in maintaining and reifying (part or all of) traditional gender roles tend to exhibit a blindness to women's sexual violence in war and conflict. As a result, stories of women's wartime sexual violence are either silenced, or produced and reproduced in ways that deny women's agency in violence, and characterize women who do commit violence as singular or aberrant.[63] Accounts of women's violence "become systems of signification which are productive (or reproductive) of their subject women" specifically and women more generally.[64] If violent women are differentiated from an ideal understanding of what is expected of *women as women*, then no further accounting for their violence is necessary, and the (false) conception that women are or could be *fundamentally* peaceful or nonviolent does not require interrogation.

I argue that an interest in maintaining that ideal notion of womanhood is a key reason that women's motivations for committing political violence are often analyzed differently than men's motivations. In addition to distinctions between women's commission of war crimes and men's similar behaviors, politically violent women are themselves characterized as distinct from normal or real women. "Real" or "normal" women are seen as incapable of committing violence generally and the sexual violation of women specifically. "Real" women are peaceful, conservative, virtuous, and restrained—feminine; violent women ignore those boundaries of womanhood."[65] Because the stories of sexually violent women conflict with the ideal-typical notion of peaceful femininity, violent women fit uneasily (if at all) in political discourse. Their decisions to engage in political violence are rarely framed as voluntarily taken, and, when they are, they, by definition, need different explanatory theories than men's violence, which is more normalized.

Sexually violent women, though, are "women" as much as any other "women" are women—and defining femininity as nonviolent does not make it that way. They commit sexual violence in war and conflict, as much as anyone does—and defining sexual violence in war and conflict as something women do not do does not change that. In this book, I argue that sexually violent women, like sexually violent men, cannot be accounted for by or disaggregated by the "biological sex" of the body of the perpetrator. While deconstructing these categories will be a majority of the work of this book, it is important to recognize (and critique) some of the costs associated with deconstructing traditional notions of the sex of perpetrators of sexual war crimes.

Misconception #5: If Women Are the Perpetrators of (Political and Sexual) Violence in War and Conflict, It Is No Longer Important to Look at Women as Victims, or at the Gendered Impacts of War and Conflict

One common result of recognizing that women commit any sort of proscribed or illegal violence in global politics is the erasure of the gendered nature of victimization in conflict. A significant portion of the few stories that *are* told of women's conflict sexual violence characterize it as *reverse gender subordination*—where women are by definition no longer the victims when they become perpetrators.[66] Barbara Ehrenreich's discussion of the prison abuse at Abu Ghraib is an example of such a discourse—she argues that women committing sexual violence demonstrates the ultimate success of (and current unnecessity of) the feminist movement, since women who can abuse women are now by definition equal to men and therefore not in need of whatever the feminist movement had to offer.[67] In other words, some argue female war criminals show that women's unequal and sex-specific victimization in war is over—that women cannot both be victims of conflict violence (as a class) and perpetrators (as individuals or as a group)—it has to be one or the other.[68]

This might be because recognizing women perpetrators distorts frames that characterize sexual violence in war and conflict as a crime that men commit against women. But women *have* participated in, encouraged, and led such violence. This often seems paradoxical to observers looking to make sense of gender subordination, both generally and in war and conflict. If wartime rape is an ultimate site of women's marginalization, why do women subordinate women?

The answers to these questions, I argue, are both uncomfortable and straightforward. While gendered orders in the world often position women differently than men, we often mistake that difference in positioning for a difference in nature. While similarly positioned people often feel empathy or solidarity with those who suffer the same plight, we often mistake that as a natural solidarity or community among women. As a result, we expect women who have experienced gender subordination to be less likely to enact gender subordination. There are a number of flaws with this logic, though. The first, discussed above, is that the assumption that women have something in common because they are women is problematic on a variety of levels. The second is that it assumes that men's likelihood to subordinate women on the basis of gender comes from a place where those men are not subordinated on the basis of gender. But, as a significant amount of feminist scholarship has noted, men are often subordinated on the basis of gender, and/or subject to expectations of gendered power structures that are at odds with their personal sense of desire and/or identity.[69]

Instead, I suggest that "men," "women," and people who fall into either/or or neither/nor category *all* live in a world of gendered structures and gendered expectations that shape what opportunities they have, what they are expected to do, and how their choices are reacted to in the public sphere. People are not obligated to and do not always act within the expectations of those gendered structures. Gender subordination is not something that *men* exclusively do to *women*, but rather something any people can do to any people on the basis of gender-based expectations. Who is doing the perpetrating, then, does not change the nature of an act of gender subordination—either for the perpetrator or (most importantly) for the victim. I contend that women's (individual or group) participation as perpetrators of sexual violence does not necessarily mean that women (individually or as a class) are not victimized disproportionately in war and genocide or by that sexual violence. Instead, many of the women in this book are sexually victimizing and subordinating other women on the basis of gender, while they themselves live in and experience a highly gender-hierarchical world.

It is, then, worth engaging thinking about what it means to characterize women as victimized on the basis of gender in war and conflict. This book builds on the argument that the *practices* and *impacts* of genocide, war, and conflict are gendered along many axes.[70] War and conflict often affect people positioned as women differently than they affect people positioned as men in a number of ways.[71] Work, and income, are often distributed along what scholars of gender have identified as "gendered divisions of labor," which are often exacerbated during war and conflict, leaving "women" operating with more responsibilities and less resources.[72] People often understood as women are assumed to be protected from wars (given their status as by-definition civilians), regardless of whether or not protection is provided. This discursive double bind means that, in practice, women are often the majority of wars' civilian victims, and experience war with sexualized divisions of labor.[73] For people positioned as women, war and conflict often end decades after the shooting stops—where the lasting effects of infrastructural damage, food and health-care deprivation, social structure breakdown, and governance destruction and reconstruction often influence their lives in a continuing way, particularly at home where the influence is the least visible.[74] Often, women's experiences of sexual violence in war and conflict also continue long after the shooting stops—in the form of social stigma, rejection by family, long-term internal injuries, and children born as a product of wartime rape.[75]

Women are not the only ones who experience genocide, war, and conflict as gendered. Often, people understood to be men are expected to fight in wars regardless of their personal preferences.[76] That is because idealized masculinities are often associated with soldiering, where men achieve manliness, and membership in social and political communities, through the chivalry associated with providing protection (and glory) to their nation (and their women) by making and fighting in wars. This call to service as "just warriors" or citizen-soldiers has affected many otherwise unwilling soldiers, and led to a significant amount of death and destruction in war and conflict.[77]

Feminist scholars have argued that these gendered roles in war and conflict, and their resultant gendered impacts, are not incidental or coincidental, but a necessary element of the ways that wars and conflicts are framed, justified, and performed.[78] This argument suggests that the "visible" gendered violence of war and conflict (for example, sexual violence committed against women by men) is a symptom of an even larger problem of the gendered nature of war and conflict.[79] This orientation is crucial to understanding why characterizations of sexual violence in war and conflict as incidental or coincidental are not only inaccurate but problematic, theoretically and practically.

Misconception #6: Sexual Violence in War and Conflict Is Incidental or Coincidental, Not a Common, Deliberate, and Strategic Weapon of War

Discussion of sexual violence in war and conflict that either assumes away women perpetrators or sensationalizes them often, though not always, shares the assumption that sexual violence is an incidental or coincidental part of war. Much of the policy and jurisprudential activism around sexual violence in war and conflict suggests that war and the rape that happens during it are separable—that it is possible to fight wars and conflicts paying attention to *jus in bello* rules, including, but often not limited to, restraint from sexual violence.[80] This assumption has led many to study the variation in sexual violence in war and conflict, looking for commonalities among conflicts where sexual violence is higher or lower.[81] While these researchers find a number of conflicts in which wartime sexual violence is low, neither these nor any other identifiable researchers claim that wars *without* gendered and/or sexual violence have occurred.[82]

Instead, sexual violence *in war* is as old as war itself. During wars, rape "becomes a metaphor for national humiliation . . . as well as a tactic of war used to symbolically prove the superiority of one's national group."[83] The use of this tactic is, according to the feminist literature, overdetermined. War *is* sexual violence, and therefore it is not surprising but expected that it includes sexual violence.[84] Soldiers who fight in wars are often motivated to fight using both gendered and sexually charged language (and related stereotypes), which suggests that the manliness of soldiers is proved by the degree to which they are able to feminize other soldiers—either directly or by taking dominion over "their" women.[85]

The number of conflicts in which war rape has been prevalent, when collected, is stunning. Feminist political theorist Robin May Schott finds references in ancient texts from Homer's *Iliad* to the Christian Bible, and recounts particularly brutal instances of war rape in World War II, the former Yugoslavia, the Rwandan genocide, and the Democratic Republic of Congo.[86] Before these extreme examples were recognized, sexual violence in war and conflict had "been characterized by physical invisibility—in the double sense that civilian casualties are often invisible in official casualty statistics and in the sense that rape does not always leave visible signs on the bodies of victims."[87] Yet "organized rape has been an integral aspect of war for a long time."[88]

Although sexual violence has been a weapon of war throughout history, only recently has it been explicitly recognized as such. In Schott's words, "with this physical invisibility has gone political invisibility."[89] Since the early 1990s, there has been an upswing in the recognition of rape and other gender-based violence as war crimes and/or crimes against humanity in the institutions and conversations of international law.[90] While the punishment of wartime rape had previously been very inconsistent, the 1990s saw it broadly classified as a war crime in international jurisprudence.

Saying that sexual violence is a "weapon of genocide" and a "weapon of war" does not equate or even compare the experiences of individual or collective rape and individual or collective death. If genocide is an explicit attempt to exterminate a group of people (be it on the basis of race, ethnicity, religion, culture, or some other axis), then rape is used as a weapon of genocide when rapes are committed intentionally and systematically to further the cause of that extermination. The purposes that rape as a weapon of genocide can serve include destroying collective consciousness, forced impregnation (and therefore racial or ethnic impurity), destruction of household (economic and social) units, and national/ethnic humiliation. If war is an attempt to conquer, humiliate, destroy, or remove the enemy, sexual violence in war and conflict can be (and is) used as an instrument of those ends in similar ways.

Seeing sexual violence as a weapon of war, though, is only part of the picture. Many who recognize rape as a weapon of war fail to understand it as gendered. That fallacy is addressed next.

Misconception #7: Sexual Violence in War and Conflict Is Not Gendered

K. R. Carter defines war rape as "a crime—and, in the context of my argument, also a weapon—that can be sex/gender neutral."[91] Carter characterizes it as "sex/gender neutral" because it is a weapon that can be used against both women and men, and because "men are . . . victims of rape as a weapon of war."[92] In this understanding, it is not the sex or gender of the body/ies committing sexual violence, or the sex or gender of the body/ies victimized by that violence. Instead, what makes sexual violence worth considering as a weapon of war is the pure volume of the destruction that rape causes—to men, to women, to children, and to societies as a whole.[93] Many who either ignore or sensationalize women's perpetration of war rape do so sharing, explicitly or implicitly, Carter's assumption that the commission of rape *on* multiply sexed bodies constitutes it as both sex- and gender-neutral.

This book argues that sexual violence in war and conflict is neither sex- nor gender-neutral. It is not sex-neutral because those committing the sexual violence are attentive to the sex of the bodies they are victimizing, both for their own sake and for the signification of the violation as an act of sexualized power.[94] Wartime rapists communicate emasculation to "enemy" men and express their own masculinity on male and female bodies differently.[95] Even if war rape were sex-neutral, however, its sex neutrality would not lead to gender neutrality.

Instead, being victimized in sexual violence in war and conflict is an experience shared by those understood as biologically female and those feminized in political and social relations. A number of feminist scholars argue that the prevalence and even possibility of war rape is a key threat both to women's security and to the possibility of achieving gender equality.[96] Judith Gardam sees wartime rape as a cornerstone of gender subordination, arguing that "nowhere is women's marginalization more evident than in the attitude of the law of armed conflict to rape, an experience limited to women."[97] Gardam argues that "rape is . . . an integral part of the system ensuring the maintenance of the subordination of women."[98]

Sexual violence in war and conflict can be seen as an attack on the "enemy" state or nation in two different ways. First, "it is a symbolic attack on men's virility and their ability to protect their women."[99] As Jan Jindy Pettman explains, "rape functions as a strategy to deliver a blow against a collective enemy by striking at a group of high symbolic value."[100] Second, conflict sexual violence directly and materially threatens a state or nation's ability to sustain itself through cultural and biological reproduction. Characterized as "occupation of the womb,"[101] forced impregnation is "committed systematically" and "generates mass terror, panic, and destruction"[102] through the physical but also symbolic consequences of these acts.[103] In other words, forced impregnation causes both a fearful emotional reaction and a physically destructive impact. Even though many of these observations about the gendered nature of different forms of sexual violence in war and conflict are accurate, many of them are still framed in ways heavily reliant on understanding men as the perpetrators of the violence, and women as its victims, an assumption discussed in more detail below.

Misconception #8: For Sexual Violence in War and Conflict to Be Gendered, Men Have to Be the Ones Committing It

A widely held but rarely discussed viewpoint in a number of the policy and jurisprudence communities that deal with sexual violence in war and conflict frames it as a gendered phenomenon, as seen in recent jurisprudence of sexual violence in war and conflict. The term "genocidal rape" is a relatively new term, used to specify a particular subset of sexual violence in war and conflict wherein rape is used as a tool of genocide—of extermination of a national, religious, or ethnic group. This new term signifies changes in thinking about the moral status of sexual violence in conflict. While sexual violence *in war* is as old as war itself, the ethical and legal status of that violence has changed significantly over time, place, culture, and conflict. Some (especially ancient) war stories account for women's sexual enslavement as one of the victors' spoils at the end of the conflict.[104] Others characterize sexual violence in war and conflict as a violation of the property rights of a man to whom the raped woman is understood as belonging.[105] Recently, in international law, sexual violence in war and conflict has been characterized as a violation of women's human rights, a reification of gender inequality, a war crime, and sometimes an act of genocide.[106]

With a similar outlook, the International Criminal Tribunal for Rwanda (ICTR) decided that occurences of rape can "constitute genocide in the same way as any other so long as they were committed with the specific intent to destroy, in whole or in part, a particular group, targeted as such."[107] Accordingly, the court decided that "the rape of Tutsi women was systematic and was perpetrated against all Tutsi women and solely against them."[108] In fact, the ICTR and the International Criminal Tribunal for the Former Yugoslavia (ICTY) have been the leading courts in identifying and prosecuting the crime of genocidal rape, though those identifications and prosecutions have resulted in fewer convictions than some advocates for women's rights and women's security argue are appropriate. The ICTR provides arguably the first jurisprudential definition of rape in international law, explaining that "while rape has been defined in certain national jurisdictions as non-consensual intercourse, variations on the act of rape may include acts which involve the insertion of objects and/or the use of bodily orifices not considered to be intrinsically sexual."[109] It followed that characterization with the explanation that rape is a type and magnitude of force, rather than the mechanizations of particular actions, "used for such purposes as intimidation, degradation, humiliation, discrimination, punishment, control or destruction of a person."[110] In ICTR jurisprudence, one can be guilty of genocidal rape either by having committed the rape oneself or by commanding, aiding and abetting, or inciting it.[111] To find a defendant guilty of genocidal rape, two elements are necessary: an act listed as an act

of genocide must have been committed, and it must have been specifically targeted towards a national, ethnical, racial, or religious group with
the special intent necessary for genocide—destruction of the group.[112]
Citing the European Court for Human Rights, the ICTR discussed the
physical and psychological scarring that results from genocidal rape as
evidence that it constitutes a crime against humanity.[113]

Still, most discussions of genocidal rape (and wartime sexual violence
more generally) assume that if women are (largely, individually and collectively) its victims, men are exclusively the perpetrators. Many court
cases either implicitly or explicitly define the victims of genocidal rape
as female and the perpetrators as men who violate them. Many arguments for conviction of genocidal rapists, and indeed the convictions
themselves, specify women as the population of the victims and one or
many men who did the victimizing. They assume, implicitly or explicitly, that the male sex of the perpetrator is a constitutive feature of the
gendering of the violence.

Women's commission of wartime sexual violence is often invisible
in these narratives, then, by definition. Some feminist scholars see it as
important not to lose the long-overdue recognition of women as victims
of sexual violence in war and conflict because of the very few women
who perpetrate the crime. In conflict sexual violence jurisprudence, this
is upheld by a number of different characterizations of the sex/gender
of victims/perpetrators. Combing through cases of war rape jurisprudence suggests additional ways the sex of the perpetrator of war rape is
assumed to be male. First, many cases employ a characterization of war
rape as primarily a crime of the commission of a sex act, and as therefore
primarily a sexual crime. This understanding of the sexualized content
of the crime (as opposed to seeing the crime as a combination of sex and
power, or as a crime of power) seems implicitly to limit its perpetrators
to men (who are assumed to be sexual) and its victims to women (who
are assumed not to desire base sexuality). Second, heavy reliance on the
concept of gender justice[114] as a justification for the prosecution of sexual violence in war and conflict seems to help to conflate gender justice
(which should be about masculinities and femininities, masculinization
and feminization, as well as women and men) and sex justice (a sense
that men are the "bad guys" who oppress women, and that sex discrimination is both dichotomous and one-directional). Third, the particular

reliance on the idea that what makes sexual violence in war and conflict so terrible is women's innocence[115] defines not only women victims as incapable of violence, but also women perpetrators. These elements are visible in the discussions below of specific cases of women's sexual violence against other women during conflict.

This book suggests that it is important to disaggregate, but continue to understand, both sex justice and gender justice. A woman (or a man) being raped *by a woman* makes her (or him) *no less raped* for the sex of the perpetrator. An act of rape being committed *by a woman* makes it no less gender subordinating for the victim, male or female. The gendered nature of sexual violence in war and conflict is not limited to, or mapped on to, the sex of the perpetrator.

This argument, however, does not mean to suggest that recognizing women as perpetrators of sexual violence in war and conflict does not change that violence should be conceptualized. Such an assumption can lead to the silencing of stories of female perpetrators, male victims, and male and female victims of female perpetrators. Instead, I mean to suggest that seeing female perpetrators (and sexual violence in war and conflict as an act of feminization rather than an instantiation of masculinity) changes the way that sexual violence in war and conflict is conceptualized. The changes this re-visioning inspires are complicated and require retheorizing not only sexual violence in war, but both gender and war.

Misconception #9: Including Women Perpetrators in the Analysis of Sexual Violence in War and Conflict Does Not Necessarily Change How Wartime Sexual Violence Is Defined, Understood, and Theorized

Approaches to the perpetration of sexual violence in war and conflict that ignore women perpetrators often continue to assume that the perpetrators are exclusively male. While accounts that sensationalize women's violence change the face of the perpetrators, they also treat women perpetrators differently than male perpetrators. In that context, accounts of sexual violence in war and conflict and accounts of that violence perpetrated by women are substantively different. I argue that this approach is fundamentally flawed.

A surface exploration might suggest that "adding" women perpetrators *should not* change theories of sexual violence in war and conflict. After all, I have been making the argument that wartime sexual violence is not *something different* because women do it. Indeed, I reiterate, conflcit sexual violence *is not* something different because women do it. That said, theories of sexual violence in war and conflict were often constructed *assuming men are the perpetrators* and *assuming an essential masculinity to the male perpetrators*. The combination of those assumptions are problematic, because they not only leave out women perpetrators, but any characteristics associated with femininity (e.g., emotion, impulse, relationality) which might go into motivating the commission of sexual violence in war and conflict, and any characteristics associated with masculinity that might be present in its performances, its victims, and/or its significations. Theories constructed *by men, about men, assuming masculinity* are partial not only because they leave out women *as people* but also substantive considerations related to femininity.[116]

I argue that gender analysis is crucial to understanding the occurrence of, meanings of, and representations of (women's) sexual violence, against each other and more generally. To this end, the book rethinks not only women's sexual violence but men's as well. It suggests that such rethinking is a necessary part of theorizing sexual violence in war and conflict (and the accompanying gender subordination) as something *people* do, rather than as something *men* do. Including previously obscured gender inequalities in accounting for people's sexual violence in war and conflict "allows us to see how many of the insecurities affecting us all, women and men alike, are gendered in their historical origins, their conventional definitions, and their contemporary manifestations."[117] Recognizing that women sometimes commit sexual violence in war and conflict, this perspective argues, is insufficient. Instead, that recognition should be accompanied by rethinking the phenomena of sexual violence in war and conflict to account for not only the women but the gendered complexities that were previously absent from narrow and sex-biased accounts.

Misconception #10: Post-Conflict Justice for Sexual Violence
Necessarily Relies on Being Able to Disaggregate the Sex of
Perpetrators and the Sex of Victims

As discussed above, jurisprudence and even scholarly analysis about sexual violence in war and conflict seems to rely fairly firmly on the idea that men are its perpetrators. This book argues that the assumption that all perpetrators of sexual violence are men actually hinders post-conflict justice in a number of ways. It creates spaces of invisibility around women perpetrators, around women victims of women perpetrators, and around male victims generally. These spaces of invisibility, I argue, are not necessary to post-conflict justice, even if those who promote them might see them as an essential shortcut. Instead, they are conceptually problematic (since women can and do play roles in perpetration) as well as practically problematic (since they make it more difficult to identify and punish women perpetrators and to provide justice to their victims).

Instead, the theoretical reformulations inspired by seeing both women and femininity in the perpetration of sexual violence in war and conflict can be translated into suggestions for dealing with rape among women more effectively in prosecutions, and therefore more accurately accounting for occurrences and gender dynamics of sexual violence in war and conflict. These hopes rest in a few foundational principles on which the law of wartime rape should be conceptualized. First, it is crucial to understand that gender subordination is not about *being* male or female in some absolute sense, but instead about perceived membership or even association in/with those groups. Second, those perceived associations have only *subordinating* impacts because gender categorization and association is at its foundation a power relationship, where association with masculinities augments power and association with femininities disempowers.

As I mentioned above, then, it is best not to see gender subordination as something men *do to* women or women *do to* women, but to understand it instead as a discursive constellation of gender-based power relationships (and related expectations) based on the perception of maleness and femaleness, masculinity and femininity. Such an interpretation resolves the apparent paradox of female perpetrators of conflict sexual violence victimizing individual women in acts that also subjugate women as a social category.

The key to rewriting conflict sexual violence jurisprudence successfully, in my view, will be to preserve the "gender justice" paradigm in which war rape is politically and jurisprudentially condemned, while breaking down the sex and gender essentialism that maps that "gender justice" paradigm into understanding women as necessarily the innocent victims and men as necessarily the violent perpetrators. An alternative conceptualization might begin with seeing war rape as an act of *feminization* of the victim and the victim's group, regardless of the biological sex of the perpetrator or the victim. Such an approach would prove more descriptive of *what happens* in war rape and (therefore) more useful in jurisprudential situations of prosecuting rapists and policy situations of protecting victims. This sort of thinking can serve as the foundation for a gender-conscious practice of post-conflict justice around sexual violence.

Seeing Rape among Women: An Outline

This book, then, looks to pair critical feminist theorizing and the analysis of women's sexual violence in war and conflict. By "critical feminist theorizing," I mean analysis that seeks to identify and discover the implications of genderings in global politics. It is "neither just about women, nor about the addition of women to male-stream constructions, it is about transforming ways of being and knowing."[118] Looking through "gender lenses" is a way to filter knowledge, such that

> [t]o look at the world through gender lenses is to focus on gender as a particular kind of power relation, or to trace out the ways in which gender is central to understanding international processes. Gender lenses also focus on the everyday experiences of women *as women* and highlight the consequences of their own unequal social position.[119]

The stories about women who commit wartime sex crimes in this book are about women, but they are also (and more) about gender. Particularly, scholars studying gender and global politics have emphasized that gendered power relations are not inherent to relations between people understood to be women and people understood to be men (or even between men and men or women and women).[120] Instead, in the case of the subject matter of this volume, gender relations happen among parties in war and conflict, among war crimes perpetrators, and between perpetrators and their victims. Many of these gendered relationships, including many of those in the pages of this book, are ones in which "institutional hierarchies are *naturalized* by feminization and thus are effectively depoliticized," where "feminization as devalorization" intersects race/ethnicity, class, gender, nationality, and other cleavages in global politics.[121] Since "gender is relational," "*privileging who and what is masculinized is inextricable from devaluing who and what is feminized*"—one requires the other.[122] Therefore, instead of looking at women wartime rapists as if "women" were either a natural category or one separate from men or masculinity, the chapters in this book study those women as gendered actors, navigating gendered relationships, and living in a gendered world.

Chapter 1, "Conditions That Drove Them to the Brink of Death: Gender, War, Genocide, and Sexual Violence," starts this process by discussing the relationship between gender, war, and genocide. It introduces the concept of gender in more depth, detailing the complicated relationships between sex, gender, and gendered expectations and receptions of human behavior. It then applies this analysis to war and conflict, suggesting that the conceptual structure, causes, performance, and results of war and conflict are profoundly laced by gendered expectations, gendered competition, and gendered inequities. Suggesting that there are gendered dimensions both to war generally and to ethnic conflict specifically, the chapter makes the argument that gender analysis is necessary to understanding the dynamics of gender, war, and conflict. It then expands on the argument in this introduction that sexual violence in war and conflict is gendered and endemic to war and conflict. It argues that understanding sexual violence in war and conflict as gendered adds explanatory power to understandings of war and to understandings of gender.

Chapter 2, "Man-to-Man Communication: The Impossible Existence of Rape among Women," suggests that the analysis in Chapter 1 is a significant part of a discursive structure that makes the recognition of women wartime rapists almost impossible and even-handed treatment of the ones who are recognized unlikely. It argues that the current media, scholarly, and jurisprudential treatments of wartime rape are structured around narratives that require women victims and male perpetrators. It examines the assumptions about *what men are, what women are,* and *what men and women signify in war and conflict* that are necessary to require male perpetrators of female victims in war rape narratives. The chapter argues in turn that each of these assumptions are problematic. It contends that the discursive impossibility of women wartime rapists is not only troublesome for the analysis *of* sexual violence in war and conflict, but is also a linchpin of current (gender-unjust) justifications for and motivations for the perpetration of conflict, war, and genocide.

The discursive impossibility of women perpetrators of sexual violence in war and conflict in chapter 2 is coupled with the stories of those very women in chapter 3, "The Unforgettable Wound: Seeing Rape among Women in Conflict." This chapter explores rape among women in conflicts across the world—Darfur, Armenia, Germany, the former Yugoslavia, Rwanda, and the Democratic Republic of Congo. These cases were selected to show a variety of conflicts in which women engaged in a variety of types of sexual violence. This chapter suggests that the women rapists in these conflicts are not more inclined to sensitivity, reservation, or non-violence than men are. It notes, however, that these women are also not seen as the same as men, even when their behaviors are similar and the perpetrators claim similar motivations. Instead, these women are often held up as examples of the problems with, and therefore the need to control, femininity. In each of these stories, there is a "double move of sensationalizing *that women rape women* and distancing women rapists both from agency in their own actions and from normal femininity."[123] It compares their discursive impossibility to the information that we have about these women, their lives, their crimes, and their motivations.

Chapter 4, "There's No Evidence Women Are Any Worse at Rape than Men Are: Understanding Women, War, and Rape," constructs a theory of sexual violence in war and conflict aware of women perpetrators and the role of not only masculinities but also femininities in the creation and perpetuation of wartime sexual violence. It begins by suggesting, in general terms, that the underlying problem of the devaluation and devalorization of femininity needs to be addressed to address these manifestations of that problem. That problem can only be addressed in a world where values associated with femininity are "more universally valued in public life" and "women's agency in their decisions is as recognized as men's agency in theirs."[124] I suggest that a path towards those goals starts with recognizing the contingent and contextual nature of *all* interaction and *all* decision-making, not only women's. Taking this as a starting point, Chapter 4 critically engages existing theoretical approaches to sexual violence in war and conflict. It suggests reformulations of those theoretical approaches that help to understand sexual violence in war and conflict, even as it is among women. In so doing, it uses feminist theorizing to construct an argument that the characterization of sexual violence in war and conflict as gender subordination is not inaccurate—instead, inherited notions of what that gender subordination is are oversimple. Revisiting the discussion of sex and gender in chapter 1, this chapter makes the argument that seeing gender subordination more complexly can strengthen theories of wartime sexual violence, regardless of the sex of the perpetrator. The chapter concludes by suggesting a way forward to theorizing gender subordination (in war and outside of it) that accounts for the dynamics of masculinization, feminization, and gender subordination, acknowledging that women can be the perpetrators of those acts in addition to being (and sometimes while being) their victims.

Chapter 5, "The Wrong of Rape: How Women Rapists Change Criminal Jurisprudence," turns from theorizing to practice. It suggests that accounting for rape among women in post-conflict justice is complicated, given that it complicates (and sometimes contravenes) some of the political forces that have drawn important attention to the commission of the war crime of rape. Expanding on the discussion of the possible directions for war rape jurisprudence above, it suggests complications for the current "gender justice" paradigm of post-conflict justice for sexual violence. It suggests that a new paradigm for evaluating war rape should rely on an understanding that gender subordination is both structurally systematic and substantively fluid. Gender subordination relies on both the delineation of gendered categories based on perceived associations with sex, and on the inscription of power on those gendered categories. This creates a situation of both incomplete independence and unequal power. This chapter uses that understanding of gender subordination to explain that women, both as individuls and as a group, can be seen as victims of women's acts of sexual violence *without* that victimhood denying women's capacity to exercise political and/or violent agency. It introduces the idea of gender/violence as a war crime to explore the enforceability of this more complex notion of gender subordination.

In conclusion, chapter 6, "One of the Most Abiding Myths of Our Time: Re-visioning Women, War, and Rape," suggests that this reconstruction of conflict sexual violence jurisprudence could be carried over into policy and advocacy work on war rape specifically and on gender subordination in war and conflict generally. It puts forward a frame for reconceptualizing the relationships between gender, war, and sexual violence in the policy world with an aim towards decreasing both wartime sexual violence specifically and gender subordination generally *without* essentializing, sensationalizing, or ignoring violent women. It does so by reframing two recent conflict sexual violence cases in the terms of the lessons learned about impossibility, visibility, and gender subordination in this book. In so doing, it suggests that rape among women is not something sensational, unmanageable, or strange for scholars, media, or courts—at least, it does not have to be.

1

Conditions That Drove Them to the Brink of Death

Gender, War, Genocide, and Sexual Violence

Women were raped. . . . [The rapes] weren't an expression of
sexuality or sexual need or sexual gratification. It was an attempt to demonstrate the sexual act as an expression of violence . . . tarnishing the honour of any family. . . . A woman
forced by day to clean up the blood of beaten prisoners and
by night repeatedly raped; prisoners forced to commit sexual
acts or even sexual mutilations upon other prisoners. . . . The
lucky ones in camp, those who were not forced to participate
in a loved one's murder, or sexually mutilated, or beaten to
death over a period of agonizing days, or subject to other
torments, nevertheless endured conditions that drove them
to the brink of death.[1]
—Excerpt from a Sentencing Hearing at the International
Criminal Tribunal for the Former Yugoslavia

The old adage that "war is hell"[2] rings true in ways even those who first
popularized the phrase might not have intended—because war, as this
chapter's epigraph exemplifies, is a special kind of hell for its civilian
victims, most of whom are targeted for a cause they did not choose, or
just for being a certain race, ethnicity, or religion. The passage, from a
war crimes sentencing hearing, discusses the terrible tortures of rape
and sexual violence in the conflict in the former Yugoslavia, and the
(gendered) hell that the perpetrators' victims experienced. This chapter
argues that war and genocide are *gendered* hell, and that the *gendered*
part of that phrase is crucial to understand fully the events themselves.

This chapter explores the relationships between gender, war, genocide, and sexual violence to lay the foundation for the argument that
war, genocide, and sexual violence therein are *gendered*, and need to

be analyzed as such for the fullest understanding of what they are, how they happen, how they can be stopped, and how they should be dealt with jurisprudentially. It begins by introducing the concept of gender in more depth, discussing the relationships between sex, gender, and gendered expectations and readings of people and event in global politics. A second section uses gender analysis to theorize war and conflict, suggesting that there are gendered dimensions to war generally and ethnic conflict specifically. A third section turns to the analysis of sexual violence in war and conflict, suggesting that it is a systematic part of gendered war and gendered genocide, and appropriately theorized as such. The chapter concludes by situating this within the book's analysis of rape among women.

Gender

As mentioned in the introduction, popular misconceptions of gender characterize it as reducible to biological maleness or femaleness and/or the traits that are seen to go with those biological configurations. Male bodies and female bodies are expected to contain masculine and feminine people who fill gender roles in orderly ways. This *does not mean* that expectations about what women are and what men are constant over time, place, and culture—instead, it means that, across all of those differences, there are expectations of what women are and what men are. Gender roles both differ and change, but the existence of gender roles as an ordering principle of social and political life seems to endure.

Gender role expectations seem to endure despite the mounting evidence that people do not fit into the categories of biologically male and biologically female,[3] that the retreat to biology as fundamental is conceptually and empirically flawed,[4] that bodies can be and are socially constructed,[5] and that sex, gender, and sexuality are *social orders* rather than *natural orders*. In other words, not only is there nothing essential about *being a woman* or about *being a man* that makes a person fundamentally one way or another, the very ideas of *being a woman* and *being a man* are inseparable from the social contexts in which they are read and interpreted.

It might at first glance appear that the argument in this chapter is internally contradictory—that there is nothing natural,[6] essential, or biological about gender but that war and genocide are *gendered*. A brief discussion of what it means to be *gendered* in this context shows that the argument is not internally inconsistent, however, and that both parts of it are necessary to understanding the complexities of gendered war(s) and gendered genocide(s).

First, it is important to note, as many feminist scholars have pointed out before, that gender being performative, socially constructed, and non-essential does not make the experience of gender any less *real* in the lives of people who live global politics (or even in the lives of people who both live and research global politics). Given that, expectations about the ways gender influences what people do and how they do it are almost overwhelmingly present in social and political life—from the different treatment of male children and female children to the suggestion that men and women who are in politics do (and should) behave differently.[7] Initially, then, it looks like gender can be accounted for in the expectations of people understood as men and people understood as women, and the difference among them. The (different) expectations of people understood as men and people understood as women can be called *gender normativity*—the expectation that gender rules can be used to predict, explain, and indeed *order* behavior. Under gender-normative social and political structures, maleness and femaleness, masculinities and femininities, serve as organizing principles for social and political life, by which people and behaviors are categorized, and with which people and behaviors are read.

A brief explication might be helpful en route to unpacking that account: the passage that starts out this chapter, about the rapes in the Bosnian genocide, begins with the observation that "women" were raped. Here, "women" is the literal subject of the sentence (*women* are the victims of the rape). But it is also a signifier of a number of different understandings of women/gender—some universal(izable), others specific to the reader and/or interpreter. The first sentence implies that women are disproportionately victimized. The passage implies that it is especially *bad* to abuse a woman ("a woman forced by day . . ." is more specific than "a person forced by day . . ." because the sex of the victim is an aggravating condition of the victimhood). It characterizes rape not only as a sex-specific experience to and for women, but as an expression of gendered power rather than as an act of sex and sexuality. It relates women's sexuality to familial honor (implying strongly that this relation is local to Bosnian Muslim culture in the omitted part of the text).

In other words, taking the *sexed* terms out of the passage would impact its meanings and significations. Replacing the words "women" and "woman" with "people" and "person" would make the passage *still* descriptive of the war crimes of torture, rape, and even genocidal rape. The passage would still account for terrible human rights abuses which are both normatively shameful and subject to prosecution in international law. While it would mean the same thing in those senses, it would also mean something very different: the feminine as the subject and the signifier here matters to the implications about what the crime is and how it is committed. While no one would disagree that doing those things *to a man* would be a terrible thing to do, them being done *to a woman* is at once a different kind of offense (against those presumed innocent, in need of protection, and protected) and *somewhat normal* (given that sexual violence in war and conflict against women has become a feature of most if not all wars, conflicts, and genocides).

So, in a sense, gender has both everything and nothing to do with understanding the act/crime/experience being described. On the one hand, the person's perceived sex, gender, gendering, and sexuality has nothing to do with the occurrence of the event; on the other hand, it has everything to do with its perpetration, its reading, its experience, its reporting, and even its punishment. *Gendered orders* produced by and reinforced by *gender-normative* understandings of how people do (and should) live and act cannot be divorced from how life is read *and even experienced*.[8] In this way, as Laura Shepherd describes, gender is "a noun, a verb, and a logic that is product/productive of performances of violences and security."[9] As Judith Butler explains, this makes sex "a regulatory ideal" whose materialization is forced, where "what constitutes the fixity of the body, its movements, will be fully material, but the materiality will be rethought of an effective of power."[10]

In other words, gender becomes manifest in "a series of demands, taboos, sanctions, injunctions, prohibitions, impossible idealizations, and threats."[11] These demands and threats affect the behavior, behavioral expectations, and living conditions of people understood to be men and people understood to be women, both structurally and in everyday life. While the process by which *gender normativity* and *gender orders* are enforced affect people similarly, the *content* and *result* of those orders differs. If, in Butler's words, "the boundary, forming and deforming of sexed bodies is animated by a set of founding prohibitions, a set of enforced criteria of intelligibility,"[12] the *standards of intelligibility* set different criteria for people understood to be men and people understood to be women. Gender is not just derived behavioral standards and derived difference, then—it is derived inequality. Gender normativity includes the distribution of not only roles but power, regard, and privilege based on perceived associations with sex-based characteristics.

Scholars of gender identify perceived associations with sex-based characteristics using the terms "masculinities" and "femininities." These are pluralized for two main reasons. First, as discussed above, masculinities and femininities vary over time, place, and culture, though their existence seems relatively stable. Second, and perhaps more importantly for the discussion in this book, "masculinity" and "femininity" in social and political life is not a dichotomy, but a spectrum. R. W. Connell's description of the existence of "hegemonic masculinities" twenty years ago sets the stage for the analysis of multiple gender tropes; Connell suggests that there are dominant masculinities (e.g., particular understandings of physique, career, behavior, and the like) which are held as ideal, and other masculinities that are subordinated to the ideal-typical hegemonic masculinities.[13] An easy example of this relationship that Connell uses is the subordination of nonheterosexual masculinities to heterosexual masculinities. Connell suggests that it remains true in many societies that the notion that the ideal man is straight, and that other masculinities are less ideal.[14] As a result, "straight" is a standard to which men are expected to aspire, and by which they are measured. The ideal-typical, or hegemonic, masculinity in any given society at any given time stands at the top of (often otherwise multidimensional) gender hierarchies and gendered orders. Other masculinities, and femininities, are (to varying degrees and in varying ways) subordinated to those ideal-typical masculinities.

Placement along those hierarchies has then been described as *masculinization* and *feminization*. This is the association of people (and states and other actors) with traits associated with masculinities and femininities, men and women. To *masculinize* is to associate with masculinities, and to *feminize* is to associate with femininities. These two words function in many similar ways in terms of the processes of genderings and the manifestation of gendered performances, but thinking about them in terms of gendered power relations shows their differences. Masculinization is associated with affirmation, valorization, upward mobility, potential, and success; feminization is associated with rejection, devalorization, immobility, and limits. As Cynthia Enloe has argued, "patriarchal systems are notable for marginalizing the feminine," acting to "infantilize, ignore, trivialize, or even actively cast scorn upon what is thought to be feminized."[15] As V. Spike Peterson explains, the effect of this feminization is a reduction in "legitimacy, status, and value" that is "simultaneously ideological (discursive, cultural) *and* material (structural, economic)."[16] Gender normativity produces gendered orders that normalize "the marginalization, subordination, and exploitation of feminized practices or persons," such that routinized feminization can be associated with routinized devalorization.[17] Mary Hawkesworth explains that "the underlying logic of feminization" is "a vindictive construction of femininity" which relates it to (and relates to it) the "weak, violated, silenced, docile, obedient, humiliated, and craven."[18] That is why, as Spike Peterson argues, feminization is not limited to those people understood to be women or female, but extends across people, states, and other actors that display or are seen to displace traits associated with femininity.[19] In other words, "not only subjects, but also concepts, desires, tastes, styles, ways of knowing . . . can be masculinized or feminized."[20]

I argue that sort of gendering occurs frequently in everyday life in global social and political relations. It has two important manifestations: an organization among things (people, actors, behaviors) that are perceived to be in conformity with gender-normative orders and things that are not, with the valorization (and centrality) of the masculine and the devalorization (and marginalization) of the feminine, and an organization of hierarchies initially generated by "other" characteristics (e.g., race, class, religion, national identity) in terms of masculinities and femininities, masculinizations and feminizations. It is then possible to think about gender *as hierarchical* in global politics. This understanding of gender is necessary to show the ways in which war and genocide can be thought of as *gendered* in global politics.

War

In the introduction, I briefly discussed the argument that women are victimized disproportionately on the basis of gender in war and conflict. In response to the myth that the rise of women perpetrators has decreased the need to pay attention to the victimization of women, I pointed out the ways that the political, social, and economic hardships of war are often distributed in gender-biased ways that reproduce and deepen preexisting gendered divisions of labor and gendered role expectations in households, communities, and even nations. I suggested that the ways disproportionate victimization of women civilians is just one of a number of ways that gender orders construct and impact people's war experiences—outlining the gendered expectations of men to act as "just warriors," providing protection and being willing to fight for righteous causes along with the (parallel) expectation that women act as "beautiful souls" who need protection, and whose protection often provides justification for making and fighting wars.

These are examples of the ways that gender orders manifest in and are reified by the making and fighting of wars. This section will talk more about how that comes to be, focusing on combating the (frequent) assumption that the presence and performance of gender hierarchy is incidental to, or orthogonal to, war and conflict. Instead, it will suggest that war and conflict in global politics are structured by, and inseparable from, gender in *both senses* outlined above—as an organization of events and actors, and as a tool of valorization and devalorization. In order to make this argument, an engagement with the question of *what war is* and how political scientists traditionally theorize it might help to lay the foundation for the discussion.

Traditional definitions of war include a number of common elements. First, most definitions of war share the understanding that war is *violent*, where there is an intention to "kill and injure people and to destroy military and economic resources."[21] Second, most definitions characterize war as something that occurs *between* two or more political groups—where it is important that two or more groups exist; that of the two or more groups that exist, at least two *actually fight*; and that those groups are political in nature.[22] Some scholars limit the actors who they think commit wars to recognized states in the international system, while others hold a broader interpretation that includes not only states, but international organizations, nongovernmental organizations, sub-state insurgent groups, and other possible actors.[23] A third traditional element of what counts as a war is a notion that wars have longevity and are *sustained*, differentiable from "organized violence that is more limited in magnitude or impact."[24]

With traditional definitions of war come traditional accounts of war. In IR theorizing, these are most often causal accounts of war organized by the "level" of analysis on which the causal account focuses, or the type of issue that it prioritizes. The "levels" of analysis that explanations of war and conflict focus on include the system level (Kenneth Waltz's "third image"), the state level (Waltz's "second image"), and the individual level (Waltz's "first image").[25] Issue-based explanations for war focus on any number of possible problems in the international arena—from state dissatisfaction with existing international orders[26] to religious disputes.[27]

System-level theories of war fall predominantly within a paradigm of international theorizing called realism, and account for war as made possible by anarchy among states in the international arena.[28] In these accounts, the lack of central authority among states forces them to look out for their own survival, which produces both defensive and aggressive tendencies in a search for the only guarantor of survival—relative power and relative supremacy.[29] System-level accounts of war from outside the realist paradigm emphasize the *management* of anarchy through manufacturing security,[30] the cycles of ebb and flow of warfare throughout international history,[31] or cycles of change of world-systems or international governance orders.[32]

State-level theories of war have come to take two fairly different forms: dyad-level theories that address the causes of war *between* two states and monad-level theories that address the ways that states can cause wars. Dyad-level accounts of war tend to explain war by reference to rivalries between states, economic interactions among states, or traits thatstates have in common. Focusing on the large percentage of wars that happen between a small number of actors, rivalry theorists try to understand how states come into repetitive conflict.[33] Some emphasize path dependency, while others pay attention to the steps that commonly lead to war.[34] Other theorists, largely working from liberal perspectives on international theorizing, suggest that states that are trade-dependent on each other have a lower propensity to become involved in wars and conflicts.[35] Perhaps the most popular dyadic account of the causes of war, though, is called "the democratic peace," which argues that states that are democracies do not make conflict withother states that are democracies.[36] Still other dyad-level theories focus on other commonalities states might have, including but not limited to settled borders,[37] Western culture,[38] or (relative) gender equality.[39] Monadic accounts of war that look for how and why states cause wars look at the economic structures of societies,[40] the role of military elites,[41] coalition politics,[42] and various forms of cultural conflict.[43]

First-image, or individual-level, theories of war also come in two major types. Some theories focus on leader decision-making, suggesting that attention be paid to who makes war decisions and how their personalities and psychological makeups come into play.[44] Looking at bureaucratic politics, organizational decision-making, leadership styles, and risk propensity, these approaches see understanding leaders' decisions as key to understanding war.[45] Other first-image theories of war making and war fighting emphasize various aspects of (or perceived aspects of) human nature to account for when and how wars are fought. Classical realists, for example, suggested that the fundamental evil present in human nature is responsible for the propensity to war in international politics.[46] More recently, scholars interested in taking lessons for war theorizing from evolutionary biology look to understand war propensity through Darwinian mechanisms of survival through reproduction.[47]

Not all theorizing about war focuses on the causes of war, however. Some work focuses on how war is practiced by belligerent states and parties—strategy, tactics, and logistics. The study of strategy looks at the ways that militaries go about using military operations to achieve policy goals, including maneuver, attrition, and punishment, in service of offensive or defensive objectives.[48] Much of the analysis of strategy assumes that wars are fought, and strategies are deployed, by large states with large, organized, standing military forces.[49] Still, recently, scholars have shifted the study of strategy to include terrorism and counterterrorism, preemption, intentional civilian victimization, and/or siege warfare.[50] While scholars of strategy are focused on macro-level military operations, scholars of tactics are interested in the micro-level puzzle pieces that make up those macro-level strategies.[51] Tactical choices include how to attack or defend, what weapons to use, what targets to select, and the like.[52] Some scholars are interested in whether tactical choices are motivated by perception, efficiency, or the development of technology.[53] Others are interested in the ethical dimensions involved in particular tactical choices—what weapons and uses of them are morally acceptable to use in war, and which are not?[54] Still other scholars focus on logistics—"moving, supplying, and maintaining military forces"—arguing that logistical plausibility is a condition of possibility for the making and fighting of all wars, as well as the deployment of all strategies and tactics.[55]

Critical war theorizing is often less interested in the causes of wars or the sources of choices of how to fight than it is in the discourses of war-making and war-fighting, the conditions of possibility of political violence, and the signification of events and decisions associated with war. "Critical Security Studies" often focus broadly on the politics of security rather than narrowly on military operations.[56] Enlightenment-based critical theorizing is interested in understanding broadly the ways that injustice, everyday violence, and war are linked, for the purpose of trying to make the world less unjust, less violent, and less plagued by wars.[57] Relatedly, human security theorists are interested in contextualizing war *within* other threats to people's community, economic, environmental, food, health, personal, and political security, as well as how war exacerbates these threats to people's security.[58] Copenhagen school theorists contribute an interest in how some things come to be *securitized* (that is, objects of security discourse and practice), while other things with very similar characteristics do not.[59] Poststructuralist or postmodern war theorizing studies both war and war discourses in a way that "does not look for a continuous history, but for discontinuity and forgotten meanings; it does not look for an origin, indeed, it is assumed one cannot be found; and it does not, finally, focus on the 'object of genealogy itself' but on the conditions, discourses, and interpretations surrounding it."[60] In this view, war is a continuum, a practice, and a symbolic politics.[61] In other words, war as traditional theorists understand it is inseparable from the performative symbolic politics surrounding it—*it is produced, and productive.*[62] In this context, causal theory makes less sense than constitutive theory as a tool to study war and conflict.[63]

Though war theorizing is incredibly diverse, much of ignores gender analysis in whole or in part. As I discussed above, gender analysis looks for gender in global politics and reads the ways that gender dynamics impact the ways that global social and political life is structured and experienced—something I have referred to as gender orders. As J. Ann Tickner explains, the "distinctive features" of feminist analysis are "asking feminist questions and building knowledge from women's lives."[64] Building on this methodology, I (along with other feminist scholars) see gender as an ordering principle for war and conflict, but most war theorizing either omits gender or reduces it to a variable with the assumption that women behave differently than men. Feminist work in IR has made the argument that these omissions leave out more than just the detail of how gender matters—they make it impossible to come up with a full understanding of what war is, how it works, and its many dimensions, including but not limited to sexual violence in war and conflict.

For starters, feminist theorists have suggested that the importance of attention to security narratives surrounding war—that "traditional conceptions of violence as an identifiable *thing* or *given* limit our imagination," and it is therefore important to engage in "a rethinking of security and violence as *made*."[65] Such a rethinking leads to a broader view of what war is than traditional theories often see—where the violence that is *made* is linked from the everyday to the international.[66] Looking not only at the battles that happen on battlefields, feminist war theorizing has paid attention to the tools that make war possible, the militarisms that are conditions of possibility of war and conflict, the ways that wars are lived and experienced in homes as well as in militaries, the long-reaching impacts of war and conflict especially at the political margins, and the similarities between violence traditionally understood as war and human insecurity, structural violence, and economic deprivation.[67] Looking at war with a long view shows the ways that gender and war are co-constituted—where traditional gender roles are a condition of possibility of war-fighting, and war-fighting reifies traditional gender roles.[68] Feminist war theorists have argued that "without the relationships between gender and nationalism, protection racket logic . . . , just warriors and military service, war as we know it would be unthinkable."[69]

Understanding the co-constitution of gender and war has led feminist theorists to look at the ways wars are lived and experienced, rather than at traditional macro-political understandings that focus on cause or even signification.[70] While it is important to understand the gendered dimensions of the systemic, dyadic, monadic, and individual levels of war-making and war-fighting, feminists have suggested that it is equally important to understand war as felt, lived, and embodied.[71] In terms of the traditional areas of war theorizing, feminist analyses have suggested that the international system, the structure of states, the distribution of resources within states, and the leadership of states are touched by gendered power dynamics that make them gendered orders.[72] This is the first element mentioned above—that war is structured by gender as an organization of events and actors.

The second element—that gender is an axis of valorization and devalorization in war—can be seen in feminist theorizing of the strategies, tactics, and logistics of war-making and war-fighting. Feminists have pointed out the way that current practices of military strategy rest on gendered assumptions and rely on gender-stereotypical understandings of enemies.[73] They have suggested that contemporary strategies—like intentional civilian victimization and the deployment of private military and security companies—are often analyzed without reference to gender, but rest on gendered structures of valorization and devalorization.[74] Gendered strategies are built on and reinforce gendered tactics, including both tactics traditionally understood as gendered (e.g., wartime rape and forced impregnation), as well as tactics traditionally seen as gender-neutral (the development of wartime technologies, the use of women and femininity as weapons of war, and the gendered nature of logistical choices and deployments).[75] Gender operates across these strategies and tactics as an axis on which victors show victory and dominance over the vanquished—demonstrating their own masculinity in opposition to the feminization of those who they are looking to conquer or even eliminate.[76]

These very different understandings of what war is and how it is practiced have implications for thinking about the practice of sexual violence in war and conflict, which is the subject of the analysis of this book. Feminist insights take a broad look at what counts as war, and therefore what counts as wartime sexual violence.[77] They also provide more explanatory leverage about what wartime sexual violence is, what it signifies, what it communicates, and how it comes to be made possible.

Along these lines, feminist attempts to look for where women are in conflict[78] have often focused on experience. Feminist accounts of what happens to women in war and conflict have paid attention to the fact that most women have little say in the making of most wars, yet are disproportionately wars' civilian victims.[79] Gender analysis has demonstrated the ways that war has sex-specific negative impacts on women, from economic deprivation to physical abuse to familial destruction.[80] Scholarship that takes account of those impacts has come to frame militarism, and the violence that is its inevitable result, as masculinist.[81] By *masculinist*, the scholarship means that it is violence that is made possible by prizing values associated with masculinity (particularly bravery, aggression, and dominance) over values associated with femininity (particularly solidarity, compromise, and interdependence).[82] Most masculinist violence is committed by people understood to be men, often in fulfillment of gender-role expectations that are product and producer of gendered orders. Many victims of masculinist violence are people understood to be women. At the same time, not all perpetrators of masculinist violence are men, and not all of its victims are women.

Thinking about conflict violence this way might augment both the understanding provided by and the explanatory leverage of theorizing about it. Part of that expanded explanatory leverage might be ways to understand the relationships between war and genocide, wartime sexual violence and genocidal sexual violence. Since a significant amount of the sexual violence in war and conflict in this book took place during genocides, this is an important relationship to explore. The next section explores the existing research and legal cases identifying what genocide is, analyzing its causes, constitution, and history, and relating war and genocide.

Genocide

International law classifies genocide as a war crime with two elements, per the 1948 Geneva Convention on the Prevention and Punishment of Genocide: an intent element ("intent to destroy, in whole or in part, a national, ethnical, racial or religious group as such") and a physical element (killing, causing serious bodily harm, deliberately inflicting conditions of life calculated to bring about physical destruction, attempting to prevent births, and forcibly transferring children).[83] Committing genocide is classified as a crime, as is conspiracy to commit genocide, incitement to commit genocide, attempts to commit genocide, and complicity.[84] This definition evolved from Raphael Lemkin's characterization of the Nazi systematic murder of European Jews with the intent to destroy them—he described it as "a coordination plan of different actions aiming at the destruction of essential foundations of the life of national groups, with the aim of annihilating the groups themselves."[85]

The term was rarely used in international law with anything but historical reflection until the early 1990s, when it was used frequently in reference to the wars in the former Yugoslavia,[86] and then to the 1994 Rwandan genocide.[87] The world's first conviction in international court for the crime of genocide happened in 1998—the defendant was Rwandan Jean-Paul Akayesu.[88] That "first" was surrounded and followed by a number of other "firsts"—including but not limited to the first conviction for genocidal rape[89] and the first time the United States government formally identified an ongoing conflict as genocide.[90]

In academia, a field of genocide studies has developed, interested in understanding what genocide is, how it is related to similar concepts, theories of the causes and significations of genocides, studies of empirical cases where genocides have occurred, questions of when and how to prevent or intervene in the commission of genocide, and how to adjudicate genocides that have been committed.[91] The formation of the Association of Genocide Scholars[92] and of a number of centers of Holocaust and genocide studies at universities across the globe[93] are often inspired by the paired missions of understanding the commission of genocide and stopping it.

A number of theories have developed to attempt to account for how the mass killing that is genocide comes to happen, often committed in large part by ordinary people who might, in other circumstances, be considered civilians.[94] Herbert Kelman, for example, suggests that state permissiveness about mass violence creates a routinization of dehumanization that not only allows but encourages ordinary citizens to engage in genocide.[95] In analyzing the Nazi genocide, Daniel Jonah Goldhagen argues that genocides are born of long-standing sentiments in one group against another.[96] In the case of the Nazi genocide, he calls the sentiment "eliminationist anti-Semitism," which dehumanized the target people *before* the violence was permissible, and led to an explosion of violence once it became permissible. R. J. Rummel uses the term "democide" to refer to people who have been killed by their or other governments, and suggests that many if not all genocides have been in some way government sponsored. After an intense study of these democides, Rummel contends that democratic governments are less likely to engage in genocidal violence—and that genocide can (and should) be combatted with political openness, political competition, and leader accountability.[97]

Work from different disciplinary backgrounds in genocide studies often has different foci.[98] Work in criminology often focuses on how and when people's moral compasses can become so out of line with reality as to make the commission of genocide seem acceptable.[99] Sociologists often address the group and inter-group dynamics from which genocides spring, and the question of the social origins of genocide.[100] Political scientists who study genocide often focus on the role (or failure) of political, military, and economic institutions in the commission of or prevention of genocide.[101] Legal scholars frequently focus on the legal status of the actors who commit genocide and their victims, as well as legal tools for the prevention and punishment of genocide.[102] Geographical research on genocide often focuses on the spatial constitution of genocide—including but not limited to the ways that competing spatial claims aggravate tense relationships and the ways in which the elimination intent in genocide is often a spatial intent.[103]

The question of the relationship between war and genocide is neglected in much of this work. Yet war and genocide are closely related in a number of ways. The most obvious of these relationships is that many genocides take place in the context of wars, either by one belligerent against another or by one belligerent against a group that is not directly involved in the war. Sometimes genocides start wars, where the victims (or parties looking to protect the victims) fight back; sometimes genocides end wars, where a victor in a war looks to exterminate the vanquished. Sometimes, genocides happen during wars, and are ended with the end of the war and the defeat of the perpetrator. Sometimes genocide is used by one side or another in an intrastate war. Sometimes, though rarely, genocides are perpetrated outside of the context of what is traditionally understood as war. Much less rarely, events traditionally understood as war do not include acts understood as genocide. War and genocide are clearly not unrelated, yet conflating them into "warandgenocide"[104] would also clearly be theoretically and empirically unrepresentative of how either happen.

Perhaps for this reason, some have attempted to understand the intersection (or lack thereof) between genocide and war. Some have argued that there is a fine line in war between mass civilian victimization and genocide.[105] Others have categorized genocide as a war crime, that is, a crime that occurs within the context of war-fighting.[106] Still other theorists have found it crucially important to understand the ways that genocide *expands* war—since it is not normally (only) committed by the sorts of soldiers that kill other combatants on battlefields.[107] In this view, genocide is an extension of and an extreme form of war.[108] Martin Shaw has made the argument that "the problems of genocide and war are so intimately linked that we need to see them within a common frame," especially when it comes to causes and effects.[109] Conscious of the politics of naming, some scholars express concerns that conflating war and genocide can be done for instrumental and political purposes, and that there is little intellectual purchase to be had from the conflation.[110] I agree, and look to trace sexual violence in war and conflict across war, genocide, and other conflicts rather than conflating them.

Gender analysis does not necessarily look to sort out the ways in which genocide might fit into, extend, or fall outside of traditional definitions of war. Instead, the continuum approach to violence and war outlined above applies to the question of genocide as well—feminist analysis has been more concerned with the conditions of possibility of violence, the human impacts of violence, and the interlinkings of violence than the existence or intersections of particular categories of violence. While the events traditionally read as war and the events traditionally understood as genocide have important features that distinguish each, my approach is as interested in the things that are common between those different events as the things that make them different. A view of the gendered aspects of both war and genocide shows gender as an organizing principle of both, and gender as a tool of valorization and devalorization in both. Across many instances of genocides, practices, strategies, and tactics display many of the gendered patterns and significations that one can see in the practice of war and conflict violence more generally.[111] Genocide, war, and other sorts of violent conflict in global politics also share the common feature of sexual violence in war and conflict. Whether it is (called) war rape, wartime sexual violence, genocidal rape, or gender-based violence, sexual violence in war and conflict has a number of common themes and significations that can be read across (types of) conflict(s). Chief among these common themes are the central role that sexual violence in war and conflict plays in the gendering of war, conflict, and genocide, and the gendered nature of the planning and performance of that violence. It is to that argument that the next section turns.

Sexual Violence in War and Conflict

Sexual violence is a strategy and tactic (depending on how one sees it)[112] used in most wars and conflicts. Whether it is the recent discussion of rapes in Libya[113] and Syria[114] or the historical tales of the Rape of Berlin[115] or even the documentation of war rape in Greek and Roman history,[116] most wars and conflicts in recorded human history have included some rape and sexual violence[117] (though the levels vary). As discussed briefly in the introduction, war rape is traditionally thought of as a crime *men* do to *women*, but is actually a gendered part of the practice of war and genocide regardless of the sex of the perpetrators or the victims.[118] Many feminist scholars argue that war rape is feminizing, that it is a cornerstone of women's oppression, and that it is an integral part of, rather than incidental to, war, genocide, and violent conflict in global politics more broadly.[119] This analysis leads them to suggest that "wartime rape is a key war tactic because of the symbolic function it serves of attacking (and corrupting the purity of) women as a way to communicate dominance over the enemy state and/or nation."[120] In this way, sexual violence in war and conflict "works to install a disempowered masculinity as constitutive of the identities of the nation's men."[121]

In this way, sexual violence in war and conflict is an expression of masculinization of the perpetrator and feminization of the victim—whether perpetrators are understood as states, militaries, organizations, or individuals, and whether victims are understood as the person towards whom violence is committed, the people (presumably men) charged with that person's protection, or that person's family, nation, state, or ethnic group. Given the multitude of ways that conflict in global politics *is* sexual violence, that it *includes* sexual violence, and that it is a condition of possibility for (and made possible *by*) sexual violence, it is important to think about the multiple layers of sexual violence in war and conflict.

As noted in the introduction, there are a number of ways that sexual violence in war and conflict serves to signify domination and defeat, or as a tool of oppression. Empirical research has shown rape used as a metaphor for national humiliation, a signifier of conquest, a tool of feminization, and a tool of extermination.[122] A number of analysts of sexual violence in war and conflict have identified it as a key source of women's insecurity, arguing that it attacks women's bodies and re-productive capabilities, individually and collectively.[123] The collective element—that sexual violence in war and conflict is an attack on *femininity* and/or *women* as well as its individual victims, has led feminist lawyers to link war rape and the maintenance of gender subordination across the globe.[124]

There has been a history of inconsistency in the recognition of victims of sexual violence in war and conflict and punishment of perpetrators in many different arenas. Since the early 1990s, progress has been made in getting rape and sexual violence recognized as war crimes in international law.[125] Changes in law have been called "revolutionary" by analysts, and credited to "growing mobilization and influence of non-governmental or-ganizations articulating the importance of the rights of women."[126] Chang-ing jurisprudence has been accompanied by militaries taking action to discourage soldiers from committing sexual violence,[127] and international organizations have been constructing legal frameworks interested in rec-ognizing, preventing, and punishing war rape.[128] These frameworks have come to recognize the criminality of a number of different sorts of sexual violence in war and conflict, including domestic violence, sexual assault, kidnapping, trafficking, forced marriage, forced prostitution, forced im-pregnation,[129] enslavement, rape, and molestation.[130]

Courts have also started to recognize that war rape and genocidal rape are similar crimes but have some differences. Where war rape is understood as a crime against its victim, women generally, and perhaps even the nationality of the opponent, genocidal rape is seen as perpetrated "with the specific intent of destroying ethno-religious groups."[131] This jurisprudential distinction was first adjudicated in a US court, but repeated in jurisprudence at the ICTR, where it was found that rape constitutes "genocide in the same way as any other so long as they were committed with the specific intent to destroy, in whole or in part, a particular group, targeted as such."[132] Accordingly, in the *Akayesu* case, the court found that the rape of Tutsi women was "systematic and perpetrated against all Tutsi women and solely against them," which made the act genocidal rape.[133] Genocidal rape is often fatal itself and part of a strategy "not only to kill the victim but to corrupt and or end the purity of the victims' racial or ethnic group."[134]

The passage that starts this chapter is a description of a group of rapes many would consider to be genocidal that took place in the former Yugoslavia. The description of these rapes by the ICTY accounted for what happened not as an "expression of sexuality or sexual need or sexual gratification" but instead as "an attempt to demonstrate the sexual act as an expression of violence."[135] The violence sex crimes in war and conflict express is *gendered*—it is an act of feminization and violence towards femininity. It cannot be understood otherwise—hundreds of thousands of stories of war rape include the gendered element of the subordination of women and femininity and the feminization of the men who are (most often) the victims' supposed protectors and (sometimes) the victims themselves.

For these reasons, as I have argued before, "the very normalization of rape as a weapon of emasculation and the sexual violence in war that accompanies it suggests that sex, sexuality, and violence are more closely linked" than traditional analyses might acknowledge.[136] This is why feminist scholars seek "new understandings of security in the face of systemic gendered violence (war, rape, domestic violence)" in order to highlight "the security issue of the relationship between sexual and international violence."[137] In other words, if genocide, war, and conflict were as gender-neutral as traditional accounts of their meaning, causes, and consequences often report, then sexual violence in those events, when visible at all, would have to be considered incidental or orthogonal—a curable bad part of otherwise redeemable enterprises, or at least a separable bad part of generally bad enterprises. If, instead, gender, war, and conflict are fundamentally *ordered* and *performed* along gender lines, then sexual violence and international violence are intimately linked, and "the terrible combination of sexual abuse, abstraction, and dehumanization found in war rape can be found across a wide variety of war tactics, all of which are gendered."[138] That description is most accurate about sexual violence in war and conflict.

Gendered Sexual Violence in War and Conflict and Rape among Women

At this point the reader might wonder why I spent the time and effort to construct an account of sexual violence in war and conflict as gendered and an attack on femininity (and, by proxy if not directly, women), given that the title and premise of this book suggests that it will explore women's perpetration of sexual violence in war and conflict. After all, does women's perpetration not deconstruct the account of sexual violence in war and conflict as an act of emasculation of the men who are supposed to protect the women victims, or of the men victims themselves?

As I suggested in the introduction, I argue that men do not have to be the perpetrators of sexual violence for it to be a gendered phenomenon. On the contrary, understanding that women perpetrate an act of gender subordination that attacks women, attacks femininity, and emasculates men when they perpetrate sexual violence in war and conflict adds complexity to understandings *both* of that violence and of gender orders in global politics more broadly. However, to understand the gendered nature of *both* men's and women's commission of sexual violence in war and conflict fully, we must understand the variety of ways in which women's commission of that violence is set up as impossible in traditional policy and academic narratives.

Several of the producers of that invisibility have come up in the (accurate) narratives of gendered conflict and gendered sexual violence in war and conflict throughout this chapter: the (apparent) gender neutrality of theories of war and genocide that really masks the gendered elements of those violences; the characterization of sexual violence as orthogonal to, incidental within, or removable from war, genocide, and conflict; and the implication that gender subordination happens to women only when it is perpetrated by men. All three of these producers of invisibility of women's perpetration of sexual violence in war and conflict are explored in the next chapter, along with jurisprudence, scholarship, and policy advocacy that is (perhaps unwittingly) complicit in that invisibility, and therefore in empirically and conceptually incomplete accounts of sexual violence in war and conflict specifically, and war and conflict generally.

2

Man-to-Man Communication

The Impossible Existence of Rape among Women

The mass war rapes can be understood as an element of communication—the symbolic humiliation of the male opponent. By dishonoring a woman's body, which symbolizes her lineage, a man can symbolically dishonor the whole lineage. . . . Thus, sexual violence against women became a tool of genocide for destroying the enemy's honor, lineage, and nation.[1]
—Cindy S. Snyder, Wesley J. Gabbard, J. Dean May, and Nihada Zulcic, "On the Battlegrounds of Women's Bodies: Mass Rape in Bosnia-Herzegovina"

This description of sexual violence in war and conflict resonates with accounts of sexual violence during conflict as gendered. It suggests that *men* victimize *women* in gendered ways. This chapter argues that the *gender analysis* in this description holds—and is important, even when women are the ones doing the victimizing. The common perception that sexual violence needs to be committed by men towards women to be gendered is inaccurate.

Particularly, if we read this chapter's epigraph next to the one in chapter 1, it appears to tell a coherent story of men victimizing women on the basis of gender, as a message both about women and to men. In this sense, war rape can use entrenched heteronormative gender orders that delineate traditional families to bring dishonor not only to the woman who is raped in the story, but also to the men who are charged with protecting her from that dishonor, and to the families (and by extension states and nations) who are the intended target of that dishonor. That's why sexual violence in war and conflict has been characterized (appropriately) as "attacking women, violating their bodies and abusing their reproductive capabilities."[2]

The narrative is disrupted, though, when we see that the epigraph that begins chapter 1 is *about a female* perpetrator, Biljana Plavšić. *A woman* was charged with, and pled guilty to, crimes against humanity, including charges that she incited, and commanded, the rapes of uncounted and uncountable Bosnian women with the intent of exterminating the Bosnian ethnicity. This book makes the argument that *a woman* being charged with a gendered war crime is not at odds with the ways that gender, war, genocide, and sexual violence therein *should* be read, but does contradict the ways that the relationships among those things are often read. Across a wide spectrum of analysis—in media outlets, in scholarly research, and in jurisprudential decision-making, descriptions, definitions, and prosecutions of sexual violence in war and conflict make the existence of female perpetrators of that violence discursively impossible. By "discursively impossible," I do not mean an imagined impossibility—I mean that the ways in which sexual violence in war and conflict is read, understood, described, and even prosecuted *obscure* the existence of perpetrators *and victims* who fall outside of the sex-stereotypical assumptions that go along with their characterizations of that sexual violence.

Some of the ways that women perpetrators (and their victims, and male victims) of sexual violence in war and conflict are made invisible across these outlets were discussed in the introduction to this book in the form of common misperceptions about how women's relationship to sexual violence in war and conflict is best understood. Many of the misconceptions about the stability of the category of woman, women's commonalities, and women's peacefulness close observers' minds to the possibility of women wartime rapists. Assumptions about the gender neutrality or incidental nature of sexual violence in war and conflict might lead to the unreflective use of traditional sex and/or gender terms. Misconceptions about women's perpetration erasing victimhood or obstructing justice might cause observers to turn a politicized blind eye to that perpetration. In other words, the assumptions outlined in the introduction help overdetermine the impossibility or invisibility of women who commit sexual violence.

Other ways that women perpetrators of sexual violence are made invisible can be seen in descriptions of gender, war, and genocide as gendered. Gender role expectations that characterize men as strong and autonomous and women as peaceful and sensitive can create blinders not only to male victims but also to women perpetrators. A misconception that women have a sense of solidarity with other women *because they are women* can make it especially difficult to see when women victimize other women on the basis of gender. War theorizing's tendency to frame as gender-neutral not only conflicts and events but also theories and research that omit women, women's roles, and the existence of femininity make it difficult to see where women are in conflict at all, not to mention in perpetration of sex crimes. Characterizations of genocide that suggest that family units are the key to the production and survival of national, ethnic, religious, or racial groups make it difficult to see women as anything other than the biological and social *reproducers* of groups (and therefore the targets and victims of sexual violence). Seeing women as serving an exclusively reproductive role makes the notion of women as *destructive* a discursive impossibility. Notions of sexual violence in war and conflict that suggest that it is something *done to* women by men make it difficult to see the times when women do victimize women on the basis of gender, or when gendered attacks do not map one to one onto the lines of (perceived) membership in biological sex categories.

Many of these conditions of invisibility of female perpetrators of sexual violence in war and conflict are reducible to assumptions about *what women are, what men are*, and *what men and women signify in war and conflict* that are product and producer of gender orders in global politics. This chapter starts with a brief retelling of the gender-ordered account of sexual violence in war and conflict necessary to create the discursive impossibility of women perpetrators, implicating not only traditional, masculinist accounts of gender but also feminist accounts that conflate women and femininity. A second section introduces the impossible women and men that the discursive impossibility makes invisible—women perpetrators, male victims, and women victims of women perpetrators. A third section then makes the argument that standard accounts of sexual violence in war and conflict are structured around narratives that indeed require women victims and male perpetrators. It pays attention to scholarly and media accounts as well as jurisprudence that defines, prosecutes, and punishes sexual violence in war and conflict. The chapter then argues that the discursive impossibility of women's perpetration of sexual violence stands in defiance of the empirical evidence that many women (not just Bijana Plavšić) engage in rape, in inciting rape, in molestation, in sexual enslavement, and in other sexual and sexualized abuse in the contexts of war, genocide, and other conflicts. It contends that the discursive impossibility of these women rapists is not only troublesome for understanding what wartime rape is, how to stop it, and how to adjudicate it, but also for understanding justifications for and motivations for the perpetration of conflict, war, and genocide more generally *as well as* the current structure of gender orders in global politics.

Possible Women

Traditional, gender-subordinating accounts of what women are in war and conflict assign them several roles. First, women are that which men are assigned to and burdened to protect; men's honor is tied to providing protection to innocent women who are assumed to be unable to protect themselves.[3] In fact, Grotius's account of the civilians who are physically and mentally incapable of fighting in war and conflict includes three groups: children, women, and the elderly.[4] As I mentioned earlier, Thucydides's account of the Peloponnesian War casts women as possessions to be taken control over at the end of a battle by the victor.[5] Jean Elshtain's description of this stereotyped role that women are to play uses Hegel's notion of the "beautiful soul"—characterizing the idealized (and ideal) woman in war as innocent of both its cause and its prosecution, peaceful, and in need of protection from the violence.[6]

The perception that women need protection and men should provide that protection is the foundation for a second role that traditional accounts of what women are have women playing in war and conflict— the *cause* for which men fight wars. As Joshua Goldstein notes, men will fight wars *for women* when they have no other motivation to fight.[7] As I have argued before, "the gendered protection racket can even be characterized as creating a condition of possibility for war, since innocent, defenseless women (and their love and virtue) *to fight for* motivate men to fight, even absent other motivation."[8] This fighting *for women*, though, is (often) not at women's request or in response to their need, but instead in response to a stereotyped notion of what women are and what they need. Often, the threat to women is understood as an important consequence of defeat—a concern voiced as loudly by Nazi Germany in 1945 as by the United States in the twenty-first-century war on terror.[9]

A third role that women play in traditional, patriarchal accounts of war is as *available to* soldiers who are fighting for them to be used in supposed furtherance of the cause being fought for.[10] This availability has a number of different dimensions. Some women are seen as willing to open their homes to soldiers who are traveling to fight, and responsible not only for doing so but for providing for soldiers' food and shelter needs while they are in the area.[11] Others are seen as willing to travel with militaries to provide food, entertainment, medical care, and morale to traveling soldiers in order to (if indirectly and nonviolently) help them to win battles and wars.[12] Still others are understood as sexually available to men who "need" gratification as they fight, defend, guard, or travel—and therefore as useable as entertainers, or even prostitutes, bush wives, or rape victims.

Traditional, patriarchal accounts of the nature of "women" and their experiences in wars do not often pay attention to the suffering women experience, but when they do, it is often if not always a story of how the enemy is so evil that they are willing to victimize innocent women and children to gain strategic or tactical advantages.[13] In those stories, the evil of the enemy can be measured by the abuse that they exact on women civilians, and the "good guys" would never do anything like that, even when the "bad guys" do it first.[14] In most if not all of the cases where these narratives are popularized, the abuse of civilian women is not one-sided but happens on both sides of the war, genocide, or conflict.[15] Feminist gender analysis broadens the spectrum of possible women in wars,[16] showing the ways that women are often left out of war decision-making[17] but subject to sex-specific, disproportionate harms[18] in masculinist wars and conflicts.[19]

Accounting for war, genocide, and sexual violence therein as gendered is, I contend, crucially important to understanding how all three come to be, and how all three are related. Gender orders in global politics—from the prizing of hegemonic masculinities to the expectation of the existence of heteronormative families as foundations for building states, nations, and racial/ethnic groups—are central to understanding the meaning, causes, and dynamics of violence in global politics. At the same time, an oversimple reading of the many, many ways that sexual violence in war and conflict is gendered might lead to allowing one of the simplest misconceptions discussed in this book to take over—the misconception that femininity and feminization are associated with, happen only to, and are found only in those people (or states or organizations) who are understood to be women and feminine; and that masculinization, masculinities, masculine violence, and emasculating are associated with, happen only to, and are found only in those people (and states and organizations) who are understood to be men and masculine. The simple conflation of men/masculinity and women/femininity *within* progressive, feminist readings of gender in global politics can lead to the same result as conservative, patriarchal readings of gender reach when thinking about how women are positioned as relates to sexual violence in war and conflict: that women are its victims, its potential victims, and those people who need to be protected from its (possibly inevitable) attempted perpetration by enemies. Women auxiliaries, victims, and potential victims, then, are wars' possible women.

Impossible Women

These idealized notions of gender roles serve to deepen the discursive impossibility of women perpetrators of sexual violence in war and conflict. If women are wars' peaceful constitutive others for whom others must fight and die because they are *incapable* of protecting themselves from the inevitable barrage of masculinist violence, then being perpetrators of sexual violence is quite literally the least likely role for women in war, genocide, and other conflicts. This makes it unlikely that women perpetrators, when and if they exist, are visible to analysts, scholars, media reporters, and legal systems. This unlikeliness is compounded when the misconception that women *are all* something—that is, that women have something in common, and that one of the things that they have in common is one status—either as perpetrators or as victims. Therefore, if women are sexual violence's victims, they cannot be its perpetrators; if they cannot be its perpetrators, looking for and looking to understand women perpetrators is a pointless exercise.

But women perpetrators of sexual violence in war and conflict *do exist*, however invisible accounts of sexual violence make them. They exist across different conflicts, across different sorts of conflict, across different geographical regions, across different cultures, across different religions, and across different time periods. I have already introduced some of them—Ilse Koch in World War II Germany and Biljana Plavšić in the former Yugoslavia. Many others will be introduced throughout the remainder of this book. While some books that talk about *things women do*—whether it is engage in political leadership, serve in the military, or commit acts of terrorism[20]—focus on what those women have in common *as women* and how they differ from men, this book is more interested in the complex layers of gendering that come to *both* make women perpetrators impossible and stereotype the ones that are recognized.

For example, Pauline Nyiramasuhuko was the first woman charged with genocidal rape in an international court. Sita Balthazar states that "the ICTR established an incredible precedent by being the first tribunal ever to charge a woman with genocidal rape."[21] This "incredible precedent" was apparently incredible because of the sex of the perpetrator—Nyiramasuhuko is a woman. Before and during the 1994 Rwandan genocide, Nyiramasuhuko was a cabinet member in the Rwandan government as the minister for family and women's affairs. She was charged both with rape as a crime against humanity and rape as a violation of the Geneva Convention.[22] Reports of Nyiramasuhuko's time in office suggests that she openly campaigned to "get rid of all Tutsis" and was one of the key planners of the genocide that took place in the summer of 1994.[23] Prosecutors presented evidence that she instigated the strategy of genocidal rape, that she directly commanded troops to commit rape, that she established a system of sexual slavery, and that she engaged in sexual torture.[24]

Nyiramasuhuko is one of the few women perpetrators of genocidal rape who have garnered the attention of media outlets, scholars, analysts, and courts.[25] While most women perpetrators remain excluded from both official and unofficial narratives of the conflicts in which they commit sexual violence, Nyiramasuhuko has received a disproportionate amount of attention. This attention has combined gendered and racialized exoticism, and framed Nyiramasuhuko as "other" to femininity and civilization. News stories, scholarly analysis, and even legal analysis emphasized the particular horror of woman-on-woman sexual violence in her case.[26] As Mark Drumbl has explained, "the outsize attention showered upon *Prosecutor v. Nyiramasuhuko* is animated neither by its jurisprudential novelty nor by its progressive development of the law, . . . [but] by the fact that the case concerns a purportedly novel kind of subject . . . to wit, the female atrocity perpetrator."[27]

Framed around this purported novelty, most of the narratives about Nyiramasuhuko involve a double move of distancing her from the ideal-typical woman, who is understood as incapable of the violence Nyiramasuhuko committed, and discussing the particular flaws in femininity that make the sort of atrocities that she committed possible.[28] In other words, a number of analyses of her behavior suggest that *appropriate femininity* is entirely nonviolent, but *femininity gone wrong* can manifest in extreme forms of violence.[29] Some coverage suggests that it is the very rareness of women perpetrating sexual violence in conflict that makes this case interesting, since "this sort of crime committed by a woman seems almost unfathomable because, historically, it is men who commit or instigate rape."[30] In fact, "she is not just a woman who ordered rape, but she is a mother—and grandmother—who ordered women to be raped in front of their own children."[31] This ignores both that women do, though less frequently than men, commit sexual violence, and that sex is not a determinant of one's criminal ability or criminal engagement. Still other coverage suggests, as I mentioned above, that the existence of women who commit sexual violence in war and conflict cancels out "myths" of "the special victimization of women."[32] This ignores that the majority of Nyiramasuhuko's victims *were* women, victimized *because they were women*, and relies on an oversimplistic understanding of the victim/perpetrator dichotomy, as I will discuss later in this book. Nyiramasuhuko herself also projected a gendered narrative of her involvement in the Rwandan genocide, both when asked in interviews and as a defense in court. Her argument suggested that women are pacifist, gentle, and victimized, and therefore incapable of the sort of violence of which she was accused. In fact, Nyiramasuhuko contended that her status as a mother proved her innocence of genocide, claiming to a reporter that "if there is a person who says a woman—a mother—killed, then I'll confront that person."[33]

Amid all of these gendered narratives, the apparent paradox that there was an overwhelming amount of evidence suggesting that Nyiramasuhuko was indeed one of the planners and more extreme perpetrators of the Rwandan genocide *and sexual violence within it* remained, and contributed to a trial that lasted almost a decade, with a fair amount of media attention surrounding it. Still, as we are reminded by Drumbl, "Nyiramasuhuko may reflect a new kind of international convict, but she is far from a new kind of perpetrator, whether in Rwanda or wherever episodes of mass atrocity erupt."[34]

The publicity surrounding Nyiramasuhuko's case can be contrasted with the silence around a number of other cases of women's perpetration of war crimes, sexual or otherwise. For example, many of the news stories surrounding Nyiramasuhuko's conviction suggested that she was the first woman who had perpetrated sexual violence in war and conflict and the first woman convicted of genocide and/or rape as a crime against humanity.[35] Not only was she not the first such woman, she was not even the first *Rwandan* woman convicted of committing such crimes during the 1994 genocide.[36] Nicole Hogg documents that hundreds, possibly even thousands, of Rwandan women were convicted of genocide-related offenses in courts in Rwanda before Nyiramasuhuko was convicted by the ICTR.[37] Still other women, like Consolata Mukangango, Maria Kizito, and Beatrice Munyenyezi, were convicted in the domestic courts of other countries for genocide-related offenses.[38] Other women (most notably the former president's wife, who it has been strongly suggested played a role in his assassination to set off the genocide) continue to elude trial despite a widespread understanding that they committed war crimes.[39]

Though significantly less attention is paid to these women than is paid to Pauline Nyiramasuhuko, many of the same gender tropes dominate the discourses that analyze their participation when such discourses exist. For example, a few of the women who engaged in perpetration were nuns, and both the horror of woman-on-woman crime and the role of sisterhood in covering up their crimes are emphasized in accounts of their perpetration.[40] In Nicole Hogg's terms, the "ordinary women" who committed crimes of genocide and sexual violence in Rwanda in the summer of 1994 were numerous, but less visible in media coverage, legal analysis, and scholarly work.[41] The sensationalized female perpetrator

of sexual violence in the Rwandan genocide and those women perpetrators whose stories are silenced or near-silenced *together* show a couple
of important things.

First, they show that there *were* women perpetrators of the Rwandan
genocide, including sexual violence therein. Second, they show the discursive impossibility of women perpetrators: if women are the peaceful
victims of men's masculine violence, and the post-conflict peacemakers,[42] and perpetrators and victims have to be different classes of people,
then *women* cannot be perpetrators of the genocide and/or its sexual
violence. Third, they show the untenable nature of the gendered discourses that render their actions impossible—not only can classes of
people that contain, or are, victims *contain* perpetrators, perpetrators
can be victims and victims can be perpetrators. Finally, they suggest
that the structures of gender order that is necessary to construct women
perpetrators of sexual violence in war and conflict as impossible need to
be wholesale deconstructed, given that they produce inaccurate understandings of, and expectations of, what women do during conflict, war,
and genocide.

Impossible Women in Standard Accounts of Sexual Violence

It could be suggested that the account of possible and impossible women
in narratives of conflict and sexual violence therein laid out above is
oversimplified, and unrepresentative of some of the complex realities in
the news, scholarly, legal, and policy communities. Undoubtedly, there
is some "truth" to that—the complexity of existing accounts of war, conflict, and genocide cannot be captured in a two-chapter discussion of the
major directions of, and vectors in, that work. Still, I contend that there
are important themes in scholarly, jurisprudential, and media discussions
of sexual violence in war and conflict that render women perpetrators
(and, by extension, their victims) invisible, impossible, and skewed.

Scholarly Research

As discussed previously, there has been a significant and increasing
amount of attention to sexual violence in war and conflict in scholarly
literature, not only in political science but across a number of scholarly

disciplines. Though these narratives differ on a number of axes, what they overwhelmingly share is the (implicit or explicit) identification of "war rapist" with being sexed male.[43] For example, a key piece on the psychology of war rape poses the problem of understanding rapists' motivations as "why men rape in wartime when they would not do so in peacetime."[44] While the article is not *about* war rapists *as sex specific*, it identifies war rapists as men and then asks why those men commit the crimes that they do—at once making women war rapists impossible and rendering their motivations moot or nonexistent.

In fact, that article, by Nicola Henry, Tony Ward, and Matt Hirschberg, makes a number of assumptions similar to those in many other pieces of the scholarly literature on war rape, identifying it as a phenomena of "male violence against women."[45] Many of the studies that are concerned with the causes of sexual violence in war and conflict observe that "not all men engage in wartime rape; in fact, anecdotal evidence suggests that most men do not," and therefore examine what distinguishes male rapists from male non-rapists, or what triggers the times that men rape.[46] Within this framework, there is no discursive space for women perpetrators.

A number of other scholarly research projects looking for the causes of sexual violence in war and conflict sex the perpetrator as they try to understand *him*. For example, Lisa Price's project looks to "find the man in the soldier-rapist" to "comprehend the thinking process of a man who would commit war rape."[47] Presumably, the project is not "finding the man in" women wartime rapists, or "comprehending the thinking process of a man" within women wartime rapists. Instead, the framework of who a wartime rapist is and how *he* comes to commit the crime of sexual violence in war and conflict excludes the woman wartime rapists as a possible subject of investigation. Similarly, Jill Trenholm and her coauthors ask the question of "why soldiers rape" in a way that appears sex-neutral. The next question, however, that clarifies what is meant by "soldiers," suggesting that the project will explore "what helps a soldier manage difficult situations and what it means to be a 'man.'"[48] The research team follows up by recognizing, like others "that it is not all men, but mainly military men, official and unofficial, who perpetrate this violence."[49] The term "soldier" in their analysis, then, is not sex-neutral, but is associated with men as soldiers, and therefore as (actual and potential) wartime rapists. This article, like countless other articles concerned with the causes of wartime rape, limits the category of "rapist" to men.[50] This trend carries over from, and is carried over to, a number of studies on the general causes of rape, both inside of and outside of international armed conflict.[51] While very little if any of this work creates a one-to-one pairing of "men" and "rapists" (that is, all rapists are men but not all men are rapists), it does draw sex-exclusionary boundaries around the category of rapists that renders the woman rapist impossible.

This rendering can be found in work in disciplinary IR about sexual violence in war and conflict, as well as in feminist analyses. One of the more recent examples is K. R. Carter's argument that disciplinary IR should take rape seriously as a weapon of war, even when the idea of weaponry is considered in a traditional sense.[52] As discussed earlier, Carter suggests that war rape is *in theory* "sex neutral."[53] Still, Carter suggests that "systematic rape is perpetrated overwhelmingly by men, and, in some cases, provides a form of male bonding that only further encourages this weapon's use among the male sex."[54] Arguing that "women and girls *are particularly targeted*" leads Carter to assume that men target women because of their sex—the consideration that women could target women because of their sex does not seem to enter into her theorizations.[55] Though Carter recognizes the male victims of wartime rape, she suggests that it is a signal that "individual males are progressively turning this [(sexed and gendered)] power against other men."[56] Some other research that recognizes male victims leaves the implied perpetrator as male only.[57] This work suggests the importance of paying attention to the victimization of men, but carries a (parallel?) silence for women perpetrators—it tells a story of men victimizing men and men victimizing women; women victimizers still often remain outside the realm of possibility.[58]

Discursive exclusion of the possibility of women perpetrators also permeates some feminist research about what sexual violence in war and conflict is, the conditions of its possibility, and the motivations of its perpetrators. For example, reacting to the ongoing rapes in the former Yugoslavia in 1992, psychologist Ruth Seifert described men as rape perpetrators and "women as such" as the victims, suggesting that "in military conflict, the abuse of woman is part of male communication."[59] As Seifert explains, "the rape of women carries a message: a man-to-man communication, as it were, telling the other side that they are incapable of protecting 'their' women and thus hurting their manly pride."[60] For war rape to be a man-to-man communication, by definition, the perpetrator (the one doing the communicating) must be a man looking to communicate with another man. In this account, like in many others, the very explanation of what war rape is *makes impossible* a woman engaging in war rape. If it is war rape, the perpetrator must be male; if a woman does the perpetrating, the crime committed must be something other than war rape.

Engaging further with feminist research shows that most of the identification of men as the perpetrators of sexual violence in war and conflict is implicit rather than explicitly exclusive, but is nonetheless a powerful feature of extant discussions and writings. Feminist research into sexual violence in war and conflict has paid a significant amount of attention to the gendered dynamics of both conflict generally and sexual violence in it specifically, leading a recent reviewer of the literature to suggest that feminist research has "pioneered a view of sexual violence as a form of social power characterized by operations and dynamics of gender."[61]

One exemplar of this sort of analysis is Lene Hansen's work on sexual violence in Bosnia and Herzegovina. Hansen argues that rape in this conflict targets *both* individual female victims *and* the masculinity of the nation's men, given the constitution of that masculinity being based on the ability to protect.[62] Critiquing the simplicity of the notion of gender in many public policy discourses about war rape in the Balkans, Hansen argues that "rape is gendered [to them] inasmuch as it is an act of military men attacking threatened women."[63] In Hansen's view, the gendering of war rape is significantly more complex, and involves significations about women, femininity, race, ethnicity, and religion, as well as multiple masculinities. In this way, Hansen views war rape as an "identity-producing practice"[64] and a "symbolic reflection of masculinist mythology" in a way that stresses "the ways in which women are treated as signs exchanged among men."[65] The depth of theoretical analysis of gendering that Hansen provides is welcome, and a significant improvement both on the literature that oversimplifies the gendering of sexual violence in war and conflict. That said, the remaining oversimplification in Hansen's account is that it does not seem to question the idea that war rape is, in her words, an act of military men attacking threatened women. She argues that war rape is *more than* that, but does not question the fundamental characterization *either* of women as war rape's victims or of (military) men as its (exclusive) perpetrators.

The assumption that perpetrators are *men* reverberates across a number of studies. For example, describing the Democratic Republic of Congo, Anna Maedi documents that "sexual violence perpetrated by armed groups against girls and women is particularly rampant" and theorizes it as a "*modus operandi* of the war."[66] In describing what happened to the victims that she interviewed, Maedi explains that they were victims of "whole groups of men."[67] Maedi's victims do not all identify their rapists as men explicitly, but the description of who rapists are in the article implies that rapists are (and must be) men.

Even feminist accounts of how perpetrators come to engage in sexual violence in war and conflict seem to assume the maleness of the perpetrator, either explicitly or implicitly. Explicitly, noted feminist lawyer and sexual violence litigator Catharine MacKinnon describes rapes as "being done by *some* men against *certain* women for specific reasons" as "a policy of men posturing to gain advantage and ground over other men."[68] MacKinnon's *theorization of what war rape is* requires maleness in the perpetrator. Still, even some critics who call for making MacKinnon's theorization more complex replicate the assumption that the perpetrators of conflict sexuality are male in sex.

Another example is feminist analysts Maria Eriksson Baaz and Maria Stern's impressive study of the motivations of perpetrators of wartime sexual violence in the Democratic Republic of Congo.[69] As they discussed existing theorizations of sexual violence in war and conflict, Eriksson Baaz and Stern critiqued the simplistic notion of "rape as a weapon of war" in many studies, which "is presented as somehow self-explanatory through its implied universalized storyline of gender and warring."[70] Using material from interviews with perpetrators, Baaz and Stern suggest that discourses about men's sexual needs underpin discussions of *why* the perpetrators raped. They explain that "the main ideal of masculinity which the soldiers drew upon to explain sexual violence was that of the (hetero)sexuality of the male fighter."[71] As such, in "post-conflict" Democratic Republic of Congo, "sexual violence at the hands of armed men persists, and has possibly even increased."[72] Even in this complicated analysis, though, it remains the masculinities *of men* that inspire *men* to commit sexual violence in war and conflict, and *men's* sexual violence persists, post-conflict.

Both the primary and secondary explanatory literatures about sexual violence in war and conflict reify this understanding of men as the actors who do the committing of wartime sexual violence. A number of different accounts develop different nuances. For example, Paul Kirby observes that the feminist literature sees "rape as either a weapon of war; a reward for troops; a result of breakdown of social constraints; the consequence of a 'root cause' of masculinity, or the expression of frustration-aggression and male trauma."[73] Inger Skjelsbaek suggests that there are three sorts of theories of sexual violence in war and conflict: essentialist (that characterize all women as victims), structuralist (that characterize only some women as under threat), and social constructionist (that allow that both men and women can be victims).[74] Others characterize sexual violence as an instrumental[75] way to achieve war aims,[76] an expression[77] of either group cohesion among men[78] or the subordination of devalued masculinities of "others" and "enemies," and a "spiral of violence" from humiliation, mistreatment, and victimization.[79]

These accounts have very little in common. What they *do* have in common, however, is that, like much scholarship about sexual violence in war and conflict, they assume and/or suggest that the perpetrators of that violence are men. This assumption renders female perpetrators discursively impossible. I argue, primarily, that each of these accounts gain (rather than lose) explanatory, analytic, and significatory leverage by questioning and deconstructing the assumption that all perpetrators of sexual violence in war and conflict are men. Still, questioning that assumption in scholarly work about sexual violence in war and conflict is only one part of the puzzle: the assumption replicates and is replicated in jurisprudential and media discussions of the same issues.

Jurisprudence

The history of the (domestic and international) law of sexual violence in war and conflict is complicated, and war rape's current legal status is contested and difficult. Most legal histories of the law of war rape explain that no one has ever considered war rape *legal*. Instead, "rape has long been prohibited by the laws of war and has been incorporated into various modern Codes of Military Conduct."[80] While sexual violence has generally been understood to be illegal in war and conflict, "prosecutors have not traditionally prosecuted these [sex] crimes as war crimes" despite the longtime existence of laws under which they could have been prosecuted.[81] The laws under which sexual violence in war and conflict could be prosecuted include (throughout history) countries' "domestic" laws and (more recently) the international laws of war and international criminal law.[82]

Currently, rape is formally illegal in the legal systems of every country in the world, though different countries have starkly different definitions of rape and constituencies that they include in the categories of perpetrator and victim.[83] Different countries at different times have enforced rape laws to different degrees, and experienced different rape prevalence and different citizen attitudes towards sexual violence.[84] Domestic laws have been used in many situations to bring criminal proceedings against perpetrators of sexual violence in war and conflict.[85] Perpetrators have also been the subject of civil proceedings around the world looking to hold them financially and morally accountable for their commission and commanding of sexual violence in war and conflict.[86] For example, "in the United States, civil proceedings have been commenced under the Alien Tort Claims Act and the Torture Victim Protection Act against Radovan Karadzic, who has command authority over the Bosnia-Serb military forces."[87]

Domestic laws are supplemented by international legal prohibitions that either directly outlaw sexual violence in war and conflict or can be used as a jurisprudential justification for prosecuting that violence. For example, the Geneva Convention Relative to the Protection of Civilian Persons in Time of War states that "women shall be especially protected against any attack on their honour, in particular against rape, enforced prostitution, or any form of indecent assault."[88] While some legal scholars hail this as the first formal prohibition of sexual violence in war and conflict in international law, others express concern that the gender essentialism inherent in it can be as much a part of the problem as a part of the solution to the perpetration of sexual violence. As Christine Chinkin observes, "it is noticeable that these provisions do not impose a blanket prohibition against sexual abuse, but rather oblige States to offer women protection against attacks on their honour and accord them special respect."[89] In other words, the law in the Geneva Convention treats states as protectors and women (victims) as in need of protection, rather than recognizing the human rights and/or human dignity of the victims and the responsibility of the perpetrators for the violations of their bodies.

In 1993, the UN Commission on Human Rights defined wartime rape as "a deliberate and strategic decision on the part of combatants to intimidate and destroy 'the enemy' as a whole by raping and enslaving women who are identified as members of the opposition group" and suggested that it is important to think about it as a violation of the laws of war and as an individual war crime.[90] Yet, as Chinkin has argued, "despite this impressive body of formal prohibition, the incidence of rape in armed conflict has been widely ignored, underplayed, or tolerated. Rape is too frequently regarded as an unfortunate but inevitable side-effect of conflict, or as an anticipated bonus for soldiers on all sides."[91]

In other words, the legal prohibitions against wartime rape, formal and informal, often do not result in prosecutions, and even less often produce convictions or compelling evidence that they had actually dissuaded the perpetration of sexual violence in war and conflict. Some legal scholars have recognized that there are as many international legal frameworks that are silent on sexual violence in war and conflict as there are that prohibit it.[92] Even when these "silent" frameworks could be interpreted to outlaw sexual violence as torture or some other human rights violation, this is different than formal inclusion.[93] It is, then, both easy to interpret these provisions not to include rape and difficult to find an operational definition of forms of sexual violence in war and conflict and/or the elements of the crimes that they constitute. Chinkin explains that a number of post-conflict justice proceedings have ignored sexual violence in war and conflict because it was perpetrated by both the victors and the vanquished.[94]

There has also been some definitional confusion resulting from the ambiguity of the law. As Magdalini Karagiannakis explains, "when there is no definition for an offence in international criminal law, such a definition may be derived from the principles that form the basic common denominators of that offence in major legal systems."[95] Since those principles are very different in different legal systems, a significant amount of international jurisprudence has differed in important ways on what crime sexual violence in war and conflict is, what the elements of that crime are, and how it is to be prosecuted. These complexities led feminist legal scholars in the early 1990s to talk about war rape prosecution as a "long silence" that "needed to be broken."[96]

The break in the silence about wartime sexual violence in international criminal law came from jurisprudence in the ICTY and the ICTR in the mid-1990s.[97] The establishment of these two courts, and mandates including sex crimes, resulted in the first convictions for rape as a crime against humanity in international court.[98] The ICTR Statute detailed the elements of rape as a crime against humanity:

> [A] physical invasion of a sexual nature, committed on a person under circumstances which are coercive. Sexual violence which includes rape, is considered to be any act of a sexual nature which is committed on a person under circumstances which are coercive. This act must be committed: (a) as a part of a widespread or systematic attack; (b) on a civilian population; (c) on certain catalogued discriminatory grounds, namely: national ethnic, political, racial, or religious grounds.[99]

Many analysts have seen the jurisprudence in the ICTR as the most progressive on sexual violence in war and conflict in the history of international criminal law, particularly the decision in the *Akayesu* case.[100] The *Akayesu* case suggested that sexual violence in war and conflict constitutes not only torture or a crime against humanity, but also genocide. The court explained that rapes can "constitute genocide in the same way as any other [crime] so long as they were committed with the specific intent to destroy, in whole or in part, a particular group, targeted as such."[101] Not only did this create another legal foundation on which to prosecute sexual violence in war and conflict, it suggested that the victims of that violence are *both* the individuals who are violated and the states, nations, ethnic groups, or religions of which the individual victims are members. In this view, the distinct crime of genocidal rape has the "specific intent of destroying ethnic-religious groups."[102] This understanding built on, and was discussed by, the work of a number of legal scholars who identified *rape as genocide* as a distinct crime from both *war rape* and *genocide*. Catherine MacKinnon's analysis is a good example of this legal thinking.

MacKinnon was one of the first scholars to call rape genocidal, describing the situation in Bosnia as

> rape under control. It is also rape unto death, rape as massacre, rape to kill and to make the victims wish they were dead. It is rape as an instrument of forced exile, rape to make you leave your home and never want to go back. It is rape to be seen and heard and watched and told to others: rape as spectacle. It is rape to drive a wedge through a community, to shatter a society, to destroy a people. It is rape as genocide.[103]

While MacKinnon's recognition of the collective dynamic of genocidal rape was important, and its recognition in a court decision in *Akayesu* groundbreaking, a closer look at this analysis suggests that there remain problems with the jurisprudence of sexual violence in war and conflict even here, both generally and for the recognition of female perpetrators and their victims. For example, in the same decision, the ICTR decided that women were the victims of the genocidal rape that occurred, explaining that, in Rwanda, "the rape of Tutsi women was systematic and was perpetrated against all Tutsi women and solely against them," which is what made it genocidal rape.[104] While that statement and others of the court did not explicitly suggest that *all* women are victims and *all* perpetrators are men, it did, with the scholarly work it followed, define the crime of genocidal rape by the sex of its victims—so that, in this jurisprudence, the crime takes place only if its victims are women.

While the *Akayesu* decision was initially hailed as a sea change in the international law addressing sexual violence in war and conflict, it came to be characterized as a decision which was substantively "groundbreaking but" ultimately "has had little effect on other prosecutions."[105] It was seen as ineffective for two reasons. First, other decisions went back on its logic.[106] This is reflected in the low conviction rate of both the ICTR and the ICTY on charges related to gender-based and sexual violence in their respective conflicts. For example, the conviction rate of those charged with rape in the ICTR is 32.5 percent, which is lower than the 36.9 percent conviction rate for all charges, and (notably) the 68 percent conviction rate for genocide.[107]

The many acquittals were often based on narrow definitions of rape, burden of proof issues, the general nature of allegations, doubt that leadership of rape constituted rape, lack of eyewitnesses, questions of credibility of witnesses, and the defendants' willingness to plead guilty to other charges to get rape charges dropped.[108] Legal procedure, then, can and should, get some of the blame for the disappointing records of both the ICTR and the ICTY on rape *convictions* despite relatively progressive jurisprudence. At the same time, a number of legal scholars have argued that the flaws in these tribunals' jurisprudence do not end with the procedural difficulties of obtaining convictions for rape and other conflict-related sexual violence. Instead, they suggested that there were some *substantive* problems with the jurisprudential grounds for the tribunals' decision-making.

As Katie Richey explains, "*Akayesu* . . . did not recognize the act of rape as a crime against humanity on the grounds that the singular act of rape denied the victim her humanity."[109] Instead, the legal logic that declares rape a crime against humanity or a crime of genocide emphasizes the *collectivity* of the victim of the crime. Richey suggests that "when we speak of rape as a violation of humanity as collective, it is difficult to discern to whom the law is recognizing harm."[110] She is concerned that the harm to the body politic subordinates the harm to individual bodies, both skewing the crime and making it less likely that prosecutions of perpetrators of sexual violence in war and conflict will ultimately result in convictions.[111] Even her progressive analysis, though, is stuck with the idea that all victims of sexual violence are women, as she is concerned that, in its collectivization, "the crime [of genocidal rape] is abstracted from the bodily violation of the raped woman."[112]

Richey is not the only analyst to have shown concern about the effectiveness of the explosion of legal activity surrounding wartime sexual violence in the ICTR and ICTY, however. While there is a widespread understanding that "international legal response to the wartime experiences of women has been a recent, and seemingly successful, effort by feminists at visibility," many scholars wonder if that visibility comes at a price, and is unrepresentative of the experiences of victims of sexual violence in war and conflict.[113] For example, Christine Chinkin suggests that "despite the importance of an affirmation of the illegality of rape in armed conflict, some reservations about the role of the [International

Criminal] Tribunal [for the Former Yugoslavia] from the perspective of survivors of rape must be expressed."[114] Particularly, Chinkin is concerned about the ways that the legal frameworks that have been put in place to address wartime sexual violence are perpetrator-focused rather than victim-focused, and therefore display insensitivity to victims and produce inadequate remedy for those who are victimized.[115] As Chinkin explains, "the focus of the Tribunal is on punishing wrongdoers, not on providing compensation and support to those who have suffered the harms."[116]

Even these concerns, though, are often framed in the legal community to require a revitalization of the analysis of women's roles as victims of sexual violence in war and conflict. Chinkin's analysis protesting the dehumanization of the victims, for example, is put forth in explicitly sexed terms. She contends that

> [w]omen are raped in all forms of armed conflict, international and internal, whether the conflict is fought primarily on religious, ethnic, political, or nationalist grounds, or a combination of all of these. They are raped by men from all sides—both enemy and "friendly" forces.[117]

This book is not arguing that Chinkin's account is *false*—only that it is incomplete and gender essentialist, and that its incompleteness is reflected in and reified by even the most progressive jurisprudence of sexual violence in war and conflict, which assumes (though rarely if ever explicitly states) that it is a crime committed *by men victimizing women.* This notion reifies the discursive (and legal) impossibility of both female perpetrators and their (male and female) victims of sexual violence in war and conflict.

Since the celebration of, and criticism of, the initial conflict sexual violence jurisprudence at the ICTR and the ICTY, another high-profile court where these crimes can be prosecuted has begun trying cases. The International Criminal Court (ICC) was created by the Rome Statute of the International Criminal Court, which was signed in 1998 to go into force in 2002.[118] The ICC is a voluntary-membership organization with 122 state parties and an additional 31 signatories with limited jurisdiction.[119] At the time of this writing, it has prosecuted war criminals in seven cases, all in Africa.[120]

The initial outlook for the handling of sexual violence in war and conflict at the ICC was fairly positive. Building on the momentum from the ICTY and the ICTR, "the Rome Statute codified a wide range of sex-based crimes and provided jurisdiction over war crimes, crimes against humanity, and genocide based on sexual violence."[121] This codification included a formal definition of rape as a war crime, in the ICC *Elements of Crimes*, which has four distinct elements:

1. The perpetrator invaded the body of a person by conduct resulting in penetration, however slight, of any part of the body of the victim or of the perpetrator with a sexual organ, or of the anal or genital opening of the victim with any object or any other part of the body.
2. The invasion was committed by force, or by threat of force or coercion, such as that caused by fear of violence, duress, detention, psychological oppression or abuse of power, against such person or another person, or by taking advantage of a coercive environment, or the invasion was committed against a person incapable of giving genuine consent.
3. The conduct took place in the context of and was associated with an international armed conflict.
4. The perpetrator was aware of the factual circumstances that established the existence of an armed conflict.[122]

The ICC definition of sexual violence in war and conflict has not sat idly by in the first decade of ICC jurisprudence. Quite the contrary, "the ICC has brought a range of sexual violence charges across several of the Situations under its purview."[123] Still, the ICC has yet to *convict* a defendant of sexual violence charges.[124] Kelly Dawn Askin describes the ICC's recent failure to convict Germain Katanga, a Congolese militia leader, of sexual violence in connection with an attack on civilians in Eastern Congo in 2003 as "a devastating blow to the victims of sex crimes, and for the survivors of rape and sexual slavery from Borogo."[125] While the ICC has some of the tools to prosecute sexual violence in war and conflict, its use of those tools has been unbalanced. Some legal scholars blame the absence of sexual violence convictions in the ICC on prosecutorial ineffectiveness, calling the prosecutorial structure "flawed and inconsistent."[126] Still others suggest that many of the problems that the ICTR and ICTY experienced with the procedural and substantive challenges of sexual violence convictions carry over to the ICC, and are being inadequately addressed by the "gender strategies" of the court, which reduce victims to pawns.[127]

These flaws in ICC jurisprudence specifically and international jurisprudence generally regarding sexual violence in war and conflict have led scholars and practitioners of international law to express concern with how effective international criminal law really is in either addressing or deterring it. As Doris Buss details, what initially look like a string of victories for those concerned about gender-based violence in war and conflict in the ICTR, the ICTY, and the ICC might be less successful than they appeared.[128] She suggests, "in short, the Tribunal decisions, and the statute of the ICC appear to have satisfied, at first blush, feminist concerns about the possible marginalization and even erasure of sexual violence through the prosecution process."[129] This appearance might be deceptive, however, as Buss explains when she explores the question of "how successful have the Tribunals been in drawing attention to *all* dimensions of violence against women?"[130]

Put another way, Buss thinks that it is important to explore what jurisprudence on sexual violence in war and conflict functions to do. Still, Buss asks the question in sex-specific terms, both above and as she explores the question, "what is it we see when we make violence against women visible as an international criminal law issue?"[131] Buss shares others' concerns that emphasizing the collective nature of victimization in sexual violence in war and conflict obscures individual victims, but adds analysis of what that means *for women*, and for gender equality.[132] She explains that there is a difficulty in rape jurisprudence where the need to emphasize the collectivity of both perpetration and victimization within the frameworks of gendered nationalism that are a condition of possibility for their occurrence can overshadow both its "women victims" and the "broader context of gender inequality."[133]

Buss explains that it is important to highlight "the egregious violence done to women," but that "raising the visibility of sexual violence does not . . . translate into an awareness of the systemic nature of violence against women."[134] Looking back at the jurisprudential successes and visibility of early convictions in the ICTR and ICTY of perpetrators of sexual violence in war and conflict, Buss worries that it is possible that visibility is a double-edged sword. She explains that "sometimes, as Cynthia Enloe notes, making rape visible as a matter of political concern can be 'dangerously easy.'"[135] What Buss and Enloe mean is that it is sometimes easy to get attention for oversimplified narratives of human tragedy, but that such attention can both reify faulty assumptions about situations and make it difficult to draw attention to complexities and find working solutions to address problems.

Sherri Russell-Brown goes further, to express the concern that jurisprudence and law-making around genocidal rape takes the gender out of rape by focusing on the ethnicities, national groups, racial groups, religious groups, and political groups targeted by the rapes, rather than the women targeted, individually or collectively.[136] If genocidal rape is a crime against a state or a group, then it becomes *less* or even *not* a crime against the individual victims who are violated in the commission of the rape. The impacts of this approach, some scholars suggest, go far beyond the silencing of the individual victims. Instead, some scholars recognize that the victims are not only silenced but also appropriated and instrumentalized in favor of the nationalist cause of the state or group to which the victims belong. Christine Chinkin worries that "the pain of women raped and abused in armed conflict has often been appropriated by males for propaganda purposes."[137] What Chinkin means is that the men who are seen as the supposed or potential protectors of the women who are violated hold up the violation of *their women* as evidence of the evil of the enemy, the enemy's wrong in the conflict, and why *they* must continue to combat the enemy. All of these significations of the victimization of women share a neglect of the actual plight of the victims, and many of them reify the sexist assumption that the violation of women's honor is a violation of a society as a whole. For these reasons, Janet Halley characterizes the understanding of war rape as a collective crime in international criminal jurisprudence as producing a "problematic convergence of feminism and nationalism" that risks the exploitation of and silencing of women rape victims by the victim's friends, relatives, ethnic groups, and states.[138]

In reaction, a number of legal scholars have pointed out problems that they see as fundamental with the structure of current prosecutions, from the more careful characterization of the collective nature of sexual violence in war and conflict to focusing on survivors. For example, Julie Mertus, in critiquing the structured questioning of witnesses in proceedings in the ICTY, argues that "some survivors wanted to look the men who raped them in the eye and accuse them publicly."[139] Christine Chinkin emphasizes the need to see the *men* and *masculinity* in perpetrators explicitly to improve jurisprudence, describing sexual violence in war and conflict as "a question of power and control which is 'structured by male soldiers' notions of their masculine privilege'" and must be identified as such to be properly legally addressed.[140]

Even these critiques, however, default to the description of sexual violence as something that *men* do to *women*. While the text of the legal and jurisprudential structures of the Geneva Conventions, the ICTR, the ICTY, and the ICC do not *explicitly* characterize rape as torture, genocide, and/or a crime against humanity as a sex-specific crime, the implicit understanding that it is such a crime surfaces in a number of the descriptive sections of individual court decisions, which account for women as men's victims. This is replicated in some of the text of relevant legal decisions and analysis, which has a sexed *subtext*—the ICTR definition of rape as "physical invasion," for instance, is a traditional description of what happens when a man rapes a woman, and may or may not be what happens when a man rapes a man, when a woman rapes a man, when a woman rapes a woman, or when the sex of the rapists is not identifiable or the first priority of violated rape victims. The ICC maintains the language of bodily *invasion* in its understanding of wartime rape. As Judith Butler has explained, these codings function to create an understanding of which bodies can be violated and which bodies can violate in a hierarchy of bodily vulnerability.[141]

The hierarchy of bodily vulnerability in the law of sexual violence in war and conflict exists implicitly *in the jurisprudence* and explicitly in its analysis. The ICTR *did* convict a woman of rape as a crime against humanity.[142] In that text of that conviction, the issue of the defendant being a woman was not overemphasized.[143] In fact, a cursory reading of the *Nyiramasuhuko* decision might lead one to believe that this book is all for naught, and that international criminal jurisprudence surrounding sexual violence in war and conflict really is both sex- and gender-neutral in its identification of perpetrators.[144] At the same time, the prosecutorial strategy of the ICTR prosecutors focused only on Nyiramasuhuko's command role, and therefore only on the *men* she commanded to violate *women*, leaving the traditional structures of who is a perpetrator of *the act* of sexual violence in war and conflict (and who is its victim) largely intact. There is, for example, no analysis of the potential for less-than-voluntary perpetration on the part of soldiers under Nyiramasuhuko's command, though there has been extensive analysis of the less-than-voluntary nature of the abuse committed by "bush wives" under the command of male soldiers in Sierra Leone who may have been similarly situated.[145] I suggest that this is because, while the courts had a framework for a woman who played a supervisory role in *traditionally inflicted* sexual violence in war and conflict (by men on women), they did not have a framework to analyze the victimization of *men and women* by a woman. The apparent gender neutrality in the definition of the crime of rape, in this situation, "does not safeguard against the effective influence of pervasive and enduring symbolic constructions pertaining to male and female sexuality."[146]

If these sexed dichotomies of the classes of perpetrators and victims remain influential in the definitions of sexual violence in war and conflict and the court decisions about it, they can also be found in the legal scholarship and legal activism looking to critique and extend existing international criminal law addressing sexual violence in war and conflict. A number of the legal critics of the vagueness, inefficiency, and imprecision in the international criminal law of sexual violence in war and conflict *explicitly* label rapists as men and victims as women, and rely on those dichotomies to perform the analyses that they present. Often, these critiques are justified by the demand for attention to *the women* who are victims, and *the men and masculinities* who are both perpetrators and targets. While gender analysis is essential to understanding the possibility, perpetration, signification, and prosecution of sexual violence in war and conflict, that gender analysis is *hampered* rather than *facilitated* by the oversimplistic assumption that because *most* perpetrators are male and *most* victims are female, sexual violence crimes are crimes perpetrated by men against women. Instead, the crime of sexual violence in war and conflict can be best understood as *gendered* but not *sex essentialist*, where the former promotes complicated gender analysis that enhances understanding of the crime and the latter obscures both some commissions of the crime and some dimensions thereof.

Media Accounts

It is not only in international law over the last twenty years where sexual violence in war and conflict has seen increased visibility. Media coverage has also spiked significantly. Some suggest, in fact, that media coverage of sexual violence in war and conflict increased while sexual violence itself did not.[147] Even those who are not arguing that the media coverage exaggerates have suggested that sexual violence in war and conflict becomes a different phenomenon to the public when it is seen in real time, and that the media (broadly speaking) has a role in how that sexual violence is seen and understood.[148] Some see that media coverage as either net or completely a positive development—drawing attention to abuse *during the conflict* that may not have otherwise been noticed until after the conflict or even at all.[149] Others, however, worry about media distortion, media sensationalization, media manipulation for political purposes, media participation in conflicts, or the necessary oversimplification of complex stories when they are presented in the media.[150] These challenges have become all the more complicated as the media outlets available to audiences around the world are both increasingly global and increasingly diverse. In addition to the newspapers, radio stations, and television stations from which people got news decades ago, now many people around the world have access to both reading and *writing* social media.

Seeing media outlets as an important part of structuring narratives of possibility and impossibility around sexual violence in war and conflict is important, as is seeing the ways media narratives' assumptions can be replicated in critical engagements with the role of media in conflict. This section starts with a review of media narratives of sexual violence in war and conflict in two situations—the conflict in the former Yugoslavia in the 1990s and the 2014 kidnapping of Nigerian girls by Boko Haram. Those two cases were selected because the sorts of media used and the stories the media told are wildly different, yet each case's media coverage renders the sexually violent woman impossible. In these short analyses, I am interested in understanding the dimensions of the characterizations of the victims and perpetrators as reported, and the ways that media portrayals shape (or do not shape) perceptions of the nature, direction, and constitution of sexual violence in war and conflict.

THE FORMER YUGOSLAVIA

Dubravka Zarkov's analysis of the media narratives in the conflict in the former Yugoslavia deals with media reports from the Serbian media and the Croatian media leading up to and during the conflict. Zarkov argues that the Serbian and Croatian media both participated in the "war" even before it became a war.[151] In other words, Zarkov suggests that both partisans' media outlets were themselves parties to the conflict— engaging in nationalist politics for predisposed friendly audiences.[152] As Zarkov describes, though, the media "sides" treated sexual violence very differently:

> While in the Serbian media the female body supported production of the Serbs as a collective victim of the war, in the Croatian media, the female body was crucial in producing Croatia as the ultimate victimized Self. The reasons for this striking difference lie in the different contexts within which the media war and the ethnic war operated in Serbia and Croatia.[153]

In other words, the rape of Serbian women was emphasized in the Serbian media as the key to putting Serbia collectively at risk—the vulnerability of Serbian women to "other" men served as a mandate for the legitimacy of protecting Serbian (exclusive) collective identity. The rape of Croatian women was emphasized in the Croatian media as a reason that Croatia needed to be an independent state, able to provide protection to its (female) citizens. While this difference may seem slight to an audience outside of the conflict, it was importantly reflective and reflected in the different ways that media outlets related to the populations they served. As Zarkov explains, "the media war in Serbia had to seek its legitimacy in the people. . . . In Croatia, the political situation was quite different . . . the media war and the ethnic war there made the establishment of an independent state their objective."[154] While the *direction* of the mobilization of nationalism in each of these situations was different (and therefore took shape differently), *both* narratives of sexual violence in war and conflict relate the violation of women to the violation of group, state, and nation. In this way, "the media war was about *production of ethnicity*, with notions of femininity and masculinity and norms of sexuality as its essential ingredients."[155] In each of these narratives, women (individually and collectively) and by extension the group to which the women "belong" are the victims of wartime sexual violence, and the (often explicit, sometimes understood) perpetrator are men of the "other" group that pose a threat *through sexual violence* to the existence, dominance, and/or exclusivity of the "other" group. There is both a nationalist element and a racialized dynamic to these tellings.

Zarkov sees the racialized dynamic as she looks at the way that the Croatian media covered the rapes of Croatian women differently than the way that it covered the rapes of Bosnian Muslim women, as well as in the particular emphases and blindnesses of the international media coverage of the sexual violence in the conflict. Zarkov explains that the Croatian media discussion of the rapes of Croatian women deemphasized the brutal details of attacks and focused on the violation of the woman and of Croatia, while it provided a significant amount of detail about what happened to Muslim women as they were raped—including specifics about how women were violated and brutalized.[156] Zarkov contends that this difference demonstrated a sense of voyeurism about the victimization of the racialized other alongside a protective discourse about the women within the group.

"Voyeurism" is one of the words a number of analysts use to describe the Western media coverage of the sexual violence on all sides of the conflict, especially inflicted by the Serbs on the Bosnian Muslim population.[157] As Lene Hansen describes, "stories of mass rape of Bosnian women by Serbian forces went on the front pages of western media in 1992 and 1993."[158] While part of the level of coverage of that sexual violence, which Zarkov describes as "fervent in reporting rapes of women,"[159] some worried that the Western media attention to the sexual violence in the conflict was motivated less by a genuine concern for the victims and more by a narrowly tailored political engagement. Much like Zarkov worried that the media coverage *from outlets within* the conflict used sexual violence in war and conflict as a vehicle for partisan engagement, Hansen saw a similar move in the the international media, where coverage of the horrors of the sexual violence of the conflict was used by a variety of constituencies to encourage external intervention. Hansen points out that this was often a difficult line to walk for advocates interested in wielding media coverage to get attention for and intervention in the injustices which were occurring without either making the problem worse, or marginalizing the victims.[160] She explains that "the dilemma become how to use the media to mobilize support for intervention when the same media attention might construct the victims in problematic—sexualized—ways."[161]

Zarkov notes that the many political pressures on Western media outlets from those with a political interest in intervention and the political pressures that Western media outlets looked to *create* combined to make the coverage not only a partial representation of what happened but also blind to perpetrators and victims that fell outside of the idealized notions of what sexual violence in war and conflict is, who perpetrates it, and who is victimized by it.[162] For example, she states that "the international media . . . shied away from the topic of sexually assaulted men. In coverage that relied heavily on images of starving Muslim men behind barbed wire and on tear-stained photos of raped women, no one saw a photo of raped men."[163] This, Zarkov argues, was not a coincidence or intentional discrimination against men. Instead, it is a result of, and a reification of, a particular narrative of sexual violence in war and conflict in which *men* victimize *women*—therefore male victims (and, I would add, even more so women perpetrators) become impossible to imagine and to report. She concludes that the level of sympathy that would be produced from reporting the rape of men would, media outlets likely suspected, be lower than the level of sympathy that would be produced from reporting the rape of women. This (likely accurate) reading is an overdetermined verdict based on understanding women as in need of the protection that men provide, men's masculinity as dependent on providing protection, and women as biological and cultural reproducers of state and nation.[164]

These codes for what women are, what men are, and what conflict is as it relates to sex and gender combined to produce multiple media narratives of the sexual violence in war and conflict in the war in the former Yugoslavia with remarkably consistent features, despite different audiences and different political purposes. The consistent features of the media narratives about the sexual violence in the Serbian media, in the Croatian media, and across Western media outlets included emphasis on the victimization of women, attention to that victimization as a *collective* affront to the social fabric of the nation/ethnic group rather than an offense against the individual person who was violated in a particular instance of rape, the characterization of the perpetrator of individual and collective rapes as both male and masculine, the assertion that there is something *worse* about the crime of rape when it is the result of or used in service of the extermination or oppression of an ethnic group, state, or nation. A narrative with these features has no room for people who are not, in Mibenge's words, the perfect or legitimate victim.[165] Being a victim of a woman perpetrator is discursively impossible, and therefore disrupts narratives of legitimation of victimhood. It is therefore left out in (and left out by) partisan media outlets with either an intentional interest in inciting a particular direction or change in the conflict or with an interest in preserving existing gender orders.

#BRINGBACKOURGIRLS

The kidnappings in April 2014 of an undetermined number of Nigerian schoolgirls by the insurgent group Boko Haram happened in an entirely different media context. The media context differed in location, time, international political climate, and (perhaps most importantly) available media outlets. While the newspapers, television channels, and radio stations that covered the conflicts of the 1990s (for the most part) continue to be major sources of news and information for many people around the world, as many people also (or in the alternative) use social media to both learn and communicate. The advent of the internet as a source for transmitting and receiving news has made the reporting process significantly more interactive, and as a result often lay persons "report" and "engage" across multiple (social) media platforms.

The kidnapping of the Nigerian girls was covered by mainstream media outlets, and then became the subject of a social media campaign (largely on Twitter, with hashtag #bringbackourgirls), and then the social media campaign was covered in the mainstream media. Boko Haram[166] has been carrying out attacks in Nigeria since 2009, causing instability in the Nigerian state. In April 2014, an estimated 250 to 350 girls were kidnapped from the Government Secondary School in Chibok. In CNN's initial report, the kidnappers were described as "dozens of gunmen" who were "heavily armed" and kidnapped the girls "as the students slept in their dormitories."[167] Most of the news coverage both in Nigeria and beyond refers to the victims of the violence as schoolgirls.[168] The students were at the time between ages sixteen and eighteen.[169]

Early in the ordeal, the kidnapping was mentioned in some international media outlets, but did not receive a significant amount of coverage. A story in *Ms.* begins by introducing the threat that Boko Haram is to traditional security concerns, describing it as a terrorist group fast learning to disrupt Africa's largest economy in its most populous state and control its vast oil resources.[170] The author then continues that "those lenses, for the moment, don't interest me. Here's what does: the abduction and selling into sex slavery [of] over 200 girls in Northern Nigeria and the appalling lack of US media coverage."[171] This story has several key significations for thinking about narratives of gender and sexual violence in war and conflict. The first signification is that the capture of women and girls is *not* a traditional security issue, and does not fit within the purview of power politics, international political economy, and international terrorism as traditionally understood. In this account, the author directs the reader to look *outside* of that traditional domain to see what happened to the Nigerian girls. The second signification is that the abduction of the girls *necessarily* involves sexual abuse, which is one of the primary reasons that the kidnapping of the girls is normatively and practically problematic. The third signification is that the US media has a responsibility to be covering the kidnapping of the girls regardless of its falling outside of traditional security concerns, and its failure to do so is morally repugnant. While I would argue that sexual violence against women and girls *is* a key part of "traditional" security concerns, and "traditional" security concerns play a key role in the commission of sexual violence in war and conflict, even stories that do not frame the kidnappings in this language feature gendered accounts of the perpetrators and the victims.

One of the genderings is the continued use of the labels "girls" and "schoolgirls" to refer to the persons who had been kidnapped. On the one hand, that is an accurate description in a number of contexts—though some people think of people who are eighteen as women rather than girls, many of the persons kidnapped were younger; they were in a school dormitory when they were kidnapped. On the other hand, the injury of a number of children and young adults in a number of other situations has been characterized with more diverse vocabulary—either by identifying the victims by name, or as children, or as men and women, or as people.[172] While the use of this gendered terminology *does* highlight the sexist behavior of Boko Haram (which is well-known for abusing women and girls, believing it is acceptable to enslave and sell women),[173] it also invokes stereotypes about the age and gender of the people who were kidnapped. As I argued in a blog post during the media coverage of #bringbackourgirls, in the media, the kidnapped persons in Nigeria are "at once Cynthia Enloe's 'womenandchildren' and *literally* women children."[174]

By Cynthia Enloe's "womenandchildren," I mean that they are defined as a group by their helplessness and need for protection, which is related to a conflated notion of femininity and infantilism. The stories about the kidnapped girls both in mainstream and social media emphasize the gendered risks that the girls face as they remain in the custody of their captors. The media coverage of the kidnapping spiked around the time that someone understood to be a leader of Boko Haram suggested that the organization would be putting the kidnapped girls up for sale.[175] An Associated Press story explains that the leader suggested that "he will sell the abducted schoolgirls 'in the market' and 'marry them off,' referring to them as 'slaves.'"[176] Any boys who were kidnapped were assumed to be "boy soldiers" and not "sex slaves."

This report and others of sexual violence fueled the sense of emergency in both mainstream and social media.[177] A number of news stories quoted the leaders of Boko Haram as suggesting that the proper role of girls is to get married, and that these girls would be doing so whether they accepted that as their proper role or not.[178] A Fox News reporter worried that the girls "could face a life of misery, as slaves or child brides sold for a pittance in markets across the globe" when they are "forced into the sex trade."[179] Some reporters have even gone so far as to write critically about the use of the sanitized language of "forced marriage" when the experience that they are anticipating the girls experiencing is really repeated rape—repeated by the same man who claims her as his "wife" without her permission or with her consent only under duress.[180]

While some news stories express concerns about the girls being forced into servitude,[181] others find it important to highlight that the reality is that the girls have likely already been the victims of rape and sexual abuse.[182] For example, *Buzzfeed World* reports Dr. Valerie Obote, the national president of the Medical Women's Association of Nigeria, suggesting that "'the first thing those men [Boko Haram] will be thinking of is sexual violence,"[183] an assumption that the Nigerian government was reported to have shared.[184] The news stories that emphasized (actual or potential) sexual violence of which the kidnapped girls either were or would be the victims were many, and most stories that did not focus on that aspect of the plight of the victims often at least mentioned or alluded to it.[185]

Sexual violence is not the only harm of feminized vulnerability that newspaper stories about the kidnapping feature. They also suggest that the girls are vulnerable to religious conversion and political radicalization. A *Global Post* report explains that "the danger of waiting for so long to free the Chibok girls is that the group can radicalize these girls, to the point that by the time they are released, they . . . become part of the problem . . . brainwashing, indoctrination is part of the strategy of the insurgency."[186] This concern about the girls' vulnerability is repeated and apparently validated in a number of media reports which discussed a May 12 video that Boko Haram released featuring some of the kidnapped girls.[187] In the video, Boko Haram members announced that many of the girls who had been Christian had converted to Islam.

The fact that the girls remained missing (as they still do as of this writing) combined with speculation about their vulnerability to both violence and corruption inspired growing mainstream media coverage in the month of May 2014, as well as a social media campaign on twitter, with #bringbackourgirls. The tweeting of "#bringbackourgirls" started as an adaptation of the #bringbackourdaughters that some of the Nigerian families of kidnapping victims had used. #bringbackourgirls began being used about a week after the kidnappings took place, and "its usage spiked from a few thousand tweets to roughly 250,000 on April 30, when the kidnappers threatened to sell the girls before quieting down again."[188] The #bringbackourgirls campaign not only received a significant number of followers and retweeters on Twitter, but got the attention of the United States' political and social elite. As *The Independent* reported, Michelle Obama tweeted a picture of herself with the hashtag, which drove up traffic significantly.[189] As a result, "two days later [after Michelle Obama joined] the use of the hashtag spiked at more than 488,000 occurrences on Twitter."[190] A number of other well-known politicians and activists, including President Obama and celebrity activist Angelina Jolie, joined the #bringbackourgirls campaign.[191] While there is little centralized information about the movement, it seems to have been a combination of demanding that someone do something to find the girls and informing people who do not know what happened to them of the tragedy.[192]

The explosion of the #bringbackourgirls hashtag on Twitter was heartening to many, who saw it is activist investment in the cause of finding and saving the Nigerian girls who were in peril of abuse.[193] Others were less enthusiastic, concerned that it was "doing nothing as activism."[194] Those critics wondered whether or not there were any teeth behind the demand to "bring back our girls," and what would happen if the demand was not complied with. Dan Hodges asked, "Where are our girls? A month ago everyone wanted to know. . . . But they weren't brought back. So the world put down its signs and moved on."[195] Hodges suggested that the Twitter campaign succeeded only in giving Boko Haram attention and motivation to act with impunity. He argued:

> Here's how Boko Haram have responded to us taking a stand. According to reports, the terror group last week assaulted a village called Kumma-bza in the Damboa district of Borno state. The attackers left 30 dead, and kidnapped 60 women and young girls, and 31 boys. . . . What are we going to do now?[196]

Whether or not #bringbackourgirls did anything to contribute to the (lack of, or attempts to) rescue the kidnapped girls from their captors, it was picked up in the mainstream media, where stories about the kidnapping incident proliferated, and many of them used the language of the Twitter activists. The demand to #bringbackourgirls moved from Twitter to the blogosphere to newspapers and television stations.

Two problematic trends can be identified in the proliferation of the #bringbackourgirls story. The first, discussed above, is the use of gendered language to describe the girls and the related assumptions about and characterization of feminized peril. The second is the instrumentalization of existing sexual violence in war and conflict and/or the risk of sexual violence towards particular political ends. For example, analysts have suggested that the Nigerian government exploited the kidnappings for electoral gain without putting significant effort into recovering the kidnapping victims.[197] Specifically, Suman Varadani reports the Nigerian government identifying the act of kidnapping the girls as "international terrorism" and declared the matter of their return important to "protect our democracy, our national unity, and our political stability."[198]

This association of the of the ability to protect girls with national sustainability *within* Nigeria is matched by outside states volunteering to intervene when Nigeria demonstrates its *inability* to protect the girls. As *The Globe and Mail* reports, "U.S. troops and drones are providing support in the form of intelligence gathering, surveillance, reconnaissance, and any other activity."[199] Samantha Nutt characterizes this as "the risk that comes with campaigns such as #bringbackourgirls. . . . [T]hey can turn into an open invitation to endless interventionism."[200] Like the media narratives about sexual violence in war and conflict in the former Yugoslavia, the media narratives about the (actual and potential) sexual violence against the kidnapped Nigerian girls can be wielded instrumentally in service of nationalist protection or of liberal interventionism.

#bringbackourgirls and the media coverage of both the hashtag and the kidnapping that inspire it are not talking about the whole conflict in Nigeria, which has been going on for at least the last five years, nor are they talking about all of the sexual violence in the conflict in Nigeria. All of the victims of the April 2014 kidnapping *are* female, and there is no evidence that there were women among the perpetrators of this particular kidnapping, though there is evidence that there are women who are members of Boko Haram.[201] So, on one hand, this is a story *about* the female victims of male perpetrators. On the other hand, the *feminization* of the female victims and the *emasculation* of those who are seen as having been responsible for providing them protection contain elements that idealize gendered notions of perpetrators and victims which may or may not map onto the male perpetrators or female victims of this particular act of sexual violence in war and conflict. Women perpetrators are discursively impossible (whether or not they exist) in this narrative because women are signified as *girls*, as in need of help, as in need of rescue, as vulnerable to sexual assault, as vulnerable to political or religious conversion, and as owned by the families, communities, and even global community to which they belong. While the stories that talk about Boko Haram's abuse of women importantly reveal the group's misogyny, many of them (even inadvertently) entrench a number of the gendered stereotypes that the group's distorted views of women rely on, and themselves distort gender roles in conflict, in Nigeria and elsewhere. These narratives limit what Nigerian women are and what Nigerian men are, along with constraining their possible roles in sexual violence in war and conflict.

#BRINGBACKOURGIRLS, THE FORMER YUGOSLAVIA, AND MEDIA ACCOUNTS

These two examples demonstrate a common theme in the many media narratives surrounding two extensively covered instances of sexual violence in war and conflict: the sexual violence on all sides of a decade-long conflict in the former Yugoslavia, and the kidnapping of hundreds of girls from a Nigerian school in April 2014. The events do not have a lot in common, either in what happened or in terms of the media atmospheres in which they were situated. In terms of the perpetrators, evidence suggests that there were a number of female perpetrators of the sexual violence in war and conflict in the former Yugoslavia, while there is no evidence that women participated in the kidnapping of the Nigerian girls. At the same time, these two cases of media coverage share a number of important characteristics. Both present a particular image of women as the *receivers* of sexual violence in war and conflict, of which they are co-targets with what it appears that they "stand for"—whether that is ethnic groups (Yugoslavia), religious sects (both conflicts), or Westernization (Nigeria). Violation of the women is a violation of the values, or valued institutions, for which they stand. If women are, institutionally and individually, the targets of the violence *because they are women*, these media accounts assume away the possibility that *women* can target women *because they are women*, and characterize the perpetrators as collectively male while characterizing the victims as individually and collectively female. Such narratives are closer approximations to the "truth" of the sexual violence in some conflicts than others, but always engage in gender-stereotyping, gender-limiting, gender-signified discourses that make the picture substantively if not representationally partial.

A number of critics blame this partiality on the media outlets' inherent flaws or intentional manipulation of the "facts" of the conflict. For example, Zarkov was concerned that media outlets were partisans to the conflict, trying to convince their "domestic" audiences to commit to nationalist fervor. Dan Hodges was concerned that media "activism" about the kidnapping of the girls in Nigeria was being substituted for and taken to be material action, when headlines and hashtags were not really improving the lives of chances of rescue of the kidnapped girls. David Mitchell worried that "instant reporting from the field has resulted in the rapid sensationalization of public option, to make some kind of action a moral imperative" without specifying the correct action or paying attention to the complexities of the situation.[202]

Jennifer Green suggests that these problems are a side effect of some of the general problems that news coverage faces in reporting events that go on in global politics, and may not be specific to sexual violence in war and conflict.[203] She explains that any given news reporting is subject to both selection bias (competition over space, reporting norms, editorial concerns, and limited access to the subjects of reporting) and description bias (with a preference for reporting "hard news" over "soft news").[204] Sexual violence in war and conflict often appears to be "soft news" and its subjects (whether perpetrator or victim) are often difficult to access, yet stories about women being abused are often heavily reported, especially when a political competitor or enemy is doing the reporting. For these and other reasons, it is important to note that reports of sexual violence in war and conflict may be partial, misrepresentative, or even untrue.

In fact, Robert Hayden suggests that wartime sexual violence narratives published in media outlets can rise to the level of propaganda. He explains that "the representation of rape and rape victim varies with the different nationalist governments and the information media they control, which is not surprising; the use of reports of sexual violence, whether true or not, is a common propaganda techniques."[205] As a result, "women's experiences of war are highly misrepresented in mainstream media," including silence towards most women's experiences and distortions of others, creating "gendered coverage of women in war."[206]

This gendered coverage is sometimes an incidental or at least unconscious reproduction of gendered political values in the context of the media outlets, as much a product as a producer of gendered accounts of war and conflict. However, as Hayden and Augusta Del Zotto have explained, and the analysis of the former Yugoslavia above suggests, media outlets may not only be passive agents of the reproduction of gender-stereotyping and gender-subordinating perceptions of conflict and sexual violence therein, but active participants in both perpetuating conflict and subordinating women therein.

Paying attention to the conflicts in both the former Yugoslavia and Rwanda, Yaschica Williams and Janine Bower suggest that it is important to "ask questions about the role of news media in shaping and re-inforcing perceptions of genocide," particularly as media outlets publish conflict-inciting op-eds or propaganda, and/or frame particular events in a way that would be violence inciting intentionally.[207] Patricia Weitsman found that media outlets sometimes perpetuate the negative labeling of children born of genocidal rape and assume and/or encourage their rejection by their mothers' families, ethnic groups, states, or nations.[208] For these and other actions, it is actually legally possible for media outlets to be found responsible for having committed crimes against humanity, including inciting rape.[209]

Even the media outlets at the other end of the spectrum, the ones that are just trying to report what happened to women, perhaps even to help the women, often end up presenting distorted stories, or creating distorting impressions. For example, Tamara Tompkins suggests that media outlets' exponential increase in covering sexual violence in war and conflict starting in the 1990s (unintentionally, and perhaps even counter to the intentions of the reporters and news outlets) created the impression that wartime sexual violence was a new phenomena. She explains that

[w]artime rape has never before been so aggressively and immediately reported. Certainly it has never been exposed in mainstream media forums in such grisly detail. Would the horrified, and seemingly paralyzed, watching world be further horrified to know that the phenomenon of wartime rape, including rape conducted on a systematic basis and massive scales, is nothing new?[210]

I agree but argue that the distortion that sexual violence in war and conflict is new is not the only distortion these stories perpetuate. Another distortion is the discursive impossibility of female perpetrators of sexual violence through the framing of that violence as a crime

that *men do to women,* and the concomitant classification of perpetrators of sexual violence as men and the victims as women. Whether
that is or is not the sex distribution of perpetrators and victims in any
given conflict, most media narratives, like most scholarly accounts and
most legal accounts, *frame* sexual violence in war and conflict in a way
that makes other perpetrators (and other victims) unimaginable *by
definition.* In media outlets, this oversimplification is overdetermined.
Media outlets have little space to explain events as concisely as possible,
and rely on metaphors and readers' existing knowledges and understandings to complete the rest of the picture. For sexual violence in
war and conflict, readers' existing knowledges and understandings are
often centered around stereotypical notions of the capabilities of people understood to be men and people understood to be women. These
assumptions, and media narratives' tendencies not to question them
(and to sensationalize exceptions), limit men, women, and conflicts
unrepresentatively, not least by constructing the discursive impossibility of women perpetrators.

The Analytical Costs of Making Women Perpetrators Impossible

The forces making women perpetrators discursively impossible might
be seen as overwhelming. They include but are not limited to the
misperceptions about women's relationships with war, conflict, and violence; the gendered nature of war and conflict; and scholarly, legal, and
media structured narratives accounting for sexual violence in war and
conflict. The forces that make disrupting narratives of men's sexual violence and women's victimization itself dangerous are also important to
heed. First, urging "attention" to women perpetrators of sexual violence
can become a slippery slope, slipping easily from "attention" to sensationalizing, singling out, and paying disproportionate heed to those
women. Second, pointing out the existence of women perpetrators can
easily be capitalized on to downplay the extreme suffering of women
victims, a move which is both non sequitur in terms of the political
reality of the existence of women perpetrators and women victims and
problematic for trying to explain and understand sexual violence in war
and conflict. Third, suggesting that it is important to recognize women
perpetrators can easily be misunderstood as a claim that women *as*

women commit wartime sexual violence for different reasons or in different ways than men *as men* do, or that women's sexual violence is somehow a more egregious war crime than men's sexual violence. Fourth, calling attention to the invisibility of women's perpetration of sexual violence in war and conflict as a product of gender subordination in global politics might accidentally be read as a suggestion that women's perpetration is a result of gender liberation or is gender liberating. That could not be further from the point that this book is trying to make. Finally, the suggestion that women's perpetration is important to analyze might be misread as resting on a claim that women constitute a large, or at least statistically significant, portion of the overall number of perpetrators of sexual violence in war and conflict. As the introduction to this book states, there is every reason to believe that a number of women perpetrators exist, across conflicts and throughout history, but no reason to believe that they are more than a couple of percent of the perpetrators in any given conflict, if that. Instead, their *existence* is conceptually significant.

Those pitfalls are important to heed, especially when looking to pay attention to the suffering of victims and the gendered nature of sexual violence in war and conflict, avoiding sensationalism in favor of rethinking how that violence is presented and analyzed. Still, that overall gendered misrepresentation is problematic enough that the risks of trying to understand the discursive impossibility of women's perpetration are worth the corrective—understanding its complexities, and debunking its myths, is not only a worthwhile payoff but one of the only available steps forward in the attempt to put a real dent in the (increasing) prevalence of sexual violence in war and conflict.[211]

The following chapters, then, focus on first making *visible* some of the women perpetrators of sexual violence in some of the conflicts in recent history. These accounts are not meant to be either comprehensive or representative—instead, they are meant to explore the information that can be found about women perpetrators despite the multiple layers of discursive impossibility piled on their actions. This book also looks to explore what seeing female perpetrators, and coming to understand both the possibility and existence of their actions, means for how it is possible to understand not only sexual violence in war and conflict, but also men and women, masculinity and femininity. The remainder of the book builds on that analysis to try to develop an account of sexual violence in war and conflict as *sexed* and *gendered,* but not either sex or gender essential—deconstructing the notion that sexual violence is the purview of *male perpetrators* victimizing *women* (and, by extension, the men that are perceived to be responsible for their protection) and reconstructing an understanding of sexual violence in war and conflict as *feminizing.*

3

The Unforgettable Wound

Seeing Rape among Women in Conflict

The consequence of our refusal to concede female contributions to violence are manifold. It affects our capacity to promote ourselves as autonomous and responsible beings. It affects our ability to develop a literature about ourselves that encompasses the full array of human emotions and experience. It demeans the right our victims have to be valued. . . . Perhaps above all, the denial of women's aggression profoundly undermines our attempt as a culture to understand violence, to trace its causes and to quell them.[1]
—Patricia Pearson, *When She Was Bad: How and Why Women Get Away with Murder*

This chapter looks to investigate women's commission of sexual violence in war and conflict in the spirit of Patricia Pearson's concern. We will return to this point at the end of the chapter, but it is worth discussing for a bit at the outset: this book and this chapter do not strive to enumerate all of the instances of women's perpetration of sexual violence in war and conflict, or the demographic traits of women perpetrators, their motives for doing what they did, or the sex- or gender-specific consequences of women's engagement in perpetration. While all of those are laudable (if possible) goals, the goal of this analysis is to demonstrate that "the impossible woman"—the woman perpetrator of sexual violence in war and conflict—exists, and that her existence is more than an anomaly. "She" exists not only in one conflict or in one part of the world or in one period of time, but across a wide variety of conflicts, a wide variety of time periods, and a wide variety of cultural, religious, language, national, class, and gender orders in global politics.

As discussed previously, it is not that women perpetrators of sexual violence in war and conflict do not make appearances in legal, scholarly, and even media coverage of war criminals. Instead, when those women appear in those accounts, the timing of their appearances, the framing of their actions, the significations of gender stereotyping, and the analysis of their motivations all serve to reify a notion of their impossibility similar to the implication of the majority of accounts of sexual violence in war and conflict, which are silent as to not only the existence but the possibility of women perpetrators.

The complexity of how female perpetrators of sexual violence in war and conflict are presented and understood, with the complexity of thinking about that sexual violence in light of women's perpetration, can be seen in many accounts of women's involvement across many conflicts. For example, a 2004 Amnesty International report implicated women in encouraging men to rape by singing songs of racial hatred and destruction of the feminine in Darfur, as the Janjaweed committed a high level of racially targeted sexual violence.[2] As Amnesty reported:

> The songs of the Hakima, or the Janjaweed women as the refugees call them, encouraged the atrocities committed by the militamen. The women singers stirred up racial hatred against black civilians during attacks on villages in Darfur and celebrated the humiliation of their enemies, the human rights group said. . . . Amnesty International collected several testimonies mentioning the presence of Hakima while women were raped by the Janjaweed. The report said: "Hakima appear to have directly [physically] harassed the women who were assaulted, and verbally attacked them."[3]

This report was repeated in a large number of news sites and internet blogs, and included in academic accounts of the conflict. The *Hakima*[4] play a role in conflict in Sudan historically, as anthropologist Isam Mohamed Ibrahim explains: "they sing the bravery, strength, and cavalry values. The *Hakima* plays a dominant role here. She incites the men to fight bravely. She also sings the defects of others."[5] This is consistent with psychologist Phyllis Chesler's description that the *Hakima* women provide support to the men and "utter racial insults to the women being raped."[6]

Chesler, a psychologist who focuses her scholarly attention on "deviant" women, attempts to explain the motivation behind women's participation in the Sudanese ethnic conflict in an article for *Frontpage* magazine. She first explains that she is "not surprised by the behavior of the Janjaweed women" because, "like men, women also internalize sexist values [and] . . . cling to the status quo; even to one that demeans them."[7] Chesler accounts for women's participation in and encouragement of *sexist* sexual violence by their internalization of sexist norms, given the power of sexist norms in society. Chesler suggests that the sexual violence is *masculinist*, even when women are committing it. The women committing it are characterized as snowed by sexism, and therefore inadvertently, rather than knowingly, perpetrators.

This sort of analysis, however, is uncommon among scholars, media outlets, and legal analysts who pay attention to the existence of the Janjaweed women who were accused of inciting sexual violence in the conflict in Darfur. Instead, what most of the depictions of these women have in common is a characterization of women's participation in violence against women as both unique and somehow more twisted and more serious than men's "normal" perpetration of sexual violence against women in war and conflict. News articles discussing the Janjaweed women are about women's encouragement of rape, rather than about the rapists that they encouraged to commit rape, or the victims of those rapes.

Several layers of difficulty shroud coverage of and discussions of women's perpetration of sexual violence in war and conflict. Like in Darfur, many discussions of sexual violence in war and conflict omit both the existence of female perpetrators and the possibility of that existence, framing perpetrators as male and victims as female. Also like in Darfur, much of the coverage of women's engagement in sexual violence in war and conflict sensationalizes it, overfocuses on it, and creates gendered and distorted images of the female perpetrators. This chapter looks to recognize the existence of women's perpetration of sexual violence without perpetuating distortions or sensationalizing.[8]

A 2007 report identified the existence of sexual violence in war and conflict within *ongoing or recent* conflicts in 51 countries across the globe.[9] Most of those conflicts give evidence of women's perpetration of political violence; in many, there is evidence of women's perpetration of sexual violence in war and conflict. Determining *how many* women commit sexual violence in *how many* conflicts is a different project than this book looks to accomplish. Instead, this chapter looks at several cases of women's perpetration of sexual and sexualized violence in conflict since the beginning of the twentieth century, selecting for variety in type, location, circumstance, and conflict. It does so not claiming that the cases presented here are representative or typical—quite the opposite, in fact. I argue that there is not a representative or typical female perpetrator of sexual violence in war and conflict—or a representative or typical perpetrator of sexual violence in war and conflict more generally. Instead, my purpose in exploring these cases is to explore the twinned *existence* and *invisibility* of female perpetrators of sexual violence.

This chapter explores five cases of women's perpetration of sexual violence in war and conflict: in the Armenian genocide, in World War II Germany, in the former Yugoslavia, in the Rwandan genocide, and in the Democratic Republic of Congo. It provides some information about the conflicts in which this violence occurs, but, for purposes of space, very little detail about the background of each conflict situation. In providing information about these female perpetrators of sexual violence in war and conflict, this chapter looks neither to downplay the horror of the crimes that women (were alleged to have) committed nor to sensationalize sexual violence in war and conflict either generally or *because* women were its perpetrators. Instead, it provides background information for the analysis in later chapters for leveraging women's perpetration to contribute to understanding gender, women, and sexual violence, and the relationships among them.

The Armenian Genocide

The Armenian genocide, or Armenian holocaust, is the name generally given to the slaughter of Armenians in the Ottoman Empire, which reached its peak in 1915–1916.[10] While the term "genocide" is not used by the Turkish government, it has been used by a number of states in the international arena, as well as a number of scholars.[11] Helen Fein's characterization of the Armenian genocide as the "first modern ideological genocide of the [twentieth] century" has garnered a fair amount of consensus both among historians of the late Ottoman Empire and among scholars of genocide.[12] Conservative estimates suggest that around 700,000 people died during the extermination of the Armenians and other minority groups,[13] while others suggest that it could have been as many as 1.5 million.[14] During the commission of these killings, there was a significant amount of documentation, both from foreign state intelligence and from missionaries and journalists who were in the Ottoman Empire at the time.[15] The Ottoman government suggested that they were simply putting down pro-Russian revolutions, but even their allies in World War I stopped believing that and made it clear that they would hold the Ottoman government responsible for the crimes against humanity that were being committed.[16] While the word "genocide" did not arise until later,[17] scholars of genocide suggest that what happened in the Armenian genocide is one of its textbook cases.[18] In 1998, the Council of Europe Parliamentary Assembly resolved to "commemorate the anniversary of what has been called the first genocide of the 20th century" and "salute the memory of the Armenian victims of crimes against humanity."[19] Recently, the Armenian genocide has been recognized by the government of Brazil,[20] and the subject of controversy about President Obama's failure to recognize it formally.[21]

Katharine Derderian argued that, in the perpetration of the Armenian genocide, there was a "definite link between genocidal and gender ideologies."[22] Derderian's description is consonant with many of the historical accounts put forth by scholars who study the Armenian genocide, which recount a significant amount of gender-based abuse, including but not limited to rape, sale into sex slavery, and targeted killing. S. D. Stein's description is an example: "at one place, the new bride of a priest was raped repeatedly by the raiders, while her husband, the priest, watched her torment. The priest saw her die before his eyes, and then he himself was killed after being mutilated terribly."[23] A number of other terrible experiences for women are chronicled in histories of the Armenian genocide.[24] This has led scholars like Derderian to suggest that the link between genocidal and gendered ideologies during the genocide ran deep, with gender being a key axis on which genocide was perpetrated.[25] As she details:

> Gender ideology influenced the perpetration of the Genocide, beginning with the separation and massacre of men, which left Armenian women and children defenseless. Rape, kidnapping, sexual slavery, and forced

conversion to Islam furthered the genocidal program, in which women and girls represented a productive and reproductive forced targeted for forced labor and biological assimilation.[26]

Most historical accounts describe this genocide as one carried out *by men* against men and women.[27] Several close studies of the genocide, however, have revealed that there were women perpetrators of genocide generally and of genocidal sexual violence specifically. As Stein notes, witnesses to the genocide pointed out that women played a role in the killings.[28] He recounts one incident where victims "had their hands tied behind their back and were rolled down steep cliffs. Women were standing below and they slashed at those who had rolled down with knives until they were dead."[29]

A study by Eliz Sanasarian notes that women were indeed involved in the Armenian genocide as perpetrators, and their perpetration often victimized other women. Sanasarian interviewed a number of survivors of the Armenian genocide, and recounts stories of women beating other women, killing other women, sexually violating other women, and selling other women (and girls) into sexual slavery.[30] The commission of sexual violence in war and conflict *by women towards women* is left out of most accounts of the Armenian genocide.

Sanasarian explains that, while women were more likely than men to survive the genocide, both as perpetrators and as victims, they were more likely than men to have been sexually violated during it. In other words, women did constitute the majority of the victims of sexual violence in war and conflict in the Armenian genocide. Still, the victimization of women did not mean that all women were either overall peaceful or left out of the realm of the perpetration of sexual violence specifically. Sanasarian expected that she would find that women played stereotypically feminine roles during the genocide, as rescuers, or protesters for peace. It turns out, instead, that women were represented in the ranks of the perpetrators, and not overrepresented in the ranks of the rescuers. Women's roles in selling other women into sexual slavery were particularly salient in the narratives of the survivors whom Sanasarian interviewed. In the survivors' words and in Sanasarian's telling of their stories, (most often Turkish) women were described as sexually abusing and then selling Armenian women who had been brought into their households (often, ironically, by their husbands for protection) because they were jealous of their husbands' (imagined or actual) sexual relationships with these women (who were often in their early teen years).[31]

Sanasarian relates first-hand accounts from personal interviews with women who experienced the Armenian genocide, often as children or young adults. She explains that "one survivor's story was typical. She was abducted by a Turk during the deportation. He took her home; his wife and neighborhood women tied her up and tattooed her. Tattooing was the primary mark of slavery."[32] Another one of Sanasarian's interviewees describes being forced into marriage by a woman in the household that was supposedly protecting her from being hurt or killed. The victim's sister recounted the story, starting with the man who had taken her and her sister in. Sanasarian provides details:

> To assure their safety, he took them to his house. The mother-in-law of the officer pressured the respondent's sister into marrying a Turkish neighbor. When she refused, the woman beat her and called soldiers telling them to take her away. The frightened sister then consented to the marriage.[33]

Women's participation in sexual violence in war and conflict in the Armenian genocide, when it is recognized, is often described in terms of their status as jealous housewives, rather than in any terms that would make them either responsible for their violence or comparable to male perpetrators. Even Sanasarian looks to gendered household dynamics for an explanation of how and why women could come to do such heinous violence to other women. She wonders if women wanted to "rid their lives of the presence of young female intruders" in part because they were "perceiving the child as a future second-wife in the household."[34] Sanasarian notes that the perpetration of sexual violence by women on women did not stop at the end of the formal killing, or with the breakup of the Ottoman Empire. Instead, she documents a "post-genocide" practice of selling girls who had been orphaned by the genocide as mail-order brides from the orphanages where they were staying.[35] Her article does not have an account of women's motivation for engagement in selling other women as mail-order brides.

Sanasarian's study of the roles that women played in the Armenian genocide concludes that "women acquired all possible roles traditionally ascribed to men; they were perpetrators and collaborators in genocide."[36] While there is not any evidence of women raping other women in the Armenian genocide, that does not mean that women did not commit a variety of other offenses that constitute sexual violence in war and conflict, including forcing other women to have sexual relations with men. Sanasarian's study, while it samples a relatively small number of victims, suggests that a not insignificant percentage of victims have stories of their experiences of the genocide that include female perpetrators. Female perpetrators sold or forced other women into sexual slavery or other nonconsensual sexual relationships, women tattooed and enslaved other women themselves, and women engaged in physical torture of other women. In the Armenian genocide, the "impossible" female perpetrator existed, if hidden just outside of the reach of traditional analyses of war rape and below the surface of most accounts of what constitutes both genocide and sexual violence in war and conflict.

Nazi Genocide

The Nazi genocide needs little introduction—it is one of the most historically memorable events in the twentieth century.[37] Under the control of Adolf Hitler and the Nazi party, the German military, German police, and everyday Germans engaged in an extermination attempt targeted at Jews, Roma, Slavs, communists, homosexuals, Jehovah's Witnesses, and others whom the Third Reich considered to be genetically inferior to Aryan Germans.[38] These killings took place not only in Germany, but in the many places Germany occupied and/or controlled during the lead-up to and fighting of World War II. In the Holocaust, as it has come to be called, it is estimated that more than 60 percent of the population of Jews residing in continental Europe were killed, along with literally millions of other people.[39] Tens of thousands if not hundreds of thousands of Germans and other Europeans became killers during the Holocaust.[40]

Most of the attention in history, political science, and legal literatures to the Nazi genocide focuses on the killing that occurred therein, and with good reason. The overall death toll of the Nazi genocide is a unique distinguishing feature—it was, both in scale and in level of cruelty, historically with few if any precedents, and therefore shocking.[41] A new body of international law developed *in response to* the Nazi genocide in order to classify what the Nazis had done as a different sort of crime than normal "war crimes" or "crimes against humanity"—but as genocide.[42] As other genocides have unfolded over the years, however, it has become obvious that they often if not always included tools of dehumanization and extermination in addition to and other to killing—including but not limited to sexual violence, enslavement, forced impregnation, and forced migration.[43] Looking back at the Nazi genocide, the historical record suggests *not* that it was without sexual violence, but instead that, in contemporary accounts, the violence of mass murder overshadowed the reports of sexual violence that did exist.[44]

Another part of the genocide that often slipped under the radar was the existence of women perpetrators.[45] As I suggested in the introduction to this book in the discussion of the image of Ilse Koch, very few women were recognized as perpetrators of the Nazi genocide.[46] While it was well-known that women participated, their participation was rarely discussed or prosecuted.[47] When women were recognized as perpetrators, it was often in their capacities as the wives or mistresses of male perpetrators, or with the understanding that they were mentally ill, depraved, or crazy.[48] Women's engagement in sexual violence was, to the extent that I am able to find, not mentioned in official jurisprudential or policy discussions, despite discussions of men's sexual violence and even of women's engagement in other forms of perpetration of genocide.[49]

Still, there is a significant amount of evidence that women participated in sexual violence against other women, both at prison, concentration, and extermination camps and in situations where women were responsible for providing other women medical care.[50] While the "image of Ilse Koch" carried over to many women who either were at the time or have since been recognized as perpetrators of the Nazi genocide, many of them received significantly less attention than Koch herself.[51] Still, we have some information about other women who are alleged to have engaged in sexual violence at prison camps. For example, Dr. Herta Oberheuser, resident physician at Auschwitz, was alleged to have committed a number of crimes of torture against the women prisoners there.[52] Among the crimes she is said to have committed are rubbing glass and sawdust into wounds, amputating limbs, removing vital organs, and killing by injecting oil into women and girls, all the while suggesting that these actions were for the sake of experimental science.[53] She was well-known for operating on healthy women as a part of her "experimentation."[54] Sources that did recognize Oberheuser's engagement in torture and sexual violence during the Nazi genocide often paired that recognition with a characterization of her as a mentally unstable monster incapable of normal social interaction.[55]

Another woman whose perpetration of physical and sexual violence in prison camps has been alleged is Dorothea Binz, who also worked at Auschwitz, as a guard.[56] Binz's job was training other guards to keep order at concentration camps, and she is credited with training some of the most brutal guards who worked at Nazi camps during World War II.[57] At the height of Binz's career in the Nazi prison camp system, she was in charge of training the guards who controlled around 50,000 women and children prisoners. During that time, she allegedly supervised gas chamber killings, shootings, starvations, and freezings.[58] Binz is reputed to have set trained fighting dogs on prisoners. In addition to her supervisory roles, there is evidence that she personally beat, slapped, kicked, shot, whipped, and sexually abused women prisoners.[59]

Irma Grese has also been accused of sexual violence towards other women. As Sarti explains:

> Survivor accounts related repeatedly that Grese not only beat prisoners, she sexually abused them as well. Sexual abuse, in one sense, is more humiliating than physical abuse alone, but both abuses combined and administered by one's own sex were among the most horrifying of all crimes perpetrated by these women.[60]

These women are a few whose stories have made it into the history books, and sometimes into the realm of political and legal analysis. Some of them had greater roles of authority than the women whose names did not make it into the history books, others had traits (or alleged traits) that caught the fancy of potential audiences. While it is possible to know these women's names and piece together some stories of what they did during the Nazi genocide, there are many other women who were clearly either perpetrators of or complicit in genocide, and who may or may not have committed sexual violence within the scope of that perpetration or complicity, but whose names and stories remain untold. Still, it is possible to know that these women existed, as many historical accounts now recognize women prison guards by numbers if not by name. For example, James Waller notes that there were around 3,950 women guards at Ravensbrück, another Nazi prison camp.[61] Very little information is available about those women, individually or collectively.

Most of the information that is available about female prison guards characterizes them as pawns of their husbands, or as teenagers who were carefree and unable to grasp the broader consequences of their actions. Stories that suggest that women perpetrators of sexual violence (or any violence at all) under the Nazi regime made choices pair that suggestion with characterizations that the women were mentally ill or emotionally unstable, or even examples of the creativity of femininity carried to its (dangerous) extremes.[62] They were, therefore, characterized as at once having committed crimes that constituted genocide and having been incapable of the intentionality that made their actions truly disturbing.

Nowhere is this internal contradiction more obvious than in the telling of the stories of the women who seem to have been responsible for the most systematic sexual violence that women committed against other women during the Nazi genocide: women who engaged in the forced sterilization of other women in hospitals, mental facilities, and even concentration camps.[63] Nazi ideology that motivated the commission of the genocide relied on a notion of the production of a genetically ideal, and genetically pure, population.[64] Many Nazi policies, therefore, focused on encouraging reproduction of Germans whom the Reich and the Nazi Party saw as ideal, and stopping the reproduction of populations seen as genetically inferior.[65] This stopping of reproduction included not only killing, but eliminating the reproductive abilities of people who were not killed.[66]

In many genocides, sexual violence included forced impregnation as a major element of the strategy of extermination—using pregnancy to destroy the purity of the racial or ethnic group that was under attack.[67] The Nazis thought about this differently—they were not interested in destroying the purity of Jews or other groups; instead, they were primarily focused on destroying their existence.[68] As such, the Nazi regime often actually punished between-race sexual violence, particularly rape—not because it was a violation of the rights or the humanity of the victim, but because it was a violation of Nazi population policies that could have a negative impact on the achievement of the party's goals.[69] There is, perhaps for this reason, little if any evidence of the use of forced impregnation during the Nazi genocide.[70] Instead, the great majority of Nazi sexual violence towards victims of the genocide came in other forms—including medical experimentation on pregnant women, whipping the groin and breast areas, and forced sterilizations.[71]

Nurses and other medical professionals in Nazi Germany played a large role in the sexual violation of other women.[72] The best evidence of this phenomenon is in psychiatric facilities, where Nazi doctrine suggested that the mentally and physically handicapped patients were a part of genetically inferior groups whose reproduction needed to be prevented.[73] As a historical study on nurses in Nazi Germany notes, "there was no question in the minds of the *Geisteskrankenpflege*'s contributors that proposed eugenic measures, and especially sterilization, were necessary and justified."[74] In nurse training, it was emphasized that "eugenics was not an intellectual fad but rather a decades-old *science* whose 'significance' had finally been recognized and incorporated into state policy."[75] Characterized as "grading fertility according to racial value," Nazi policies suggested that "just as the prevention of infectious diseases was obviously preferable to treating them once they had appeared, preventing the spread of genetic deficiencies by taking analogous steps was a matter of common sense."[76]

Eugenic policies included both "positive" incentivization, like providing "marriage loans for nonpredisposed partners" for the purpose of "filling the gene pool with racially pure and healthy offspring," and "negative" ones that "would ensure that undesirable elements tapered off and eventually disappeared."[77] This framed sterilization as a positive public policy contribution to shaping the population, rather than as an individual punishment for being undesirable. When nurses were being trained to sterilize undesirable people, the humanity of sterilization was emphasized, particularly inasmuch as the ability to both have and enjoy sex was maintained. Forced sterilization targeted women, who were framed as the source of the problem of substandard reproduction.[78] Nazi policy statements suggested that many mothers were dirty, ugly, poorly behaved, and into drinking, smoking, and other vices, and passing those vices on to their children, characterized as "genetically ill" and "asocial."[79] The category of "genetically ill" people were split into two subcategories: "the 'good' ones demonstrated their sense of responsibility by volunteering to be sterilized, while the 'bad' ones reproduced with abandon."[80] Good or bad, though, "all were subject to sterilization" which was discussed as deserved, but not punitive.[81] Often, patients in psychiatric institutions were offered the opportunity to leave in exchange for submitting to sterilization, which was an alternative to remaining at the psychiatric institution and paying for one's 'hospitalization' there.[82]

We know that forced sterilization was a part of Nazi official policy, both in psychiatric institutions and in situations where sterilization looked to be more efficient than killing to end the target genetic line. We know that these sterilizations, like many of the euthanasia programs in Nazi Germany, were largely carried out by health professionals, particularly nurses.[83] We know that the overwhelming majority of the nurses who perpetrated forced sterilizations did so in response to both trainings and commands that instructed it both as a matter of policy and as medically necessary.[84] We also know that the majority of nurses who perpetrated forced sterilizations were women.[85] While some of these nurses stood trial after the defeat of Nazi Germany,[86] many neither took nor were forced to take any responsibility for their actions.[87] Historians estimate that tens of thousands of nurses participated in the forced sterilization of about half a million people over the course of the Nazi reign.[88]

Between tens of thousands of women prison, concentration camp, and death camp guards, and tens of thousands of nurses, it is clear that a number of women engaged in the perpetration of the Holocaust, and their participation has been heavily documented elsewhere. In fact, women's participation in sexual violence—whether it is sexual violation in concentration camps or compulsory sterilizations in hospitals—is also relatively well documented (in contrast to many other conflicts across history, but in line with other Nazi atrocities). At the same time, most if not all of these accounts of women's engagement in sexualized beatings, women's sexual violation of other women, and women's sterilization of other women stop short of accounting for the violence *as sexual violence*. As mentioned above, that may be because the horrors of the killings in the Holocaust tend to overshadow detailed and pointed analyses of other violence. It may also be because of the impossibility of women perpetrators of sexual violence against other women—especially given that most accounts of women's engagement in these acts focus either on the insanity of the female perpetrator or on the ways in which the violence was "sold" to women by their superiors to appear acceptable or even humane. While, in the Holocaust, there is little evidence of women's direct engagement in the rape of other women, there is evidence that women engaged in a number of acts that constitute sexual violence, sexualized beatings, sexually assaulting women prisoners, and sterilizing women patients against their will. The impossibility of these women *sexual* perpetrators may have kept accounts of their behavior out of mainstream scholarly, media, and legal accounts of the Holocaust for quite a while, but the combination of new evidence and rereading old accounts of the Holocaust provide ample evidence that the impossible Nazi woman engaging in sexual violence in war and conflict not only existed, but was a systematic part of the perpetration of the Nazi genocide.[89]

The Former Yugoslavia

A series of political crises in the 1980s among the republics that made up the Socialist Federal Republic of Yugoslavia developed into a series of conflicts during and after the breakup of Yugoslavia in the 1990s.[90] Yugoslavia had been a federation composed of six states: Bosnia and Herzegovina, Croatia, Macedonia, Montenegro, Serbia, and Slovenia, where each republic had its own governmental system and the federal government mediated.[91] The Socialist Federal Republic of Yugoslavia was governed for most of its history by Josip Broz Tito, who had been president-for-life.[92] After his death in 1980, Yugoslavia was less politically stable.[93] One trigger for the conflict that ensued was Slobodan Milošević's coming to power in Serbia in 1987. Milošević sought control over the autonomous province of Kosovo (which was within Serbia, and where a number of Kosovar Albanians had been advocating for independence since the early 1980s).[94] This was met with opposition from the other Yugoslav republics, an issue that came to a head in a number of 1990 elections at the end of the Cold War, where communist parties lost power everywhere but Serbia and Montenegro.[95] Many of the communist parties were defeated by explicitly nationalist leaders who led four of the Yugoslav republics to declare their independence from Yugoslavia.[96] These declarations of independence, however, did not resolve either rising ethnic tensions among the former Yugoslav republics, or the fate of the ethnic minorities of Serbs, Croats, and Bosniaks within the other republics.[97] Intense negotiations for a peaceful breakup of the former Yugoslavia with the European Union and other interested parties ended without much success,[98] especially since Serbia's leadership was unsatisfied with guarantees of Serbian territorial integrity and protection of Serbs outside of Serbia.[99] On April 6, 1992, the European Union formally recognized the independence of Bosnia and Herzegvina, and the Republika Srpska, or the Republic of the Serbian People of Bosnia and Herzegovina, declared its independence with a stated interest of joining the Serb Republic.[100] Years of war ensued, with the most intense conflict going on in Bosnia and Herzegovina.[101]

What ensued has been characterized as both ethnic cleansing and genocide, with some debate on how to categorize it within the historical record.[102] Whatever the label, more than 100,000 people (80 percent Bosniak) died in the next few years.[103] One of the most well-known incidents of mass killing and violence happened in the summer of 1995, when the Bosnian government had lost control of all but a few towns in eastern Bosnia, but held Srebrenica, Zepa, and Gorazde, which the United Nations had declared "safe havens" to be protected by peacekeeping forces.[104] On July 11, 1995, however, Bosnian Serb forces defeated the Dutch peacekeeping forces in Srebrenica and took control of the civilian population there.[105] The Bosnian Serb forces separated the civilians on the basis of their sex, sending women and children on buses to Bosnian-controled territories (sometimes while or after sexually assaulting them), and killed the men and boys onsite.[106] More than 8,000 men died that day, which the ICTY recognized as an act of genocide.[107] At the end of the conflict, between 100,000 and 200,000 were killed, with ten times as many displaced.[108] While most of the ethnic cleansing was perpetrated by Serbia and the Serb Republic against Bosniaks and Croats, ethnically motivated killings took place on all sides of the conflict.[109]

Women participated in, and sometimes led, the violence in the wars that broke up the former Yugoslavia.[110] One of the most high-profile female perpetrators is a woman named Bijana Plavšić, who served as acting president of the Republika Srpska both shortly after it declared its independence in 1992 and then again from 1996 to 1998.[111] Before going into politics, Plavšić had a successful career as a biologist, which she later used to further her political agenda of ethnic cleansing.[112] As one academic observer noted, she "used her knowledge of biology to convince people to share her ethnic hatred" and argued that "Bosnian Muslims were 'genetically deformed Serbs.'"[113] Plavšić's academic addresses and political speeches advocated ethnic cleansing and ethnic purity, and sometimes even implied that rape was a tactic that could or should be used to achieve these goals.[114] There is evidence that troops under both her direct and indirect commands engaged in commanded, ethnically targeted rape. Many of her comments involved sex and sexuality in the discussion of ethnic purity.[115]

After the conflict died down, the ICTY charged Plavšić with a number of war crimes, including "genocide, crimes against humanity, and war crimes for a series of crimes, including rape crimes, committed by the Serb military, political, and government authorities," which were alleged to have been committed with her blessing and sometimes under direct her command.[116] It is alleged that Plavšić both conceived of and oversaw the Serbian use of rape as a weapon of genocide.[117] The passage that starts chapter 1 in this book is a small part of hundreds of pages of accusations against Plavšić that were discussed explicitly at her ICTY sentencing hearing.[118] They include accusations of repeated rape, sexual mutilations, and forced commission of sexual assault.[119]

Plavšić's sentencing hearing was the only airing of charges against her in international court, because she never stood trial, reaching a plea bargain instead.[120] Plavšić pled guilty to crimes against humanity charges, including accepting responsibility for rape charges.[121] She received a sentence of eleven years, truncated in part because of her willingness to admit responsibility for her crimes.[122] While she was serving her sentence, Plavšić retracted her admission, arguing that "she had admitted to committing war crimes because she was unable to gather enough witnesses to testify on her behalf" and because she did not want to endure the unpleasantness of a trial.[123] She was released early, having served about 60 percent of her sentence, because of her poor health and because it was judged that she had demonstrated adequate remorse.[124]

Media and scholarly retellings of Plavšić's involvement in the genocide in the former Yugoslavia are often narrated with gender-based characterizations, as well as the language of sex and sexualization. Several accounts put forward rumors of Plavšić's sexual involvement with warlords, and discuss her military leadership sexually.[125] Often alongside these sexual characterizations, there are narrativizations of Plavšić *mothering* the men who committed the actual violence, including challenging their masculinity and engaging in "goading."[126] Other stories told of her mental instability. For example, many newspapers repeated Slobodan Milošević's calling her a "female Mengele."[127]

Gender was also prominent in discussions of what punishment Plavšić would receive once she pled guilty to some of the charges against her.[128] At her sentencing hearings, people who testified on Plavšić's behalf suggested that, as a woman, she was inherently less responsible for her behavior and merited a lighter sentence.[129] Many elite world leaders also came to Plavšić's defense, suggesting that she was either personally or as a result of her sex unable to have committed the crimes of which she was accused.[130] These defenses characterized her as a caring, feminine peacemaker who was being unfairly accused of men's crimes.[131]

While Plavšić got significant attention both from international jurisprudence systems and from media (in both a positive and negative light), most of these accounts portray her as if she was the only woman who was involved in the commission of mass atrocities during the breakup of the former Yugoslavia. Her singularity is emphasized over and over again, especially in stories that engage in the most sensationalist coverage of the combination of her gender and her crimes. At the same time, it is incredibly unlikely that Plavšić was the only female perpetrator of ethnically motivated violence generally or sexual violence specifically in this context, both given its widespread occurrence and other, lesser-known accounts of female perpetrators.[132] Whether or not there were other women in the former Yugoslavia who participated in the planning and perpetration of sexual violence in war and conflict, Plavšić is another "impossible" woman perpetrator—a woman whose defenders hailed her femininity as evidence of her innocence, and whose critics faulted her hypersexuality and "hysteria." While there is no direct evidence that Plavšić engaged in sexual violence in war and conflict herself, there is ample evidence that she was *responsible* for that violence, both in the planning stages and as a commander when it was being carried out.[133] This "impossible" woman *led* the perpetration of sexual violence in war and conflict as a national leader, while president, vice president, and a member of the command of the Republika Srpska military forces, and, if her most recent interviews and writings are to be believed, remains convinced of the justice of her actions.[134]

Rwanda

Like the histories of the other conflicts in this chapter, the history of the genocide in Rwanda is long and anything but simple.[135] Rwanda was one of Africa's first organized states, composed of people understood to be Hutu, Tutsi, and Twa, with an organized government before the European colonization of many African states.[136] Rwanda managed to avoid some of the worst consequences of the slave trade,[137] but was ultimately colonized, first by Germany and then by Belgium.[138] Movement among the groups in early Rwanda was fluid, where a change in a person's economic status could be read as a change in their ethnic group membership.[139] In 1890, the German Empire was given Rwanda and Burundi in exchange for renouncing its claims on Uganda, but border disputes stopped the final borders from being set until 1900.[140] Upon their arrival in the late nineteenth century in Rwanda, the Germans found a monarchy which considered the Tutsi King semi-divine, crediting him with the economic prosperity of the country, which was biased in favor of Tutsi citizens.[141]

Colonization seems to have put a halt both to fluidity and to peaceful interaction between Hutu and Tutsis in Rwanda.[142] Perhaps the Germans' biggest influence on Rwandan government was their importation of the extremes of European thinking about race to the country.[143] The Germans characterized the Tutsis in Rwanda as descended from Europeans, citing evidence that Tutsis were taller, friendlier, and more willing to convert to Catholicism, and favored them.[144] Control of Rwanda shifted from Germany to Belgium at the end of World War I,[145] and, while the governmental structure did not change much, Belgian involvement in Rwanda was more active than German involvement had been.[146]

The Belgian government instituted the system of forcing Rwandan residents to carry ethnic identity cards which ultimately both killed the flexibility in group membership and was used to identify victims in the 1994 genocide.[147] They did so because they became convinced that the combinations of Tutsi's larger skull size (which was read as a larger brain size), taller height, and lighter skin made them more akin to Europeans than Hutus, and therefore racially superior.[148] Both the colonial government and the Roman Catholic Church, which provided most of the education in Belgian Rwanda, reinforced differences between Hutu and Tutsi, segregating them in educational institutions, residence areas, and professional situations.[149]

Rwandan independence was marred by ethnic violence, when, in 1959, assassinations of Hutu politicians at the alleged hands of the Tutsis occurred.[150] A number of Tutsis were killed in retaliation, and Tutsi leaders accused the Belgians of helping the Hutu killers.[151] This violence was accompanied by a change in the local authority in Rwanda, which became dominated by Hutus to the exclusion of Tutsis, many of whom who fled Rwanda for Uganda and the Congo.[152] An elected president, Grégoire Kayibanda, was in office for about a decade, but his administration was plagued by inefficiency and corruption.[153] In 1973, the defence minister, Juvénal Habyarimana, overthrew the government, suspended the constitution, and imposed a ban on political activity.[154] Habyarimana, who held power until he was killed in 1994, was characterized as a moderate on racial and ethnic issues in Rwanda.[155] From his takeover in 1973 until 1990, he ran Rwanda as a one-party state, but in 1990 announced his openness to multiparty governance.[156]

On October 1, 1990, Rwanda was invaded by the Rwandan Patriotic Front (RPF), a majority-Tutsi group of veterans of the Ugandan war.[157] In theory, an August 1993 ceasefire called the Arusha Accords ended that invasion. In that agreement, Habyarimana agreed to share power with the RPF and the Tutsi population.[158] Before much progress could be made in the establishment of that government, however, Habyarimana was assassinated.[159] Extremist Hutu groups (including the president's wife, Agathe) have most often been held responsible for the assassination.[160] The president was killed April 6, 1994, and an interim government of extremist Hutus started killings on the morning of April 7, with evidence that a list of targets had been developed before the assassination.[161]

The Rwandan genocide has been characterized as the most "efficient" genocide in the history of the world, measured by the percentage of the target population that was killed and by the speed with which the killings took place.[162] In the hundred days of the genocide before the RPF took power in Rwanda, it is estimated that between 800,000 and 1,000,000 Tutsis and moderate Hutus were killed, and more were raped or otherwise injured.[163] The final death toll accounted for between 70 and 80 percent of the Tutsi population of Rwanda being killed over the summer of 1994.[164]

More than 100,000 Rwandans were ultimately arrested for the perpetration of the Rwandan genocide, including a number of women.[165] Reva Adler, Cyanne Loyle, and Judith Globerman explain that "statistics from the Rwandan justice system indicate that in 2004 approximately 3,000 women, representing some 3.4% of the Rwandan prison population, were incarcerated in Rwandan prisons for genocide-related crime."[166] The participation of women in the Rwandan genocide was not, according to observers, unprecedented. Women had participated in ethnic violence in large numbers in Rwanda before, including during the conflict over the 1973 coup, which the British organization African Rights suggest was "the beginning of their [women's] widespread participation in violence."[167]

Perhaps this history of women's involvement in government is why women's engagement in the perpetration of the Rwandan genocide in 1994 is among the best-documented instances of both ordinary women and those in leadership positions engaging in political violence. As Donna Maier notes, "the involvement of female leaders in the Rwanda genocide (cabinet officials, nuns, journalists, nurses, and teachers) is striking and well-established."[168] Adler, Loyle, and Globerman suggest something similar, explaining that "women's involvement in the planning and implementation of the 1994 genocide at all societal levels has been well-described."[169] Adler and her collaborators suggest that the high visibility of women in the Rwandan genocide "compels us to reexamine the specific roles of women in collective ethnic violence."[170] For that reason they look to "develop a theoretical model explaining why rank-and-file Rwandan women assaulted or murdered targeted victims during the 1994 Rwandan genocide" with the goal of identifying "attitudinal risk factors for genocidal behavior" in female perpetrators.[171] In this endeavor, the researchers sought to identify the range of women's perpetration of the genocide, and discovered that "women's participation ranged from working as main architects of the violence to acting as individual killers in small communities. Most commonly, women denounced victims and looted victims' homes as well as their bodies."[172]

A number of high-profile women have been accused of perpetration of genocide without explicit reference to their committing sex crimes, though there is no way to know whether that omission is because those women did not commit such crimes, or because their commission of such crimes went under the radar. Those women included, but are not limited, Agathe Habyarimana (the president's wife);[173] Agnes Ntamabyariro (the minister of justice in the provisional government in Rwanda in the summer of 1994);[174] prominent radio journalist Valerie Bérmeriki (who worked for Radio Télévision Libre des Mille Collines);[175] and Odette Nyirabegenzi, Rose Karushara, and Euphrasie Kamatamu (part of the Kigali local government).[176] While the first lady of Rwanda has hailed Felicitee Semakuba as a heroine during the genocide who used her power to save Tutsis with whom she was close,[177] witnesses who talked to African Rights told a different story, suggesting she perpetrated genocide, from shooting into crowds to throwing grenades. Her crimes were characterized as all the more serious because she committed them while pregnant.[178]

Adler and her collaborators then looked to find out what they could about the women who had perpetrated these and other crimes during the Rwandan genocide, but suggested that perpetrator-narratives were more available from men than from women.[179] While many men were willing to talk about how and why they did what they did during the genocide, the researchers explained that "much of what we know about female genocide participants in all of these realms has been gathered from the eyewitness accounts of victims and bystanders; little has come from the perpetrators themselves."[180] The researchers therefore looked to interview female perpetrators, and found fourteen women who were willing to talk about their involvement in the genocide.

Many of their interview subjects discussed the ways that they had been perpetrators of the genocide, including leading militias to the potential victims, participating in attack groups, revealing victims, killing victims, and distributing weapons.[181] Others admitted to committing crimes during the genocide but were unwilling to describe them directly.[182] Among Adler, Loyle, and Globerman's interviewees, there was a wide range of the level of responsibility that the women took for their actions. While most of them admitted to having made bad decisions or engaged in poorly considered behavior out of fear or some other motivations, "some participated deliberately and with conviction."[183] Those included "a small number of women . . . [who] used the genocide as an opportunity to improve their financial circumstances or to advance 'professionally' by assuming positions of authority during the time of upheaval."[184]

Many victims of the genocide have identified a number of the perpetrators as female. An observer explained that some women "'were actively involved, killing with machetes and guns' while others 'acted in support roles—allowing murder squads access to hospitals and homes, cheering on male killers, stripping the dead and looting their houses."'[185] Victims told of women being beaten, and children being killed, by female perpetrators.[186] Still, the prosecution of female perpetrators has been characterized as uneven—women perpetrators have protested being disproportionately punished and international observers have expressed concern that women perpetrators were let off more easily than their male counterparts.[187]

Those who see women as underprosecuted point out that the death penalty for the crimes associated with the genocide (when it was still legal in Rwanda, before 1998), was given out disproportionately to male perpetrators, where "only six women (.2%) have been sentenced to death for genocide-related crimes, and only one woman was in fact executed."[188] They also point out that there is a differential conviction rate for women who had been arrested within Rwanda for the genocide, where "the acquittal rate for women charged with genocide-related crimes is 40%."[189] The acquittal rate for men was only 27.6 percent.[190] This unwillingness to prosecute, convict, and punish women, critics argue, is replicated in the international legal arena, where "only one woman, Pauline Nyiramasuhuko, has been indicted by the International Criminal Tribunal for Rwanda, on charges that she incited troops to rape and kill hundreds of women in the university town of Butare."[191]

At the same time, Mahmood Mamdani noted that many Rwandan women felt singled out by prosecutions, because they thought that they were being prosecuted for lesser crimes than men were in order to prosecute women because they were women.[192] Mamdani quotes Aloysius Inyumba, the RPF minister in charge of women's affairs, in 1995, explaining that "I have 838 women in prison. One woman said to me, I have only killed eight; there are people who have killed more and are free."[193] While this shows the difficulty of finding perspective in who counts as a perpetrator in a conflict with such unspeakable horrors, it also shows tension when gender becomes a key descriptor of either perpetrators or victims of genocide.

While media and legal coverage of women's involvement in Rwandan genocide far exceeds the attention given to women's violence in other conflicts, it still remains quite limited, both in substance and in quantity. This is especially true when it comes to discussions of women's perpetration of sexual violence. While there is some discussion among scholars and in the media of Pauline Nyiramasuhuko's involvement in both murderous and sexual violence during the genocide, her engagement in political violence is often treated as singular and her engagement in sexual violence is minimized.[194] While victims testified that Pauline raped and ordered the rape of young girls before they were killed,[195] this feature of her perpetration is deemphasized in a number of accounts of the genocide.

Pauline, it appears, was nowhere near the only woman who perpetrated sexual violence during the Rwandan genocide. African Rights, a British organization that conducted a number of victim interviews in 1994 and 1995, published a book detailing the perpetration of genocidal violence by dozens if not hundreds of women, told through the accounts of their victims and other observers. Many of these descriptions include accounts of women personally perpetrating, ordering the perpetration of, or facilitating the perpetration of, sexual violence. For example, African Rights provides descriptions of Léoncie Nyirabacamurwango victimizing a girl who was being protected by her mother during the genocide. The girl, described as a daughter of Sylvestre Muhiza who held a fake Hutu ID, lived with Nyirabacamurwango's mother to protect her from the genocide. According to an observer, "Mme Leoncie forced her to take off all her clothes and took her to the roadblock herself where the girl was once again raped before being killed."[196] Here, Nyirabacamurwango committed sexual assault (by forcing the girl to take her clothes off) and facilitated rape (by bringing her to the roadblock to be raped) and murder (by delivering her to killers when she had been in no immediate danger).

Another account depicts a Hutu woman named Maman Aline as committing rape on a wealthy Tutsi businesswoman, Speciose Kara-kezi.[197] As African Rights explains it,

> The *Interahamwe* refused to kill her because she had given them money. Maman Aline demanded to kill the woman herself. There were some displaced women from Gizozi who had pointed sticks. They tried to penetrate her vagina with them. They opened her legs and Maman Aline penetrated her vagina with a stick.[198]

Other women are alleged to have offered rape as a spoil of war to the soldiers under their command for dutiful obedience to killing orders. For example, Bernadette Mukarurangwa "recruited bands of men and used rape (as well as other incentives) to bribe them into killing."[199] She is described as commanding soldiers to "take up your machetes, kill all the Tutsis, don't spare a single one."[200] During one killing spree, a witness recounted that "certain *Interahamwe* had taken in Tutsi girls to rape. Bernadette ordered them to be killed [too], as well as the children of Hutu women married to Tutsis, regardless of sex."[201]

These women came from different economic backgrounds, different sources of authority, and different areas of Rwanda. All they shared were the perpetration of sexual violence during the Rwandan genocide. These and other women are identified as not only having committed sexual violence towards other women, but as engaging in behavior that encouraged an air of permissibility surrounding attacking women *because they were women*, which led other men and women to see this sort of violence as part of the "war" against Tutsis, and therefore acceptable behavior during the genocide.

Women were also identified as "cheerleaders" for male rapists throughout the genocide, similar to the description of the behavior of Sudanese women that begins this chapter.[202] They are described as engaged in "support" of male rapists by singing.[203] One woman who is accused of genocide by engaging in this sort of singing insists that she did nothing wrong, because she did not individually either rape the women who were raped or shed their blood.[204]

The accusation that a woman physically committed rape seems to throw off more readers than the suggestions that women assaulted

other women, sold them into sexual slavery, performed forced sterilizations, and ordered women's rapes. Still, while the Rwandan genocide
is the source of the most detailed descriptions of women's perpetration of acts described as rape, it may be the available level of detail
about these acts, rather than the acts themselves, which is unique to
the Rwandan genocide.

As Janie Leatherman details, "in the Rwandan genocide, both men
and women were among the perpetrators. Hutu women from all seg-
ments of society (even nuns) carried out rapes, either using objects or
ordering men to commit rape of Tutsi women."[205] The Rwandan genocide is the first of the cases explored in this book where there is direct testimony evidence that, in addition to committing other forms of
sexual violence and ordering or commanding rape, women actually engaged in the commission of rape and sexual assault against individual
women victims. It was not just one "impossible" woman, or a nameless
group of "impossible" women—but a significant and documented group
of perpetrators, both of genocide and of sexual violence. The volume
and range of sexual violence perpetrated on women by "impossible"
women in Rwanda further debunks the idea of the impossible female
perpetrator of sexual violence in war and conflict, and suggests that it is
important to look actively at sexual violence when interested in where
women are in war and conflict, and at women when looking for the perpetrators of sexual violence in war and conflict.

Democratic Republic of Congo

The conflict in the Democratic Republic of Congo cannot be seen as
unrelated to the Rwandan civil wars and genocide, but it cannot be seen
as the same conflict, either. The 1994 genocide in Rwanda saw the mass
exodus of Rwandans.[206] Most of the refugees to the Eastern Democratic
Republic of Congo were Hutus who migrated there after the RPF gained
control in Rwanda in the late summer of 1994.[207] Estimates of the number of Rwandan Hutus who took refuge in the DRC range from one
to two million.[208] The United Nations High Commissioner for Refugees (UNHCR) suggested a nontrivial number of those refugees were
perpetrators of the Rwandan genocide.[209] Most of those were perpetrators from the *Interahamwe*.[210] A 1996 invasion of the Eastern DRC

(then called Zaire) by Rwanda and Uganda (aided by then opposition leader Laurent Kabila) was ostensibly to rid the area of perpetrators of the Rwandan genocide, but Congolese leaders and some observers expressed concern that other motivations also played a role.[211] In 1998, Kabila, now president, ordered Rwandan and Ugandese forces out of the DRC, and enlisted the military aid of Angola and Zimbabwe.[212] Nine states total have fought in the conflict, which has taken place almost entirely on Congolese soil.[213]

Laurent Kabila was succeeded upon his 2001 assassination by his twenty-nine-year-old son, Joseph.[214] When Joseph Kabila won a 2006 election in the DRC, a Tutsi-led organization, the National Congress for the Defense of the People (CNDP), increased its military activity in pursuing Rwandan Hutus in the Eastern DRC.[215] A 2008 peace agreement that included twenty-two armed groups looked promising, but fighting continued.[216] Military cooperation between the Rwandan government and the Congolese government began in early 2009, with the goal of removing the last of the Rwandan genocide perpetrators from the Eastern DRC.[217] This cooperation has increased the stability of the region, but between government military activity, the remaining Rwandan opposition factions, and the presence of the Ugandan Lord's Resistance Army (LRA) in the region, a significant amount of instability remains in the Eastern DRC at the time of this writing, and some believe that it may be getting worse.[218] Over almost two decades of off-and-on fighting, it is estimated that 5.4 million people have died.[219] The conflict has been described as one of the worst in the world in terms of the high prevalence of rape and sexual violence, as well as the death rate.[220] Language labeling the DRC a failed state,[221] and the war an intransigent conflict,[222] has been used with increasing frequency.

A 2010 *Washington Post* report suggested that "the prevalence and intensity of sexual violence against women in eastern Congo are 'almost unimaginable,'" where, for example, "4500 cases of sexual violence have been reported in just one eastern province since January [nine months], though the actual number is surely much higher."[223] A United Nations official described rape in the area as "'almost a cultural phenomenon'" which had become "'all too common'" such that "'intensity and frequency is worse than anywhere else in the world.'"[224] The intensity of the sexual violence is paired with the intensity of the killing, where reports suggest that the combination of the conflict and "conflict-driven humanitarian crisis" continue to kill 45,000 Congolese every month, which, put into perspective "is equivalent to the entire population of Denmark or the state of Colorado perishing within a decade."[225]

A significant amount of the coverage of this conflict suggests that it is one perpetrated by groups of men fighting, and that women and other civilians are their collateral damage. Stories tell of women victims:

> Mukeya Ulumba, 28, recounts the epic losses she has suffered in recent months. Several of her relatives and neighbors were killed when antigovernment rebels stormed their village last November, moving from house to house in a murder spree that lasted for hours. Ulumba and her husband managed to flee with their four children, leaving behind their life's possessions, a ravaged community of torched houses, and the bloodied corpses of family members and friends.[226]

While there is overwhelming evidence of the gender-based abuse of women in the long-running conflict in the Democratic Republic of Congo, there is also evidence that a significant amount of that violence, including sexual violence, is perpetrated by women. A team of doctors did a population-based survey of almost 1,000 households in the Eastern Democratic Republic of Congo in 2010 to get a sense both of the prevalence of sexual violence and of who the perpetrators were, and who they victimized.[227] They noted that previous population-based surveys had used narrow definitions of rape and failed to ask for any information "about perpetrators, circumstances, mental and physical health consequences of the violence, or establish if the violence was community based, conflict-related or violence against men."[228] In the survey, 29.5 percent of women and 15.2 percent of men had been exposed to conflict-related sexual violence.[229] Of those, "41 percent reported a female perpetrator, most typically a female combatant."[230]

This statistic seems oddly placed in a conflict where there are whole studies of sexual violence in war and conflict, often with focus groups and ground-level interviews, that do not acknowledge either the possibility that men can be victims or the possibility that women can be perpetrators.[231] Also, unlike the accounts that surface in other conflicts, the women perpetrators in the Eastern Democratic Republic of Congo have not been identified by name, singled out, or sensationalized. Still, a number of victims are speaking out about the prevalence of women committing sexual violence in war and conflict in the area. A Congolese United Nations employee explained to *Time* magazine, "women who were raped for years are now raping other women . . . some take sticks or a banana, others take bottles or knives."[232] Accounts of women's perpetration often leave the perpetrator nameless and faceless:

> In 2005, Valerie, who was then a 17-year-old girl, was going to farm her family's land in Congo when she met a group of bandits on the edge of a forest stealing crops—two men, two women and a girl. While the men cut maize and dug out cassava roots, the women removed Valerie's clothes and started to touch her. They used their hands and sticks "like animals," Valerie recalls. The first time she was raped by an unidentified armed man, at age 15, she was left to bear her assailant's child, but this time, her uterus was destroyed. Valerie will never give birth again and no man will marry her as a result.[233]

This victim's narrative ends by characterizing being raped by a woman as "'an unforgettable wound,'" where "'male rape is everywhere, but when it's women, it's incomprehensible. Its like a curse.'"[234]

Unlike in a number of other conflicts, there is evidence of the prevalence of women's commission of sexual violence in war and conflict—and that prevalence is fairly high, with more than a third of the victims of sexual violence reporting a female perpetrator. That high percentage is all the more notable in that the conflict in the DRC is one with a high volume of sexual violence. Impossible women perpetrators have raped and violated men and women in this brutal conflict. In the Eastern DRC, not only is the impossible woman perpetrator of sexual violence *possible*, she borders on the norm.

Conclusion

As mentioned at the outset of this chapter, the conflicts explored in depth here are not the only conflicts in which there is evidence of women's perpetration of sexual violence. There has also been empirical work done exploring women's engagement in sexual violence during the Cambodian genocide,[235] during the civil war in Sierra Leone,[236] and during the ongoing conflict with ISIS/Daesh in Iraq and Syria.[237] Still, whether it is the cases detailed in this chapter or others, there is not a lot of information about women's perpetration of sexual violence in war, conflict, and genocide available, especially compared to the available information about sexual violence in war and conflict more broadly.

As those who did the empirical study of sexual violence in the Eastern Democratic Republic of Congo noted, a significant amount of women's sexual violence in war and conflict probably goes under the radar when focus groups, interviews, and other on-the-ground studies do not ask questions about the perpetrators of the violence, particularly as relates to their sex and/or gender.[238] As inquiries into women's sexual violence in the Armenian genocide and in the Nazi genocide show, sometimes definitions of sexual violence in war and conflict are so narrow (often limited to penetrative rape by a person with a penis using that penis) that behavior that is clearly women's sexual violence towards other women (including forced sterilization, selling into sexual slavery, and forced marriage) are not recognized in the same analyses that attempt to quantify, explain, and account for sexual violence in war and conflict. As the Rwandan situation shows, even studies that pay a significant amount of attention to women's violence tend to gloss over or sensationalize (or some combination of both) occurrences of women's sexual violence towards other women. As the case of the former Yugoslavia demonstrates, sometimes women who *are* held accountable for the commission of sexual violence in media, political, or legal narratives are made singular in analysis and discussion of their behaviors. The unavailability of names or descriptors of female perpetrators in the Eastern DRC seems to stand in stark contrast to the naming of the women who committed sexual violence in Rwanda and in the former Yugoslavia at first glance, but when it is looked at in a different light, there is a lot of similarity in these moves. One erases the impossible woman while the other emphasizes her impossibility.

A 2013 *Time* magazine article on the women rapists in the Eastern Democratic Republic of Congo helps to frame these discourses and put their commonalities into perspective.[239] The article asks "How can a woman rape?" (before answering the question), suggesting that it is appropriate women's capacity sexual violence in war and conflict seem mysterious to readers.[240] This appropriateness of mystery, echoed in a number of other news reports and even scholarly articles which acknowledge women's perpetration (though such reports remain a very small minority of surveyed discussions of sexual violence in war and conflict), can help to provide an understanding of the ways that women's perpetration of this sort of violence can be alternatively (or even simultaneously) ignored, silenced, or sensationalized. It contributes to the taboo attached to women's perpetration of sexual violence in war and conflict.

If this book were a study of the women who commit sexual war crimes, of their demographics, of their motivations, or of their testimonials, the evidence of women's commission of sexual violence in war and conflict in this chapter would be woefully inadequate, and present significant problems for data analysis. In some of the older conflicts, it is possible that evidence of women's perpetration of sexual violence in war and conflict worthy of data analysis, if it ever existed, has disappeared with the deaths of the victims and/or their families. In some of the more recent conflicts, finding comprehensive data about women's perpetration may be possible with extensive fieldwork, working around taboos, different definitions of sexual violence, continuing violence in some regions, idealized collective memories, gender essentialisms, and victim fears. This work is very important, and has the potential to provide a significant amount of leverage on important questions about the nature, causes, and consequences of sexual violence in war and conflict, both in particular conflicts and generally.

This book is meant to encourage that sort of inquiry, but it is secondary to the point of its particular analysis. The argument of this book is less interested in the frequency, causes, and consequences of women's commission of sexual violence in war and conflict than it is in the simultaneous *existence* and *silencing/marginalization* of women perpetrators, in media, scholarly, and legal analyses. The puzzle it looks to account for is how constructions of women, femininity, and sexual violence in war and conflict reinforce the impossibility of women perpetrators, and how recognizing their possibility as subjects changes the nature of thinking about (and prosecuting) that violence. It is to those questions that subsequent chapters turn.

4

There's No Evidence Women Are Any Worse at Rape than Men Are

Understanding Women, War, and Rape

"I do feel like there is this sort of unspoken agreement that girls look out for other girls. . . . And not that you expect a guy to violate you, and I don't walk down the street expecting to be raped by a man, but you don't really expect it from a woman because they're meant to be on your side." Stephanie told news.com.au that she hasn't had counseling yet. "I couldn't deal with it (reporting the attack)," she said.[1]
—A news.com.au story about woman-on-woman sexual violence, by reporter Andy Park

The passage above was taken from a news interview with a woman who was a victim of another woman's sexual violence in a non-conflict situation. It highlights the combination of the assumption that women will not be the perpetrators of sexual violence and the feeling of surprise and betrayal when they are. The victim here says that the fact that she was assaulted by a woman made the assault harder for her to see and recognize at the time, and more difficult for her to comprehend afterwards. At the same time, the female perpetrator did not make the assault any less real, or any less a violation of the victim's body. In this story, Stephanie *was* assaulted by a woman. Earlier, we found that the "impossible" woman perpetrator of sexual violence in war and conflict exists in a number of different conflicts, times, places, and cultures. At the same time, for theorizing gender, war, and conflict, recognizing the existence of the "impossible" woman perpetrator of sexual violence in war and conflict does not make her, or her act, easily comprehensible. Like for Stephanie, the apparent paradox of the situation makes it difficult to place women's (conflict) sexual violence within existing frames of understanding.

James Waller has suggested that there is no evidence that women are any worse at killing than men are.[2] While that statement seems counterintuitive because it is normatively undesirable to be "good at" killing, Waller's point stands: while women's violence is often less frequent, and often less noticeable, than men's violence, it is no less competently committed, and no less possible. Contrary to the framing of violent women as impossible, women commit conflict violence, including but not limited to sexual violence in war and conflict—and the women who do are not anomalous. Still, recognizing women as perpetrators raises as many questions as it answers.

What does the realization that women commit sexual violence in war and conflict do to the theorization of sexual violence as the subordination of women? In important ways, it should mean little if anything, this chapter argues. Theorizations of sexual violence in war and conflict that rely on essentialized notions of the sex of the perpetrator to understand the gender dynamics inherent in the violence are flawed anyway—that was the argument in the introduction to this book. It argued that there are several common errors in the theorization of sexual violence in war and conflict: the assumption that the category of "woman" is easily discernible, the assumption that "men" and "women" necessarily have commonalities with other members of "their" sexes, the assumption that women are more peaceful than men, the assumption that women's motivations for violence must be different than men's, the assumption that women's perpetration of war crimes means that it is no longer important to look at the gendered victimization of women, the assumption that conflict violence is incidental rather than common, the assumption that sexual violence in war and conflict is not gendered, the assumption that men have to be the perpetrators of gendered crimes, and the assumption that justice for sexual violence in war and conflict relies on the ability to disaggregate the perpetrators by sex. A theoretical approach to sexual violence in war and conflict that did not make any of those assumptions either implicitly or explicitly would *already* be able to accommodate the notion that women are among the perpetrators of that violence. In other words, "adding" women *should not* change theorizing sexual violence in war and conflict, because they never should have been "subtracted"— sexual violence in war and conflict *is not* something different because women do it.

As discussed throughout this book so far, however, most understandings of sexual violence in war and conflict, implicitly or explicitly, make at least one of those assumptions. In so doing, most of them constitute sexually violent women as impossible and therefore stand as incomplete accounts. In this way, the flaws in theorizations of sexual violence in war and conflict revealed by the recognition of female perpetrators preexisted that recognition. Still, the recognition of women's perpetration of sexual violence in war and conflict from the Ottoman Empire to the Democratic Republic of Congo betrays both theoretical and empirical flaws in each of those assumptions that require rethinking, and, therefore, a reconceptualization of the notion of what it means to read sexual violence in war and conflict as a gendered phenomenon. As suggested in the introduction, approaches to sexual violence in war and conflict that ignore women perpetrators often continue to assume that perpetrators are exclusively male, and continue to associate the perpetration of sexual violence, maleness, and masculinity. Accounts that recognize but sensationalize women's perpetration of sexual violence in war and conflict rely on distinguishing male perpetrators from female perpetrators in order to explain not only the motivation for the act, but the act itself. Most accounts, then, are constructed by men, about men, and assuming masculinity. They are therefore partial, and recognizing women's perpetration reveals the extent of their fragmentation. At the base of this problem, as Desire Lwambo argues, is a problem with the confusion of gender issues and women's issues—where there is an assumption that women cannot be the perpetrators of rape, and men cannot be its victims, if it is to be understood as gendered—since gender is associated with women.[3] This and other problematic assumptions and associations often leave theorizations of sexual violence in war and conflict reliant on dichotomized, essentialized understandings of sex and gender.

After deconstructing the problematic, sex-biased assumptions about what sexual violence in war and conflict and who perpetrates it, what is left? If none of the above assumptions can be incorporated into understanding what sexual violence in war and conflict *is*, how can it be understood? If it is not sex dependent, *or degendered*, then what is it? This chapter looks to address that question, by rethinking not only sexual violence in war and conflict *when women commit it*, but generally. It looks at the properties of sexual violence in war and conflict when it is seen as something *people* do, rather than as something *men* do—without ignoring the gendered pressures and gendered power relations of global politics generally and of conflict(s) specifically. Perpetration, then, remains multifaceted, but another dimension becomes recognizable: the *sex identity of the perpetrator* and the *sex identity of the victim* are relevant to and only to the degree that they are part of the construction of gender order in the mind of the perpetrator that is a condition of possibility of the perpetration of the act. From this perspective, recognizing that women sometimes commit sexual violence is insufficient—the recognition should inspire rethinking sexual violence in war and conflict to account not only for women but also for the gendered complexities the existence of women perpetrators reveals. As Chiseche Salome Mibenge frames it, "the lens must be adjusted, and the view must move from quick studies of 'sex in war' to serious analyses of the operation of 'gender and violence' in humanitarian crises as well as in humanitarian interventions."[4] Like Mibenge's rethinking, the one in this chapter rethinks both the subject of the sentence (sex/gender) and the predicate (war/conflict/crisis).

In that spirit, this chapter looks to understand sexual violence in war and conflict aware of women perpetrators and the role of not only masculinities but also femininities in the creation and perpetration of sexual violence. It begins by suggesting that one of the key aspects of gender subordination is the devaluation of traits and values associated with femininities, and that gender subordination must be addressed at least in part by finding a path to a point where values associated with femininity *and* the experiences of women in global politics are valued in global social and political life.[5] This rethinking starts with the recognition that people are interdependent and their autonomy is relational. This means that all decisions (not just women's) are contextualizable, and contingent on their social and political atmosphere. All decisions, though are also *decisions* people make—it's not just men who make choices. Taking this as a starting point, this chapter critically engages existing theoretical approaches to sexual violence in war and conflict. It suggests reformulations of those theoretical approaches that help to understand war rape, even as it is among women, based on rethinking the visibility and intelligibility of (gendered) perpetrators and (gendered) victims by seeing sexual violence in war and conflict as a gendered practice in a relationally autonomous social world, built on gendered background knowledges.

Femininities, Gender Subordination, and Sexual Violence

It is true (and fairly well-known) that "worldwide, most crimes against the person are perpetrated by men" and women are most often the victims of those men's crimes.[6] That may be why many theorizations of sexual violence in war and conflict in a number of different conflicts around the world have focused on male perpetrators and women victims. The mean, median, and modal occurrence of sexual violence in war and conflict involves a male perpetrator and a female victim. Still, many war sex crimes are committed by people who are not men, and many are committed against people who are not women. This subset of war sex crimes, though, has not distracted attention from theorizing sexual violence in war and conflict as something men do to women. For example, as Adler and her co-authors have noted, "investigators who have explored the motivations of genocide perpetrators have focused principally on male participants."[7] Even when it is recognized that women can commit war crimes, the focus is on "women's tendency to commit more 'gender-consonant' crimes such as looting or denouncement," and there is a clear demarcation between the crimes that women commit and the crimes that men are seen to commit.[8]

This assumption that there are crimes that women commit and crimes that men commit is especially prevalent in the analysis of sexual violence in war and conflict, where it is so expected that men are the perpetrators and women are the victims that there is very little analysis of *why* the perpetration of those crimes is sex-specific, *how* that sex-specificity comes to be, and *how it is possible* that most victims of sexual violence in war and conflict are women. The assumed naturalness of the dichotomy of the male perpetrator and the female victim has several implications that we have already discussed at some length: it renders female perpetrators impossible, it renders the victims of female perpetrators (and male victims generally) invisible, it reifies a victim/perpetrator dichotomy, and it leads to the assumption that when women commit *men's* crimes there is something scarier about those behaviors, since they are a deviation from natural capacities.[9]

Still, as I have argued, many reactions to the recognition that women commit violence generally and sexual violence specifically are also inappropriate, inaccurate, and misleading. In the groundbreaking study of the number of victims of sexual violence in the Democratic Republic of Congo who identify their perpetrators as female discussed in chapter 3, the realization that a significant number of the perpetrators were women led the authors to quit using the term "gender-based violence" to describe rape during that conflict.[10] The authors of that study explained that "the term *interpersonal violence* is used in place of *gender-based violence* to include all types of violence between women and men."[11] I argue that violence is not *gender-neutral* because it defies sex specificity. Quite the opposite, it is important to understand the complexity of the genderings of sexual violence in war and conflict.

Along those lines, lawyer Lara Stemple, expressing concern when discovering "how few tools were at my disposal when the victims of sexual abuse were male," critiques the removal of gender analysis from gendered crimes when, though there is not a consistent *sex* of perpetrators and victims, the crimes clearly have gender-based motivations, gender-based impacts, and gender-based implications.[12] Stemple explains that there are sex problems all over rape advocacy and jurisprudence: men's rights advocates are resistant to understanding it as a gender-based crime; feminists are often resistant to the recognition of male victims and/or female perpetrators; and "gender nonconforming people . . . did not fit comfortably within the essentialist two-sex binary presented."[13] Stemple suggests:

> Instead of belonging to any one constituency, the phenomenon of rape is instead part of a larger whole, related, of course, to the exercise of domination, the violation of bodily integrity, and the subjugation of its victims. And, yes, rape is almost always about gender, which is not to say it is always about women.[14]

Sexual violence in war and conflict is very nearly always gendered. The claim that it is very nearly always gendered does not imply that it is about or centered around women. As discussed in the introduction, women are not the only people who have genders, or who experience daily life *as gendered*—and genderings include a wide variety of masculinities and femininities. That's why, in Stemple's words, "sex-based framing reinforced an us-versus-them dualism" which she describes as "generally useless and frequently counterproductive."[15] Stemple then distinguishes between feminist approaches to sexual violence in war and conflict that focus on the evils of male perpetrators from the ones she finds more useful—those that "value equality and inclusion, that interrogate structural hierarchies, and that examine intersecting forms of oppression."[16] While she sees that "undoing rape requires thorough attention to gender in all its forms," "thorough attention to gender in all its forms" *includes* deconstructing the dichotomy of the male perpetrator and the female victim.[17]

This starts with, Stemple argues, recognizing and stopping the conflation of the terms "gender" and "women," which happens across a wide range of communities, from neo-conservative pundits to radical feminists.[18] Stemple points to the frequent use of the phrase "violence against women" as interchangeable with "gender-based violence," and as a special category in many legal and advocacy approaches to a wide variety of human rights issues.[19] Rather than this essentialism, she calls for "a comprehensive *gendered analysis* of sexual violence," which she contends "has much to contribute."[20] Stemple argues that this is especially the case when we think about female perpetration of sexual violence, where it is important to "'absorb more holistically the experiences of women who would wield strength, aggression, and violence in all its forms.'"[21] Though "sympathetic to concerns about compromising decades of work to tell a story about rape as a tool of male dominance and female subordination," Stemple contends that "this narrative risks obscuring other vectors of gendered oppression that are actually operating" and that "balance" should be a priority."[22] The path to doing that is, in her view, to "move beyond the female victim/male perpetrator focus."[23]

As Rosemary Grey and Laura Shepherd recognize, "conflict-related sexual violence is multidimensional, and its perpetration, prevention, and punishment raise a complex set of issues," but "narrow envisioning of violation has led to a partial understanding of how gender matters in/to conflict-related sexual violence."[24] In this view, the "presentation of sexual violence as a women's issue is characteristic of the literature on sexual violence" which either uses sex as a shortcut since women victims are the majority or simply pays less attention those who constitute a minority of the victims despite recognition of male victims.[25] They critique a tendency *"to envision the politics of the violence in terms of the female victim*: women are targeted because they are vulnerable/disempowered; because they are seen to embody the nation under attack; because they are the 'spoils of war'; because violating woman emasculates her male 'protector' and so on."[26]

Stemple's ideas (especially understanding rape as *about gender*, but not always about women; and thinking of sexual violence as gendered while getting away from the male perpetrator/female victim dichotomy) are excellent building blocks from which to think about retheorizing sexual violence in war and conflict, maintaining a feminist framework while recognizing and considering female perpetrators. Grey and Shepherd contend that the first step to a theoretical reformulation is "paying serious and sustained attention to the ways in which assumptions about who is an appropriate victim of violence and who is its perpetrator constitute the parameters of our engagement."[27] At the same time, their piece is largely focused on examining the first half of that statement— the analysis of who is an appropriate victim of violence, with an emphasis on the omission, exclusion, and underattentive analysis of/towards male victims of sexual violence in war and conflict. What is missing from that account, however, is an understanding that those *very same* assumptions tend to contribute to the invisibility of women perpetrators. The question of how to get around that is not answered in either Stemple's or Grey and Shepherd's work. What does theorizing sexual violence as *gendered* even when the sex of the perpetrator is an unstable referent *mean*?

While recognition of male victims is important to deconstructing the sexed dichotomy that men are the perpetrators of sexual violence in war and conflict and women are the victims, it is only part of the work that needs to be done. The recognition of male victims might *not* include the recognition of female perpetrators—men might be (or might be assumed to be) victimized by men, and women might be assumed to remain victims and not perpetrators—just no longer *all* of the victims. Buried under even more layers of invisibility is the possibility that women are victimized *by women*. If sexual violence in war and conflict is seen as something that *men* do to *men and women*, then the paradigmatic thinking has changed some, but not enough. In those views, whether explicitly (by the classification of women as victims) or implicitly (by the failure to give serious attention to women perpetrators), what Johanna Bond calls *victim essentialism* for women can remain intact. As Bond explains:

> Victim essentialism limits women's discursive space in several ways. First, when women are defined exclusively, or even primarily, as victims of sexual violence, they are perceived as lacking agency. As non-agentic members of the community, they are unable to actively participate in reimaging or rebuilding the community. Second, when women are equated with sexualized victims, they are often consulted on matters related to sexual violence. The terrain of sexual violence represents the discursive territory that women are allowed to occupy.[28]

This victim essentialism *limits the recognition of women in conflict* to the arena of sexual violence victimhood, and limits victims to women. In addition to constructing victimhood in female terms, it constructs *capacity to victimize* in male terms. In other words, the male perpetrator/ female victim dichotomy makes the male victim *and* the female perpetrator impossible, as well as sexual violence towards (and by) gender nonconforming bodies, and what might be termed non-heterosexual sexual violence in war and conflict (man-on-man or woman-on-woman).[29] Since all of these impossible people—female perpetrators, male victims, and gender nonconforming bodies—exist in sexual violence in war and conflict, the question of how to theorize them is puzzling.

Recognition of victim essentialism has led some scholars to trace the problems with international criminal jurisprudence about sexual violence in war and conflict to inherent gender biases both in social order and in law.[30] As Chiseche Salome Mibenge explains, "gender groups are traditionally divided into two monolithic units: men and women. This division is erroneous as it tends to make invisible subgroups and cultures within a dominant gender group and also conceals the hierarchies and hegemonic power within a single gender group."[31] Mibenge, describing the ICTR's gender jurisprudence, suggests that its "dominant narrative of gender and violence is monolithic and overly exclusive."[32] Mibenge is critiquing several dynamics. First, she is suggesting that membership in sex categories is not clear and straightforward. She is concerned not only that the category of "women" is difficult to define, but also that courts' ease in defining it comes with the baggage of associating women with certain characteristics of femininity, and therefore with lower or even invisible social status. She is concerned that "the exclusive portrayal by the laws of war of all women as 'mothers,' 'nursing mothers,' or 'pregnant women' strips women of individuality and focuses legal protection in women's sexual reproductive potential."[33] In other words, women become defined by their sexual violability and their reproductive capacity, and are treated by courts with emphasis on those traits, rather than as men's equals against whose bodies a crime was committed.

Second, Mibenge is expressing concern that the focus on the positioning of people identified as "men" and people identified as "women" in sexual violence in war and conflict obscures the different positions that people classified *within* those groups occupy—that there are hierarchies *among men* and *among women* within any given social, political, ethnic, racial, or religious group in conflicts, and that those hierarchies affect and matter to what happens to people in and around sexual violence in war and conflict. In their extreme form, those hierarchies are reflected in the perpetration of sexual violence in war and conflict by one member of a (perceived) sex class against another member of that (perceived) sex class. Even when they do not reach those levels, though, sexual and/or gender identity, class, race, ethnic, religious, and national differences *among* those understood to be men and those understood to be women significantly impact not only whether but how they experience sexual violence in many conflicts, and therefore need to influence the legal conceptualization of what that sexual violence is and how it should be addressed.

Third, Mibenge is concerned that the notion that there are positions that *men* have and positions that *women* have related to sexual violence in war and conflict creates idealized notions of victimhood to which victims must aspire to be recognized. She explains that "the price of inclusion in an essentializing justice process" is the appearance of normalcy—it "requires a 'perfect' or 'legitimate' victim who is allowed to gain access to justice but required to adjust their testimony of atrocity to fit the script provided by the dominant narrative."[34] The script of the dominant narrative includes a female victim violated by a male perpetrator in particularly ways made intelligible as "legitimately rape" and in need of saving or avenging by the men charged with her protection. This "criteria of intelligibility operates to constitute a field of bodies" that *can be raped* and a field of bodies that can be held individually responsible for their rapes.[35] This is complicit in the discursive and legal impossibility of female perpetrators.

Judith Butler expresses concern that this constitution of intelligibility causes problems far beyond poor policy and media reactions to sexual violence in war and conflict. She explains that "it may be that certain identifications and affiliations are made, certain sympathetic connections amplified, precisely in order to institute a disidentification with a position that seems too saturated with injury."[36] In other words, her logic suggests that the *impact* of the discursive construction of the ideal victim of sexual violence as *violated by a man* is a sympathetic association that serves to construct a further wedge between traditional understandings of sexual violence in war and conflict and its actual complexities.

In this view, there is a risk that visible *recognition* of sexual violence in war and conflict is, in Cynthia Enloe's words, *dangerous*, perhaps even more dangerous than silence, for the victims.[37] This recognition is resignifying an ineffective norm against an oversimplified notion of sexual violence in war and conflict. As Butler explains, "the resignification of norms is thus a function of their inefficacy, and so the question of subversion, of working the weakness in the norm, becomes a matter of inhabiting the practices of its rearticulation."[38] There is a lot in Butler's analysis, but the first key point for this chapter's argument is that the continued *repetition* of the norm against sexual violence in war and conflict is not (necessarily/only/at all) a victory of visibility transgressing gender inequality, but a resignification of its ineffectiveness, especially given the prosecutorial record on related offenses. In Mibenge's terms, it is important to recognize the material harm produced by this resignification of standards that render women perpetrators (and many male and female victims) discursively impossible. She explains that "the pain that law and justice inflict, the omissions they make, the control they keep, the freedoms they confiscate, and the oppression they legitimate are part and parcel of their protection mechanisms."[39]

Rejecting victim essentialism, then, is about redressing the harms caused by the idealized victim narrative, both insomuch as it makes discursively impossible this book's subject, women perpetrators, and insomuch as that discursive invisibility shows the problematic structure of the idealized victim norm being constructed around sex-essentialist notions of perpetrator and victim for understanding, prosecuting, and stopping conflict-related sexual violence. As Butler explains, such subversion is necessarily done from the inside, that is, within media, scholarly, and legal analysis of sexual violence in war and conflict, "inhabiting processes of rearticulation" of definitions, standards, notions, and prosecutorial strategies.[40] This inhabitation, though, must not only be within the walls of jurisprudence and legal analysis, but also engage media coverage, which reifies and is reified in the discussion of what constitutes, and how to pursue, justice for sexual violence in war and conflict. This requires thinking about gender, war, genocide, and sexual violence in these contexts.

Rethinking Visibility in Sexual Violence Analysis

At the same time, it is difficult to argue either for *less* visibility of sexual violence in war and conflict, or for *more* visibility of the (often sensationalized) female perpetrators of such violence. Instead, it *seems* possible to make an argument for rethinking gender-based accounts of sexual violence in war and conflict. Maria Eriksson Baaz and Maria Stern, for example, look to change inherited "grids of intelligibility" as they "query the seemingly cohesive and certainly compelling narrative of wartime rape, unpack its prevailing logics, explore its limits, and examine its effects."[41] One of these authors' critiques is of the frequent failure to interrogate a "'Gendered' Story," where "it is the gendering of perpetrators and victims of war which constructs rape as a weapon via its power and efficiency."[42] Baaz and Stern make the argument that the ties between the *sexed* story where men commit sexual violence against women and the gendered story where sexual violence in war and conflict is an act of feminization mean that the gendered story *both* maintains essentialisms and has other deleterious effects on the conceptualization of sexual violence.[43] One of the key other effects about which Baaz and

Stern express concern is that the "gendered story" simultaneously normalizes sexual violence in war and conflict (as what is expected to show masculinity situationally),[44] denies the gendering of "other" conflict violence,[45] and places the "gendering" of sexual violence in war and conflict between the violence and humanity.

I think Baaz and Stern have correctly identified an important problem. The narrative of sexual violence in war and conflict as *gendered* remains too closely tied to the biological essentialism of explanations of sexual violence that relied on men's inherent sexual needs as the motivator.[46] After all, if it is people (men, women, and others) victimizing people (men, women, and others) in sexual violence in war and conflict, using sex- and gender-neutral terms seems not only accurate but the only appropriate response. In this framing, it would be defined and understood as sexual violence during conflict, regardless of who perpetrates it and who is victimized. In theory, such a framing would allow for the recognition of male victims, female perpetrators, and gender nonconforming bodies without the baggage of the sex-essentialist current terminologies and assumptions. In this view (as will be discussed in chapter 5), not only would sexual violence in war and conflict be easier to *theorize* in a world in which is its considered, its place in international criminal law would be easier to discern, since it would be a variety of torture and of crimes against humanity without the need for sex- or gender-specific jurisprudence to understand the nature and severity of the crime.

This analysis has appeal, especially because one of the key problems of thinking about sexual violence in war and conflict is assumptions concerning who perpetrates that violence (and therefore who its victims are).[47] It is further problematic to insist or even imply that the genderings of sexual violence in war and conflict are divorced from, separate from, or nullify the genderings of violence more generally, either in the global political arena or in any other forum.[48] Still, I am skeptical that undoing gendered stories of sexual violence in war and conflict would be any more effective than looking to give either more or less attention to female perpetrators outside attempts to change the frameworks of intelligibility.

Instead, I argue that the suggestion that the "gendered story" of sexual violence in war and conflict should be deemphasized is problematic, and that de-gendering accounts of that violence is both idealistic and inaccurate. I characterize it as idealistic for two reasons. The first reason is that it assumes that sex and gender discrimination happens only *between* and *across* sexes, while empirical reality suggests it is both much more complicated and much more widespread. Assuming that the eradication of sex distinctions is accompanied by the eradication of sex subordination feels idyllic rather than reasonable. The second reason that I characterize it as idealistic is because it assumes that sexual violence in war and conflict would be thought of as a serious crime without reliance on the logic that women's inherent innocence and inability to defend themselves is *why it is so bad to do*. Advocacy for sex- and gender-neutral terminology, theorizing, and jurisprudence about sexual violence in war and conflict assumes that de-sexing and de-gendering the analysis of it would make it easier to prosecute, while I worry it would make it easier to ignore. The significations of women as those who need protection, who are vulnerable to violation, whose sexual purity is valued, who are the biological and cultural reproducers of state and nation, and who are (only) wars' victims are key to many of the discourses (legal, media, and scholarly) is what finally garnered attention *towards* the severity and normatively and legally problematic nature of sexual violence in war and conflict. Removing those significations from thinking and talking about the victims of sexual violence in war and conflict may take it *off* the radar of international politics and international criminal law—since it would invalidate the logic of a number of court decisions and policy resolutions condemning sexual violence in war and conflict.[49] While I am not certain of this result, it would at the very least be a *risk* of de-sexing sexual violence, in theory, in jurisprudence, and in practice. In my view, this risk is not worth taking, especially given the volume and severity of sexual violence in war and conflict around the world, and the uphill battle that victims must already fight to get recognition, even when they fit the "ideal victim" mold Mibenge discussed.[50]

To that end, I disagree with Baaz and Stern that the sex essentialism in the relationship between the "sex story" and the "gender story" is a necessary part of a "gender story" of sexual violence in war and conflict. I also disagree with them that the normalization effect of the "gender story" is a necessary direct and proximate result of the "gender" framing. Unlike Baaz and Stern, I make the argument that characterizing sexual violence in war and conflict as gendered is a part of a larger story of understanding gender/violence in a gendered/violent world[51]—inside and outside of the domains traditionally understood as "conflict."

Still, I am not advocating the maintenance of inaccurate, gender-essentialist stereotypes because there is a risk of a decrease in the attention to sexual violence in war and conflict if those stereotypes are removed from the discourses of that violence. Instead, I am arguing that the suggestion that sexual violence in war and conflict is gender- and sex-neutral is equally if not more inaccurate. I called the assumption that taking away sex distinctions takes away sex subordination idyllic above—what I meant by that is that there is a significant amount of evidence that *men and women* can and do subordinate *men and women* based on sex and gender, not to mention those who fall outside of prescribed sex dichotomies. Sex and gender subordination is a significant part of women's perpetration of sexual violence in war and conflict, as well as men's victimization, and other sex-transgressive performances of sexual violence. Accordingly, I am suggesting that the inaccurate, gender-essentialist stereotypes that have often dominated theorizations of sexual violence in war and conflict be *replaced* with more complicated, and more nuanced, understandings—as sexed, as sexual, and as gendered. Such understandings would not rely, as Stemple suggested, on the male perpetrator/female victim dichotomy. This move is important not only because of the question of how to get victims the attention that they need, but also because sex- and gender-neutral framings of sexual violence in war and conflict are as inaccurate as (if not more inaccurate than) gender-essentialist framings that suggest that women can only be victims, and the perpetrators of women's victimization must be men. Wartime sexual violence *is* sexed, sexual, and gendered, and all of these observations matter in theorizing it. To do so fully, both women perpetrators and the "gender story" need to be visible, and reconciled.

Reformulating Gender Subordination in Gender-Based Accounts

This returns to the question that went unanswered above, however—how is it possible to theorize sexual violence in war and conflict as gendered if it is not something that *men do to women*? The answer, I argue, lies in carefully incorporating a number of the insights of feminist theorizing about gender into thinking about sexual violence in war and conflict. Rather than relying on a sex-dichotomized notion of which *people* commit sexual violence in war and conflict, it is appropriate to focus on *what happens* when that sexual violence is committed—its conditions of possibility and significations. Specifically, I argue that it is important to look at *what happens* when sexual violence in war and conflict is committed in terms of genderings—masculinities, feminities, masculinization, and feminization—rather than in terms of the sex of the bodies doing the committing of that sexual violence in war and conflict.

This is not meant to diminish the agency of perpetrators (discussed in the next section) or to move from an agent-based notion of sexual violence in war and conflict to a structure-based understanding. Instead, it is meant to suggest that *the acts* of sexual violence and the *actors* that perpetrate them can be understood, and understood as gendered, without explicit reference to or implicit understanding of who the perpetrator is (particularly his or her perceived or assigned biological sex). The male perpetrator/female victim dichotomy is, as many of the examples so far in this book have shown, problematically false. The basis of its popularity is its reifying and being reified by both the general gender stereotypes that women are weak, passive, in need of protection, and at risk of violation and that men are aggressive, physically and sexually. This is compounded by the fact that the majority of perpetrators of sexual violence in war and conflict *are* people understood to be men and the majority of victims of such sexual violence *are* people understood to be women. Many accounts of sexual violence in war and conflict suggest that the later empirical observation is a result of, and a reaffirmation of, the gender stereotypes that predict it.

A deeper look at sex and gender offers another approach that accounts not only for the "normal" commission of sexual violence in war and conflict by men towards women, but for the other sexual violence in war and conflict that does not easily fit that model. As mentioned in the introduction, gender expectations of people assumed to be men include toughness, autonomy, aggression, rationality, confidence, and (hetero)sexual desire.[52] In most cultures and institutions most places in the world, masculinities are valued over femininities—where people understood to be men, and people and institutions understood to be masculine, hold a place of dominance over people understood to be women, and people and institutions understood to be feminine.[53] Those people and institutions can be seen as associated with gendered expectations like sensitivity, (inter)dependence, passivity, emotionality, quietness, innocence, grace, care, and purity.[54]

I argue that this account of gender subordination is wrong, or at the very least incomplete. This reading of gender subordination would, for example, suggest that Pauline Nyiramasuhuko's ordering and presiding over the rapes of hundreds if not thousands of women was not gender subordination because gender subordination must be done by men to women—or even it must be done by men *to be* done to women. The traditional implied naturalness of women's position on the bottom of gender hierarchies that men enforce and dominate is a significant part of what makes women perpetrators of sexual violence in war and conflict impossible and/or invisible. It also (as discussed below) normalizes men's commission of sexual violence in war and conflict (and perhaps even sexual violence more broadly). Rather than thinking of gender subordination as something men do to women, I contend that it should be thought of as "based on perceived membership in and relationship with, rather than some sort of absolute and actual membership in, sex classes."[55]

In that sense, it is not that men and/or women are doing the abusing in their biological capacity as men and/or women, whatever that might be.[56] Instead, it is that men and/or women are doing the abusing in response to, and in relation to, hierarchies in social and political life that are structured around expectations around and values assigned to masculinities and femininities.[57] I have referred to this, in the introduction and elsewhere, as *gendered orders* and *gender order*.[58] By gendered orders, I mean that alignment with values associated with masculinities is a signifier of value and dominance, and alignment with values associated with femininities is a signifier of subordination and devaluation. Gendered orders are rarely visible, and most often take the form of unspoken assumptions about the ways that social and political organizations work.[59] As I have discussed before, "while it is possible to see manifestations of gender orders everywhere—from women's economic inequalities to the ways men and women are expected to dress—it is not possible to *see* gender[ed] orders."[60] Still, looking for manifestations of gendered orders can aid in understanding where they are and how they structure social and political relations.

Manifestations of gendered orders can be found in the subordination of women, and in sexed and gendered expectations of what women and men do. Association between people understood to be women and femininities, and people understood to be men and masculinities is one of the default placements of people within gender hierarchies (and therefore gendered orders), but it is by no means the only placement within those orders, and by no means always static. Instead, there are forms of masculinities (e.g., hypermasculinities[61] and hegemonic masculinities) that subordinate other masculinities, and associate them with femininities. Likewise, *feminization* is the political act of associating a person or group with values associated with femininity and/or devaluing those traits associated with femininity (often simultaneously). Feminization *as devalorization* can happen to any one or any group, organization, nation, or state.[62] The very gendering that has been used to hold back, subordinate, and oppress women for decades, centuries, and millennia is not *necessarily* sex-specific, even if it is manifest in largely sex-specific ways. Instead, men and/or women can *feminize* men and/or women by associating them with values associated with femininity, and devaluing those characteristics or traits.[63]

In this view, gender subordination is a *class relationship* where femininities are valued less than masculinities, and people often try to classify and associate not only themselves but (friendly or enemy) others along gender hierarchies of those associations.[64] This gender subordination is not tied to biologically male bodies and biologically female bodies, but is instead "fundamentally a power relationship in which those perceived as female/feminine are made less powerful than those perceived as masculine/male."[65] This sort of gender subordination can be seen as, in some ways, socially fluid (that is, people can manipulate their and others' placement along gender hierarchies in some situations).[66] Thus, "gender[ed] orders exist, but balances among masculinities, and even among masculinities and femininities, change over time, place, and culture."[67] Despite this fluidity, this reading suggests that gender subordination is a systematic force with perhaps even more reach than most envision—not only is perceived membership in gendered categories "inscribed with gendered power,"[68] acts of *gendered disempowerment* happen even when biological sex is not directly involved in the labeling and classification of people.[69] Gender, then, functions to structure social hierarchies, where the dominant are associated with masculinities and the subordinate are associated with femininities.[70] People, groups, and states that are in competition, then, often attempt to associate themselves with masculinities (masculinization) and to associate their enemies with devalued femininities (feminization).[71]

I suggest that *gendered orders* account for the ways in which people, groups, and states often compete in political violence. In this understanding, "gender[ed] orders are key to understanding international political orders" and "global political actors contest for relative position along a gendered hierarchy among them."[72] By this I mean that association with masculinities and femininities, both in any given interaction and more generally, are symbolic of status among people, nations, and states. Therefore, reading power onto a person, nation, or state in international politics is by association masculinizing, and reading masculinization onto a person, nation, or state is by association empowering; reading disempowerment onto a person, nation, or state in international politics is by association feminizing, and reading feminization onto a person nation, or state is by association disempowering. Many variations on these basic associations form the basis for the salience of gender orders in global politics.

If *gender orders* are the organizations of hierarchies based on association with values associated with masculinities and femininities, a *gender order* is a particular organization of those values and traits (and of the people and groups associated with them) that makes a particular social or political event or organization possible. In other words, a *gender order* is the normalized hierarchy among gendered values in a given place or context. The gender order in times of "peace" and the gender order in times of "war" are not disconnected, but they are also not the same. Like Cynthia Enloe thinks of wars as having gender histories,[73] I think of wars related to interruptions in or changes of established or "peacetime" gender orders.[74]

With a number of other feminist scholars, I have argued elsewhere that the gender order in many wars and conflicts require particular sorts of behavior that meet expectations associated with the (perceived) biological sex with which one is identified.[75] Those expectations often *differ* from peacetime gender expectations, but are often no less (and sometimes even more) structured.[76] For example, expectations associated with masculinities in peacetime in a particular society may revolve around household support, marriage, sport, or other indicators of social status *among men*, while expectations associated with masculinities during conflict in the same society could revolve around willingness to kill and die and/or victory in battle.[77] Expectations associated with femininities in peacetime in the same society might revolve around chastity, marriage, and motherhood, while expectations associated with femininities during conflicts might involve various sorts of troop support, maintaining domestic political economies, or even soldiering.[78]

Of course, this is an oversimplified account of peacetime and conflict gender roles, which have been explored in more detail and with more complexity elsewhere in this book and in other studies of gender, war, and conflict. The point of that brief exploration was to suggest that conflict preserves the existence of gender hierarchies and some of the particular expectations related to masculinities and femininities, while others change as conflict goes on. Often, the interruption of gendered orders can be used as a weapon in conflict, and the restoration of the pre-conflict gender order can be a "symbol that a conflict has subsided and normal life can be resumed."[79] Expectations of men *as men* and of women *as women* are molded around the (pre-conflict and conflict) gender(ed) orders of masculinities and femininities, rather than attached to the biological sex of the people who live, enforce, or fall victim to gender subordination.

In this view, gender subordination is complex product and producer of gendered orders and gender order—rather than tied to the sex of the subordinator and the sex of the subordinated. Men can subordinate men on the basis of sex and gender, as women can subordinate women—and these same-sex subordinations are just two of the many variations of biological sex "pairings" across which sex and gender subordination can take place. *Anyone* can utilize the power of sex and gender hierarchy against *anyone else*. In this view, though, access to the tools of gender subordination is not equally distributed, and it is therefore not equally likely that *anyone* utilizes the power of sex and gender hierarchy against *anyone else*.[80] Instead, the reified nature of sex and gender hierarchy, and the differential power different people hold within it due to their perceived associations with both biological sexes and social genders, mean that the demographics of gender subordinators and the gender subordinated are likely to be skewed in the direction of the male perpetrator/female victim dichotomy—perhaps one of many reasons that this inaccurate dichotomy remains so popular. In other words, it is not a coincidence that most of gender subordination's perpetrators have been men and most of its victims have been women in many if not most contexts—but a product of the feminization of women, the association of women and femininities, and the devaluation and devalorization of femininities.

Sexual violence in war and conflict, then, is neither sex-neutral nor gender-neutral. Still, the *sexed* and *gendered* nature of that sexual violence does not stem from the (assumed) maleness of the perpetrators or the (assumed) femaleness of the victims. Instead, the significant percentage of perpetrators who are male and the significant percentage of victims who are female stem from and are overdetermined by the sexed and gendered nature of sexual violence in war and conflict. The interesting theoretical question, then, for those looking to recognize male victims, female perpetrators, and victims and perpetrators that are either/or or neither/nor, is what the sexed and gendered nature of sexual violence in war and conflict looks like, is, and is constituted from. From this perspective, I contend that it is important to see the gendered nature of that sexual violence as stemming from gendered orders of social and political life, which incentivize masculinism in self and feminization of the Other, *individually and collectively*, in war and conflict—*in men and women*.[81] Incentives to feminize the enemy state/nation are not necessarily less strong for people identified as women than it is for people identified as men.[82] The difference in their rates of perpetration come not from some natural difference in ability, predisposition, or incentive structure, but instead from a difference in preexisting social constraints in the same gendered orders that structurally motivate the behavior to begin with. Men and women's undifferentiated *capacity* to commit sexual violence in war and conflict, though, is only part of the story—and the fact that it is only part of the story is what makes the idea that sexual violence can/should be read as neutral both inaccurate and normatively problematic. The rest of the story is the context of the constraints of *gendered orders*.

When I suggest that sexual violence in war and conflict is contextualized in the constraints of gendered orders, I mean that people understood to be women are positioned differently vis-à-vis material opportunities, social expectations, and socialization than people understood to be men as a result of the gender order in which they live and experience war and conflict. Therefore, the gendered world in which men and women live affects their positions as relates to perpetration of and victimization in sexual violence in war and conflict. When I suggest that this sexual violence is contextualized in its own gendered orders, I mean that the messages of masculinization and feminization contained in practices of sexual violence in war and conflict serve as a gendered incentive structure for perpetration that meshes with preexisting gendered social orders. Thus, rather than being sex- and gender-neutral, sexual violence in war and conflict, like other gender subordination, can be seen as the product and producer of multiple layers of gendered expectations, gendered hierarchies, and gendered orders. In these terms, women, individually and collectively, can be seen as victims of gender subordination generally and sexual violence in war and conflict specifically, even as women are perpetrators.[83]

Women Perpetrators, Relational Autonomy, and Practices of Sexual Violence

Noting that women act as perpetrators of gender subordination generally and sexual violence in war and conflict specifically is an important step towards reconceptualizing traditional notions of sexual violence in war and conflict, which make women perpetrators impossible. It is not the only step towards such a reconceptualization, however. Instead, as Caron Gentry and I have argued,[84] recognizing women's involvement in violence requires rethinking *what that violence is*. That is not because men and women commit violence in different ways or for different reasons than men do—instead, it is because theoretical approaches to the commission of violence formed when it was understood to be something largely if not exclusively committed by men, and therefore filtered through the lenses of masculine social values.[85]

Gentry and I have argued that male-centered approaches to theorizing individual violence fail to accommodate violent women, and that, correspondingly, most descriptions of the violence of women deal with their violence *as women*—men's violence is violence, and women's violence is *women's violence*.[86] Therefore, many ostensibly sex-neutral theories of people's violence are not applied to violence that women commit—not because they are carelessly overlooked, but because they are, implicitly or explicitly, constructed around the assumption that men are the people who "normally" commit individual violence. Their construction around male actors can take one of two forms: the characterization of the violent individual as male, or the use of masculine stereotypes, traits, and understandings to explain violence. In both of these ways, much of the theorization of people's violence in global politics generally, and people's sexual violence in global politics specifically, were shaped with an eye towards the male perpetrator. Therefore, even applying these ostensibly sex-neutral theories to women perpetrators does not solve their theoretical problems. That is because applying those theoretical approaches to women is essentially "adding women and stirring," where the standards and expectations have been set by masculine discourses that neglect feminine traits, experiences, and knowledges.[87] In these terms, recognizing women's violence shows *not only* that most approaches to individual sexual violence omit women's perpetration, but that their gendered assumptions cause problems for their ability to explain the perpetration of sexual violence in war and conflict (and violence more generally) whoever perpetrates it.[88]

Perhaps this is why scholars who have an interest in why women perpetrate individual (sexual or other) political violence have steered clear of traditional accounts of people's violence in global politics, and instead used gendered assumptions about women's nature to account for women's violence as *women's violence*.[89] For example, as she discusses women's motivations for committing acts of self-martyrdom, Mia Bloom focuses on *female-specific* motivations like avenging personal losses and redeeming family honor.[90] Caron Gentry and I have argued that there are two major problems with explaining women's violence with sex-specific logics.[91] First, woman-specific approaches to women's violence often feature sex-essentialist stereotypes (assumptions that women *as women* by nature have something in common) as well as sensationalized notions of femininities' negative qualities.[92] Second, we have argued that it is inappropriate to separate theoretical approaches to men's violence and theoretical approaches to women's violence.[93] This bifurcation involves a number of inaccurate assumptions, including but not limited to the assumption that men and women have fundamental differences, and the assumption that men's violence is not gendered and women's violence is gendered. We suggest that both women's violence and men's violence (along with the violences of people who are both/and or neither/nor) are gendered in many ways—they are committed by individuals whose identities and social contexts are gendered, and who live in gendered worlds with gender-hierarchical consequences and implications of political action/activity.[94] Sex-specific theories of women's violence often obscure agency[95] in women's violence and obscure the genderings of men's violence.

On these grounds I contend that theories about sexual violence which assume that men were the perpetrators cannot be representative of the constitution and motivations of men who committed that sexual violence, much less of those of women perpetrators. Instead, like the understanding they present of who perpetrated sexual violence, they were partial understandings based on the privileging of values associated with masculinities over values associated with femininities. This is true not least of the assumption that perpetrators of sexual violence in war and conflict are *actors* in the traditional sense—where their choices are fully "freely" made without social, political, or economic constraints.

Feminists thinking about gender subordination in the structure of social and political life have questioned both the content and the utility of this traditional notion of agency. Broadly defined, agency is the understanding that people and states that are *agents* have some unrestrained ability to act, sometimes independent of or even against the political and social structures within which they experience life. Feminist theorists have argued that autonomy is associated with, and defined by, masculine-biased notions of human interaction. While the masculine is often identified as, and operated as, autonomous, the feminine is often identified as, and operated as, controlled and dependent. The understanding of autonomous decision-making most often deployed in theories of political life is one that suggests, in line with social contract theorizing, that any autonomy people have ceded to others is to the state, and that ceding was voluntary in exchange for protection.[96] Feminist theorists have suggested that this assumption that people choose their obligations and limits on their freedom either directly or indirectly is both partial and gendered.[97]

Though the assumption of fully autonomous decision-making is gendered and problematic, it also features prominently in a number of ostensibly gender-neutral theories of individual violence. Many rational-actor approaches to people's violence suggest that violent people are making rational choices to engage in individual violence—that is, weighing the costs and benefits independently. Many approaches to people's violence that are based in psychology build sex-specific models to explain personal violence, mostly relying on men's experience *as men* to account for the existence of political violence, and frequently failing to account for women's violence. In most existing theories of people's violence in global politics, masculinity (either directly or in the form of masculinized notions of rationality and autonomy) is a key part of accounting for violence.

When women's violence is recognized, sex-specific theories are often used to address it as well. Many of these theories downplay women's role in choosing their violence.[98] In fact, in a number of sex-specific approaches to women's violence, women are framed as having lost control—over their will to live, over their need for revenge, over their sanity, or over their sexuality.[99] Violent women are then framed as at once incapable of choosing violence, but more dangerous because their violence has to have been inspired by a loss of control over the worst elements of femininity.[100] Implicit in these framings is the notion that women's choices are socially constrained by the boundaries of femininity, and that women's behavior outside of those boundaries is by definition a *dysfunction* both of the woman and of the gender norms. Men's violence is *abnormal but expected*; women's violence is *outside of the realm of expectation*—and this distinction comes from gendered assumptions about people's roles having significant salience.

If there is no substantive difference in men's violence and women's violence because they are men and women, then, the gendered notions of choice and agency underplaying interpretive differences about men's and women's violence need to be reexamined without abandoning what is known about the genderings of global and local social and political life. My first reaction is to suggest that, whatever level of agency in violence *anyone* has, women have—women are not more or less agential in their choices to commit violence than men are.[101] Such a reaction, however, validates masculinized notions of agency and violence, and suggests that adding women to accounts of men's sexual violence in war and conflict is adequate. Such an approach would suggest that women, like men, commit war crimes—and women, like men, commit those war crimes for reasons that traditional accounts of sexual violence in war and conflict can understand and explain. This approach, however, leaves an unrepresentative, and masculinized, model of the individual perpetrator of sexual violence in war and conflict intact.

Instead, as Caron Gentry and I have suggested, feminist theorizing (appropriately) questions a "reactive" autonomy notion of agency in political violence, and possibly the utility of the notion of agency at all.[102] With Nancy Hirschmann, we have found it important to recognize relational autonomy, where people maintain individual identity and decision-making capacity, but decide within constraints that are sometimes involuntarily assumed and always complicated.[103] Hirschmann recognizes the involuntary assumption of obligation as sex- and gender-unequal, and therefore sees gender bias in the structures of obligation in social and political life.[104] In other words, "people understood to be women often are assigned obligations that they have not agreed to, implicitly or explicitly."[105] In these obligatory situations, often, people do make *choices*, but those choices are limited by their situations as well as by other constraints imposed by the social, economic, political, and/or familial resources available. In Hirschmann's words, "desires and preferences are always limited by contexts that determine the parameters of choice."[106]

Instead, Hirschmann characterizes choice, obligation, and responsibility as responsive and intersubjective.[107] This means that independence is contingent, and one of the things it is contingent *on* is gendered social expectations of men and women, masculinities and femininities.[108] In this view, political choice is a matter of *gendered* position, and a question of degree, conditioned at least in part of gendered orders.[109] Therefore, decisions are made *with fellow constrainees*[110] and/or *within constraints*, where constraints are more or less restrictive based on a number of social and political factors, but never outside of constraints entirely. In this interpretation, the existence and identity of the self and other are mutually dependent, mutually vulnerable, and mutually socially constructed. Choices are, then, neither entirely free nor entirely constrained—therefore characterizations on both extremes are inaccurate, and often gendered.

Thinking about choices to perpetrate violence as relationally autonomous and within the context of gender orders helps to frame sexual violence in war and conflict as a practice rather than an act.[111] Emanuel Adler and Vincent Pouliot describe practices as "socially meaningful practices of action which, in being performed more or less competently, simultaneously embody, act out, and possibly reify background knowledge and discourse in and on the material world."[112] Rather than being what *agents do* or what *structure dictates*, practices are "dynamic material and ideational processes that enable structures to be stable or evolve, and agents to reproduce or transform structures."[113] While Adler and Pouliot do not explicitly use the concept of relational autonomy, their concept of practice can accommodate and be complemented by it. Adler, Pouliot, and others engaged in studying practices in global politics suggest that, while the concepts of behavior, action, and practice are often used as if they are interchangeable, they are conceptually distinguishable—where *practice* is socially structured and reiterated. In this parlance, *international* practices are "socially organized activities that pertain to world politics, broadly construed."[114] These organized activities are performances, which "have no other existence than in their unfolding or process."[115] Practices are also *patterned*—which means that, while they do not recur uniformly, they "generally exhibit certain regularities over time and space."[116] Not every action or performance, however, is a practice—because "social recognition is . . . a fundamental aspect of practice," which has "a public . . . an audience able to appraise the practice."[117] Because it is communicative, "practice rests on *background knowledge*, which it embodies, enacts, and reifies all at once."[118] In this way, "practice weaves together the *discursive and material* worlds," where discourse at once *is* practice and makes practice intelligible.[119] Practice-based approaches in IR emphasize "the everyday, highlight embodied capacities such as know-how, skills, and tacit understandings" at the same time they link the everyday to the everyday in macro-level global politics.[120]

It is fairly straightforward, in these terms, to think of sexual violence in war and conflict as a practice, both in each instance in which it occurs and at the macro-level in global politics. Sexual violence in war and conflict *is the everyday*, but everyday, everywhere there is a conflict. Its practice is socially meaningful with little (though some) variation wherever and whenever it is practiced. Its occurrence serves to reify the background knowledge of gender inequality that serves as its backdrop at the same time. Rather than being *what agents do* or *what structure dictates*, sexual violence in war and conflict has both material and ideational elements—processes that, each time they are enacted, contribute to their own institutionalization. It is at once *socially organized* and has no existence outside of each unfolding, which signifies a particular politics, not only of gender, but of state, nation, and humanity. It is *patterned*—that is, though it does not recur uniformly, there is a regularity to sexual violence in war and conflict over time and space. This regularity produces social recognition, by perpetrators, by victims, and by targets. Sexual violence in war and conflict has "a public"—in fact—many publics: its immediate victim(s), a "domestic" audience of the rapists' allies, a "foreign" audience of the rapists' opponents, and a "removed" audience of international communities. All of these audiences have (separate but linked) background knowledges about *what* sexual violence in war and conflict *is*—which its practice "embodies, enacts, and reifies all at once"—both on the macro-political level and everyday.

Thinking about sexual violence in war and conflict as a practice has a number of advantages, both in terms of considering how it happens and in terms of theorizing its significations.[121] In considering how sexual violence in war and conflict happens, a practice-based approach can account both for the gendered capacities and know-how that are a condition of possibility for it and the tacit understandings that produce its frequency and severity. Such an approach can also situate thinking about sexual violence in war and conflict as everyday, as embodied, social, and gendered.[122] The next section rethinks sexual violence in war and conflict as a gendered practice, taking into account the existence of women perpetrators. Such an approach asks what background knowledges are required for the practice of sexual violence in war and conflict, and what it embodies and enacts. It also moves away from both gendered understandings of agency and the gendered deployment of the idea of agency to legitimate, make recognizable, or make visible people's violence in global politics.

Background Knowledges and Sexual Violence

In looking for the background knowledges of sexual violence in war and conflict, one of the most important inherited knowledges, reified with every new act of sexual violence in war and conflict, is that this violence is normal in conflict. For those vulnerable to victimization by sexual violence in war and conflict, conflict is an inherently (sexually) insecure state, where the risk of sexual violation is always present. For those who perpetrate or witness the perpetration of sexual violence, conflict is an inherently (sexually) permissive state, where a victim's permission is less needed (or no longer needed at all) to engage in sex, and where rape can act as a punishment and an act of humiliation to the (individual, collective, or both, enemy). In other words, there is a normalization of sexual violence in war and conflict—where a particular script of such violence is assumed to be perpetrated. This script of sexual violence in war and conflict that is normalized is one where a male perpetrator on one side of the conflict rapes a female victim perceived to belong to the other side of the conflict.[123] As a number of scholars of sexual violence have noted, a combination of expectation, impunity, and social chaos contribute to the normalization of men's of commission rape in war, thought about as sexual violence in war and conflict.[124] This seems to be an assumption shared by approaches that cast sexual violence as endemic in conflict and those that see it as tangential.

The normalization of the existence of sexual violence in war and conflict and of the (assumed) male perpetrator, however, does not only impact thinking about what that violence means. Instead, the delineation of "conflict rape" and "genocidal rape" from "[regular] rape" *regularizes* non-conflict sexual violence.[125] Not only are the normative implications of this distinction problematic, as discussed in the introduction, the lines between the beginning, "during," and "after" of a conflict are not as clear as the language of "war rape" or "conflict sexual violence" or "genocidal rape" make it seem.[126] On top of that, many of the components of sexual violence in war and conflict that might make it distinct from "[regular] rape" exist in "[regular] rape" as well.[127] As Copelon explains:

> The line between war and "peace" is not so sharp. Gang rape in civilian life shares the repetitive, gleeful, and public character of rape in war.

Marital rape, the most private of all, shares some of the particular characteristics of genocidal rape in Bosnia: it is repetitive, brutal, exacerbated
by betrayal; it assaults a woman's reproductive autonomy, may force her
into hiding, to flee her home and community, and is widely treated as
legitimate by law and custom.[128]

In my view, Copelon's suggestion does not invalidate the notion about
thinking of sexual violence in war and conflict, but it does suggest that
there are background knowledges to conflict sexual violence other than
the normalization and expectation of its occurrence. Another background knowledge is the existence and perpetration of "[regular] rape,"
which is a condition of possibility of its subspecies, conflict sexual violence, war rape, and genocidal rape.[129] The background knowledge of
the omnipresence of rape (and the possibility of rape) is available both to
potential perpetrator and to potential victim (and to persons or groups
who are in both positions).[130]

Another (related) element of the background knowledges of sexual
violence in war and conflict, reified every time it is performed, is that
this violence is *gendered*, both in is discourses and its materiality. Copelon suggests that, at its base, sexual violence in war and conflict is an
expression of the objectification of women *as victims*, especially given
that "their" men are most often the targets. She explains:

The fact that the rape of women is also designed to humiliate the men
or destroy "the enemy" itself reflects the fundamental objectification of
women. When a woman is attacked because she "belongs" to the enemy
or because of her relationship to male targets, raping her is a means to humiliate, indeed, to feminize, the men who are powerless to protect her. As
such she is also being attacked on the basis of gender, as man's property,
lacking separate identity, dehumanized and subservient.[131]

Thus, each "performance" for the "audiences" of sexual violence in
war and conflict—the direct victim, the direct target, the perpetrators'
allies, and the victim's (perceived) allies is gendered—is gendered differently. The gendered dehumanization of the direct victim, the gendered
emasculation of the direct and proximate targets, and the gendered masculinization of the direct perpetrator and his/her allies *all communicate*

gendered messages. This is true *regardless* of the sex of the perpetrator or the sex of the victim. Thought of this way, the socially meaningful component of the practice of sexual violence in war and conflict cannot be located or parsed without reference to gender, because the sexualization, domination, subordination, and in-group bonding in sexual violence in war and conflict cannot be understood without reference to masculinities, femininities, and the construction of power relationships among them. The gender-hierarchical message of sexual violence in war and conflict is a process that, each time it is enacted, contributes to its own institutionalization.[132] Its gendering is both material (in that a physical act of feminization has occurred) and discursive (in that a signification of feminization has been communicated). Sexual violence in war and conflict is also is *socially organized* (in that it is part of the social institutions of militarization, of conflict, and even of the state), with a particular politics of *feminization as devalorization* paired with a politics of *sexual violence as feminization*. These politics are part of the gendered orders of conflicts, and the gender order of militarism.

In this way, normalization, regularity and gender subordination are background knowledges for the practice of sexual violence in war and conflict, and their reification happens through its practice. This reification is both discursive and material—in that it creates and legitimates a pattern of sexual violence in war and conflict and that the pattern's repetition repeats the effectiveness of the messages of sexual violence for the perpetrators' supporters and their opponents. While *the messages* are a significant component of sexual violence in war and conflict, it is also important to understand the practice as *embodied*. As Rhoda Copelon explains, "rape is transposition of the intimate into violence."[133] At the core of being a victim of sexual violence in war and conflict is (usually) being grotesquely physically violated, whereas at the core of perpetrating sexual violence is (usually) using one's body or an extension thereof to cause grotesque physical violation. Thus, both the enactment and the experience of sexual violence in war and conflict is an *embodied* practice, where people's bodies (as victims and as perpetrators) are both the site of inscribed violence and the site of the inscription of messages of gendered subordination.

It should be noted that there is nothing essential about the practice of sexual violence in war and conflict that makes a person a perpetrator and not a victim, or a victim and not a perpetrator. While relative power dynamics in conflict contexts often make it improbable that a victim of one perpetrator's sexual violence has the ability to inflict sexual violence on others, it is not unheard of. Much more commonly, a perpetrator turns his/her victims into perpetrators, either physically coercing them into violating others or encouraging their participation in violation.[134] Even more often than actual victims become actual perpetrators, "the line between victim and perpetrator is blurry" because "victims often experienced abuse at the hands of acquaintances, neighbors, relatives, tribesmen, and other intimates."[135] As such, the intimacy of the practice of sexual violence in war and conflict is not only embodied, but social—where often the victims and perpetrators share not only common background knowledges (about gender, and race, class, and conflict dynamics), but also common social groups and experiences. In this sense, it is best to describe sexual violence in war and conflict as a gendered, embodied, intimate, and iterated social practice, enacted within the context of the background knowledges of normalization, repetition, and gender subordination.

Conclusion

The goal of this reformulation is to follow up on my previous suggestion that understandings of sexual violence in war and conflict should change "with the realization that women can and do participate in it."[136] It is important that the reinterpretation happen without "trying to add or fit women to theories, the terms of which were set before women's violence was considered."[137] Instead, a gender-conscious reinterpretation of sexual violence in war and conflict should strive to "understand the phenomenon of perpetration *as if* women as *both* perpetrators and victims mattered in theoretical formulation."[138] This necessarily needs to rely on a more complicated notion of gender subordination—one that does not rely on the sex of the perpetrator to recognize either the act or its victims.

I contend that an account of sexual violence in war and conflict that sees it as a gendered social practice with gendered background knowledges can accomplish this, while avoiding many of the pitfalls of other possible approaches. Such an understanding captures many of the important dynamics of conflict sexual violence without resorting to reliance on sex- or gender-essentialist understandings of perpetrators or victims, or on dichotomized distinctions between men/women, war/"not war," agent/structure, and perpetrator/victim. It does not require either a decrease of attention to gendered stories of conflict sexual violence that often inspire attempts to obtain justice or an increase in sensationalized attention to women's perpetration. This approach is mindful of Mibenge's critique of the attraction of counterproductive attention as well as of Stemple's critique of silence around gendered war crimes.

It also provides theoretical space for understanding the discursive and material elements of the practice of sexual violence in war and conflict, and for parsing its reification by both enactment and prosecution. Such an approach might be able to co-opt current recognition of sexual violence in war and conflict to resignify more complicated, and more effective, norms—in Butler's terms, "inhabiting the practices of its rearticulation" of gendered sexual violence in war and conflict.[139] The question of the feasibility of rearticulation in the policy, media, legal and scholarly worlds remains, however. It is to the question of legal context that the next chapter turns—asking how jurisprudence of sexual violence in war and conflict needs to change with this theorization in mind, to account both for women perpetrators and for the practice-based understanding of sexual violence in war and conflict that acknowledging women perpetrators and the gender orders in which they perpetrate that violence inspires.

5

The Wrong of Rape

How Women Rapists Change Criminal Jurisprudence

Look what they did. They violated my honor. . . . They swore
at me and they filmed me. There was whisky. I was tied up.
They peed on me.[1]
—From a *Guardian* news story quoting Iman al-Obeidi
about how she was raped

When Iman al-Obeidi burst into a Tripoli hotel in April 2011 pleading
with journalists from abroad to stop her from being sexually abused
by members of the Libyan military, the internet caught on, and the
story went viral almost immediately.[2] On the one hand, attention to
the story was overdetermined: it happened in a hotel full of journalists, at a time when there was a fairly strong international consensus
that the Qaddafi regime was problematic and dangerous,[3] at the same
time that there was a significant amount of media attention being
given to women's situation in Arab Middle East and North Africa.[4]
At the same time, at least some of the attention to al-Obeidi's story
can be attributed to the account fitting neatly into common understandings of who commits sexual violence in war and conflict, who
is victimized by it, and why it is wrong.[5] Al-Obeidi constituted
Mibenge's "ideal victim."[6]

Al-Obeidi was a Libyan woman running from Libyan men whose
presumed evil was overdetermined, claiming helplessness and describing what happened to her as a violation of her honor and purity.[7] This
framing concurs with many used in the reporting and jurisprudence of
sexual violence in war and conflict.[8] It suggests that at least part of the
egregiousness of the commission of sexual violence in war and conflict
lies in its sex-specific violations of femininity by men (often, brown men
who are described in racialized terms).[9] As discussed earlier, the sexed

nature of how *victims* are understood—that is, that a part of understanding *victimization* in sexual violence in war and conflict is about seeing the victim as sexed female and/or feminized—contributes heavily to the invisibility of female perpetrators of sexual violence in war and conflict.

At the same time, those very sexed tropes have been instrumental in marshaling the political will to develop a jurisprudential system that identifies and punishes wartime sexual violence in international law. In fact, Mibenge argues that, despite shortcomings, "the legal value of rape as a crime in humanitarian law has progressed remarkably."[10] As Mibenge explains, "over the last ten years, the extraordinary developments in gender jurisprudence ushered in by the *ad hoc* tribunals and the International Criminal Court reflect the international community's willingness to combat and redress crimes of sexual violence as a specific means of warfare, and there is a strong indication that such crimes constitute *jus cogens*."[11] *Jus cogens*, or a generally accepted blanket prohibition, is generally understood to be the highest level of clarity that a precedent in law can have.[12] In other words, sexual violence in war and conflict is almost universally classified as a violation of international law—despite its fairly recent explicit criminalization.[13] An optimistic reading suggests that the general prohibition, as well as each specific decision to prosecute sexual violence in war and conflict "is grounded in the determination that a raped woman's body is not analogous to a misappropriated piece of goods."[14] A pessimistic reading suggests that the *jus cogens* prohibition against sexual violence in war and conflict is enforced as a mark of civilization—that the "we" of international society judges the "other" by how "they" treat "their" women. In either case, the number of prosecutions of sexual violence in war and conflict has increased significantly in recent years.

The first conviction in international court for rape charges was in 1998. On February 22, 2001, three Bosnian soldiers were convicted of war crimes in the International Criminal Tribunal for the Former Yugoslavia (ICTY) *solely* for rape.[15] Debra Bergoffen notes that this was unprecedented, and emblematic of three important things: "the decision to prosecute, the condemnation, and the classification of rape as torture, as a crime against humanity."[16] At the same time, as discussed throughout this book, the jurisprudential attention to sexual violence in war and conflict has been both uneven and narrow—and legal definitions have often appeared to be sharper than their ultimate utility has borne out. There is reason to be concerned about some of the attention to sexual violence in war and conflict being counterproductive to ending gender subordination, given its reliance on and construction of gender-based notions of ideal victims and perpetrators.[17]

When I suggest that the jurisprudential attention to sexual violence in war and conflict has been uneven, I echo a concern of Rhoda Copelon, who doubted that the war rape trials in the ICTY and ICTR were indicators of the permanent arrival of a condemnation of sexual violence in war and conflict, in international law or elsewhere. In Copelon's view, "the fact that rape of women in the wars in the former Yugoslavia captured world attention provides no guarantee that it will not also disappear from history, or survive, at best, as an exceptional case."[18] To provide evidence for her point, Copelon discusses a number of the cases of sexual violence in war and conflict that remained invisible during the hypervisible ICTR and ICTY prosecutions. She explains that, "by contrast, the rape of fifty percent of the women of the indigenous Yuracruz people in Ecuador by mercenaries of an international company seeking to 'cleanse' the land went largely unreported. Similarly, the routine rape of women in civil wars in Peru, Liberia, and Burma, for example, has only drawn occasional attention."[19]

When I suggest that jurisprudential attention to sexual violence in war and conflict has been narrow, I am suggesting that the gender stereotypes discussed thus far in the book influence the existence, shape, and result of prosecutions, punishments, and victim rights.[20] These stereotypes matter across systems of jurisprudence, from judgments about witness reliability[21] to definitions of what counts as rape and what does not count.[22] As Lori Girshick explains, "the law presumes heterosexuality, and assumes a female victim and a male perpetrator."[23] This presumption that men are the perpetrators of sexual violence is often not explicit in either the text of decisions or the legal frameworks on which courts rely.[24] Instead, it is the pairing of presumed heterosexuality and the the assumption that women are the victims that "sets up a presumed opposition with men as perpetrators—the implication is that if *women as women* are victims, then *men as men* are the persons doing the victimizing."[25] As Lara Stemple has argued and several of the cases in this book have demonstrated, "this sex-based framing reinforced an us-versus-them dualism that was generally useless and frequently counterproductive."[26]

When I suggest that legal definitions of rape have often appeared to be sharper than their utility has borne out, I am following a line of feminist legal critics of sexual violence jurisprudence. For example, Joanna Bourke, in her history of rape, suggests that many legal definitions of rape "have an aura of meticulousness—until explored more carefully."[27] Standards shift, where some statutes and courts require evidence of semen, while others require vaginal penetration by a penis, while still others have a broader notion of what rape is.[28] While the wide variety of definitions might be seen as a field trying to find definition, or space for victims to define what is happening to them, often it is instead a paved path back to reliance on the unevenness and narrowness discussed above.

This chapter, turning from theorizing the invisibility (and possibilities for visibility) of women's perpetration of sexual violence in war and conflict to the practice of jurisprudence, looks to explore the ways in which both the unevenness and narrowness of prosecutions for sexual violence in war and conflict might be corrected by rethinking the gendered assumptions behind current jurisprudential practices. In it, I suggest that accounting for sexual violence *by* and *among* women in post-conflict justice is complicated, given the ways that it confounds and sometimes even contravenes some of the political forces that have been crucial to drawing attention to sexual violence in war and conflict to begin with, as well as some of the logics that motivate prosecution. The chapter proposes reformulations for the current "gender justice" paradigm of post-conflict justice, focusing on changing operationalizations of gender, perpetration, and victimization to account for the gendered influences on autonomy and power that are constitutive of the perpetration of sexual violence. In so doing, it sketches a path where it is not only technically possible (as in the current system) but feasible and probable that women, individually and collectively, can be seen as victims of women's perpetration of sexual violence in war and conflict, without making invisible, individually and collectively, the women who perpetrate those war crimes.

Gender, Rape, and the Law

The making invisible of women perpetrators of sexual violence in war and conflict (and, by extension, making invisible the victims of women's perpetration) is not the only harm involved in the gendered and heterosexist assumption that this is something that men do to women. As Mibenge explains, this jurisprudence "sequesters women into the private sphere but fails to acknowledge the trespass of war into that gendered space."[29] The sequestering of women into the private sphere in this sense is overdetermined, by the sexed and gendered treatment of sexual violence in war and conflict outside of the legal sphere and the reification of these stereotypes in jurisprudence. That reification impacts not just the women who perpetrate sexual violence or the women who are victimized by it, but instead women as a socially identified group. In this way, arguments that *seem to* prioritize women's rights and women's bodies, which have been the linchpin of developing sexual violence in war and conflict jurisprudence, can actually have the performative and practical impact of gender subordination.

For example, Katie Richey argues that "the wrong of rape must be identified first and foremost as a crime against the raped woman's bodily integrity and sexual autonomy. It should not be subordinated to the harm done to the body politic."[30] This argument both feels and is meant to be progressive—it contains recognitions of the gendered nature of sexual violence in war and conflict, critiques of the instrumentalization of women's bodies by states and by soldiers, and prioritization of women's autonomy. All of these are issues that mainstream analyses of sexual violence in war and conflict often struggle with, in the legal world and outside of it—and all are, in my view, normative goods. At the same time, Richey's argument entrenches some gendered assumptions while eschewing others—positioning women's bodies as victimized by rape, and those (victimized) women's bodies as at the center of a liberal notion of rights redemption. As the organization African Rights noted in its 1995 study of women perpetrators of the Rwandan genocide, "focusing exclusively on women as victims of genocide does not help the survivors" (of their violence).[31]

Still, the only strong counternarrative to the entrenchment of the notion that women are the victims of sexual violence in war and conflict, exclusively, has been the recognition that men can also be victimized, either by feminists[32] or by anti-feminist men's rights activists.[33] However, correcting the narrowness and unevenness of attention to sexual violence in war and conflict is not (just) about recognizing male victims, and/or making visible women perpetrators. Instead, it is about reformulating how that violence is understood. The legal arena is no exception to that need. As Lara Stemple explains, "rape is an integrated part of a larger whole of subjugation, bodily violation, and victimization."[34] Rape is always gendered, but it being gendered does not mean that it is about women and only women.[35] In this sense, Copelon identified "the power of the intimate" as a weapon of both gender subordination and war.[36]

Reformulating Richey's understanding, in these terms, suggests that the wrong of rape needs to be identified first and foremost as a crime of feminization, violating the raped victim's bodily integrity and sexuality. As Stemple argues, "neither I nor most scholars who seek to challenge the sex-based certainties of international law advocate for the erasure of gender considerations."[37] Instead, law must acknowledge *both* that people do not fit perfectly into sex categories *and* that sex categories are not the only signifier of gender relations. The framework that suggests that sexual violence in war and conflict is a crime committed by men against women leaves out gender-nonconforming people,[38] same-sex victims and perpetrators, and female perpetrators with male victims. As a result, the idea that women abuse men, that men abuse men, or that women abuse men is *by definition* excluded.

The difficulty, though, lies not in helping the law imagine other categories of victim and perpetrator, and/or non-heterosexual sexual abuse—but in fitting those categories and pairings into a framework which both acknowledges that sexual violence in war and conflict is gendered and that sex categories do not map directly onto gender. These complexities are essential to having a legal framework for sexual violence in war and conflict that both commands attention and has the ability to take account of the breadth and depth of sexual violence in war and conflict. In Stemple's words, the problem is "how movements for transformative gender change can ever describe inequality ('women are victims') without reinscribing sex-based stereotypes ('women are victims')."[39] This is a key problem in contemporary conflict sexual violence jurisprudence.

Querying the "Gender Justice" Paradigm

Critiquing the framing and process of conflict sexual violence jurisprudence, however, does not provide a way forward. I take seriously Butler's suggestion that it is important to inhabit the practices of rearticulation from the inside—to think about how to revise conflict sexual violence jurisprudence rather than ignore or discard it. It becomes incumbent, then, I think, on critics of conflict sexual violence jurisprudence to make an effort to understand how it is understood by those engaged in it, and by those advocating for its development, to look to change how it works.

This chapter examines what some have identified as the "gender justice" paradigm for conflict sexual violence jurisprudence.[40] While there is no definitive account of the "gender justice" paradigm of international conflict sexual violence jurisprudence, a number of observers have identified several of its salient features. One key feature is a commitment to increasing the quantity of prosecutions of sexual violence in war and conflict, with the understnading that thorough investigation and prosecution will lead to more convictions, and convictions are signifiers of the provision of justice.[41] The underlying assumption of this part of the gender justice paradigm is that the prosecution of any given occurrence of sexual violence in war and conflict *against women* provides justice *for women* and constitutes a just response to this violence.

A second key feature of the gender justice paradigm is a commitment to women's entitlement to what is understood as basic human dignity and human rights.[42] This entitlement, "with roots in liberal feminist political philosophy," looks to construct "the conditions required for free and rational choice" in a world where gender subordination can "disable women's agency by limiting their capacities to reason and act independently."[43] In this approach to gender justice, the focus of attempts to obtain justice rely on *making space for* women to act in decision-making capacities—that is, making sure that they have capacities to actualize their equality. Doris Buss suggests that "the insistence on the formal recognition of harm done to women in armed conflict was, at its root, a claim to justice," and the continued failure to recognize those harms fully serves to "position women as less important than men."[44] This is one of the key problems of sexual violence in war and conflict in the gender justice paradigmatic approach—that the treatment of women *as women* as *less than agents* and (therefore) *less than human* is a key source of gender subordination in global (and even local) politics. The gender justice paradigm therefore suggests the redress of sexual violence in war and conflict against women will enable women's agency.

A third key feature of gender justice advocacy, frequently paired with the promotion of women's entitlement to basic humanity, is women's entitlement to the positive rights generally understood as human rights.[45] These include obligations to respect basic human rights, obligations to protect from bodily harm, and obligations to provide basic needs.[46] The underlying assumption of this feature of gender justice jurisprudence is that holding women equal to men in global politics involves making sure that sex-based violations of women's human rights and bodily integrity are taken seriously, and holding women equal to men in global politics is a desirable transgression of gender subordination. The key parts of this argument are made explicit in Catharine MacKinnon's *Are Women Human?*, which argues that taking women seriously *as humans* requires taking seriously women's human rights, not only when they are similarly situated to (and therefore have/need the same rights as) men, but also when they find themselves situated differently than, or even in opposition to, men.[47]

A fourth key feature of the gender justice paradigm is that it looks to erase discrimination *against women*.[48] Goetz classifies this as a "negative liberties" approach, exemplified best by the Convention on the Elimination of Discrimination against Women (CEDAW).[49] Gender justice jurisprudence advocates often focus on "integrating" gender crimes into the prosecution mechanisms of other, more recognized war crimes to provide equal legal protection to the women victims.[50] The underlying assumption of this feature is that providing women negative liberties and equal protection of the law is a condition of possibility of women's equality with men, which is an important part of (if not the sum total) of redressing gender subordination.

These assumptions of the gender justice paradigm can be found frequently in the theory and practice of the international jurisprudence of sexual violence in war and conflict. While there are disagreements *within* the gender justice paradigm (should a positive or negative rights approach be used to define war rape?), it coalesces around "reference to emancipatory projects that advance women's rights through legal change, or promote women's interests in social and economic policy" and commitment to a politics of the rejection of women's (and some-times gender) subordination.[51] This is why references to these assump-tions can be seen in the work of many feminist scholars and practitioners of politics and law.[52] In the view of many of these scholars, prosecu-tion of each occurrence of sexual violence against women approximates justice for women, not least because it creates space for women to act as agents, is a condition of possibility of women's basic humanity (and therefore of women's equality to men, who are assumed to be human), and is a transgression against discrimination *against* women in social and political life. Seeking "gender justice," then, can be seen as implicat-ing self-determination (self-development, recognition, and democratic freedom), equality of gendered consequences, and diversity.[53] Seeking these things *for women* means that "gender justice" jurisprudence *about women as victims* looks to empower women, to hold them equal to men, and to pay attention to women's special needs in particular jurispruden-tial situations.[54]

A number of critics of the legal situation of women maintain that many of the foundational tenets of the "gender justice" paradigm re-main fundamentally appropriate for combating gender subordination.[55] Rather than discarding the gender justice paradigm completely, some critics suggest that it is the misinterpretation[56] or its ineffective deploy-ment[57] that causes any deficiencies of conflict sexual violence jurispru-dence. Others, however, contend that the "gender justice" approach is *prima facie* insufficient or even fundamentally counterproductive.[58] The argument that the gender justice paradigm is insufficient is based on the contention that law is not enough. For example, Beth Van Schaak argues that "strong, positive law is irrelevant where a commitment to gender justice does not infuse all stages of development and implementation of a prosecutorial strategy."[59] In other words, Van Schaak is concerned that prosecution is always left to prosecutorial discretion, and prosecutors may choose not to seek justice for, or may be willing to plea bargain in, cases of sexual violence and sexual abuse. The existence of laws inspired by an interest in gender justice, then, may not be sufficient for the development of jurisprudence in substantive accordance with the intent behind those laws.

The argument that the gender justice paradigm is fundamentally counterproductive frames gender equality law as not only inadequate by itself but potentially problematic. The gender justice paradigm assumes that law produces the results from a well-formulated expression of its intent. It also relies on the assumption that the law of sexual violence in war and conflict is constructed outside of, and free or innocent of the politics of, the conflict in which the sexual violence is being committed. Alternate readings, however, suggest that those assumptions, along with the "gender justice" approach that they embody, are deeply problematic. For example, Nicola Henry paints a picture of the law of sexual violence in war and conflict that frames it as *constructing* memories of the conflict that the jurisprudence addresses, and therefore inseparable from the conflict. As Henry explains, "the law shapes, selects, and institutionalizes the way the past is remembered . . . through authoritatively declaring what crimes are deserving of international recognition and justice, and which crimes are to be relegated to the forgotten abyss of history."[60] If the law is a tool of substantive recognition, then "law as a space of ritual plays an important role in the construction of collective memory."[61] In this view, "a criminal trial is a significant public opportunity for the collective mourning of victims that can help them and the general public come to terms with a traumatic and violent past."[62]

At the same time, the collective mourning of victims needs to be fit into the rigid model of the ritual of the law, where individual mourning of victims can sometimes be bastardized. As Henry explains, "it is the inanimate evidence—the parts devoid of humanity and of pain and suffering—that are the most valued parts of the trial. It is not the witness herself, as an autonomous individual, who testifies, rather the witness essentially *becomes or is equivalent to the evidence* and as such her evidence testifies to the truth or otherwise of the case."[63] This is because the *focus* of an international court is on "prosecuting defendants" rather than on creating or recognizing individual or collective narratives of perpetrators or victims.[64] When victims are recognized, it is often in a way that either only recognizes Mibenge's ideal victims, or looks to repair victims to meet that mold. The focus on prosecution means that the stories of the participants in, and victims of, sexual violence in war and conflict, "are not fully told through the law."[65]

The justice the gender justice paradigm looks to provide is a forum for the testimony, healing, and vindication for the victims of the sexual violence in war and conflict. This is a difficult aim to follow through on in a system where, often, direct evidence provided by the victim does not establish the accused's responsibility or culpability.[66] As Nicola Henry worries, there are "inherent limitations of the law—of language, process, and outcome" that mean that it "may offer little in the way of justice and vindication for rape crimes."[67] Beyond that, though, if conflict sexual violence jurisprudence *creates* memories of sexual violence in war and conflict, it institutionalizes its idealized victims and makes seeing nontraditional victims (and perpetrators) all the more difficult.

But it is not just the inability to bring individual victims their "justice" that makes the gender justice paradigm problematic. Instead, as Hilary Charlesworth, Christine Chinkin, and Shelley Wright contend, "male-defined substantive, procedural, and conceptual structures may serve to undermine, marginalize, or obscure women's experiences of warfare."[68] This is why feminist legal advocates often argue that "international rape trials are fundamentally political."[69] This politics is inherent in evidentiary assumptions, procedural decisions, labels for crimes, and the production of conflict histories. The political nature of international rape trials "create narratives that are distinct from those produced in other institutional realms" *both* in their "creation of meaning" *and* in their "re-enactment of violence."[70] One of the meanings that they produce is a distinction between the civilized (those prosecuting) and savage (those being prosecuted *and* their victims).[71] Often the meaning that these trials create is one that reifies sex and race essentialist assumptions about perpetrators and victims, and the reenactment of violence that they perpetrate asks victims to relive their trauma by testimony without providing them a tangible result.[72]

Problematizing "Gender Justice"

These problems with the politics, meaning-creation, and violence of international criminal trials for sexual violence in war and conflict stem from what I argue are misunderstandings of gender, of perpetration, and of victimization in much "gender justice" thinking about conflict sexual violence jurisprudence. These misunderstandings then spill over into and feed off of the jurisprudence itself.

The problematic understanding of gender underlying most of this thinking, is that "gender justice" often means "justice for women as they are positioned relative to men." While this is an important part of gender justice, reducing gender justice to women's justice vis-à-vis men has the ironic impact of dampening the potential for the achievement of either gender justice more broadly or justice for women specifically. This is because the victimization of women in sexual violence in war and conflict is not the victimization of women *as women* by men *as men*—it is instead the victimization of women (and some men and some people that are both/and or neither/nor) *as associated with and signified as related to* femininity by men (and women and some people that are both/and or neither/nor) interested in asserting (literal or figurative) masculine dominance.[73] Understanding this means that seeking protection *of women as women* from *men as men* is an incorrectly specified object in the "gender justice" paradigm, which can be a problem for its applicability to the gendered complexities of sexual violence in war and conflict, even when it is committed by those generally understood to be men against those generally understood to be women.

Recalibrating this reading of gender might reformulate traditional claims about the need for gender justice in jurisprudence. For example, as Doris Buss explains, following the post–Cold War conflict in the former Yugoslavia, "violence against women, including in conflict settings, and the erasure of women's experiences by international institutions and actors, quickly became a defining issue for activists and scholars."[74] I am not arguing that violence against women and the erasure of women's experiences by international institutions and actors are not important problems around which activism should be centered. Instead, I am arguing that activism centered around violence against women and the erasure of women's experiences should be aimed at the axes of gender subordination that associate women with femininities and devalue femininities.

When I argue that the gender justice paradigm holds a partial understanding of the phenomenon of perpetration, I mean to invoke my earlier discussion of relational autonomy and gendered practice.

The gender justice paradigm more often than not focuses on rape as a choice made by its perpetrators, and then analyzes the motivations for and impacts of that choice. For example, common soundbite analyses of sexual violence in war and conflict suggest that "rape is about power, not about sex."[75] In this interpretation, the gender subordination in sexual violence in war and conflict is in the expression of men's power over women. That view, however, is oversimplified—if rape were *solely about power* rather than about sex, then "why don't men just hit women?"[76] In other words, there is a sexual component to the perpetration of sexual violence in war and conflict.[77] Still, the sexual component is not a simple problem of sexual desire, sexual "need," or sexual desirability.[78] Instead, sexual violence in war and conflict has been appropriately understood as expressing feminization, both of the direct victims and of those (personally and as communities/states/nations) who are seen to be responsible for their protection.[79] It is also a signification of violation of the biological and cultural reproduction of the community/state/nation.[80]

Much of the analysis in the feminist literature, though, assumes that this logic applies perpetration when men violate women, or even when men violate men. It is my argument that these interpretations of the perpetration of sexual violence in war and conflict are appropriate, even when the perpetrators are female, and the victims are male and female. Sexual violence in war and conflict is a practice of gendered devalorization, regardless of the sex of the perpetrator. *Women* can *subordinate* men, women, and people who are both/and or neither/nor because of their sex and gender. Women can seek masculine valor/dominance, both individually and on behalf of the community/state/nation with which they identify. In the "gender justice" model, it is assumed that sexual violence in war and conflict is an act of injustice that is done to women *by men*. Instead, sexual violence is a practice of injustice done to those who are feminized by those seeking a masculinized dominance.

Related analysis shows the problem with the gender justice paradigm's sex-based understanding of victimization. Victimization is torture, dehumanization, and the violation of the basic human rights of the victim. Victimization is gendered—it constitutes feminization, which is devalorization, and a constitutive feature of the ways that sexual violence in war and conflict is torture, dehumanization, and a

human rights violation. The gendered power relations of masculinization and feminization are conditions of possibility of what it means to
be a victim of sexual violence in war and conflict. This sexual violence
is a part of a patriarchal system that functions to "infantilize, ignore,
[and] trivialize . . . what is thought to be feminized."[81] This feminization has impacts on legitimacy, status, value, and relative material and
discursive position/power.[82]

Seeing victimization as feminization has implications for the ways
that the gender justice paradigm suggests pursuing gender justice. Some
analysts suggest that conflict sexual violence jurisprudence *furthers* the
feminization of the victim. For example, Tshepo Madlingozi critically
describes the process by which victims offer testimony as a "transnational justice industry" that can be appropriately understood as both
voyeuristic and pornographic.[83] This understanding draws on the criti-
cisms described above that see international jurisprudence as problematically productive of meaning and risking reenactment of violence. The
product of court transcripts, then, is not limited to the result for any
victim or for any accused, but reaches to the recounting of the conflict
and the history of the state and/or group that the conflict surrounds.

Tami Jacoby's analysis of the significatory value of the status of "victim" and the social production of "victimhood" is analytically useful for
these purposes.[84] Jacoby is interested in why some victims are legiti-
mized in jurisprudential processes while others are not, asking, "Why
do *these* victims, rather than others, come to be recognized, by whom
and for what purpose?"[85] The answer Jacoby identifies is that power
is an important part not only of the act of victimization but also to
the conferral of victim status.[86] This is because "the right to define a
victim (and be so defined) is an equally salient form of power as it
grants legitimacy to some groups and not others. From this act of labeling flows a host of material and other benefits bestowed on recognized
victims, from which those who fail to get recognized are deprived."[87]
Victimhood, in these terms, becomes both a status and an identity. Victim identity is inscribed not only by victimization, but by recognition,
reconciliation, and justice processes. It is a "fundamentally contested
process."[88]

Two significant implications follow. First, if justice processes "create" victims, then Henry's concerns about the manufacture of collec-

tive memory through international jurisprudence holds weight, as does Mibenge's concern that essentialist attention to sexual violence in war and conflict might be more harmful than inattention.[89] Second, and relatedly, in the practice of conflict sexual violence, perpetrator and victim cannot be seen as dichotomous, independent identities.

That is the case in a straightforward sense—a perpetrator's perpetration does not create or constitute a *victim* even when victimization occurs. But there are also several deeper problems with the perpetrator/victim dichotomy. One problem is in the presumed sex of perpetrator and victim, where woman=victim and man=perpetrator. Instead, victims and perpetrators do not map onto particular sexes (or even particular genders or gender identities). A second problem is that not all *perpetrators* automatically create *victims*—since being a victim is a politically contested and politically produced concept.[90] The third problem with the perpetrator/victim dichotomy is that being a perpetrator does not exclude one from victim status, and being a victim does not exclude one from perpetrating sexual violence, or any other act of violence in war/conflict.[91] As Jacoby relates, "the fact is that many victims commit violence as the compelling and sad case of child soldiers demonstrates: victim and perpetrator are one and the same."[92]

For the "gender justice" paradigm, these complications in victimization and victim identity cause a lot of problems for the core assumptions about what international jurisprudence of sexual violence in war and conflict is and should look like. Discrimination, denial of humanity, denial of human rights, and victimization are related, but they are not the same things. While people understood to be women are discriminated against, denied humanity, denied human rights, and victimized in sexual violence in war and conflict, and people understood to be women are the majority of people those things happen to, complex understandings of gender, perpetration, and victimhood show that it is important not only to recognize the outliers on their own merits (that is, for their humanity, human rights, and dignity) but also *substantively* to understand what happens both to the norm (women "victims" of male "perpetrators") *and* the outliers. The existence of the outliers demonstrates the perpetrator-victim relationship as gendered, as sex-fluid, as signified by and signifier of gendered power, as potentially multidirectional, as political in nature, and as situated within gender orders. The "gender justice" paradigm relies on strict dichotomies—implicitly and explicitly—between man/woman, male/female, sex/power, and victim/perpetrator, none of which are reflective of *what happens* in sexual violence in war and conflict. As a result, jurisprudence that deploys that sort of thinking—or aims to or is encouraged to do so—is necessarily going to be, with its other problems, unrepresentative of what sexual violence in war and conflict is. The remainder of this chapter looks to sketch out what a representative jurisprudence might look like. Particularly, I argue that it is possible to put forward a new framework for legally analyzing sexual violence in war and conflict, starting with a re-interpretation of gender subordination for international law and moving forward from there.

Seeing Gender Subordination in International Criminal Law

As discussed earlier, it is possible and even necessary to reread gender subordination as discrimination based on the perception that someone is male or female and the inscription of power on those perceptions, rather than just men's abuse of women. Perpetration and victimization are practices that take place in a world of relational autonomy and gendered violence. This, combined with the social and jurisprudential production of collective memory, has important implications for thinking about criminal prosecution, trial, and punishment for sexual violence in war and conflict.[93]

It would be reasonable to perceive that these implications are theoretical only, because the system of conflict sexual violence jurisprudence could be seen as necessarily dependent on dichotomized notions (not only of sex, gender, and victim/perpetrator, but also generally on the adversarial system).[94] I argue that the inherent limitations of the law still allow for some room to escape the rigidity of those dichotomies.[95] It is possible to move away from problematic understandings of gender, as well as of victims and perpetrators.[96] First, the law operationalizing a more complicated notion of discrimination based on gender can help to change the assumption that the perpetrator is always male/masculine. Such an approach can maintain attention to conflict sexual violence as gendered, while creating space for the recognition of female perpetrators.[97]

This starts with rethinking what makes sexual violence in war and conflict criminal. There are a number of different interpretations of what makes sexual violence criminal. Some court decisions suggest that it is the nature of sexual violence in war and conflict as intentional civilian victimization, when the laws of war allow only for targeting combatants.[98] Others see sexual violence in war and conflict as a crime because they understand it to constitute torture, which is also a direct violation of the laws of war.[99] Other jurisprudence focuses on the ways that wartime rape is a crime against humanity—something *prima facie* bad to do to anyone.[100] Still other decisions focus on the aspect of human rights violations in sexual violence in war and conflict.[101] Another perspective sees the criminality of sexual violence in war and conflict not in its impact on individual victims, but in its victimization of the community/ethnic group/state/nation which is, broadly speaking, being "aimed at." Katie Richey argues that, in one way or another, these logics are all proxies for gendered understandings of female victims—sexual violence in war and conflict is a war crime because innocent women are being violated.

With Baaz and Stern, I think that these accounts have two major flaws. First, it is problematic to say that sexual violence in war and conflict *is* one thing—whether it is a weapon of war, strategic, nationalist violence, or something else.[102] It follows that finding one source of criminality across diverse sexual violence in war and conflict is difficult unless their gendered significations are the source of that criminality.[103] Second, they continue to attach what Baaz and Stern call the "sex story" to the "gender story" of sexual violence in war and conflict. While Baaz and Stern suggest decreasing reliance on the "gender story" in order to fix interpretations of sexual violence in war and conflict, I argue that it is better to understand what gender subordination is going on—to complicate, then emphasize—the gender story.[104]

One of the key links between the "sex story" and the "gender story" in international criminal jurisprudence of sexual violence in war and conflict is that expectations of men and women are translated into expectations of masculinities and femininities.[105] Further, though anyone can feminize anyone else, and anyone can display masculinized behaviors, it is true that "feminization" is often understood as something men do to women, however inaccurate that is, and however many male victims and/or female perpetrators it makes invisible. In my view, though, this logical error should not be compounded by the logical error of therefore discrediting the "gender story" of sexual violence in war and conflict. Recall that a victim being *feminized* does not mean that a man is doing the feminizing to a woman—a woman could be doing it to another woman, or to a man; or a man could be doing it to another man; or the people doing the feminizing and being feminized could be of ambiguous sex and/or gender. The decoupling of sex and gender (and the use of sex as a signifier for gender) does not make the genderings of sexual violence in war and conflict disappear. Baaz and Stern suggest, however, that not every perpetrator of war rape *means to* commit acts of feminization.[106] Perpetrators' lack of gender-based intent, however, would only detract from the "gender story" if what made sexual violence in war and conflict a crime was gendered intent. If, instead, sexual violence in war and conflict is a practice of gender subordination, the focus of criminalizing it is not either the victimization of innocent women or the gendered intent of the perpetrator.

In this view, sexual violence in war and conflict is not (only) a crime because it targets civilians, even though it often does. It is not (only) a crime because it constitutes torture, though, by most definitions of torture, it often does. It is not (only) a crime because it constitutes a "crime against humanity"—though it certainly might, depending on what understood "humanity" having in common or how one read an individual's "humanity." It is not (only) a crime because it violates its direct victim's human rights, though usually does. It is not (only) a crime because it attacks the group/state/nation/community/ethnicity of its victims, when it does. These reasons (individually) do not constitute sexual violence in war and conflict as a crime because it is not the same thing each time, or perpetrated by the same sorts of people against the same sorts of people for the same reason. They do not (collectively) constitute sexual violence in war and conflict as a crime because none of them explain what it is that is either unique about it as a crime or sufficiently similar about it to merge it with other crimes.

In other words, at the end of reading the jurisprudential grounds for the prosecution and conviction of conflict sexual violence, there remains a debate about what crime conflict sexual violence is a part of, or what constitutes a unique crime of conflict sexual violence. While each of the legal grounds enumerated above have resulted in the recognition of some commissions of conflict sexual violence as crimes and have resulted in the conviction of some perpetrators of conflict sexual violence, none has accurately captured the spectrum of either perpetrators or victims of conflict sexual violence, or the full gendered mapping of the motivations for and significations of that violence.[107] Instead, I argue that understanding conflict sexual violence as a gendered practice casts a different light on the source of criminality. I contend the source of criminality is the gendered signification of the gendered practice of conflict sexual violence.

Both conflict sexual violence as intentional gender subordination and conflict sexual violence as a result of disorder and lawlessness are gendered practices. The first is the strategic, violent deployment of gender norms.[108] The second is a demonstration that gendered hierarchies, gendered orders, and gendered expectation *remain* or are even exaggerated in times of conflict, chaos, or disorder. Rather than seeing conflict sexual violence that happens in times of (gender, military, and/or other) disorder as disrupting a story about the ways that gender subordination influences its existence and practice, I suggest that conflict sexual violence resulting from military or other *disorder* evinces the stability of gender orders that create an air of permissiveness about (or even a condition of possibility of) that violence.[109]

What both of these sorts of conflict sexual violence have in common, and share with almost every other story of how conflict sexual violence comes to be, is that they make sense because global politics is guided and constituted by a gender order—where principles of gender organization position (relatively and absolutely) people, groups, and states on the basis of association with gendered characteristics.[110] While different gendered orders (hierarchies of traits associated with particular genders, hierarchies of particular genders, or even traits associated with particular genders) exist over different times, in different places, and in different situations, gender orders (that is orders with gender as an ordering principle) endure.[111]

In this view, gender subordination is embedded in gendered structures, gendered orders, and gender order. Acts and practices that show gender hierarchy, that take advantage of gender hierarchy, that reify and reinforce gender hierarchy—acts and practices *of* gender subordination—are then constituted as gender subordination by their genderings, rather than by the intent of the perpetrator or even the (direct or proximate) impact on the (direct or proximate) victim/target/receptor. The "gender story," rephrased as such, then can accommodate a number of different types of, and different levels of, agency and/or intent, coming from the (individual or collective) perpetrator(s). If who does gender subordination and why is not a key part of the crime, then there might be room in conflict sexual violence jurisprudence to break away from idealized tropes of who perpetrators and victims are, while still paying attention to the gendered nature of sexual violence in war and conflict.[112]

Still, Baaz and Stern have a legitimate concern that the *normalization* of sexual violence in war and conflict in the gender story risks accidental complicity in the proliferation of such violence.[113] If such sexual violence is seen as a practice of gender subordination, and a gender-hierarchical global political arena endures, people and actors looking for masculine *bona fides* will inevitably commit sexual violence in war and conflict—in fact, it should be expected. The confusing result would be when it occurs less, or even not at all.[114] While an expectation of the normality of such violence does not necessarily constitute endorsement, the dual move of seeing sexual violence in war and conflict as inevitable and identifying its likely perpetrators and victims can be normatively problematic.

At the same time, I think that the argument *against* this normalization is not as straightforward as it appears to Baaz and Stern, for several reasons. First, it is important to note that people differently positioned along gender hierarchies and differently impacted by them have different motivations to engage in gendered sexual violence in war and conflict—such that the "gender" story does not predict either inevitability or evenness of the commission of that violence.[115] Variation among incentives and reactions of the incentivized will always mean both group-level and individual-level variation in conflict violence, including but not limited to sexual violence in war and conflict. In other words, there is no *norm* of conflict behavior—sexually violent or not—instead, there are webs of normative structures that are interacted with in a number of different ways in different situations at different times by different people. Second, and more importantly, *normalizing* sexual violence in war and conflict is dangerous only if it is not already a norm—even *the* norm. A significant amount of feminist research has suggested that sexual violence in war and conflict is the norm in global politics. In other words, understanding that, to a degree, this sexual violence has been *normalized* is as much an empirical observation about how conflict works (and has come to work) as a theoretical move in the "gender story" of sexual violence in war and conflict, if not more so. Both independent of and given that, the sexual violence in war and conflict is because of and interdependent with the normalization of gendered hierarchies between, among, and within nations and states. If the "gender story" sees sexual violence as normal, I would suggest that the observation is a reflection, rather than a constitution, of gendered social dynamics.

Third, and finally, if gender/violence is the *source of criminality* of sexual violence in war and conflict, there is an implication that both the "extraordinary" gender subordination in this violence and its more "ordinary" counterpart of the gender subordination in everyday life are to be rejected. In other words, seeing gender subordination (broadly interpreted) as *why* sexual violence in war and conflict is illegal, rather than basing its illegality on the violation of *women* might be both a stronger foundation for conflict sexual violence jurisprudence *and* have an osmosis effect on other instantiations of gender hierarchy in global politics.

This dynamic could shed light on sexual violence in war and conflict as an *exemplar* of both the ways that conflict/violence is always and already gendered, and the ways that the gendered structures and incentives of conflict that make possible sexual violence are inseparable from the structures and incentive structures of interstate conflict, state governance, and indeed the state system. The gendered logics of sexual violence in war and conflict are not unique to conflict sexual violence— they are instead more visible in conflict sexual violence than in other parts of war and conflict, and therefore more easily read as gendered than other parts of war and conflict. Seeing gender subordination as the source of criminality of sexual violence in war and conflict is not, in my view, creating a category of gender violence that is separate from human violence.[116] Instead, it is a part of a larger claim that human violence, inside conflict or outside of it, *is gendered violence*—and that the gendered nature of that violence is problematic.

In other words, I argue that we must cast a wider net around the "gender story" of sexual violence in war and conflict—deconstructing the essentialisms not only of the gender justice paradigm but sometimes even of its critics, and analytically confronting the complexity of gender subordination within the gender orders of global politics. Seeing gender subordination in sexual violence in war and conflict is seeing the multiple ways in which multiple gender significations and even multiple gender hierarchies manifest and are manifested in a matrix of distinct occurrences of such violence across time, space, and conflict.

Seeing gender subordination in sexual violence in war and conflict *jurisprudentially* is difficult in gender-analysis terms, because it is not as if gender lenses can see sexual violence as a (gendered) crime in the middle of (ungendered) non-criminal warfare. Instead, the very tools that gender analysis has that allows it to identify the multiple gendered dimensions in, and reflected in, sexual violence in war and conflict are the same tools that help feminist scholars identify violence as a spectrum from domestic to nuclear, and war as a gendered phenomenon from its causes to its practices to its results.[117] Those tools also, as discussed above, allow scholars utilizing gendered lenses to situate the gendered logics of sexual violence among the gendered logics of other strategies, tactics, and logistical maneuvers, as well as among the gendered logics of the causes and justifications of war-making and war-fighting.[118] That means that, for the purposes of law and trial, the "crime" of sexual violence in war and conflict is not, in either gender terms or other terms, fully distinguishable from those things currently considered non-crimes of war-making and war-fighting. The degree and mode of that gender/violence is currently considered illegal as well as normatively taboo—but every reason that sexual violence may be a war crime, a crime against humanity, torture, gendered violence, and/or a human rights violation can be applied (if not neatly, roughly) to many other forms and shades of conflict/gender/violence.

Conflict/Gender/Violence/War

Retheorizing the jurisprudence of sexual violence in war and conflict *fully*, then, would be retheorizing the jurisprudence and practice of gender/violence/war. Seeing gender subordination as itself the crime would require interrogating the gender order in the international arena, and the gendered structures of the causes, practices, and experiences of war and conflict. Yet understanding the crime of sexual violence in war and conflict outside of seeing it as a practice of gender subordination is not only an incomplete understanding of the phenomenon of sexual violence in war and conflict, it robs conflict sexual violence jurisprudence and advocacy around it of the key subjects that have inspired any "progress" that has been made in prosecuting sexual violence and/or slowing it down: that of the innocent woman victim in need of protection. To take the first step requires beginning to recognize if not deconstruct the evil of sexual violence—whether the argument is that gender subordination is a root cause, or that gender liberation would provide a path to liberation, or both. To take the second step requires showing the important ways in which sexual violence is distinguishable from other crimes of war—that is, the ways in which it is *not okay* to engage in sexual violence that may apply in part to other crimes of war, but apply wholly to none of them.

A few scholars have suggested alternate frameworks for jurisprudence that balance these concerns to some degree or another. Anne-Marie Goetz has argued that the law of conflict sexual violence's current basis on contract-like rules that soldiers should follow should be replaced with an understanding of the law of armed conflict based on reciprocity.[119] The idea behind this approach is that understandings of how people ought to be treated *as people* should inspire conflict behavior, and should inspire responses to being in conflict. In this approach, sexual violence in war and conflict would never be acceptable because it would never be acceptable to have done to self. I don't think this proposal goes far enough, however—for two main reasons. First, as many just war theorists have suggested, very often reciprocity degenerates into an excuse to match the opponent's violation of understood norms of combat justifies. Second, were that avoidable, the reasons sexual violence "would never be acceptable to have done to self" are quietly wrapped up in sexed and gendered narratives of what sexual violence in war and conflict is, how it is perpetrated, what sort of people are the perpetrators, and what sort of people are the victims. Disaggregating those things the way this book does—and making them explicit—solves for part of that problem but not all of it.

That is because there remains the "human" to whom sexual violence cannot be done, and the "other" to whom sexual violence is done (condemned, but done).

Others have suggested a jurisprudential approach to prosecuting crimes of war, conflict, and genocide focused on connectivity. Such a connectivity approach would link together many of the factors of gender/violence in conflict that are currently either poorly linked or unlinked, jurisprudentially speaking.[120] It would understand the links between citizenship and protector masculinities *within* states that make opponents *value* the safety of their women/feminized others from sexual violence in war and conflict, the masculinization of soldiers that incentivizes violating that protectability and the purity that goes with it, and the gendered *feminization* that allows "perpetrator" to dehumanize and other "victim." While these ideas sound like they would be welcome *theoretical* additions to jurisprudence and *practical* additions to prosecutorial strategies, they do not seem like they would be an easy basis on which to identify, prosecute, and prove the commission of war crimes. Particularly, connectivity understandings lend themselves more efficiently to nonindividual proceedings like truth and reconciliation commissions and post-conflict state building.[121] In individual trials, connections, interdependence, and a lack of clarity about who is originally or primarily responsible can detract from the ability to successfully identify people to prosecute and to get convictions from prosecutions.

While I do not want to suggest that trials and prosecutions should be the only venue for seeking justice for sexual violence in war and conflict, I think that walking away from the trial arena is neither feasible nor desirable. I think that it is not desirable because trials, for all their flaws, have significant funding and public will behind them—they were one of the major origins of what has come to be understood as a *jus cogens* prohibition against sexual violence in war and conflict. In other words, trials are a source of public attention, legal attention, and condemnation for sexual violence in war and conflict that did not exist before the advent of international criminal tribunals, either for particular conflicts or in the permanent body of the ICC. The popularity of post-conflict trials as a forum for delivering justice also makes the proposition of removing prosecutions from the repertoire of post-conflict justice mechanisms infeasible. To me, it is clear *both* that trials should exist, and that international criminal jurisprudence *cannot alone* be an adequate mechanism for justice for sexual violence in war and conflict.[122] The goal, then, is not reifying international criminal jurisprudence as *the source* of post-conflict justice—but finding ways to maximize the provision of justice while minimizing the contribution to or continuance of injustice.

To me, that means formally, legally recognizing the element of hierarchical gendered orders in the perpetration of sexual violence in war and conflict—whether that element comes into play in a moment of disorder where a male perpetrator sees an "enemy" woman civilian as vulnerable to attack or in a moment of order where a military command structure makes the strategic choice to command its troops to engage in sexual violence.[123] Understanding sexual violence in war and conflict as, depending on the circumstances of its perpetration, a crime against humanity, a violation of human rights, a crime of torture, and/or a crime of intentional civilian victimization, then, becomes part of the question—what legal classifications does a particular commission of sexual violence fall into that makes it actionable by courts?

Still, as discussed above, this cannot and should not be the sum total of conflict sexual violence jurisprudence—such an approach risks erasure of the gendered components of the crime and/or (possibly worse) the implication that the gendered components of the crime are normal and the extremes to which they were taken is the only problem. I suggest, then, that prosecutions for sexual violence in war and conflict avail themselves of the existing legal grounds, but charge (and ask courts to make available to them) another crime of gender/violence, described explicitly as violence committed with the implicit or explicit use of, creation of, or entrenchment of gender hierarchies. In other words, the *criminal* difference between a soldier knocking out a civilian and a soldier raping a civilian (all other factors held equal) is that the latter constitutes both gender/violence and intentional civilian victimization, where the former constitutes intentional civilian victimization.

Gender/violence, however, is not necessarily or even primarily limited to the use of rape in war and conflict. For example, the choice to separate men from women and children, killing the men with intent to cause social destruction and the starvation of women and children—is gender/violence—with an explicitly sexed/gendered/sexual component, against both men and women.[124] While such a framework, deployed poorly, risks reifying Baaz and Stern's concern about separating the "gender-based violence" from the "non-gender-based violence" as if the latter existed, thinking about that as a burden-of-proof issue rather than a separation of types of violence can provide a way around that distinction. Specifically, it is not that all conflict/violence is not gender/violence—or, put in the affirmative, conflict/violence is gendered—it is instead that the burden of proof in criminal trials is to *demonstrate* the commission of a crime *beyond a reasonable doubt.*

Many war crimes (and many crimes more generally) occur but cannot be prosecuted successfully in court because the available testimony will not meet the burden of proof.[125] It is unlikely that war crimes *outside* of explicitly gendered or sexual violence would be charged as gender/violence, not because they *are not* gendered, but because prosecutors could not prove the links between gender and that violence, and judges would be unlikely to see the charges as substantiated. In other words, a significant amount of gender/violence in conflict—perhaps even the overwhelming majority of gender/violence in conflict—could not be prosecuted.

But some could. And the laying out of standards for charging and prosecuting a crime of gender/violence would also permit an opportunity for the discursive re-telling of the "gender story' of sexual violence in war and conflict in a more nuanced way—a way that allows for women perpetrators and male victims; a way that is more even and less narrow. Gender/violence could be seen as either having an element of gender subordination intent or an element of gender subordination reification. The prosecution of gender/violence crimes could make a new "grid of intelligibility" for sexual violence in war and conflict that tells a story of it much like the one told in this book—as *gendered* but not tied to sex essentialism, as an act of gendering but not tied to a dichotomy between (male) perpetrator and (female) victim, and as significatory of gender hierarchies when committed with or without strategic intent. Such a "gender story" of sexual violence in war and conflict might correct my problems both with the current jurisprudential landscape and Baaz and Stern's.

Conclusion

One of the main goals of such an approach, of course, would be accommodating the possibility of women perpetrators of sexual violence in war and conflict *without* suggesting that women's perpetration means that it is appropriate to take the victimization of women less seriously. In 2011, I referred to the problem as the need for "preserving the understanding that women are, as a class, victimized by genocidal rape based on gender."[126] I would word it differently now—I would describe it as the need to preserve the understanding that sexual violence in war and conflict is a gendered practice which has a disproportionate effect on people associated with femininity—particularly women.

In other words, throwing the "gender story" out with the "sex story" and their problematic links, for both descriptive and jurisprudential purposes is, in my view, as problematic as maintaining the status quo "gender justice" paradigm if not more so. But modifying the "gender justice" paradigm of jurisprudence and the "gender story" about the genesis, commission, and effects of sexual violence in war and conflict seems like it might be a worthwhile move. While it is certainly not a definitive answer to the problem(s) of sexual violence in war and conflict (or even to the problem[s] of conflict sexual violence jurisprudence), it seems like an important step towards reconceptualizing this violence as a gendered crime away from sex-essentialist narratives.

In practical terms, there are three ways I see such a shift being meaningful. The first is as a discursive interruption of the dominant narratives of sexual violence in war and conflict, which tend to essentialize sex, rely on uncomplicated notions of gender, and take shortcuts to understanding complicated things like victimhood and perpetration. The second is as trial shaping. If one of the things a prosecutor is looking to prove is a gender-based component to sexual violence in war and conflict, and that gender-based component can be in intent, signification, or engagement of hierarchy, the testimony being asked of witnesses, and the evidence relevant to provide, expands significantly from the notoriously narrow and regimented testimony asked for in and allowed by war crimes tribunals. The third is as shaping the post-conflict narratives and memories that are created by the international criminal tribunal jurisprudence. As mentioned earlier in this chapter, trials tend to be at least in part constitutive of narrative histories of conflicts. If wartime sexual violence trials were more nuanced, more complicated, and more explicit in their gender analyses, then it is possible that those histories could be more complicated at well. The next and final chapter explores the implications of switching out uneven, narrow gender justice jurisprudence for a notion of post-conflict international criminal jurisprudence in which gender matters by rehearsing and counterfactually (re)creating three key moments in the international criminal jurisprudence of sexual violence in war and conflict.

6

One of the Most Abiding Myths of Our Time

Re-visioning Women, War, and Rape

Violence is masculine. Men are the cause of it, and women and children are the ones who suffer. The sole explanation offered up by criminologists for violence committed by a woman is that it is involuntary, the rare result of provocation or mental illness, as if half of the population of the globe consisted of saintly stoics who never succumbed to fury, frustration, or greed. Though the evidence may contradict that statement, the consensus runs deep. Women from all walks of life, at all levels of power—corporate, political, or familial, women in combat and on police forces—have no fault in violence. *It is one of the most abiding myths of our time.*[1]
—Patricia Pearson, *When She Was Bad . . . : Violent Women and the Myth of Innocence* (emphasis mine)

This book has argued that recognizing women as perpetrators of sexual violence in war and conflict is necessary both for its own sake and for correcting a number of assumptions in media, scholarly, and jurisprudential treatments of *what wartime sexual violence is*, when it occurs, and how it is/should be addressed. These deconstructions and reconstructions are both complicated and fraught, given the strength of the myth of women's non-violence.

Sexual violence in war and conflict, whether strategic or transgressive, is an act of feminizaton as devalorization both towards its direct victims and to the group(s) of which those victims are seen to be a part. This is often, in the media, in scholarship, and in the courts, read with a number of shortcuts and essentialist assumptions to understand sexual violence in war and conflict as an act of gender subordination perpetrated against women by men. These narratives have found some attention and success in the global political arena, in part because they make sexual violence clearly intelligible, in part because they fit with inherited notions of gender roles in wars and conflicts, and in part because they can (if not fully correctly) account for the majority of sexual violence cases in wars and conflicts throughout history.

Sexual violence in war and conflict, however, is a case where the exception reveals problems with the assumptions of, rather than proving, the rule. As discussed in chapter 1, the relationships between gender, war, and conflict—the assemblage of gender/violence/war—is complicated and multidimensional. There are gendered dimensions to wars and conflicts generally, and then to sexual violence in them specifically as well. As discussed in chapter 4, it is not that some conflict violence is gendered and other conflict violence is somehow ungendered—it is that the genderings of conflict violence vary and are complex. This leads some analysts to walk away from explicit gender analysis of conflict generally and of sexual violence therein specifically.

Such a move is a mistake—understanding sexual violence in war and conflict as gendered adds explanatory value not only for that sexual violence, but for understandings of war and gender. At the same time, too many times, understanding sexual violence in war and conflict as gendered has been reduced to what Baaz and Stern call the "sex story" and the "gender story" of that sexual violence.[2] The "sex story" suggests that sexual violence in war and conflict is caused by men's unfulfilled need for sex in conflict zones, given that sexual release is a "natural" need for men, exacerbated by the stress of battle conditions.[3] In theory, the "gender story" departs from this sex essentialism to talk about sexual violence in war and conflict as related to the expectations and conditionings related to militarized masculinities, and the feminization of the enemy (women, men, culture, and state). With Baaz and Stern, though, I suggest that most of the current instantiations of this "gender story" maintain the assumption that sexual violence's perpetrators are male and its victims are female, despite the fact that one of the moves from the "sex story" to the "gender story" is the rejection of sex essentialism. While gender-analytic narratives often either do not mention or explicitly reject the notion that sexual violence in war and conflict is something that men do to women, the accounts that they produce of that violence implicitly reify those notions. This reification can happen jurisprudentially, where the "gender justice" paradigm looks to protect women from the violence of men and/or redress violations of women's human rights when they are violated by gender-based violence. It can also happen in media coverage and scholarly analysis, where assumptions about *what women are*, *what men are*, and *what men and women signify in war and conflict* implicitly require male perpetrators and female victims.

That is why, in chapter 2, I argued that existing narratives of sexual violence in war and conflict overdetermine that rapes among women specifically (or women perpetrators generally) are discursively impossible. This discursive impossibility means that, in myriad situations in which their existence would be appropriately recognized, women who commit sexual violence in war and conflict are often ignored, underplayed, stereotyped, sensationalized, or otherwise treated differently on the basis of their sex and/or gender. Chapter 3 demonstrated that, despite their exclusion from the speakable realm of conflict analysis, women perpetrators exist. These women perpetrators are not, as some stories would depict them, freaks of nature who defy their gender and/or are crazy, broken, scarier-than-men animals who are to be at once defined out of existence and understood as monstrous and discarded as deviant. Instead, they are, like other perpetrators of sexual violence, gendered actors in gendered conflicts, beset by and situated in a number of other factors that account for sexual violence in war and conflict *whoever* commits it. As I have argued, the double move of sensationalizing women's engagement in sexual violence in war and conflict and distancing sexually violent women both from agency in their own actions and a normalized notion of peaceful femininity is both repeatedly performed and normatively and practically problematic.

The remainder of the book engaged those normative and practical problems, looking to understand the ways in which recognizing women perpetrators refigures notions of what sexual violence is, what women are, and how sexual violence in war and conflict should be dealt with in international criminal jurisprudence. While I am not arguing that international criminal jurisprudence is the most important part of post-conflict justice, either generally or for sexual violence specifically, I am making the argument that war crimes tribunals are exemplars of the implicit work of the discursive assumption that per-petrators are male and victims are female, and therefore an important potential ground for rethinking and retheorizing these ideas. Addi-tionally, since international criminal jurisprudence has been a frontier for *progress* in the recognition of sexual violence as a war crime, it is important to evaluate the ways in which it has succeeded in repre-senting sexual violence in war and conflict appropriately as well as the ways in which inaccuracies in those representations reflect and are reflected in other histories and interpretations of conflicts. To that end, I argued in chapter 4 that seeing gender subordination more com-plexly can strengthen theories of wartime sexual violence, regardless of the sex of the perpetrator—and without abandoning the produc-tive identifications of the many and multilayered was in which conflict generally and sexual violence therein specifically are sexed, gendered, and sexualized. This is a move that, as I argued in chapter 5, does not need to remain in the realm of the theoretical. Instead, some of its insights have the potential to be translated into the realm of conflict sexual violence jurisprudence, both in reframing and reenvisioning in-terpretations of the current legal grounds for the recognition of sexual violence in war and conflict as a crime and adding the possibility for legal analysis of gender/violence in conflict violence jurisprudence at the international level.

Identifying gender/violence as a war crime is not to suggest that some conflict violence is gendered while other conflict violence is not gen-dered. Instead, the idea is to suggest that the burden of proof in court cases to *identify* gender/violence is such that much gendered violence in conflict would remain impossible to charge *as a matter of law*, but some gendered violence in conflict could be clearly identified as such—with a number of potential payoffs. As I discussed in chapter 5, the potential payoffs include discursive interruption of dominant, essentialist nar-ratives; changes in the ways in which testimony is offered and valued in trial situations; and changes in the elements that trials contribute to shaping post-conflict narratives and memories.

This concluding chapter contends that it is important *both* to identify rape among women (practically and theoretically) and to conceptually and legally adapt jurisprudential practice to that recognition. It does so, first, by looking at two cases of sexual violence in war and conflict (in terms of media framing and jurisprudential process) explicitly through the lenses of the lessons learned in this book. While these rehearsals and counterfactual recreations cannot, by definition, do justice to the thousands of pages of jurisprudence, years of prosecution and defense work, years of trial, and uncountable media coverage of each case to make thorough reformulations based on authoritative evaluations of the facts of the case, they can explore the extent to which the interpretive keys that this book has critiqued shaped the ways in which each case was made intelligible (or unintelligible) to a variety of audiences, and suggest counterfactually the ways that rereadings of those interpretive keys might provide space for reenvisioning framings and "grids of intelligibility" for sexual violence in war and conflict.[4]

After rereading those cases, this chapter concludes by recommending the reconstruction of war rape jurisprudence, both for the procedural and normative justice provided by international criminal trials and for broader policy goals. It suggests that the recognition of women's engagement in sexual violence in war and conflict provides a path to reconceptualize relationships between gender, war, and sexual violence more generally that can produce both a more nuanced and more accurate account. This, in turn, could be the foundation for two more potentially important steps: decreasing wartime sexual violence specifically *without* essentializing, sensationalizing, or ignoring women's violence *and* complicating understandings of what gender subordination is and how it works in global politics.

The *Nyiramasuhuko* Case

Many of the details of the case of Pauline Nyiramasuhuko were discussed in chapters 2 and 3, and do not need to be rehearsed in great detail here. In Rwanda, though there was significant evidence that women participated in genocide-related crimes generally and genocide-related sexual violence specifically, indictment, arrest, and conviction rates for women were significantly lower than they were for men in domestic courts—a trend replicated in the ICTR, where Nyiramasuhuko was the only woman arrested and indicted.[5] Some attention in both the media and in scholarly work was paid to women perpetrators both of genocide and of genocidal rape, but most of it was either piecemeal or sensationalistic, and very little of it got a significant amount of attention.[6] While both men and women were among the perpetrators of the Rwandan genocide *as well as* both strategic and counterstrategic genocidal rape, Nyirama-suhuko was singled out, both for media horror and for prosecution, as an exemplar of the abnormal phenomenon of women's perpetration.[7]

The sex-related crimes with which Nyiramasuhuko was charged were rape as genocide and rape as an outrage to dignity.[8] The legal basis for the charge of genocidal rape was twofold: she was charged with rape as a crime against humanity and rape as a violation of the Geneva Convention on war crimes.[9] These charges were supported by evidence of Nyiramasuhuko's open advocacy of getting rid of all Tut-sis[10] and of her strategic use of rape and sexual slavery as weapons.[11] While the ICTR declined to prosecute a number of other high-profile women alleged to have been involved in the genocide, its prosecutors, judges, and media and scholarly audience showered disproportionate attention on the Nyiramasuhuko case, which included both genocidal rape charges and charges for the deaths of tens of thousands of Rwan-dans in the genocide. Many analysts have attributed this attention (even while replicating it) to the novelty of "the female atrocity perpetrator," as discussed in chapter 2.[12]

The coverage of the Nyiramasuhuko case sensationalized the transgression against gender norms that the perpetrator seemed to exemplify—distancing her from "normal" women assumed incapable of such violence, and suggesting that a woman's capacity to engage in this sort of violence heralds an end to understanding women's special victimization. This book has gone over the many problems with this sort of analysis. Suffice to say that Nyiramasuhuko was not the first female perpetrator of sexual violence in war and conflict, nor the only one in the Rwandan genocide,[13] and that sensationalism around the sex of the perpetrator demonstrates not only problematic gender analysis of *this* case, but what wartime sexual violence is, who perpetrates it, and how it should be prosecuted.

All of these problems in coverage aside, it remains true that Ny-iramasuhuko *was convicted* by the ICTR of rape as a crime against humanity.[14] As discussed in chapter 2, a surface-level reading of the decision in the *Nyiramasuhuko* case suggests that many of the cri-tiques of international criminal jurisprudence about sexual violence in war and conflict are unnecessary—since the sex of Nyiramasuhuko as a perpetrator is not overemphasized in her conviction.[15] At the same time, the sexual violence of which she was convicted was strangely "normal" and "traditional"—she was convicted for her role in commanding male soldiers to abuse female victims. While Nyiramasuhuko was an unconventional commander/perpetrator, the decision emphasized conventional perpetration, and focused on her command role in that conventional perpetration. Above and beyond that, while the decision of the court in the conviction was not clearly pinned to her sex, it was featured strongly in the prosecutorial strategy as well as the legal defense, and clearly struggled with in parts of the court's opinion.[16]

An example of the key role of Nyiramasuhuko's sex in the prosecutorial strategy in the trial is in the prosecution's opening statement, which characterizes her as

[a] woman from Rwandan society, a woman who is a minister, who is a member of parliament. A woman who lost all her civil nature: people being raped before their parents; watching their children be raped. She had lost her civil nature because in her presence, the most serious rape under the cruest conditions were applauded. She even encouraged her son to do as much. She put everything she had to the point that she was dressed in military gear to play her role of a militant minister. A woman who had lost every sense of feeling.[17]

While this paragraph in the prosecution opening would have had the same legal effect had Nyiramasuhuko been characterized either by name or as a person, the characterization of her as a "woman," and the repetition of the word "woman," serves to compare traditional expectations of femininity with Nyiramasuhuko's alleged aberrant behavior.

Perhaps uniquely in international criminal jurisprudence around wartime sexual violence, Nyiramasuhuko's defense also looked to compare her behavior to that of a "normal" woman, and to traditional expectations of femininity.[18] As the court recalls, "the Nyiramasuhuko Defence asserts that ordering killings and rapes was contrary to Nyiramasuhuko's character and that she had worked her entire life to help the women of Rwanda."[19] In the defense's argument, Nyiramasuhuko's *conformity* to traditional expectations of femininity and her previous *alignment* with causes of women's rights served as evidence that she was not capable of genocidal violence, either generally or of a sexual nature.

In making its evidentiary findings, the ICTR did not discuss either of these associations with gender. The court also declined to comment on expectations associated with femininity, or on Nyiramasuhuko's position as the first woman charged with or convicted of engagement in rape as a crime against humanity. At the same time, the court clearly struggled with the co-defendant relationship between Nyiramasuhuko and her son, and with what their mother-child relationship meant for her responsibility as a command superior for his behavior.[20] It also struggled with questions of the credibility of witnesses who were Nyiramasuhuko's husband or daughters, particularly in terms of what if any special bias was in their testimony related to their "mother" and "wife" that wouldn't be there with a more traditional family relationship between the accused and *his* family of defense witnesses.[21]

Juxtaposed against the advocates' use of gender tropes and the court's resistance to the use of such tropes were a number of allegations of sex-specific violence committed by Nyiramasuhuko and/or committed at the insistence of her command. The court found significant evidence that she had a role in making rape a strategy of the summer 1994 genocide.[22] She was convicted for directly ordering a number of rapes on a number of different occasions.[23] The court also decided that Nyiramasuhuko's commission of the crimes of genocide and rape as a crime against humanity was aggravated by her position at the time as the minister for family and women's affairs, since her behavior constituted an abuse of that position.[24] As the court explained:

> Nyiramasuhuko's position as Minister for Family and Women's Affairs during the events made her a person of high authority, influential and respected within the country and especially in the Butare *prefecture* from where she hails. Instead of persevering the peaceful co-existence between communities and the welfare of the family, Nyiramasuhuko, on a number of occasions, used her influence over the *Interahamwe* to commit crimes such as rape and murder. This abuse of general authority *vis-à-vis* the assailants is an aggravating factor.[25]

In my reading, this paragraph in the decision sends mixed messages. On the one hand, it is her "general authority" that Nyiramasuhuko abused, presumably as a member of the cabinet. On the other hand, the reference to how that authority was abused compares her actual behavior to "preserving peaceful co-existence between communities and the welfare of the family," a reading of Nyiramasuhuko's specific position *among* the cabinet of ministers, and a (presumably unique) gendered responsibility to women.

Reading the newspaper articles the day after Nyiramasuhuko's conviction might have led one to believe that she was convicted of everything of which she was accused, given the high number of convictions and the high number of accusations.[26] Looking closely at the convictions at trial, though, helps the sort of analysis in this book. For example, in considering the charge of genocide against Nyiramasuhuko, the court excluded evidence of the commission of rape, remarking at several occasions that the evidence of rape would be considered when it was appropriate—under the charges that alleged the commission of or command of rape.[27] The court's reasoning seemed to be largely that the prosecution had provided insufficient warning to the defendant that rape would be considered an act of genocide.

Additionally, though Nyiramasuhuko was convicted of rape as a crime against humanity and outrages on personal dignity for crimes of sexual violence, there were a number of instances of sexual violence *of which the court found evidence* but *for which Nyiramasuhuko was not convicted.* One example stands out: in June 1994,

> Nyiramasuhuko, in the company of at least four men and another woman and in a public place, handed out two boxes of condoms to a woman named Anastasie Muksakindi, and said: "Distribute these condom to our young men for them to rape the Tutsi, and after having raped them they should kill them. And moreover, it is these Tutsi women that steal away our husbands. Not a single one of them should survive. Rape them first and use the condom—and after that kill them. Let no Tutsi woman survive."[28]

These non-convictions seemed to center around insufficient warning of prosecution—where the prosecution underestimated the evidence they would find of crimes of sexual violence and the defense did not anticipate the additional evidence. In other words, the extent and variety of Nyiramasuhuko's perpetration of sexual violence was a surprise even to those who charged her with the crimes.

The media coverage of Nyiramasuhuko's case, and some of the scholarly reactions, echoed either the prosecution or defense's gender-based accounts of her role in the summer of 1994 genocide in Rwanda—characterizing her as either extra-criminal for her transgression of gender norms, or as incapable of the crimes of which she was accused because of her sex. While these stereotypes were not on display at Nyiramasuhuko's trial, it was clear that they were just under the surface in the prosecution, the defense, and the decision.

I have contended elsewhere in this book that a more complicated gender analysis of Nyiramasuhuko's case contradicts a number of these stereotypical, essentialist, or sensationalist narratives of her behavior. On a theoretical level, it is important to note that *women* can commit political violence, and can subordinate *women* on the basis of gender—nothing about being "women" themselves stops that from being within their realm of capabilities. Therefore, nothing about Nyiramasuhuko's being a woman renders her *incapable* of committing those crimes. It is true, as we have also discussed a number of places in this book, that people identified as women are far less likely to commit war crimes generally and war crimes of sexual violence specifically than people identified as men. To contextualize this empirical observation appropriately, and separate it from assumptions about biological capacity, it is important to realize that both women and men (and people who do not fit comfortably into either category) live within the gendered orders of local, national, and global social and political life. Therefore, for many people identified as women, it is possible that gender tropes determining them incapable of political and/or sexual violence are actually direct or indirect influences on their behavior. At the same time, that does not make people like Nyiramasuhuko *less female* for their engagement in political violence. Instead, it demonstrates that characteristics associated with masculinities and characteristics associated with femininities do not map one to one onto maleness and/or femaleness. This recognition suggests that Nyiramasuhuko is neither an affront to or a reification of women's femininity; *gender analysis* of her behavior is appropriate, but sex-essentialist analysis is not.

A more complicated story of gender and sexual violence in war and conflict still has something to say about Nyiramasuhuko's case, however. The sexual violence in which she engaged—from ordering rapes and kidnappings to distributing condoms and encouraging rape—is *gendered*. Again, this claim is not meant to suggest that "normal" or "regular" or "non-sexual"[29] violence is *ungendered*. Instead, it is meant to understand Nyiramasuhuko's violence as necessarily tied to gender significations in local and global politics. The grounds for seeing her violence as gendered, though, are largely separable from her status as a woman, with one possible caveat.

The argument that the Nyiramasuhuko's violence was gendered could rest on her persistent tendency to separate commands about what should happen to men (that they should be killed) and what should happen to women (that they should be raped and then killed).[30] It could also be seen in many of her derogatory comments towards the Tutsis, which were grounded in a characterization of Tutsi women as dirty, related to their actual or potential sexual relationships with Hutu men.[31] In other words, Nyiramasuhuko was targeting women *as women* on the basis of gendered assumptions about what constitutes a woman. In this respect, the sex-specific violence that she committed and encouraged is gendered in many ways similar to the genderings of the violence that her male compatriots committed during the genocide.

The feminization of the women who were Nyiramasuhuko's victims also was not unique to her perpetration either. As the court recognized, the commission of rape in Rwanda in 1994 was in large part strategic—an ordered, hierarchical command decision—rather than incidental or a result of military disorder.[32] The intent of the strategy of rape was the feminization of the Tutsi population (individually and collectively) and their coterminous extinction.[33] The rapes that Nyiramasuhuko commanded, like the rapes that her male co-conspirators commanded, and the rapes that the *Interahamwe* committed, were both a physical actualization of that intent (hurting or killing the ability of the Tutsis to reproduce) and a message communicating the inability of Tutsi men to defend Tutsi women (and therefore the defeat of the Tutsis).[34]

Still, much has been made about how much worse, or, at the very least, less comprehensible Nyiramasuhuko's violence was than the violence of her male co-conspirators. After all, she was a *woman* who raped. She was not only a woman but a *women's rights advocate*. And she was not only a women's rights advocate, but a *government official* accountable for the fate of women. The court determined that her position as a government official made her crimes worse, but provided mixed messages on whether her particular position made her crimes worse. These are complicated issues, but I am not sure that any suggestion that Nyiramasuhuko's status *as a woman* is necessary to decide that her position in government (as a minister) makes her crimes worse (taking advantage of authority), or even (going a step further than the court was willing to explicitly) that her particular position as minister for family and women's affairs makes her crimes worse. What makes it particularly reprehensible that these crimes were committed by the minister for family and women's affairs is not that the minister for family and women's affairs was a woman—it is that the minister for family and women's affairs is someone whose job title and job responsibility signifies that s/he would not actively harm women or commit gender-based violence. Counterfactually, both being a minister generally and the minister for family and women's affairs specifically would be (individually) aggravating factors in understanding the severity of the crimes committed by a male minister for family and women's affairs.

The suggestion that Nyiramasuhuko's treatment is due to her position as minister for family and women's affairs rather than her womanhood is not useful here. The (even counterfactual) existence of a male minister for family and women's affairs is unlikely. That is, the people who appointed Nyiramasuhuko to her ministerial post probably saw her female sex as a necessary but insufficient qualification for holding the post. This makes her biological sex not irrelevant to the conditions of possibility of her gendered violence. At the same time, the position of Nyiramasuhuko's womanhood as a necessary condition for a part of the gendering of her sexual violence is not a causal force in that gendering—it is the product of other complex parts of the gendered political orders that make womanhood a condition of possibility of her being the minister for family and women's affairs.

Thinking through a gender analysis of Nyiramasuhuko's actions during the 1994 Rwandan genocide shows her participation in genocide, conspiracy to commit genocide, and genocidal sexual violence—and those genderings as not tied to the biological sex of the perpetrator. Women *as a class* and individually were no less victimized by her violence because she was a woman committing it; her violence would be differently though no less gendered if it were committed with men as the primary victims.

It might be difficult to see this retheorizing mattering in jurisprudential terms. While I cannot rewrite twelve years of trial, hundreds of thousands of pages of testimony, and a 1,500-page decision in a few words in this chapter, I would like to suggest three substantive interventions that my adjustments to the "grids of intelligibility" of her (and others') sexual violence.[35] The first is that gender analyses demonstrate the links between rape and genocide that should make it possible to understand crimes of rape as crimes of genocide, as the ICTR had in other cases.[36] Nyiramasuhuko's actions were no less rape as genocide than Akayesu's. Second, and relatedly, the gendered logics of the perpetration of Nyiramasuhuko's crimes extended beyond the crimes that were explicitly sexually violent. The evidence that she talked about the destruction of family units, the killing of children, the femininity of Tutsi men, and women's responsibility to marry all had links to particular readings of how gender relations constituted and were constituted by Tutsi ethnicity specifically and Rwandan nationality generally.[37] Thinking about gender/violence as a potential charge to be pressed would, then, serve three functions in the Nyiramasuhuko case. First, it would provide a basis for linking her sexual violence with her other violent crimes. Second, it would supply a logic with which to recognize as crimes some of the things like condom distribution and incitement of rape that were not subject to conviction in the current international legal framework. Third, it would make the gendered logics that made the crimes that constituted "outrages to dignity" count as such intelligible as part of gender-subordinating stories sexual violence in war and conflict. These functions, together with the deconstructive function that provides a language to critique both prosecutors' and defendants' use of gender tropes, as well as the court's discomfort discussing gender, might make intervening with a different, more complex "gender story" of sexual violence in war and conflict intellectually, normatively, and jurisprudentially useful.

The *Akayesu* Case

The *Akayesu* case was decided thirteen years before the *Nyiramasuhuko* case, but also concerned the Rwandan genocide in the summer of 1994.[38] As mentioned in chapter 2, *Akayesu* has been heralded as the case where the crime of genocidal rape was identified, with the ICTR finding that rape is in fact genocide when its perpetrators rape with the targeted intent to destroy a group, in whole or in part.[39] In the case, the court found that the rape of Tutsi women was "systematic" and was "perpetrated against all Tutsi women and solely against them," which made the act genocidal rape.[40]

Jean-Paul Akayesu was not charged with rape as genocide. He was charged with genocide, and with rape as a crime against humanity.[41] The indictment suggested that the defendant had committed rape as a crime against humanity because Tutsi women who were in his governmental office lived in constant fear,[42] and that the defendant knew that acts of sexual violence were happening, was present at their commission, and facilitated them.[43] At no point was it suggested that the defendant *personally* committed rape,[44] only that he commanded, supervised, and saw it happening. In fact, originally, the defendant was not subject to any charges about sexual violence at all—the charges were amended during trial to reflect what the court characterized as witnesses' spontaneous testimony about the occurrence and severity of sexual violence.[45] Having heard testimony that suggested the presence and prevalence of sexual violence, the ICTR concluded that, in the *Akayesu* case, "the investigation and presentation of evidence relating to sexual violence is in the interest of justice."[46]

What followed was floodgates opening to many witnesses' testimony about rapes that took place at or near the defendant's government offices with his possible knowledge and tacit consent. The testimonies recounted dozens of rapes, in the forest area around the office,[47] in the cultural center,[48] with male sex organs,[49] and with wood and other blunt objects.[50] The ICTR chamber found that sexual violence had occurred,[51] and that the accused had reason to know about it, and failed to exercise his authority to stop it.[52] It therefore convicted the accused of rape as a crime against humanity, and used evidence of the accused's complicity in rape as evidence of the accused's complicity in genocide.[53]

In this finding, the court made a number of observations about its understandings of what rape is. It defined rape as "a form of aggression" where "the central elements of the crime of rape cannot be captured in a mechanical description of objects and body parts."[54] Analogizing rape to torture, the court defined rape as "used for such purposes as intimidation, degradation, humiliation, discrimination, control or destruction of a person."[55] The court continued: "like torture, rape is a violation of personal dignity, and rape in fact constitutes torture when inflicted by or at the instigation of or with the consent or acquiescence of a public official or person acting in an official capacity."[56] In the *Akayesu* case, the public position that the defendant held constituted consent or acquiescence.

Since the initial discussion of rape in the ICTR judgment did not discuss the sexual nature of rape as a war crime, the following paragraph defined "rape as a physical invasion of a sexual nature, committed on a person under circumstances which are coercive."[57] The court defined sexual violence as a broader category, inclusive of but not limited to rape.[58] It suggested that sexual violence "is not limited to the physical invasion of the human body and may include acts that do not involve penetration or even physical contact."[59] In this context, a coercive situation was described in some detail: "the Tribunal notes in this context that coercive circumstances need not be evidenced by a show of physical force. Threats, intimidation, extortion and other forms of duress which prey on fear or desperation may constitute coercion, and coercion may be inherent in certain circumstances, such as armed conflict."[60] The ICTR classified rape as a crime against humanity under ICTR Statute 3(g), and sexual violence as an "outrage against humanity" and/or "serious bodily or mental harm" under ICTR Statutes 4(e) and 2(2)(b) respectively. It saw sexual violence as a war crime when it was a part of a widespread or systematic attack, on a civilian population, and on certain catalogued discriminatory grounds.[61] The court went further to classify rape as an act of genocide.[62] It explained:

> With regard, particularly, to the acts described in paragraphs 12(A) and 12(B) of the Indictment, that is, rape and sexual violence, the Chamber wishes to underscore the fact that in its opinion, they constitute genocide. . . . Indeed, rape and sexual violence certainly constitute infliction

of serious bodily and mental harm on the victims and are even, according to the Chamber, one of the worst ways of inflict harm on the victim as he or she suffers both bodily and mental harm.[63]

In the case of the accused, the court found that "the acts of rape and sexual violence" that happened in his case "were committed solely against Tutsi women, many of whom were subjected to the worst public humiliation, mutilated, and raped several times, often in public . . . and often by more than one assailant."[64] The impact, the court suggested, was genocidal in nature:

> These rapes resulted in physical and psychological destruction of Tutsi women, their families and their communities. Sexual violence was an integral part of the process of destruction, specifically targeting Tutsi women and specifically contributing to their destruction and to the destruction of the Tutsi group as a whole.[65]

In finding that the rapes constituted genocide—as noted at the beginning of this section—the court characterized them as both "systematic" and "perpetrated against all Tutsi women and solely against them."[66]

In his unsuccessful defense, the defendant conceded that genocide had occurred, but denied complicity therein—arguing to the court that he "did not commit, order, or participate in any killings, beatings, or acts of sexual violence alleged."[67] Instead, he argued that he could not prevent it, and should not be required to have been a hero for, or a savior of, the Tutsi population.[68] While Akayesu did not deny that genocide had been committed, he did deny that there was any sexual violence in his direct control. As the court recounted, "during his testimony the Accused emphatically denied that any rapes had taken place at the Bureau Communal, even when he was not there."[69]

So what could rethinking sexual violence in war and conflict possibly tell us about this landmark case? And why analyze *this case*, with a male perpetrator and female victims, when the whole point of this rethinking exercise is to identify female perpetrators and their victims? When the traditional victim/perpetrator dichotomy not only holds, but has the ideal perpetrators and victims, in Mibenge's terms?[70] As I have argued throughout this book, rethinking theories of and legal approaches to sexual violence in war and conflict *through* the recognition of women perpetrators provides important correctives for approaching this violence more generally, recognizing the sex essentialism even in gender-based stories and progressive prosecutions, and recognizing the complexities of the gender orders in which it is perpetrated and received.

The *Akayesu* case reads very differently than the *Nyiramasuhuko* case—both because the *Akayesu* court needed to decide whether or not there was a genocide in Rwanda in the summer of 1994[71] and because it is textually clear that the court saw that its treatment of sexual violence was or would be politically controversial.[72] The court therefore spent a fair amount of time discussing the importance of prosecuting sexual violence and what constitutes sexual violence in war and conflict for the purposes of conviction. The result is what many see as the most broad-ranging of war rape definition in jurisprudential history (which does not rely on penetration or touching and does not necessarily include the use of sex organs),[73] with the attribution of the responsibility to stop sexual violence from a position of authority.[74] Subsequent courts either incorporated this definition or saw it as too broad, and much of the gender justice advocacy community bemoaned the definition not being used as much as it could be.[75]

As progressive as the *Akayesu* court was in recognizing the need to prosecute sexual violence to achieve justice, and in using a broad-ranging definition to capture not only rape but sexual torture and sexual humiliation, the basics of a "gender story" in which men=perpetrators and women=victims of sexual violence in war and conflict are clearly used and not interrogated in the case. A number of stories that query the absolute nature of these dichotomies are glossed over in the text of the decision, such as young men asking their female victims to teach them to rape,[76] and young women given a *laissez-passer* from the violence witnessing it and failing to protest.[77] There is no direct evidence of the existence of female perpetrators of sexual violence or male victims in city of Taba where Akayesu served as the local government, though general evidence from the Rwandan genocide suggests that both existed most places in Rwanda during the summer of 1994.[78] *If* there were no male victims *or* women perpetrators in Taba, though, that would be happenstance rather than a structural feature of the sexual violence in the conflict.

Yet in the decision it is treated as a structural feature of sexual violence in war and conflict, where that violence is understood to target and destroy *all* and *only* Tutsi women—and by secondary effect, their families. While there is some resonance in that explanation, asdiscussed in chapter 1, it is too simple. While Tutsi women were (largely) the victims (individually and collectively), even the trial evidence shows that some Tutsi women were exempted from the violence.[79] Much more importantly, however, are the gendered reasons why the majority of the victims were Tutsi women. These gendered reasons included reading women as the social, cultural, and biological reproducers of the Tutsi ethnicity, and as threats to the purity of the reproduction of the Hutu ethnicity.[80] The target, then, is *women because they are women*, but because that womanhood is identified with certain normalized notions of sex and gender relations that position women both low on gender hierarchies and central to reproduction.[81] Seeing sexual violence in war and conflict as a crime of gender/violence complicates the sex-based analysis in *Akayesu*.

Such a reading of sexual violence as a war crime of gender/violence also could have provided support to the *Akayesu* court's broad reading of the crimes that constitute sexual violence in war and conflict as a crime against humanity and an outrage against personal dignity.[82] The court seems to understand that violations like being forced to parade naked are sources of embarrassment for women, but does not interrogate the analysis of traditional gender roles that validate this embarrassment by highlighting women's status as mothers.[83] In other words, the court does convict for and punish humiliation that exploits traditional gendered expectations of women's modesty, but it does so without recognizing those traditional gendered expectations as part of the violence done to the women victims.

This is evident in the treatment of the testimony of another witness, called "JJ" by the court. JJ had left her one-year-old child with a Hutu family that promised it had milk for the baby, but killed the baby instead.[84] The paragraph that discusses her testimony, however, does not emphasize the horrors of the loss of a child. Instead, it discusses the special pain of rape for a mother, observing that the witness "testified to the humiliation she felt as a mother, by the public nudity and being raped in the presence of children by young men" as a source of "the heavy sorrow the war had caused her."[85] This humiliation was exacerbated by the witness's testimony that "she could not count the number of times she was raped."[86] As evidence of the long-term impact of sexual violence in war and conflict on its victims, the court recalled that "witness JJ told the Chamber that she had remarried but that her life had never been the same because of the beatings and rapes she suffered."[87] Here, the *wrong* of sexual violence in war and conflict is tied to the ways in which it inhibited witness JJ from performing the roles traditionally associated with femininity, as well as to the ways in which her expectations of feminine and maternal privacy were violated. The *Akayesu* conviction, then, relies on reification of very traditional (yet very complicated) gendered orders in Taba.

The *Akayesu* fact pattern includes more examples of the complicated ways in which gender norms constituted victims and victimization in the narrative of the Rwandan genocide. The decision, for example, tells the story of a family where the mother "begged the men, who were with bludgeons and machetes, to kill her daughters rather than rape them in front of her."[88] An initial reading of this sentence suggests that the mother was asking that the daughters be killed rather than raped and killed, but the testimony in court being given by one of the daughters suggested that, at least in this situation, killing was not the understood inevitable result. The mother was suggesting that being made to watch her daughters be raped was worse than watching them die. This was apparently a signification with which the perpetrators agreed, given that "the man replied that 'the principle was to make them suffer' and the girls were then raped."[89] The daughters survived that and a number of other rapes, but were rejected by their mother as a result. The witness recounted that "their mother asked her daughters to leave rather than continue to be tortured in front of her."[90]

In my view, the mother described here (but never mentioned by name) is both a victim and a perpetrator of sexual violence, and a perpetrator of violence more generally. The mother's request that her fifteen-year-old daughter be killed rather than raped *in front of her* includes a number of significations about gender. First, the rape of the daughter is understood (first and foremost) as a humiliation *of the mother*—that is, the violation of the daughter constitutes a humiliation of the mother, and, in the text of the explanation, this is something understood by both the potential rapist and the mother. Second, the life of the daughter is understood as less important than, or at the very least irreversibly destroyed by, the existence of the rape (in front of the mother or not), such that killing appears to be more humane than living with the stigma of rape. Third, then, the mother's pain at watching her daughter be raped is more important than both her daughter's pain from the rape and her daughter's life. The rape that the victim was subjected to, then, was also an affront against the mother on the basis of gender in the gender order of the community at the time. The mother, however, becomes both victim and perpetrator, first when she begs for her daughter's death, and then again when she disowns her daughter rather than watch her be raped or tortured. There is no evidence on the trial record or elsewhere of the indictment or prosecution of this mother for kicking her teenaged daughters out of the house, after which each suffered significantly and one died. While the witnesses are unidentifiable from the case record, and therefore any evidence of such an indictment or prosecution would be difficult to find, it seems unlikely that any existed.

The complicated gender dynamics of this particular account suggest both that the victim/perpetrator dichotomy is not as clear as it is often treated in either media reactions to sexual violence or in international war crimes jurisprudence. It also suggests that there remain gender-based dynamics between multiple layers of victims and multiple layers of perpetrators, even when expanding the definitions of perpetrators and victims and including both men and women among the ranks of both categories. A more complex gender analysis of the sexual violence in the *Akayesu* case reveals both more victims and more perpetrators than the jurisprudence or media coverage did, and demonstrates the fluidity of the victim/perpetrator positions.

Finally, a more complicated look at the sexed, gendered, and sexualized assumptions in the *Akayesu* trial and decision draws attention to the several times when the court struggles with getting witnesses to describe exactly how they were raped and what happened to them during the rapes. In the decision, the court discusses with reference to several victims and at length the difficulty extracting what the witnesses thought that rape was when they described what had happened to them, either using the term "rape" or using language about the insertion of one sex into another sex.[91] As the court recounts of witness JJ, "at the request of the prosecutor and with great embarrassment, she explicitly specified that the rapist, a young man armed with an axe and a long knife, penetrated her vagina with his penis."[92] The court is trying to balance its need for "specific evidence" of what happened to the female victims of the sexual violence in war and conflict with the women's reluctance to testify about it, but a gender analysis about this reluctance to testify is conspicuously absent. A number of feminist scholars have expressed concern about the ways that adversarial and detailed testimonial procedures replicated the violence that victims experience in conflict,[93] and, while the *Akayesu* court seems aware of the "great embarrassment" of testifying to the technical workings of rape, it does not seem to link that embarrassment to the gendered logics of sexual humiliation that underlie sexual violence in war and conflict. The analysis in this book has suggested that the gendered logics of humiliation, punishment, and feminization that underlie strategic sexual violence are not unique to the perpetration of war rape, but can also come up not only in myriad other forms of sexual violence in war and conflict but also in other forms of conflict violence, and in processes of post-conflict reconciliation and justice.

While, like *Nyiramasuhuko*, there are a lot of progressive elements of the *Akayesu* decision, and of media and scholarly reactions to it, there are a number of shortcuts in the gender analysis in the case that miss important details both about how the facts in the case worked and how the genocide in Rwanda worked. Thinking of the complexity of gender dynamics would remove the assumption that women have to be the only victims of the sexual violence to be victimized as a class, or that men must be by definition the perpetrators (and solely perpetrators rather than perpetrator/victims) in order for women as a class to be victimized. Considering a non-sex-essentialist version of the "gender story" of sexual violence in war and conflict also allows insight into the gender dynamics *among women*, and gender dynamics *that stereotype sex roles* which were both weaponized and overlooked as both weapons and consequences in the perpetration of sexual violence in the *Akayesu* case and in the Rwandan genocide more generally. The prosecutorial pursuit and court consideration of a charge of gender/violence would allow/ encourage/require the court to think about the complicated dynamics of Rwandan gender order that underlie the perception of what is wrong with sexual violence that constitute it as a crime against humanity and an affront to dignity—given that those logics are both implicitly and explicitly gendered. Such a counterfactual charge would have also provided the court leeway to talk about and justify the pursuit of conflict sexual violence charges, as well as rape as genocide charges, with a more clear theoretical logic. In this way, the more complex gender dynamics that are ignored in the decision could have attention paid to them, and the court could stray from sex-essentialist analysis of the victims and perpetrators of the violence while still accounting for, in gender terms, the horror that is sexual violence in war and conflict.

Re-visioning Sexual Violence in War and Conflict

This book has argued that gender analysis is crucial to a full understanding of the conditions of possibility for, the perpetration(s) of, the signification(s) of, and even the legal treatments of sexual violence in war and conflict—but that the *manner, depth,* and *accuracy* of that gender analysis matters. I have contended at several points throughout the book that full understandings of sexual violence in war and conflict are hampered by rather than facilitated by oversimplistic sex, gender, and sexuality analysis—especially those that make the assumption that, because *most* perpetrators are sexed male and *most* victims are sexed female, sexual violence is something done to women by men. The account of that violence in this book casts it as *gendered* but not sex-essentialist, using complicated gender analysis to enhance understandings of the gendered dynamics of not only sexual violence in war and conflict, but conflict violence and global political orders more generally. I have opposed such a framework to explicitly sex-essentialist accounts (which are increasingly rarer with the dominance of gender-justice frameworks)[94] and implicitly sex-essentialist accounts (which to some extent or another are present in almost all of the dominant scholarly, media, and jurisprudential accounts).[95]

In this concluding chapter, I have analyzed how such an approach might analyze and impact the decisions in and coverage of two cases

decided by the ICTR about sexual violence during the Rwandan genocide. These analyses have been cursory, given the breadth and depth of
the cases and the coverage thereof.[96] They also cover jurisprudence in
only one conflict, and only a small part of the (internationalized) jurisprudence about that conflict.[97] These cases are not the outrageous cases
on the fringes of conflict sexual violence jurisprudence that inspired the
critique that is the foundation for this book. I did not pick the hundreds
of cases where female perpetrators, not only of the Rwandan genocide
but of sexual violence in war and conflict around the world, were not
prosecuted, or the hundreds of cases where male victims were ignored
or downplayed because male=perpetrator and female=victim.[98] Instead,
I chose explicitly sex- and gender-conscious cases. Despite this sex and
gender consciousness, and serious efforts at gender analysis by the
court, these cases contain a number of the mistakes that the critiques in
this book highlight. Also, each case (though in a different way) contains
judgments that were at the time (and are still) considered progressive
by a significant audience in international criminal jurisprudence, even
feminist international criminal law analysis.[99]

I chose these "progressive" and "forward-thinking" cases to show the
vestiges of sex essentialism in their decision-making, and the implicitly
gendered dynamics in their analyses of the existence and perpetration
of sexual violence in war and conflict. I wanted to show not only that
vestiges of essentialist and oversimple "grids of intelligibility" remain in
those decisions and the treatment of them, but that a framework that
takes account of the complexities of gender dynamics can point out, rec-
tify, and correct those shortcomings *without* abandoning gender-based
analytical tools.

At the end of this book's analysis, like at the beginning, it remains
true that very few women are wartime rapists, issue commands to commit sexual violence in war and conflict, plan intentional sexual violation,
personally violate other women, advocate strategies of forced impregnation, force abortions or miscarriages, sell women into sexual slavery, or
use rape as a weapon of genocide. It also remains true, however, that it
is overdetermined that those very few women are either entirely invisible (given their discursive impossibility) or hypervisible[100] (given their
transgression of their discursive impossibility). Further, those very few
women, while statistically insignificant in many (though not all)[101] cases,

are significant for a number of reasons. First, their stories are a part of the history of the conflicts in which they committed violence, and need not be omitted from those histories because scholars, lawyers, courts, and media are unable to find frames to make those stories intelligible within broader accounts of sexual violence in war and conflict. In other words, women *do* commit sexual violence in war and conflict, and making that part of wartime sexual violence invisible is problematic. Second, and the feature of this book—recognizing the existence of women perpetrators of sexual violence in war and conflict forces substantive reconsideration of unexamined and oversimple assumptions about what women are, what men are, what sexual violence in war and conflict is, what conflict is, what perpetration is, and what victimization is. It does so by interrogating the coherence of the category of "woman" and the assumptions that members of that category have essential commonalities, critiquing assumptions about women's "natural" peacefulness and/or common decision-making processes, complicating the individual and collective assumed simplicity of the perpetrator/victim dichotomy, analyzing the gendered nature of sexual violence in war and conflict, and breaking down continuing sex-stereotypical notions of who perpetrates and who is victimized by that sexual violence. Such an approach, I hope, makes it possible to understand *women* victimizing *women* on the basis of *sex and gender* in wartime sexual violence (as elsewhere), paying as much attention (if not more) to the gendered dynamics of perpetration and victimization as to the sex, gender, or sexuality of the perpetrator(s).

NOTES

INTRODUCTION

1 See http://en.wikipedia.org/wiki/War_rape.

2 See http://en.wikipedia.org/wiki/Genocidal_rape.

3 International Military Tribunal, *Trials of the Major War Criminals before the International Military Tribunal*, 42 vols. (Nuremberg: 1947–1949), 3: pp.514–515; 5: pp.220–221; 32: p.267ff.

4 Alexandra Przyrembel, "Transfixed by an Image: Ilse Koch, the 'Komandeuse of Buchenwald,'" trans. Pamela Selwyn, *German History* 19(3) (2001): 369–399, p.396.

5 Egon W. Fleck and Edward A. Tenenbaum, "Buchenwald: ein vorläufiger Bericht vom 24.4.1945," in Lutz Niethammer, ed., *Der gesäuberte Antifaschismus. Die SED und die roten Kapos von Buchenwald* (Berlin: Dokumente, 1994), pp.180–198.

6 Przyrembel, "Transfixed by an Image," p.370.

7 Arthur L. Smith, *Die Hexe von Buchenwald: Der Fall Ilse Koch*, 2d ed. (Cologne: Böhlau,1994); Przyrembel, "Transfixed by an Image."

8 Przyrembel, "Transfixed by an Image," p.393.

9 Ibid., p.394, citing Gisela Bock, "Frauen- und Geschlechterbeziehungen in der nationalsozialistischen Rassenpolitik," in Therese Wobbe, ed., *Nach Osten. Verdekte Suren natioanlsozialistischer Verbrechen* (Frankfurt am Main: Neue Kritik, 1992), pp.99–133, p.126.

10 For extensive theorization of this point, see Laura Sjoberg and Caron Gentry, *Mothers, Monsters, Whores: Women's Violence in Global Politics* (London: Zed Books, 2007); Caron Gentry and Laura Sjoberg, *Beyond Mothers, Monsters, Whores* (London: Zed Books, 2015).

11 See extended discussion in Eva Stehle, *Performance and Gender in Ancient Greece: Non-Dramatic Poetry in Its Setting* (Princeton, NJ: Princeton University Press, 1997); Vern Bullough, *Cross Dressing, Sex, and Gender* (Philadelphia: University of Pennsylvania Press, 1993), p.28.

12 See discussion in Vinay Lal, "Not This, Not That: The Hijras of India and the Cultural Politics of Sexuality," *Social Text* 61 (Winter 1999): 119–140.

13 Some exceptions include the legal recognition of a third, neutral gender in Australia (Helen Davidson, "Third Gender Must Be Recognized by NSW after Norrie Wins Legal Battle," *Guardian*, 1 April 2014, www.theguardian.com), and similar legal recognitions in India, Pakistan, Nepal, and Thailand (Madison Park and Kiki

Dhitavat, "Thailand's New Constitution Could Soon Recognize Third Gender," *CNN.com*, 16 January 2015, www.cnn.com).

14 See discussions in Suzanne J. Kessler, "The Medical Construction of Gender: Case Management of Intersexed Infants," *Signs: Journal of Women in Culture and Society* 16(1) (1990): 3–26.

15 The World Health Organization reports on a number of genetic varieties of sex chromosomes (www.who.int/genomics/gender/en/index1.html), including sex monosomies, people with three or more sex chromosomes, people with a mutation on an X chromosome that incorporates part of a Y chromosome, and people with a mutation on a Y chromosome that incorporates part of an X chromosome, which, with the most common varieties of XY and XX, makes for at least seventeen biological combinations of sex chromosomes.

16 Estimate taken from Melanie Blackless, Anthony Charuvastra, Amanda Derryck, Anne Fausto-Sterling, and Ellen Lee, "How Sexually Dimorphic Are We? Review and Synthesis," *American Journal of Human Biology* 12 (2000): 151–166.

17 See, e.g., discussion in Joan Roughgarden, *Evolution's Rainbow: Diversity, Gender, and Sexuality in Nature and People* (Berkeley: University of California Press, 2004).

18 Susan Stryker, "Transgender History, Homonormativity, and Disciplinarity," *Radical History Review* 100 (Winter 2008): 145–157; Julia Serano, *Whipping Girl: A Transsexual Woman on Sexism and the Scapegoating of Femininity* (Emeryville, CA: Seal Press, 2007); Katrina Roen, "'Either/Or' and 'Both/Neither': Discursive Tensions in Transgender Politics." *Signs: Journal of Women in Culture and Society* 27(2) (2002): 501–522.

19 See, e.g., see discussions of the various types of gender essentialism in Charlotte Witt, "What Is Gender Essentialism?," in Charlotte Witt, ed., *Feminist Metaphysics* (New York: Springer, 2011), pp.11–25.

20 There are some rather sophisticated discussions of this, e.g., Judith Butler, *Bodies That Matter: On the Discursive Limits of Sex* (New York: Routledge, 1993); Helen Kinsella, "For a Careful Reading: The Conservativism of Gender Constructivism," *International Studies Review* 5(2) (2003): 287–302; Lauren Wilcox, "Beyond Sex/Gender: The Feminist Body of Security," *Politics and Gender* 7(4) (2011): 595–600.

21 I find the discussion about this in Laura J. Shepherd, "Sex or Gender? Bodies in World Politics and Why Gender Matters," in Laura J. Shepherd, ed., *Gender Matters in Global Politics* (London: Routledge, 2010), pp.3–17, particularly useful.

22 See, e.g., discussions in Joan Acker, "From Sex Roles to Gendered Institutions," *Contemporary Sociology* 21 (1992): 565–569; Judith Butler, *Gender Trouble* (New York: Routledge, 1990); Cressida Heyes, "Feminist Solidarity after Queer Theory: The Case of Transgender," *Signs: Journal of Women in Culture and Society* 28(3) (2003): 1093–1120.

23 See a significantly more sophisticated understanding in Raewyn Connell, *Masculinities*, 2d ed. (Berkeley: University of California Press, 2005). There are explicit

discussions of how this translates into expectations in politics in the leadership literature—see, e.g., Leonie Huddy and Nayda Terkildsen, "The Consequences of Gender Stereotypes for Women Candidates at Different Levels and Types of Public Office," *Political Research Quarterly* 46(3) (1993): 503–525.

24   Connell, *Masculinities*; Charlotte Hooper, *Manly States: Masculinities, International Relations, and Gender Politics* (New York: Columbia University Press, 2001). There was a special issue of the *International Feminist Journal of Politics* (14[4] [2012]), edited by Marsha Henry and Paul Kirby, that explored rethinking masculinity and practices of violence in global politics.

25   See, e.g., J. Ann Tickner, *Gender in International Relations* (New York: Columbia University Press, 1992); V. Spike Peterson and Anne Sisson Runyan, *Global Gender Issues* (Boulder, CO: Westview, 1992).

26   The place that this struck me the most was in the discussion of Ann Hopkins as an employee of Price Waterhouse (*Price Waterhouse v. Hopkins*, 490 US 228 [1989]), where a woman had been punished for masculine behavior in the workplace.

27   See discussion in Sue Rae Peterson, "Coercion and Rape: The State as a Male Protection Racket," in Mary Vetterling-Braggin, Frederick Elliston, and Jane English, eds., *Feminism and Philosophy* (Totowa, NJ: Littlefield, Adams, 1977); Iris Marion Young, "The Logic of Masculinist Protection: Reflections on the Current Security State," *Signs: Journal of Women in Culture and Society* 29(1) (2003): 1–25; Laura Sjoberg and Jessica Peet, "A(nother) Dark Side of the Protection Racket: Targeting Women in Wars," *International Feminist Journal of Politics* 13(2) (2011): 163–182.

28   See, e.g., the discussion in Cynthia Enloe's *Nimo's War, Emma's War: Making Feminist Sense of the Iraq War* (Berkeley: University of California Press, 2010), where she discusses gendered expectations and gendered spaces within gendered histories of wars.

29   See, e.g, Tickner, *Gender in International Relations*; Lauren Wilcox, "Gendering the Cult of the Offensive," *Security Studies* 18(2) (2009): 214–240.

30   See, e.g., Cynthia Enloe, *Does Khaki Become You? The Militarization of Women's Lives* (London: Pandora, 1983). See also Annica Kronsell, *Gender, Sex, and the Postnational Defense* (New York: Oxford University Press, 2012); Melissa T. Brown, *Enlisting Masculinity* (New York: Oxford University Press, 2012).

31   For discussions, see, e.g., Miriam Glucksman, *Cottons and Casuals: The Gendered Organisation of Labour in Time and Space* (London: Routledge, 2013); Juliet Webster, *Shaping Women's Work: Gender, Employment, and Information Technology* (London: Routledge, 2014).

32   Particularly, Enloe argued that "the personal is international" and the "international is personal" in *Bananas, Beaches, and Bases: Making Feminist Sense of International Politics* (Berkeley: University of California Press, 1990), p.196.

33   Enloe, *Bananas, Beaches, and Bases*.

34   For a recent discussion, see Janet T. Spence and Robert L. Helmreich, *Masculinity and Femininity: Their Psychological Dimensions, Correlates, and Antecedents* (Aus-

tin: University of Texas Press, 2014); Julia Wood, *Gendered Lives*, 10th ed. (Boston: CENGAGE Learning, 2013).

35 See, e.g., Connell, *Masculinities*; Butler, *Gender Trouble*; Selya Benhabib, *Situating the Self: Gender, Community, and Postmodernism in Contemporary Ethics* (New York: Routledge, 1992).

36 See Laura Sjoberg, "Agency, Militarized Femininity, and Enemy Others: Observations from the War in Iraq," *International Feminist Journal of Politics* 9(1) (2007): 82–101, p.83, for contextual discussion.

37 Sjoberg and Gentry, *Mothers, Monsters, Whores*; Sjoberg and Gentry, *Beyond Mothers, Monsters, Whores*; Laura Sjoberg and Caron Gentry, "Reduced to Bad Sex: Narratives of Violent Women from the Bible to the 'War on Terror,'" *International Relations* 22(1) (2008): 5–23; Laura Sjoberg and Caron Gentry, eds., *Women, Gender, and Terrorism* (Athens: University of Georgia Press, 2011).

38 Thucydides, *History of the Peloponnesian War* (431 BCE), trans. Richard Crawley, *MIT Classics*, http://classics.mit.edu/Thucydides/pelopwar.html.

39 See extended discussion in Laura Sjoberg, *Gender, War, and Conflict* (Cambridge, UK: Polity Press, 2014), pp.26–27.

40 Jean Bethke Elshtain, *Women and Wars* (Chicago: University of Chicago Press, 1988).

41 See Enloe, *Nimo's War, Emma's War*.

42 See, e.g., Adrienne Harris and Yneistra King, *Rocking the Ship of the State: Towards a Feminist Peace Politics* (Boulder, CO: Westview Press, 1989); Karen Warren and Duane Cady, "Feminism and Peace: Seeing the Connections," *Hypatia* 9(2) (1994): 4–19; Betty Reardon, *Sexism and the War System* (New York: Teachers' College Press, 1985).

43 For discussions of these movements, see, e.g., Beth Junor and Katrina Howse, *Greenham Common Women's Peace Camp: A History of Non-Violent Resistance* (New York: Working Press, 1995); Catia Cecilia Confortini, *Intelligent Compassion: Feminist Critical Methodology in the Women's International League for Peace and Freedom* (Oxford: Oxford University Press, 2012).

44 See discussion in Helen Kinsella, "Gendering Grotius: Sex and Sex Difference in the Laws of War," *Political Theory* 34(2) (2006): 161–191.

45 E.g., Susan McKay, "The Effects of Armed Conflict on Girls and Women," *Peace and Conflict: Journal of Peace Psychology* 4(4) (1998): 381–392.

46 See discussion in Elshtain, *Women and Wars*.

47 Ibid. See also Alan Norrie, *Law and the Beautiful Soul* (London: Routledge, 2013).

48 E.g., Alison Bailey, "Mothering, Diversity, and Peace Politics," *Hypatia* 9(2) (1994): 188–198.

49 See, e.g., the discussion in Naomi Black, "The Mothers' International: The Women's Co-operative Guild and Feminist Pacifism," *Women's Studies International Forum* 7(6) (1984): 467–476.

50 See, e.g., Sara Ruddick, *Maternal Thinking: Toward a Politics of Peace*, 2d ed. (Boston: Beacon Press, 1995).

51 See, e.g., Mia Bloom, *Bombshell: Women and Terror* (Philadelphia: University of Pennsylvania Press, 2011); Robin Morgan, *The Demon Lover: Roots of Terrorism* (New York: Washington Square Press, 1989); Barbara Victor, *An Army of Roses: Inside the World of Palestinian Women Suicide Bombers* (New York: Rodale Press, 2003).

52 See also Miranda H. Alison, *Women and Political Violence: Female Combatants in Ethno-National Conflict* (Abingdon: Routledge, 2008); Katherine E. Brown, "Blinded by the Explosion? Security and Resistance in Muslim Women's Suicide Terrorism," in Sjoberg and Gentry, *Women, Gender, and Terrorism*; Megan MacKenzie, *Female Soldiers in Sierra Leone: Sex, Security, and Post-Conflict Development* (New York: New York University Press, 2012); Swati Parashar, "Feminist International Relations and Women Militants: Case Studies from Sri Lanka and Kashmir," *Cambridge Review of International Affairs* 22(2) (2009): 235–256.

53 The term "opportunity structures" is used here as it is used in social movement theory, e.g., Herbert Kitschelt, "Political Opportunity Structures and Political Protest: Anti-Nuclear Movements in Four Democracies," *British Journal of Political Science* 16(1) (1986): 57–85; talking about gender specifically, see, e.g., Myra Marx Ferree and Silke Roth, "Gender, Class, and the Interaction Between Social Movements: A Strike of West Berlin Day Care Workers," *Gender & Society* 12(6) (1998): 626–648.

54 See Lori Girshick, *Woman-to-Woman Sexual Violence: Does She Call It Rape?* (Boston, MA: Northeastern University Press, 2002).

55 Erica Marlowe, "Five Thousand Lesbians and No Police Force," *Feminism and Psychology* 9(4) (1999): 398–401.

56 Sjoberg and Gentry, *Mothers, Monsters, Whores*.

57 Ibid.

58 E.g., Linda Ahall, "Motherhood, Myth, and Gendered Agency in Political Violence," *International Feminist Journal of Politics* 14(1) (2012): 103–120; Linda Ahall, *Motherhood and War: Gender, Agency, and Political Violence* (London: Routledge, 2014); Jessica Auchter, "Gendering Terror: Discourses of Terror and Writing Woman-as-Agent," *International Feminist Journal of Politics* 14(1) (2012): 121–139.

59 Todd Salzman, "Rape Camps as a Means of Ethnic Cleansing: Religious, Cultural, and Ethical Responses to Rape Victims in the Former Yugoslavia," *Human Rights Quarterly* 20(2) (1998): 348–378, p.349.

60 This dynamic is compounded by the assumption that real or proper women have an asexual or sexually conservative nature; women who commit sexual violence are a foil to that ideal.

61 See, e.g., description of Stella Kubler and other Jewish recruits of the Nazi regime in Beate Meyer, Hermann Simon, and Chana Schutz, eds., *Jews in Nazi Berlin: From Kristallnacht to Liberation* (Chicago: University of Chicago Press, 2009); or of people like Pascal Simbikangwa's conviction in the Rwandan Genocide (e.g., in Maia de la Baume, "France Convicts Rwandan Ex-Officer of Genocide," *New York Times*, 14 March 2014, www.nytimes.com).

62 Sarah Wight and Alice Myers, "Introduction" in Alice Myers and Sarah Wight, eds., *No Angels: Women Who Commit Violence* (London: HarperCollins, 1996), p.xii.

63 See extended discussion in Sjoberg and Gentry, *Mothers, Monsters, Whores*.

64 Ibid., p.57.

65 Laura Sjoberg, "Women and the Genocidal Rape of Women: The Gender Dynamics of Gendered War Crimes," in Debra Bergoffen, Paula Ruth Gilbert, and Tamara Harvey, eds., *Confronting Global Gender Justice: Women's Lives, Human Rights* (London and New York: Routledge, 2011), pp.21–34, p.30.

66 See, e.g., Adam Jones, *Gendercide and Genocide* (Nashville: Vanderbilt University Press, 2004).

67 Barbara Ehrenrich, "Prison Abuse: Feminism's Assumptions Upended: A Uterus Is Not a Substitute for a Conscience," *Los Angeles Times*, 16 May 2004, http://articles.latimes.com.

68 Sjoberg, "Women and the Genocidal Rape of Women."

69 Joshua Goldstein, *War and Gender: How Gender Shapes the War System and Vice Versa* (Cambridge, UK: Cambridge University Press, 2001); Aaron Belkin, *Bring Me Men: Military Masculinity and the Benign Façade of American Empire, 1898–2001* (New York: Columbia University Press, 2012); Paul Higate, "Drinking Vodka from the 'Butt-Crack': Men, Masculinities, and Fratriarchy in the Private Militarized Security Company," *International Feminist Journal of Politics* 14(4) (2012): 450–469.

70 Laura Sjoberg, *Gendering Global Conflict: Toward a Feminist Theory of War* (New York: Columbia University Press, 2013).

71 See, e.g., discussion in Carol Cohn, ed., *Women and Wars: Contested Histories, Uncertain Futures* (London: Polity, 2012).

72 Enloe, *Nimo's War, Emma's War*; Cynthia Cockburn, "Gender Relations as Causal in Militarization and War," *International Feminist Journal of Politics* 12(2) (2010): 139–157.

73 Sjoberg, *Gendering Global Conflict*, ch.9; Cockburn, "Gender Relations as Causal"; Tickner, *Gender in International Relations*; Cohn, *Women and Wars*.

74 See Sjoberg, *Gendering Global Conflict*, ch.9.

75 Catherine Niachros, "Women, War, and Rape: Challenges Facing the International Tribunal for the Former Yugoslavia," *Human Rights Quarterly* 17(4) (1995): 649–690; Lene Hansen, "Gender, Nation, Rape: Bosnia and the Construction of Security," *International Feminist Journal of Politics* 3(1) (2001): 55–75; Claudia Card, "Rape as a Weapon of War," *Hypatia* 11(4) (1996): 518; Catherine MacKinnon, "Rape, Genocide, and Women's Human Rights," *Harvard Women's Law Journal* 17 (1994): 5–16; R. Charli Carpenter, *Forgetting Children Born of War: Setting the Human Rights Agenda in Bosnia and Beyond* (New York: Columbia University Press, 2010).

76 Goldstein, *War and Gender*; Jan Jindy Pettman, *Worlding Women: A Feminist International Politics* (London: Routledge, 1996).

77 Elshtain, *Women and Wars*; Sjoberg and Peet, "A(nother) Dark Side"; Young, "The Logic of Masculinist Protection."

78 J. Ann Tickner, *Gendering World Politics* (New York: Columbia University Press, 2001); Laura J. Shepherd, *Gender, Violence, and Security: Discourse as Practice* (London: Zed Books, 2008); Sjoberg, *Gendering Global Conflict.*

79 See, e.g., Carol Cohn, "Wars, Wimps, and Women: Talking Gender and Thinking War," in Miriam Cooke and Angela Wollacott, eds., *Gendering War Talk* (Princeton, NJ: Princeton University Pres, 1993), p.236.

80 See, e.g., Dara Kay Cohen, Amelia Hoover Green, and Elisabeth Jean Wood, "Wartime Sexual Violence: Misconceptions, Implications, and Ways Forward," United States Institute of Peace Special Report, 8 February 2013, www.usip.org.

81 Elisabeth J. Wood, "Variations in Sexual Violence during War," *Politics & Society* 34(3) (2006): 307–342; Inger Skjelsbaek, "Sexual Violence and War: Mapping out a Complex Relationship," *European Journal of International Relations* 7(2) (2001): 211–237; Elisabeth Jean Wood, "Armed Groups and Sexual Violence: When is Wartime Rape Rare?" *Politics & Society* 37(1) (2009): 131–161.

82 Dara Kay Cohen and Ragnhild Nordas, "Sexual Violence in Armed Conflict: Introducing the SVAC dataset, 1989-2009," *Journal of Peace Research* 51(3) (2014): 418–428.

83 See Wilcox, "Gendering the Cult of the Offensive," p.233.

84 See discussion in V. Spike Peterson, "Sexing Political Identities/Nationalism as Heterosexism," *International Feminist Journal of Politics* 1(1) (1999): 34–65.

85 See, e.g., Sjoberg and Peet, "A(nother) Dark Side."

86 Robin May Schott, "War Rape, Social Death, and Political Evil," *Development Dialogue* 55 (March 2011): 47–62, pp.47–48.

87 Ibid., p.48.

88 Bulent Diken and Carsten Bagge Laustsen, "Becoming Abject: Rape as a Weapon of War," *Body & Society* 11(1) (2005): 111–128, p.111.

89 Schott, "War Rape, Social Death," p.48.

90 Catharine MacKinnon, *Sex Equality* (New York: Thomson Reuters, 2001), p.897.

91 K. R. Carter, "Should International Relations Consider Rape a Weapon of War?," *Politics & Gender* 6(3) (2010): 343–371, p.345.

92 Ibid., p.360.

93 Ibid., p.367.

94 See discussion in Debra Bergoffen, "Exploiting the Dignity of the Vulnerable Body: Rape as a Weapon of War," *Philosophical Papers* 38(3) (2009): 307–325.

95 Sjoberg and Peet, "A(nother) Dark Side"; Pettman, *Worlding Women*; Anne Mc-Clintock, "Family Feuds: Gender, Nationalism, and the Family," *Feminist Review* 44 (Summer 1993): 61–80.

96 Hansen, "Gender, Nation, Rape," p.59.

97 Judith Gardam, "Gender and Non-Combatant Immunity," *Transnational Law and Contemporary Problems* 3 (1993): 345–370, pp.358–359.

98 Ibid., pp.363–364.

99 Sjoberg and Peet, "A(nother) Dark Side."

100 Pettman, *Worlding Women*, p.190.

101 Sibohan K. Fisher, "Occupation of the Womb: Forced Impregnation as Genocide," *Duke Law Journal* 46 (1996): 91–133.

102 Kelly D. Askin, "The Quest for Post-Conflict Gender Justice," *Columbia Journal of Transnational Law* 41 (2003): 509–521.

103 See longer discussion in Sjoberg and Peet, "A(nother) Dark Side."

104 See, e.g., Sarah Pomeroy, *Goddesss, Whores, Wives, and Slaves: Women in Classical Antiquity* (New York: Schocken Books, 1975).

105 Susan Brownmiller, *Against Our Will: Men, Women, and Rape*, new ed. (New York: Open Road Media, 2013).

106 See, for example, Claudia Card, "Genocide and Social Death," *Hypatia* 18(1) (2003): 63–79.

107 See *Prosecutor v. Akayesu*, Case No. ICTR 96 4 T. (1998), 694.

108 Ibid., 731.

109 Quoted in Magdalini Karagiannakis, "Case Analysis: The Definition of Rape and Its Characterization as an Act of Genocide—A Review of the Jurisprudence of the International Criminal Tribunals for Rwanda and the Former Yugoslavia," *Leiden Journal of International Law* 12(2) (1999): 379–490, p.481.

110 Ibid.

111 Kelly D. Askin, "Gender Crimes Jurisprudence in the ICTR: Positive Developments," *Journal of International Criminal Justice* 3(4) (2005): 1007–1018.

112 Karagiannakis, "Case Analysis," p.486.

113 Ibid.

114 See, e.g., Rhonda Copelon, "Gender Crimes as War Crimes: Integrating Crimes against Women into International Criminal Law," *McGill Law Journal* 46 (2000): 217–240.

115 See discussions in Elshtain, *Women and Wars*, and R. Charli Carpenter, "'Women, Children, and Other Vulnerable Groups': Gender, Strategic Frames, and the Protection of Civilians as a Transnational Issue," *International Studies Quarterly* 49(2) (2005): 295–334.

116 I discuss this phenomenon in the broader discipline of IR in "The Norm of Tradition: Gender Subordination and Women's Exclusion in International Relations," *Politics & Gender* 4(1) (2008): 73–80.

117 Tickner, *Gender in International Relations*, p.129.

118 V. Spike Peterson, "Transgressing Boundaries: Theories of Knowledge, Gender, and International Relations," *Millennium: Journal of International Studies* 21(2) (1992): 183–206.

119 Jill Steans, *Gender and International Relations: An Introduction* (New Brunswick, NJ: Rutgers University Press, 1998), p.5.

120 See, e.g., Tickner, *Gendering World Politics*; Pettman, *Worlding Women*.

121 V. Spike Peterson, "Gendered Identities, Ideologies, and Practices in the Context of War and Militarism," in Laura Sjoberg and Sandra Via, eds., *Gender, War, and Militarism: Feminist Perspectives* (Santa Barbara, CA: Praeger Security International, 2010), pp.17–29, p.17.

122 Ibid., p.18.
123 Sjoberg, "Women and the Genocidal Rape of Women."
124 Tickner, *Gender in International Relations*, p.141.

CHAPTER 1. CONDITIONS THAT DROVE THEM TO THE BRINK OF DEATH

1 ICTY Sentencing Hearing, 16 and 18 December 2002, pp.395, 625, www.icty.org.
2 Credited to William Tecumseh Sherman, a Union general in the US Civil War, otherwise most famous for burning his troops' path across the state of Georgia.
3 See introduction, notes 13–17.
4 See introduction, notes 18–20.
5 See introduction, notes 20–21.
6 I am not even sure any longer what the word "natural" means, especially in the context in which it is most often used to *denaturalize* others' behaviors.
7 See, e.g., discussions in Michael Genovese and Janie Steckenrider, eds. *Women as Political Leaders: Studies in Gender and Governing* (New York: Routledge, 2013); Fernando Ferreira and Joseph Gyourko, "Does Gender Matter for Political Leadership? The Case of US Mayors," *Journal of Public Economics* 112 (2014): 24–39; Kathleen Dolan, "Gender Stereotypes, Candidate Evaluations, and Voting for Women Candidates: What Really Matters?" *Political Research Quarterly* 67(1) (2014): 96–107.
8 Sjoberg, *Gender, War, and Conflict.*
9 Shepherd, *Gender, Violence, and Security*, p.3.
10 Butler, *Bodies That Matter*, p.xii.
11 Ibid., pp.69–70.
12 Ibid., p.27.
13 Connell, *Masculinities.*
14 Ibid.
15 Cynthia Enloe, *The Curious Feminist: Searching for Women in a New Age of Empire* (Berkeley: University of California Press, 2004), p.6.
16 Peterson, "Gendered Identities, Ideologies, and Practices," p.19.
17 Ibid.
18 Mary Hawkesworth, "Feminists v. Feminization: Confronting the War Logics of the Bush Administration," *Comunicacion e Cidondonia* 1(2) (2006): 117–142, p.129.
19 Peterson, "Gendered Identities, Ideologies, and Practices."
20 Ibid., p.19.
21 Jack Levy and William R. Thompson, *Causes of War* (Oxford: Blackwell Publishing, 2010), p.5. They use violence to distinguish what they see as war from nonviolent protracted conflicts; see e.g., John Lewis Gaddis, *The Long Peace* (New York: Oxford University Press, 1987).
22 Levy and Thompson, *Causes of War*, relying heavily on interpretations of Carl von Clausewitz, *On War*, ed. and trans. Michael Howard and Peter Paret (Princeton, NJ: Princeton University Press, 1976), originally published 1832.

23 See, e.g., discussions in Thomas Risse-Kappen, ed., *Bringing Transnational Relations Back In: Non-State Actors, Domestic Politics, and International Institutions* (Cambridge, UK: Cambridge University Press, 1995); Mary Kaldor, *New and Old Wars: Organized Violence in Global Politics*, 2d ed. (London: Polity, 2006); Chris Hables Gray, *Postmodern War: The New Politics of Conflict* (New York: Guilford Press, 1997).

24 See discussion in Levy and Thompson, *Causes of War*, p.12. Magnitude or longevity are measured different ways by different scholars—in the democratic peace literature (discussed in more detail below), for example, it is often measured by battle deaths. Others measure it by war declaration, though that has its own problems (largely in that it rarely happens anymore).

25 Kenneth Waltz, *Man, the State, and War* (New York: Columbia University Press, 1959); J. David Singer, "The Levels of Analysis Problem in International Relations," *World Politics* 14(1) (1961): 77–92. Waltz refers to "images" while Singer uses "levels," but their division and content are fairly similar, and the terms have come to be used interchangeably in discussions about IR theorizing and research.

26 See, e.g., the power transitions research program, from A. F. K. Organski's *World Politics* (New York: Knopf, 1958) to Ronald Tammen, Jacek Kugler, Douglas Lemke, Carole Alsharabati, Brian Efird, and A. F. K. Organski, *Power Transitions: Strategies for the 21st Century* (New York: Chatham House, 2000).

27 See, e.g., Richard Little, "Religious Militancy," in Chester Crocker and Fen Hampson with Pamela Aall, eds., *Managing Global Chaos* (Washington, DC: United States Institute of Peace, 1996).

28 Patrick James, "Structural Realism and the Causes of War," *Mershon International Studies Review* 39 (1995): 181–208; Stephen Walt, "The Enduring Relevance of the Realist Tradition," in Ira Katznelson and Helen Milner, eds., *Political Science: The State of the Discipline* (New York: W. W. Norton, 2002), pp.197–220; Levy and Thompson, *Causes of War*, pp.28–29.

29 Kenneth Waltz, *Theory of International Politics* (New York: Columbia University Press, 1979); John J. Mearsheimer, *The Tragedy of Great Power Politics* (New York: W. W. Norton, 2001); Stephen Van Evera, *The Causes of War* (Ithaca, NY: Cornell University Press, 1999).

30 David Lake, *Hierarchy in International Relations* (Ithaca, NY: Cornell University Press, 2009); David Lake, "Anarchy, Hierarchy, and Variety in International Relations," *International Organization* 50(1) (1996): 1–33.

31 Karen Rasler and William R. Thompson, *The Great Powers and Global Struggle, 1490–1990* (Lexington: University of Kentucky Press, 1994); Joshua Goldstein, *Long Cycles: Prosperity and War in the Modern Age* (New Haven, CT: Yale University Press, 1988).

32 Immanuel Wallerstein, "Three Instances of Hegemony and the History of the World Economy," *International Journal of Comparative Sociology* 24 (1984): 100–108.

33 Paul Diehl and Gary Goertz, "The Rivalry Process: How Rivalries are Sustained and Terminated," in John Vasquez, ed., *What Do We Know about War?* (Lanham,

MD: Rowman & Littlefield, 2000), pp.83–110; Paul Diehl and Gary Goertz, *War and Peace in International Rivalry* (Ann Arbor: University of Michigan Press, 2000); Paul Diehl, *The Dynamics of Enduring Rivalries* (Urbana: University of Illinois Press, 1998).

34 For discussion of path dependency, see, e.g., Russell Leng, "When Will They Ever Learn? Coercive Bargaining in Recurrent Crises," *Journal of Conflict Resolution* 27 (1983): 379–419; for discussions of the steps to war, see, e.g., Paul Sense and John Vasquez, *The Steps to War: An Empirical Study* (Princeton, NJ: Princeton University Press, 2008). See also discussion in Levy and Thompson, *Causes of War*, pp.60–61.

35 See, e.g., special issue of *International Interactions* on the Capitalist Peace 36(2) (2010), including Gerald Schneider and Nis Petter Gleditsch, "The Capitalist Peace: Origins and Prospects of the Liberal Idea," pp.107–114; Erik Gartzke and J. Joseph Hewitt, "International Crises and the Capitalist Peace, pp.115–145. For a general overview of the liberal-trade perspective, see, e.g., John R. Oneal and Bruce Russett, "Assessing the Liberal Peace with Alternative Specifications: Trade Still Reduces Conflict," *Journal of Peace Research* 36(4) (1999): 423–442.

36 Zeev Maoz and Bruce Russett, "Normative and Structural Causes of the Democratic Peace, 1946–1986," *American Political Science Review* 87(3) (1993): 624–638, building on Michael Doyle, "Kant, Liberal Legacies, and Foreign Affairs, Parts I & II," *Philosophy and Public Affairs* 12 (1983): 205–235, 323–353.

37 Douglas M. Gibler, "Bordering on Peace: Democracy, Territorial Issues, and Conflict," *International Studies Quarterly* 51(3) (2007): 509–532.

38 Sebastian Rosato, "The Flawed Logic of Democratic Peace Theory," *American Political Science Review* 97(4) (2003): 585–602; John Owen, "How Liberalism Produces Peace," *International Security* 19(2) (1994): 87–125.

39 Valerie Hudson and Andrea Den Boer, *Bare Branches: The Security Implications of Asia's Surplus Male Population* (Cambridge, MA: MIT Press); Valerie Hudson, Bonnie Ballif-Spanvill, Mary Caprioli, and Chad F. Emmett, *Sex and World Peace* (New York: Columbia University Press, 2012); Valerie Hudson, Mary Caprioli, Bonnie Ballif-Spanvill, Rose McDermott, and Chad Emmett, "The Heart of the Matter: The Security of Women and the Security of States," *International Security* 33(3) (2009): 7–45.

40 See discussion in Levy and Thompson, *Causes of War*, p.83, citing V. I. Lenin, *Imperialism* (New York: International Publishers, 1939), originally published 1916.

41 Joseph Schumpeter, *Imperialism and Social Classes* (Oxford: Oxford University Press, 1951), originally published 1919.

42 E.g., Graham Allison, "Conceptual Models and the Cuban Missile Crisis," *American Political Science Review* 63(3) (1969): 689–718; Mancur Olson, *The Logic of Collective Action* (Cambridge, MA: Harvard University Press, 1971); Jack Snyder, *Myths of Empire: Domestic Politics and International Ambitions* (Ithaca, NY: Cornell University Press, 1991).

43 *Very* different perspectives on culture as a causal influence on war exist, including Samuel Huntington, "The Clash of Civilizations?" *Foreign Affairs* 72(3) (1993): 22–

29; Mark Salter, *Barbarians and Civilizations in International Relations* (New York: Pluto Press, 2002); Robert English, *Russia and the Idea of the West: Gorbachev, Intellectuals, and the End of the Cold War* (New York: Columbia University Press, 2000); Alexander Wendt, *Social Theory of International Politics* (Cambridge, UK: Cambridge University Press, 1999); Richard Ned Lebow, *A Cultural Theory of International Relations* (Cambridge, UK: Cambridge University Press, 2008).

44 Daniel Byman and Kenneth Pollack, "Let Us Now Praise Great Men: Bringing the Statesmen Back In," *International Security* 25(4) (2001): 107–146.

45 For discussion of bureaucratic politics and organizational processes, see Graham Allison, *Essence of Decision* (New York: Longman, 1971), cited and discussed in Levy and Thompson, *Causes of War*, p.165; for discussion of leadership styles, see Margaret Hermann, "How Decision Units Shape Foreign Policy: A Theoretical Framework," *International Studies Review* 3(2) (2001): 47–81; for a discussion of risk propensity, see work in prospect theory and conflict, e.g., Rose McDermott, *Risk-Taking and International Politics: Prospect Theory in American Foreign Policy* (Ann Arbor: University of Michigan Press, 2001).

46 E.g., E. H. Carr, *The Twenty Years' Crisis: 1919–1939* (New York: Palgrave, 2001), originally published in 1939 and 1945; Hans J. Morgenthau, *Politics among Nations: The Struggle for Power and Peace* (New York: Knopf, 1948). Some credit these scholars' work on human nature to Thucydides's *History of the Peloponnesian War* (431 B.C.E.), Thomas Hobbes's *Leviathan* (London: Andrew Crooke, 1651), and Niccolo Machiavelli's *The Prince* (1515).

47 E.g., Azar Gat, "So Why Do People Fight? Evolutionary Theory and the Causes of War," *European Journal of International Relations* 15(4) (2009): 571–599; Bradley A. Thayer, "Bringing In Darwin: Evolutionary Theory, Realism, and International Politics," *International Security* 25(2) (2000): 124–151; Valerie M. Hudson, Donna Lee Bowen, Perpetua Lynne Nielsen, "What Is the Relationship between Inequity in Family Law and Violence against Women? Approaching the Issue of Legal Enclaves," *Politics and Gender* 7(4) (2011): 453–492.

48 B. Lidell Hart, *The Way to Win Wars* (New York: Faber & Faber, 1942); Colin Gray, *Strategic Studies and Public Policy* (Lexington: University of Kentucky Press, 1982); Alan Stephens and Nicola Baker, *Making Sense of War: Strategy for the 21st Century* (Cambridge, UK: Cambridge University Press, 1994); Dan Reiter and Curtis Meek, "Determinants of Military Strategy: A Quantitative Empirical Test," *International Studies Quarterly* 43(2) (1999): 362–387.

49 Robert Art, "To What Ends Military Power?," *International Security* 4(1) (1980): 4–35.

50 Stephens and Baker, *Making Sense of War*, includes a good general discussion. About terrorism, see, e.g., Robert Pape, *Dying to Win: The Strategic Logic of Suicide Terrorism* (New York: Random House, 2006); for counterterrorism, see Robert W. Ortung and A. S. Makarychev, *National Counter-Terrorism* (New York: IOS Press, 2006); for preemption, see John Lewis Gaddis, "A Grand Strategy of Transformation," *Foreign Policy* 133 (2002): 50–57; Joseph S. Nye, Jr., "U. S. Power and Strategy

after Iraq," *Foreign Affairs* 82(4) (2003): 60–73; for siege, see, e.g., Neil Arya, "Economic Sanctions: The Kinder, Gentler Alternative?" *Medicine, Conflict, and Survival* 24(1) (2008): 25–41; for intentional civilian victimization, see Alexander Downes, *Targeting Civilians in War* (Ithaca, NY: Cornell University Press, 2008).

51 Edward Luttwak, *Strategy: The Logic of War and Peace* (Cambridge, UK: Cambridge University Press, 2001), p.81.

52 Ibid.

53 See, e.g., discussion of the airplane as a tactic, in Robert Pape, *Bombing to Win: Air Power and Coercion in War* (Ithaca, NY: Cornell University Press, 1996), and Derek Wood and Derek Dempster, *The Narrow Margin: The Battle of Britain and the Rise of Air Power, 1930–1940* (London: Hutchinson, 1961). For more general discussions, see Eliot Cohen and John Gooch, *Military Misfortunes: The Anatomy of Failure in War* (New York: Simon and Schuster, 2005).

54 E.g., Michal Walzer, *Just and Unjust Wars* (New York: Basic Books, 1977); Larry May, *War Crimes and Just War* (Cambridge, UK: Cambridge University Press, 2007).

55 Thomas Kane, *Military Logistics and Strategic Performance* (London: Cass, 2001), p.2; Martin Van Creveld, *Supplying War: Logistics from Wallenstein to Patton*, 2d ed. (Cambridge, UK: Cambridge University Press, 2004).

56 Ken Booth, *Theory of World Security* (Cambridge, UK: Cambridge University Press, 2007); Keith Krause and Michael C. Williams, *Critical Security Studies: Concepts and Cases* (New York: Psychology Press, 1997). These two works use the phrase in different ways, both of which have become popularized.

57 Booth, *Theory of World Security*, pp.65, 38.

58 E.g., Lloyd Axworthy, "Human Security and Global Governance: Putting People First," *Global Governance* 7(1) (2001): 19–25; Amartya Sen and Martha Nussbaum, eds., *Quality of Life* (Oxford: Clarendon, 1993); United Nations Development Program, *Human Development Report: New Dimensions of Human Security* (New York: United Nations, 1994).

59 Bill McSweeney, "Identity and Security: Barry Buzan and the Copenhagen School," *Review of International Studies* 22(1) (1996): 86–93; Barry Buzan, *People, States, and Fear: The National Security Problem in International Relations* (New York: Whitesheaf, 1983); Barry Buzan, Ole Waever, and Jaap de Wilde, *Security: A New Framework for Analysis* (Boulder, CO: Lynne Rienner Press, 1998).

60 Lene Hansen, "A Case for Seduction? Evaluating the Poststructuralist Conceptualization of Security," *Cooperation and Conflict—Nordic Journal of International Studies* 32(4) (1997), p.372, citing Jef Huysmans, "Security! What Do You Mean? From Concept to Thick Signifier," *European Journal of International Relations* 4(2) (1998): 226–255.

61 For a characterization of security as a continuum, see Chris J. Cuomo, "War Is Not Just an Event: Reflections on the Significance of Everyday Violence," *Hypatia* 11(4) (1996): 30–45; as a practice, see Lene Hansen, *Security as Practice: Discourse Analysis and the Bosnian War* (New York: Routledge, 2006); as symbolic politics,

see Michael C. Williams, *Culture and Security: Symbolic Power and the Politics of International Security* (New York: Psychology Press, 2007); Shepherd, *Gender, Violence, and Security*; Judith Butler, *Precarious Life* (New York: Routledge, 2006).

62 James Der Derian, *Virtuous War: Mapping the Military-Industrial-Media-Entertainment Network*, 2d ed. (London: Routledge, 2009); Ronnie Lipschutz, ed., *On Security* (New York: Columbia University Press, 1995) (especially James Der Derian's chapter, "The Value of Security").

63 See discussion of the distinction in Alexander Wendt, "On Constitution and Causation in International Relations," *Review of International Studies* 24(5) (1998): 101–118.

64 J. Ann Tickner, "What Is Your Research Program? Some Feminist Answers to International Relations Methodological Questions," *International Studies Quarterly* 49(1) (2005): 1–22, pp.3, 4.

65 Annick T. R. Wibben, *Feminist Security Studies: A Narrative Approach* (London: Routledge, 2011), p.106.

66 Cuomo, "Not Just an Event"; Betty Reardon, *Sexism and the War System* (New York: Teachers' College Press, 1985); Christine Sylvester, ed., *Experiencing War* (London: Routledge, 2011); Christine Sylvester, "War, Sense, and Security," in Laura Sjoberg, ed. *Gender and International Security: Feminist Perspectives* (London: Routledge, 2010), p.24–37; Rachel Pain, "Everyday Terrorism: Connecting Domestic Violence and Global Terrorism," *Progress in Human Geography* 38(4) (2014): 531–550.

67 See discussions in Cohn, *Women and Wars*; Jean Vickers, *Women and War* (London: Zed Books, 1993); Jacqui True, *The Political Economy of Violence against Women* (Oxford: Oxford University Press, 2012); Enloe, *Nimo's War, Emma's War*; Katharine Moon, *Sex Among Allies* (New York: Columbia University Press, 1997); Lois Ann Lorentzen and Jennifer E. Turpin, eds., *The Women and War Reader* (New York: New York University Press, 1998).

68 Peterson, "Coercion and Rape"; Young, "Logic of Masculinist Protection"; Sjoberg and Peet, "A(nother) Dark Side" ; Goldstein, *War and Gender*; Elshtain, *Women and War*.

69 Sjoberg, *Gendering Global Conflict*, p.265.

70 Sylvester, *Experiencing War*; Christine Sylvester, *War as Experience* (London: Routledge, 2013); Annica Kronsell and Erika Svedberg, *Making Gender, Making War: Violence, Military, and Peacekeeping Practices* (London: Routledge, 2011); Lauren B. Wilcox, *Practices of Violence: Theorizing Embodied Subjects in International Relations* (New York: Oxford University Press, 2014); Judith Butler, *Frames of War: When Is Life Grievable?* (New York: Routledge, 2009).

71 This concern started early in feminist work in international relations; see, e.g., Tickner, *Gender in International Relations*, for a discussion of the importance of structural violence and commitments to paying attention to the security of people at the margins.

72 Maria Stern, "'We' the Subject: The Power and Failure of (In)Security," *Security Dialogue* 37(2) (2006): 187–205; Laura Shepherd, "Power and Authority in the

Production of United Nations Security Council Resolution 1325," *International Studies Quarterly* 52(2) (2008): 384–404. For broad treatments, see Amy Allen, *The Power of Feminist Theory* (Boulder, CO: Westview Press, 2000); Tickner, *Gender in International Relations*; Nancy Hirschmann, *The Subject of Liberty: Towards a Feminist Theory of Freedom* (Princeton, NJ: Princeton University Press, 2004).

73 Enloe, *Does Khaki Become You?*; Enloe, *Bananas, Beaches, and Bases* (Berkeley: University of California Press, 1990); Carol Cohn, "Sex and Death in the Rational World of Defense Intellectuals," *Signs: Journal of Women in Culture and Society* 12(4) (1987): 687–718; Hanne Marlene Dahl, "A Perceptive or Reflective State?" *European Journal of Women's Studies* 7(4) (2000): 474–494; Sjoberg and Peet, "A(nother) Dark Side"; Paul Kirby, "How Is Rape a Weapon of War? Feminist International Relations, Modes of Critical Explanation, and the Study of Wartime Sexual Violence," *European Journal of International Relations* 19(4) (2013): 797–821; Young, "The Logic of Masculinist Protection;" Peterson, "Sexing Political Identities."

74 Peterson, "Gendered Identities, Ideologies, and Practices."

75 Sjoberg, *Gendering Global Conflict*, chs.7, 8. See also Cynthia Weber, "Flying Planes Can Be Dangerous," *Millennium: Journal of International Studies* 31(2) (2002): 129–147; Wilcox, "Gendering the Cult of the Offensive."

76 McClintock, "Family Feuds"; McClintock, *Imperial Leather*; Pettman, *Worlding Women*; Nira Yuval-Davis, *Gender and Nation* (London: Sage, 1997); Sjoberg and Peet, "A(nother) Dark Side."

77 See, e.g., discussion in Sjoberg, *Gendering Global Conflict*.

78 "Where are the women?" is Cynthia Enloe's trademark question—she forms research methodologies around asking where women are in global politics, what they do, and what happens to them. See, e.g., extended discussion in Enloe, *The Curious Feminist*.

79 Tickner, *Gender in International Relations*; Tickner, *Gendering World Politics*; Young, "The Logic of Masculinist Protection."

80 Hynes, "On the Battlefield of Women's Bodies"; Cohn, *Women and Wars*; Lorentzen and Turpin, eds., *Women and War Reader*, especially Cynthia Enloe's chapter, "All the Men Are in the Militias, All the Women Are Victims: The Politics of Masculinity and Feminity in Nationalist Wars," pp.50–62.

81 Enloe, "All the Men"; Young, "The Logic of Masculinist Protection"; Paul Higate and John Hopton, "War, Militarism, and Masculinities," in Michael S. Kimmel, Jeff Hearn, and Raewyn Connell, eds., *Handbook of Studies on Men and Masculinities* (London: Sage, 2005); Peterson, "Gendered Identities, Ideologies, and Practices."

82 Peterson, "Gendered Identities, Ideologies, and Practices"; V. Spike Peterson, "Sexing Political Identities"; see discussions in empirical work like Spyros A. Sofos, "Inter-Ethnic Violence and Gendered Constructions of Ethnicity in Former Yugoslavia," *Social Identities: Journal for the Study of Race, Nation, and Culture* 2(1) (1996): 73–92; Goldstein, *War and Gender*.

83 1948 Convention on the Prevention and Punishment of Genocide, Articles II and III.

84 Ibid., Article III.

85 Raphael Lemkin, *Axis Rule in Occupied Europe* (Washington, DC: Carnegie Institute for International Peace, 1944), p.179. See also, e.g., Raphael Lemkin, "Genocide as a Crime under International Law," *American Journal of International Law* 41(1) (1947): 145–151; Raphael Lemkin, "Genocide," *American Scholar* 15(2) (1946): 227–230; Daniel Marc Segesser and Myriam Gessler, "Raphael Lemkin and the International Debate on the Punishment of War Crimes (1919–1948)," *Journal of Genocide Research* 7(4) (2005): 453–468.

86 See, e.g., John Webb, "Genocide Treaty-Ethnic Cleansing-Substantive and Procedural Hurdles in the Application of the Genocide Convention to Alleged Crimes in the Former Yugoslavia," *Georgia Journal of International and Comparative Law* 23 (1993): 377–408; William A. Schabas, "Was Genocide Committed in Bosnia and Herzegovina? First Judgments of the International Criminal Tribunal for the Former Yugoslavia," *Fordham International Law Journal* 25 (2001–2002): 23–94; Thomas Cushman and Stjepan G. Meštrović, eds., *This Time We Knew: Western Responses to Genocide in Bosnia* (New York: New York University Press, 1996).

87 See, e.g., Gérard Prunier, *The Rwanda Crisis: History of a Genocide* (New York: Columbia University Press, 1995); Alison DesForges, *Leave None to Tell the Story: Genocide in Rwanda* (New York: Human Rights Watch, 1999); Alain Destexhe, *Rwanda and Genocide in the Twentieth Century* (London: Pluto Press, 1995); Helen M. Hintjens, "Explaining the 1994 Genocide in Rwanda," *Journal of Modern African Studies* 37(2) (1999): 241–286; Payam Akhavan, "The International Criminal Tribunal for Rwanda: The Politics and Pragmatics of Punishment," *American Journal of International Law* 90(3) (1996): 501–510; Philip Gourevitch, *We Wish to Inform You that Tomorrow We Will Be Killed with Our Families: Stories from Rwanda* (New York: Farrar, Straus, and Giroux, 1998).

88 *The Prosecutor Versus Jean-Paul Akayesu*, Case No. ICTR-96-4-T, decided 2 September 1998. See discussion in Jose E. Alvarez, "Lessons from the Akayesu Judgment," *ILSA Journal of International and Comparative Law* 5 (1998–1999): 359–370.

89 Also in *Akayesu* case. See discussion in Valerie Oosterveld, "Gender-Sensitive Justice and the International Criminal Tributnal for Rwanda: Lessons Learned for the International Criminal Court," *New England Journal of International and Comparative Law* 12 (2005–2006): 119–134; Copelon, "Gender Crimes as War Crimes"; Alex Obote-Odora, "Rape and Sexual Violence in International Law: ICTR Contribution," *New England Journal of International and Comparative Law* 12 (2005–2006): 135–160.

90 The United States Congress, followed by Secretary of State Colin Powell and President G. W. Bush, used the term in reference to Darfur. See discussion in Scott Straus, "Darfur and the Genocide Debate," *Foreign Affairs*, January–February 2006, www.foreignaffairs.com.

91 See, for introduction, Samuel Totten and Paul R. Bartop, *The Genocide Studies Reader* (Abingdon: Routledge, 2009); Donald Bloxham and A. Dirk Moses, *The Oxford Handbook of Genocide Studies* (Oxford: Oxford University Press, 2010).

92 See www.genocidescholars.org, the site of the International Association of Genocide Scholars, which was founded as the Association of Genocide Scholars in 1994.

93 See, e.g., the International Institute for Genocide and Human Rights Studies
(www.genocidestudies.org), Yale Genocide Studies Program (www.yale.edu/gsp/),
Montreal Institute for Genocide and Human Rights Studies at Concordia Univer-
sity (http://migs.concordia.ca), Institute for Holocaust, Genocide, and Memory
Studies at the University of Massachusetts-Amherst (www.umass.edu/ihgms/),
NIOD Institute for War-, Holocaust and Genocide Studies with the University
of Amsterdam (www.niod.nl/en), Center for the Study of Genocide and Human
Rights at Rutgers University (www.ncas.rutgers.edu/cghr), Danish Center for Holocaust and Genocide Studies (www.holocaust-education.dk), and Institute for the
Study of Genocide (www.studyofgenocide.org). Certainly this list is incomplete,
and biased towards available English-language resources, but gives a sense of the
development of a critical mass of scholarly/political interest in naming, understanding, and combatting genocide.

94 L. Edward Day and Margaret Vandiver, "Criminology and Genocide Studies:
Notes on What Might Have Been and What Still Could Be," *Crime, Law, and
Social Change* 34 (2000): 43–59.

95 Herbert C. Kelman, "Violence without Moral Restraint: Reflections on the Dehu-
manization of Victims and Victimizers," *Journal of Social Issues* 29(4) (1973): 25–61;
Herbet C. Kelman and V. Lee Hamilton, *Crimes of Obedience: Toward a Social
Psychology of Authority and Responsibility* (New Haven, CT: Yale University Press).

96 Daniel Jonah Goldhagen, *Hitler's Willing Executioners: Ordinary Germans and the
Holocaust* (New York: Random House, 1996).

97 R. J. Rummel, *Death by Government* (New Brunswick, NJ: Transaction Publishers,
1997); R. J. Rummel, *Democide: Nazi Genocide and Mass Murder* (New Brunswick,
NJ: Transaction Publishers, 1992); R. J. Rummel, "Democracy, Power, Genocide,
and Mass Murder," *Journal of Conflict Resolution* 39(1) (1995): 3–26.

98 The disciplines incorporated here are of course partial and biased towards
literatures with which the author is familiar; disciplines like health sciences and
psychology are admittedly under-covered.

99 E.g., John Hagan and Ron Levi, "Crimes of War and the force of Law," *Social
Forces* 83(4) (2005): 1499–1534; Joachim Savelsberg, *Crime and Human Rights:
Criminology of Genocide and Atrocities* (London: Sage, 2010); Joachim Savelsberg
and Ryan King, *American Memories: Atrocities and the Law* (New York: Russell
Sage Foundation, 2011); Alex Alvarez, *Genocidal Crimes* (London: Routledge,
2009).

100 E.g., Frank Chalk and Kurt Jonassohn, *The History and Sociology of Genocide*
(New Haven: Yale University Press, 1990); Eric Markusen and David Kopf, *The
Holocaust and Strategic Bombing: Genocide and Total War in the 20th Century*
(Boulder, CO: Westview Press, 1995); Helen Fein, *Genocide: A Sociological Per-
spective* (London: Sage, 1993); Zygmunt Bauman, *Modernity and the Holocaust*
(Ithaca, NY: Cornell University Press, 2000).

101 E.g., George Andreopolous, ed., *Genocide: The Conceptual and Historical Dimensions* (Philadelphia: University of Pennsylvania Press, 1994); Barbara Harff, "No Lessons Learned from the Holocaust? Assessing Risks of Genocide and Political Mass Murder since 1955," *American Political Science Review* 97(1) (2003): 57–73; Toni Erskine, *Can Institutions Have Responsibilities? Collective Moral Agency and International Relations* (New York: Palgrave Macmillan, 2004); Christian Davenport, "State Repression and Political Order," *Annual Review of Political Science* 10(1) (2007): 1–23.

102 E.g., William Schabas, *Genocide in International Law: The Crime of Crimes* (Cambridge: Cambridge University Press, 2000); Vahakn N. Dadrian, "Genocide as a Problem of National and International Law: The World War I Armenian Case and Its Contemporary Legal Ramifications," *Yale Journal of International Law* 14(2) (1989): 221–334; R. J. Strickland, "Genocide-at-Law: An Historic and Contemporary View of the Native American Experience," *University of Kansas Law Review* 34 (1986): 713–756.

103 E.g., Allan D. Cooper, *The Geography of Genocide* (Washington, DC: University Press of America, 2009); James Tyner, *The Killing of Cambodia: Geography, Genocide, and the Unmaking of Space* (Aldershot: Ashgate, 2008); Carl Dahlman, "Geographies of Genocide and Ethnic Cleansing: The Lessons of Bosnia-Herzegovina, in Colin Flint, ed., *The Geography of War and Peace: From Death Camps to Diplomats* (Oxford: Oxford University Press), pp.174–197; Elizabeth Oglesby and Amy Ross, "Guatemala's Genocide Determination and the Spatial Politics of Justice," *Space and Polity* 13(1) (2009): 21–39.

104 This is inspired by Cynthia Enloe's writing of the word "womenandchildren" to explain the conflation of femininity and infantilism in a significant amount of international security discourse. Enloe suggests that the subconscious combining of these two is representative of how they are conceptualized; I want to suggest that it would be dangerous to think of war and genocide in a similarly subconscious combination. That's why there is a section on genocide in this chapter. For full discussion and citation of Enloe's use of this term, see chapter 2, p.85, and n.174.

105 Martin Shaw, *War and Genocide: Organized Killing in Modern Society* (Cambridge, UK: Polity Press, 2003).

106 See, e.g., the characterization in Antonio Cassese, *International Criminal Law* (Oxford: Oxford University Press, 2003).

107 Paul Bartrop, "The Relationship between War and Genocide in the Twentieth Century: A Consideration," *Journal of Genocide Research* 4(4) (2002): 519–532.

108 This characterization can be seen in work as diverse as Donald Dutton, Ehor Boyanowsky, and Michael Harris Bond, "Extreme Mass Homicide: From Military Massacre to Genocide," *Aggression and Violent Behavior* 10(4) (2005): 437–473 (from psychology), and Samantha Power, *"A Problem from Hell": America and the Age of Genocide* (New York: Basic Books, 2002) (from journalism and law).

109 Martin Shaw, "The General Hybridity of War and Genocide," *Journal of Genocide Research* 9(3) (2007): 461–473, p.461.

110 Mahmood Mamdani, "The Politics of Naming: Genocide, Civil War, Insurgency," *London Review of Books* 29(5) (8 March 2007), www.lrb.co.uk.

111 Lisa Sharlach, "Gender and Genocide in Rwanda: Women as Agents and Objects of Genocide," *Journal of Genocide Research* 1(3) (1999): 387–399; Helen Fein, "Genocide and Gender: The Uses of Women and Group Destiny," *Journal of Genocide Research* 1(1) (1999): 43–63; Ronit Lentin, "The Rape of Nation: Women Narrativising Genocide," *Sociological Research Online* 4(2) (1999), http://socresonline.org.uk; Anne McClintock, *Imperial Leather: Race, Gender, and Sexuality in the Colonial Contest* (New York: Routledge, 1995); Rhonda Copelon, "Surfacing Gender: Re-Engraving Crimes Against Women in Humanitarian Law," *Hastings Women's Law Journal* 5 (1994): 243–316.

112 See discussion in Sjoberg, *Gendering Global Conflict*, chs.7, 8.

113 Sjoberg, *Gendering Global Conflict*, pp.194–195, citing Ujala Sehgal, "New Reports of Qaddafi Forces Using Rape as a Weapon of War," *Atlantic Wire*, 29 May 2011, www.theatlanticwire.com; Michelle Faul, "Hundreds of Women Raped by Gaddafi Militia," *Independent*, 29 May 2011, www.independent.co.uk.

114 See, e.g., Lauren Wolfe, "Syria Has a Massive Rape Crisis," *Atlantic*, 3 April 2013, www.theatlantic.com; Lauren Wolfe, "Will There Ever Be Justice for Syria's Rape Survivors?," *Nation*, 14 May 2014, www.thenation.com.

115 See discussions in Antony Beevor, *Berlin: The Downfall 1945* (London: Penguin, 2002); Anonymous, *A Woman in Berlin: Eight Weeks in a Conquered City* (New York: Henry Holt, 2005); Chris Bellamy, *Absolute War: Soviet Russia in the Second World War* (New York: Knopf, 2007); J. W. Messerschmidt, "The Forgotten Victims of World War II: Masculinities and Rape in Berlin, 1945," *Violence against Women* 12(7) (2006): 706–712; Atina Grossman, "A Question of Silence: The Rape of German Women by Occupation Soldiers," *October* 72 (1995): 42–63; Atina Grossman, *Jews, Germans, and Allies: Close Encounters in Occupied Germany* (Princeton, NJ: Princeton University Press, 2009).

116 See, e.g., discussion in Karen F. Pierce and Susan Deacy, eds. *Rape in Antiquity: Sexual Violence in the Greek and Roman Worlds* (London: Bloomsbury Academic, 2002).

117 For discussions of occurrences of sexual violence in war and conflict, see, e.g., Andrea Stiglmayer, ed., *Mass Rape: The War against Women in Bosnia-Herzegovina* (Lincoln: University of Nebraska Press, 1994); Sondra Hale, "Rape as a Marker and Eraser of Difference: Darfur and the Nuba Mountains (Sudan)," in Sjoberg and Via, *Gender, War, and Militarism*, pp.105–113; Takahasi Yoshida, *The Making of the "Rape of Nanking": History and Memory in Japan, China, and the United States* (New York: Oxford University Press, 2006), p.267; Grossman, "A Question of Silence"; W. Andy Knight and Tanya Narozhna, "Rape and Other War Crimes in Chechnya: Is There a Role for the International Criminal Court?," *Spaces of Identity* 5(1) (2005): 89–100; Catherine MacKinnon, "Rape, Genocide, and Women's Human Rights," *Harvard Women's Law Journal* 17(1) (1994): 5–16; Lisa Sharlach, "Rape as Genocide: Bangladesh, the Former

Yugoslavia, and Rwanda," *New Political Science* 22(1) (2000): 89–102; Hansen, "Gender, Nation, Rape."

118 Gardam, "Gender and Non-Combatant Immunity," pp.358–359; Schott, "War Rape, Social Death, and Political Evil."

119 Card, "Genocide and Social Death."

120 Sjoberg, *Gendering Global Conflict*, p.218.

121 Stjepen Gabriel Metrovic, *The Balkanization of the West: The Confluence of Postmodernism and Postcommunism* (London and New York: Routledge, 1999), p.x; cited in Skjelsbaek, "Sexual Violence and War," p.225.

122 Wilcox, "Gendering the Cult of the Offensive," discussing rape as national humiliation; Sjoberg and Peet, "A(nother) Dark Side," discussing rape as a signifier of conquest; Debra Bergoffen, "Exploiting the Dignity of the Vulnerable Body: Rape as a Weapon of War," *Philosophical Papers* 38(3) (2009): 307–325; Anne McClintock, "Family Feuds: Gender, Nationalism, and the Family," *Feminist Review* 44 (Summer 1993): 61–80; Pettman, *Worlding Women*, discussing rape as a tool of feminization; Card, "Genocide and Social Death," discussing rape as a tool of extermination.

123 Todd Salzman, "Rape Camps as a Means of Ethnic Cleansing: Religious, Cultural, and Ethical Responses to Rape Victims in the Former Yugoslavia" *Human Rights Quarterly* 20(2) (1998): 348–378; Hansen, "Gender, Nation, Rape," p.59.

124 Gardam, "Gender and Non-Combatant Immunity," pp.358–359.

125 MacKinnon, *Sex Equality*, p.897; Richard J. Goldstone, "Prosecuting Rape as a War Crime," *Case Western Reserve Journal of International Law* 34 (2007): 277. For a more skeptical view, see Katie C. Richey, "Several Steps Sideways: International Legal Developments Concerning War Rape and the Human Rights of Women," *Texas Journal of Women and the Law* 17 (2007–2008): 109–129.

126 Francis Pilch, "Rape as Genocide: The Legal Response to Sexual Violence," Working Paper, Center for Global Security and Democracy, Rutgers University (2002), *Columbia International Affairs Online*, www.ciaonet.org.

127 Christine Chinkin, "Rape and Sexual Abuse of Women in International Law," *European Journal of International Law* 5 (1996): 326–241.

128 For example, United Nations Security Council Resolution 1325 (S/Res/2001/1325); United Nations Security Council Resolution 1820 (S/Res/2008/1820); United Nations Security Council Resolution 1888 (S/Res/2009/1888); United Nations Security Council Resolution 1889 (S/Res/2009/1889); United Nations Security Council Resolution 1960 (S/Res/2010/1960).

129 Siobhan Fisher, "Occupation of the Womb: Forced Impregnation as Genocide," *Duke Law Journal* 46(1) (1996): 91–133.

130 See discussion in Sjoberg, *Gender, War, and Conflict*.

131 *Kadic v. Karadzic*, 70 F.3d 232 (2d Cir. 1995).

132 *Prosecutor v. Akayesu*, Case No. ICTR 96 4 T (1998), 694.

133 *Akayesu*, ICTR 96 4 T, 694, 731.

134 Sjoberg, *Gendering Global Conflict*, p.196, citing Pettman, *Worlding Women*.

135 See note 1, this chapter.

136 Sjoberg, *Gendering Global Conflict*, p.224.

137 Enloe, *Bananas, Beaches, and Bases*, p.38.

138 Sjoberg, *Gendering Global Conflict*, p.224.

CHAPTER 2. MAN-TO-MAN COMMUNICATION

1 Cindy S. Snyder, Wesley J. Gabbard, J. Dean May, and Nihada Zulcic, "On the Battlegrounds of Women's Bodies: Mass Rape in Bosnia-Herzegovina," *Affilia* 21(2) (2006): 184–195, p.190.

2 Todd Salzman, "Rape Camps as a Means of Ethnic Cleansing: Religious, Cultural, and Ethical Responses to Rape Victims in the Former Yugoslavia," *Human Rights Quarterly* 20(2) (1998): 348–378, p.349.

3 Enloe, *Nimo's War, Emma's War*; Jean Bethke Elshtain, *Women and War* (Chicago: University of Chicago Press, 1987); Laura Sjoberg, *Gender, Justice, and the Wars in Iraq* (New York: Lexington Books, 2006); Jan Jindy Pettman, *Worlding Women: A Feminist International Politics* (London: Routledge, 1996); Helen Kinsella, *The Image before the Weapon: A Critical History of the Distinction between Combatant and Civilian* (Ithaca, NY: Cornell University Press, 2011); Kinsella, "Gendering Grotius."

4 Kinsella, "Gendering Grotius."

5 Thucydides, *History of the Peloponnesian War*. See extended discussion in Sjoberg, *Gender, War, and Conflict*, pp.26–27.

6 Elshtain, *Women and War*; Jean Bethke Elshtain, "On Beautiful Souls, Just Warriors, and Feminist Consciousness," *Women's Studies International Forum* 5(3) (1982): 341–348; Laura Sjoberg, "The Gendered Realities of the Immunity Principle: Why Gender Analysis Needs Feminism," *International Studies Quarterly* 50(4) (2006): 889–910.

7 Goldstein, *War and Gender*.

8 Sjoberg and Peet, "A(nother) Dark Side," citing Nancy Huston, "Tales of War and Tears of Women," in Judith Stiehm, ed., *Women and Men's Wars* (Oxford: Pergamon Press, 1983), p.279.

9 Concerning 1945 Germany, see discussion in Sjoberg, *Gendering Global Conflict*, p.204–205, citing James W. Messerschmidt, "The Forgotten Victims of World War II: Masculinities and Rape in Berlin, 1945," *Violence against Women* 12(7) (2006): 706–712; Beevor, *Berlin: The Downfall 1945*; Anita Grossman, "A Question of Silence: The Rape of German Women by Occupation Soldiers," *October* 72 (1995): 43–63. Concerning the United States War on Terror, in summer 2014 as it appeared that ISIS/Daesh would consolidate control of Iraq, a number of news outlets focused their attention on restrictions on women's freedoms, women's suicides as a result of sexual violence, and the inability of the moderate government of Iraq to protect its women and children (e.g., Rebecca Col-

lard, "Thousands of Iraqis Flee to Kurdish Territory to Escape Unrest," *Time*, 13 June 2014, http://time.com ; Jessica Elgot, "11 Terrifying New Laws ISIS Will Impose on Its Iraq Caliphate," *Huffington Post UK*, 13 June 2014, www. huffingtonpost.co.uk). The mention of women in each of these pieces (and dozens more) is in a context that suggests that the danger of *losing* the war to the enemy is at least in part the danger that the enemy will violate the women the war was fought to protect.

10 See, e.g., Enloe, *Does Khaki Become You?*; Enloe, *Nimo's War, Emma's War*; Katharine Moon, *Sex among Allies: Military Prostitution in US-Korea Relations* (New York: Columbia University Press, 1997); Denise Horn, "Boots and Bedsheets: Constructing the Military Support System in a Time of War," in Sjoberg and Via, *Gender, War, and Militarism*, pp.57–68.

11 See, e.g., the American Revolution, where the Quartering Act of 1774 made explicit what had been common practice for several years: when British soldiers announced that they were going to stay in people's homes in North America, it was not optional to decline; instead, the soldiers were to be provided with food, shelter, entertainment, and medical care. Josh Dugan takes a contemporary look at the involved legal questions in "When Is a Search Not a Search? When It's a Quarter: The Third Amendment, Originalism, and NSA Wiretapping," *Georgetown Law Journal* 97 (2008–2009): 555–588. Quartering was not a uniquely New World practice, however, as is explained in Andre Corvisier, *Armies and Societies in Europe, 1494–1789*, trans. Abigail T. Siddall (Bloomington: Indiana University Press, 1979).

12 See, e.g., Holly A. Mayer, *Belonging to the Army: Camp Followers and Community During the American Revolution* (Columbia: University of South Carolina Press, 1999); Linda Grant de Pauw, "Women in Combat: The Revolutionary War Experience," *Armed Forces and Society* 7(2) (1981): 209–226; Sondra Albano, "Military Recognition of Family Concerns: Revolutionary War to 1993," *Armed Forces and Society* 20(2) (1993): 283–302; Megan MacKenzie, "Securitization and Desecuritization: Female Soldiers and the Reconstruction of Women in Post-Conflict Sierra Leone," *Security Studies* 18(2) (2009): 241–261.

13 Miranda Alison, "Wartime Sexual Violence: Women's Human Rights and Questions of Masculinity," *Review of International Studies* 33(1) (2007): 75–90; Miriam Cooke, "Saving Brown Women," *Signs: Journal of Women in Culture and Society* 28(1) (2002): 468–470; Gayatri Spivak, "Can the Subaltern Speak? Speculations on Widow Sacrifice," *Wedge* 7–8 (Winter/Spring 1985): 120–130; Yasmin Jiwani, "Gendering Terror: Representations of the Orientalized Body in Quebec's Post-September 11 English-Language Press," *Critique: Critical Middle Eastern Studies* 13(3) (2003): 265–291.

14 Huston, "Tales of War"; Wibben, *Feminist Security Studies*; Dana L. Cloud, "'To Veil the Threat of Terror': Afghan Women and the <Clash of Civilizations> Imagery of the U. S. War on Terrorism," *Quarterly Journal of Speech* 90(3) (2004): 285–306. See discussion of the complexities of retaliation in Alexander B. Downes,

"Restraint or Propellant? Democracy and Civilian Fatalities in Interstate Wars," *Journal of Conflict Resolution* 51(6) (2007): 872–904.

15 See, e.g., US discourses about the 1991 Gulf War being to protect women (Sjoberg, *Gender, Justice, and the Wars in Iraq*) compared to the U. S. military's sexual violence in that war (Madeline Morris, "By Force of Arms: Rape, War, and Military Culture," *Duke Law Journal* 45[4] [1996]: 651–782). For a non-conflict-specific discussion, see H. Patricia Hynes, "On the Battlefield of Women's Bodies; An Overview of the Harm of War to Women," *Women's Studies International Forum* 27(5–6) (2004): 431–445.

16 See, e.g., Enloe, *The Curious Feminist*.

17 Tickner, *Gender in International Relations*; Tickner, *Gendering World Politics*; Young, "Logic of Masculinist Protection."

18 Hynes, "On the Battlefield of Women's Bodies"; Cohn, *Women and Wars*; Lorentzen and Turpin, eds., *Women and War Reader*, especially Enloe, "All the Men."

19 Enloe, "All the Men"; Young, "The Logic of Masculinist Protection"; Higate and Hopton, "War, Militarism, and Masculinities"; Peterson, "Gendered Identities, Ideologies, and Practices."

20 Examples of books about the things *women do* that differ from the things *men do* include: Michael A. Genovese and Janie S. Steckenrider, *Women as Political Leaders: Studies in Gender and Governing* (London: Routledge, 2013); Eileen McDonagh, *The Motherless State: Women's Political Leadership and American Democracy* (Chicago: University of Chicago Press, 2009) (addressing political leadership); Robin Morgan, *The Demon Lover: Roots of Terrorism*, 2d ed. (New York: Simon and Schuster, 2010); Luisella de Cataldo Neuburger and Jo Campling, *Women and Terrorism* (London: Palgrave Macmillan, 1996) (addressing participation in "terrorism").

21 Sita Balthazar, "Gender Crimes and the International Criminal Tribunals," *Gonzaga Journal of International Law* 10(1) (2006–2007): 43–48, p.46. See also Danna Harman, "A Woman on Trial for Rwanda's Massacre," *Christian Science Monitor*, 7 March 2003, www.csmonitor.com.

22 Balthazar, "Gender Crimes," p.47.

23 The information quoting Nyiramasuhuko is found in Linda Melvern, *Conspiracy to Murder: Planning the Rwandan Genocide* (London: Verso, 2004); see also Stephanie K. Wood, "A Woman Scorned for the 'Least Condemned' War Crime: Precedent and Problems with Prosecuting Rape as a Serious War Crime in the International Criminal Tribunal for Rwanda," *Columbia Journal of Gender & Law* 13(2) (2004): 274–327.

24 Peter Landesman, "A Woman's Work," *New York Times Magazine*, 15 September 2002, www.nytimes.com.

25 "Rwanda: Ex-Women's Minister Guilty of Genocide, Rape," *BBC News Africa*, 24 June 2011, www.bbc.co.uk. A Google search for Nyiramasuhuko finds 317,000 results, more than 50 percent of which are distinct news stories about her crimes, her trial, and her conviction. As cited in this section and throughout

this book, a number of legal and social science scholarly articles (to my count, more than three hundred) deal with Nyiramasuhuko with a paragraph or more analysis.

26 See, e.g., Joseph Hazeley, "Profile: Female Rwandan Killer Pauline Nyiramasuhuko," *BBC News Africa*, 24 June 2011, www.bbc.com; Sukhdev Chhatbar, "Pauline Nyiramasuhuko: Rwandan Woman and First Ever Convicted of Genocide, Given Life Sentence," *Huffington Post/Associated Press*, 24 June 2011, www.huffingtonpost.com.

27 Mark A. Drumbl, "She Makes Me Ashamed to Be a Woman: The Genocide Conviction of Pauline Nyiramasuhuko, 2011," *Michigan Journal of International Law* 34(3) (2013): 559–603, pp.562–603.

28 See Sjoberg and Gentry, *Mothers, Monsters, Whores*; Sjoberg, "Women and the Genocidal Rape of Women." Drumbl, in "She Makes Me Ashamed," notes the importance of understanding the different ways that gender essentialisms were used on both "sides" of both the media coverage and the trial, where those with a political interest in Nyiramasuhuko appearing innocent invoked stereotypes of feminine and maternal peacefulness, while those with a political interest in her appearing guilty emphasized the terrors of femininity gone wrong and the horrors of woman-on-woman crime.

29 See, e.g., discussion in Laura Sjoberg and Caron Gentry, "Reduced to Bad Sex: Narratives of Violent Women from the Bible to the War on Terror," *International Relations* 22(1) (2008): 5–23, especially as it discusses the apparent flaws in female sexuality that might lead to extreme violence.

30 Alexandra A. Miller, "From the International Criminal Tribunal for Rwanda to the International Criminal Court: Expanding the Definition of Genocide to Include Rape," *Penn State Law Review* 108(1) (2003): 349–374, p.350.

31 Drumbl, "She Makes Me Ashamed," p.563.

32 Carrie Sperling, "Mother of All Atrocities: Pauline Nyiramasuhuko's Role in the Rwandan Genocide," *Fordham Urban Law Journal* 33(2) (2005): 101–127, p.102.

33 Landesman, "A Woman's Work."

34 Drumbl, "She Makes Me Ashamed," p.563.

35 See discussion in ibid., note 234, p.589.

36 See, e.g., discussion in Nicole Hogg, "Women's Participation in the Rwandan Genocide: Mothers or Monsters," *International Review of the Red Cross* 92(877) (2010): 69–102.

37 Ibid. See also Drumbl, "She Makes Me Ashamed"; Sjoberg and Gentry, *Mothers, Monsters, Whores*; Lisa Sharlach, "Gender and Genocide in Rwanda: Women as Agents and Objects of Genocide," *Journal of Genocide Research* 1(3) (1999): 387–399; Georgina Holmes, "The Postcolonial Politics of Militarizing Rwandan Women: An Analysis of the Extremist Magazine *Kangura* and the Gendering of a Genocidal Nation-State," *Minerva Journal of Women and War* 2(2) (2009): 44–63; Reva N. Adler, Cyanne E. Loyle, and Judith Globerman, "A Calamity in the

Neighborhood: Women's Participation in the Rwandan Genocide," *Genocide Studies and Prevention* 2(3) (2007): 209–233.

38 Drumbl, "She Makes Me Ashamed," citing Hogg, "Women's Participation in the Rwandan Genocide."

39 Philip Gourevitch, "The Arrest of Madame Agathe," *New Yorker*, 2 March 2010, www.newyorker.com; "Rwandan President's Widow Takes France to European Rights Court," *RFI English*, 15 January 2014, www.english.rfi.fr; "France Rejects Rwandan Extradition Request," *Aljazeera English*, 28 September 2011, www. aljazeera.com.

40 E.g., "Consolata Mukangango TrialWatch," *TRIAL*, www.trial-ch.org; "Rwanda Nuns in Genocide Trial," *BBC News*, 17 April 2001, http://news.bbc.co.uk; Leila Fielding, *Female Genocidaires during the Rwandan Genocide: When Women Kill* (Hamburg: Anchor Academic Press, 2013).

41 Hogg, "Women's Participation in the Rwandan Genocide," p.78.

42 See, e.g., discussions in Jennie E. Burnet, "Gender Balance and the Meanings of Women in Governance in Post-Genocide Rwanda," *African Affairs* 107(428) (2008): 361–386; Laura Sjoberg, "Reconstructing Women in Postconflict Rwanda," in Robin M. Chandler, Lihua Wang, and Linda K. Fuller, eds., *Women, War, and Violence: Personal Perspectives and Global Activism* (London: Palgrave MacMillan, 2010), pp.165–181; Judy El-Bushra, "Feminism, Gender, and Women's Peace Activism," *Development and Change* 38(1) (2007): 131–147.

43 A few important exceptions exist. Dara Kay Cohen (in "Female Combatants and the Perpetration of Violence: Wartime Rape in the Sierra Leone Civil War," *World Politics* 65[3] [2013], pp.383–415) suggests that women's motivations for wartime sexual violence, much men's motivations, lie in group pressure (see also Dara Kay Cohen, "Explaining Rape during Civil War: Cross-National Evidence (1980–2009)," *American Political Science Review* 107[3] [2013]: 461–477). Adam Jones (in *Gendercide and Genocide* and "Gender and Genocide in Rwanda," *Journal of Genocide Research* 4[1] [2002]: 65–49) makes the argument that men are targeted sex-specifically, sometimes by women, though I think that his argument is simplistic, and tends to conflate sex and gender.

44 Nicola Henry, Tony Ward, and Matt Hirshberg, "A Multifactoral Model of Wartime Rape," *Aggression and Violent Behavior* 9 (2004): 535–562, pp.536, 543.

45 Ibid., p.547.

46 Ibid., p.555.

47 Lisa S. Price, "Finding the Man in the Soldier-Rapist: Some Reflections on Comprehension and Accountability," *Women's Studies International Forum* 24(2) (2001): 211–227, p.211.

48 Jill Trenholm, Pia Olsson, Martha Blomqvist, and Beth Maina Ahlberg, "Constructing Soldiers from Boys in Eastern Democratic Republic of Congo," *Men and Masculinities* 16(3) (2013): 203–227, p.208.

49 Ibid., p.205.

50 Pascale R. Bos, "Feminists Interpreting the Politics of Wartime Rape: Berlin, 1945; Yugoslavia, 1992–1993," *Signs: Journal of Women in Culture and Society* 31(4) (2006): 995–1025 ("Why do some men or some armies rape, and not others?", p.995); Susan Brownmiller, "Making Female Bodies the Battlefield," in Stiglmayer, *Mass Rape*, pp.180–182 ("once he is handed a rifle and told to kill, the soldier becomes an adrenaline-rushed young man with permission to kick in the door, to grab, to steal, to give vent to his submerged rage against all women *who belong to other men*," p.181); Maria B. Olujic, "Embodiment of Violence: Gendered violence in Peacetime and Wartime in Croatia and Bosnia-Herzegovina," *Medical Anthropology Quarterly* 12(1) (1998): 31–50 ("control of women by men," p.34, and "violation of female honor is a weapon used by the men of one ethnic group against those of another," p.39); Meredeth Turshen, "The Political Economy of Rape: An Analysis of the Systematic Rape and Sexual Abuse of Women during Armed Conflict in Africa," in Caroline Moser and Fiona Clark, eds., *Victims, Perpetrator or Actors: Gender, Armed Conflict and Political Violence* (London: Zed Books, 2001), pp.55–68 ("systematic rape and sexual abuse are among the strategies men use to wrest personal assets from women," p.55); Christoph Schiessl, "An Element of Genocide: Rape, Total War, and International Law in the Twentieth Century," *Journal of Genocide Research* 4(2) (2002): 197–210 ("a group power develops that has no comparison in civilian life, enlarging the power of men alone. Soldiers have to prove their newly won superiority to a woman and her male relatives," p.197); Vesna Nikolic-Ristanovic, "War and Violence against Women," in Jennifer E. Turpin and Lois Ann Lorentzen, eds., *The Gendered New World Order: Militarism, Development and the Environment* (New York: Routledge, 1996) (characterizing the actors in war rape as the man-rapist, the woman-victim, and the man-war adversary of the rapist); Sara Meger, "Rape of the Congo: Understanding Sexual Violence in the Conflict in the Democratic Republic of Congo," *Journal of Contemporary African Studies* 28(2) (2010): 119–135 (rape as a tool to "communicate a message between men," p.121, where "the anxiety experienced by the soldiers when faced with the impossibility of fulfilling their position as 'men' is largely what motivates individual soldiers," p.128); Erin K. Baines, "Body Politics and the Rwandan Crisis," *Third World Quarterly* 24(3) (2003): 479–493 ("rape was used to remind Tutsi women of their proper place, in subservience to Hutu men" as well as "belittling of men by men," p.488); Inger Skjelsbaek, *The Political Psychology of War Rape: Studies from Bosnia and Herzegovina* (London, Routledge: 2011) ("they were targeted with this particular form of violence by men because they were women," p.36); Kathryn Farr, "Extreme War Rape in Today's Civil-War-Torn States: A Contextual and Comparative Analysis," *Gender Issues* 26(1) (2009): 1–41 (suggesting that "men have raped women and girls [and less frequently boys and men] in virtually all wars," p.6, and explaining war rape as a part of a social culture that "promotes aggressive behavior in men, devalues women, degrades 'the feminine' in men or nation-states, and views the raping of women as a part of the spoils of war," p.5).

51 E.g., William F. McKibbin; Todd K. Shackelford, Aaron T. Goetz, and Valerie
G. Starratt, "Why Do Men Rape? An Evolutionary Psychology Perspective,"
Review of General Psychology 12(1) (2008): 86–97; Cheryl Brown Travis, *Evolu-
tion, Gender, and Rape* (Cambridge, MA: MIT Press, 2003); A. Nicholas Groth,
Men Who Rape: The Psychology of the Offender (New York: Basic Books, 2001
[1979]); Martin L. Lalumiere, Grant T. Harris, Vernon L. Quinsey, and Marnie
E. Rice, *The Causes of Rape: Understanding Individual Differences in Male
Propensity for Sexual Aggression* (Washington, DC: American Psychological
Association, 2005).

52 Carter, "Should International Relations Consider Rape a Weapon of War?"

53 Ibid., p.351.

54 Ibid.

55 Ibid., p.356.

56 Ibid., p.359. It is for this reason that Carter argues (following Bulent Diken and
Carsten Bagge Laustsen in "Becoming Abject: Rape as a Weapon of War," *Body
and Society* 11[1] [2005], p.111) that "war rape is perhaps the clearest example of an
asymmetric strategy" (p.350). While I don't disagree with the idea that war rape
is an asymmetric strategy, Carter's lack of gender analysis means that some of the
ways that the strategy is asymmetric (e.g., gendered power) and some of the ways
that the strategy is symmetric (e.g., its widespread use by many sides in many
conflicts) are neglected in the analysis in the article.

57 E.g., R. Charli Carpenter, "Recognizing Gender-Based Violence against Civilian
Men and Boys in Conflict Situations," *Security Dialogue* 37(1) (2006): 83–103.

58 Dubravka Zarkov, "The Body of the Other Man: Sexual Violence and the Con-
struction of Masculinity, Sexuality, and Ethnicity, in Croatian Media," in Moser
and Clark, *Victims, Perpetrator or Actors*, pp.69–81; Sandesh Sivakumaran, "Male/
Male Rape and the 'Taint' of Homosexuality," *Human Rights Quarterly* 27(4)
(2005): 1274–1306; Sandesh Sivakumaran, "Sexual Violence against Men in Armed
Conflict," *European Journal of International Law* 18(2) (2007): 253–276; Sarah
Solangon and Preeti Patel, "Sexual Violence against Men in Countries Affected by
Armed Conflict," *Conflict, Security & Development* 12(4) (2012): 417–442; Janine
Natalya Clark, "A Crime of Identity: Rape and Its Neglected Victims," *Journal of
Human Rights* 13(2) (2014): 146–169.

59 Ruth Seifert, "War and Rape: Analytical Approaches," Women's International
League for Peace and Freedom, 1992, www.wilpf.int.ch.

60 Ibid.

61 Kirby, "How Is Rape a Weapon of War?," p.800, citing Zillah Eisenstein, *Sexual
Decoys: Gender, Race, and War in Imperial Democracy* (London: Zed Books,
2007); Elshtain, *Women and War*; Cynthia Enloe, "Margins, Silences, and Bottom
Rungs: How to Overcome the Underestimation of Power in the Study of International Relations," in Steve Smith, Ken Booth, and Marysia Zalewski, eds., *International Theory: Positivism and Beyond* (Cambridge, UK: Cambridge University
Press, 1996), pp.196–202; Carol Harrington, *Politicization of Sexual Violence: From*

Abolitionism to Peacekeeping (London: Ashgate, 2010); Patricia Owens, "Distinctions, Distractions: 'Public' and 'Private' Force?" *International Affairs* 84(5) (2008): 977–990.

62 Hansen, "Gender, Nation, Rape," p.60.

63 Ibid., p.62.

64 Ibid., p.60.

65 Kirby, "How Is Rape a Weapon of War?," p.811, citing Dibyesh Anand, "'Porno-Nationalism' and the Male Subject," in Jane L. Parpart and Marysia Zalewski, eds., *Rethinking the Man Question: Sex, Gender, and Violence in International Relations* (London: Zed Books, 2008), pp.163–180; Megan MacKenzie, "Securitizing Sex? Towards a Theory of the Utility of Wartime Sexual Violence," *International Feminist Journal of Politics* 12(2) (2010): 202–221; Dubravka Zarkov, *The Body of War; Media, Ethnicity, and Gender in the Break-Up of Yugoslavia* (Durham, NC: Duke University Press, 2007).

66 Anna Maedi, "Rape as a Weapon of War in the Eastern DRC?," *Human Rights Quarterly* 33(1) (2011): 128–147, p.128.

67 Ibid., p.140.

68 MacKinnon, "Rape, Genocide and Women's Human Rights," pp.10, 11.

69 Maria Eriksson Baaz and Maria Stern, "Why Do Soldiers Rape? Masculinity, Violence, and Sexuality in the Armed Forces in the Congo (DRC)," *International Studies Quarterly* 53(4) (2009): 495–517.

70 Ibid., p.496.

71 Ibid., p.505.

72 Ibid., pp.495–496, citing MONUC (United Nations Organization Mission in the DRC) data

73 Kirby, "How Is Rape a Weapon of War?," p.800, citing Donna Pankhurst, "Sexual Violence in War," in Shepherd, ed., *Gender Matters in Global Politics*, pp.148–160, 152–156.

74 Skjelsbaek, "Sexual Violence and War."

75 Ibid., p.807, citing Doris Buss, "Rethinking 'Rape as a Weapon of War,'" *Feminist Legal Studies* 17(2) (2009): 145–163.

76 Ibid., p.808, citing Card, "Rape as a Weapon of War."

77 Ibid., p.809.

78 Ibid., citing Philippe Bourgois, "The Everyday Violence of Gang Rape," in Nancy Scheper-Huges and Philippe Bourgois, eds., *Violence in War and Peace: An Anthology* (Oxford: Blackwell, 2003), pp.343–347; Goldstein, *War and Gender*; Matthias Bjornlund, "'A Fate Worse than Dying': Sexual Violence During the Armenian Genocide," in Dagmar Herzog, ed., *Brutality and Desire: War and Sexuality in Europe's Twentieth Century* (Basingstoke: Palgrave Macmillan, 2008), pp.16–58.

79 Baaz and Stern, "Why Do Soldiers Rape?," p.498, citing Chris Horwood, *The Shame of War: Sexual Violence against Women and Girls in Conflict* (Malta: OCHA/IRIN, 2007); George Kassimeris, ed., *The Barbarization of Warfare* (London: C. Hurst & Co, 2006).

80 Chinkin, "Rape and Sexual Abuse of Women in International Law," p.331, citing Theodor Meron, "Shakespeare's Henry the Fifth and the Law of War," *American Journal of International Law* 86(1) (1992): 1–45; Theodor Meron, "Rape as a Crime under International Humanitarian Law," *American Journal of International Law* 87(3) (1993): 424–428.

81 Obote-Odora, "Rape and Sexual Violence in International Law," p.135; Christin B. Coan, "Rethinking the Spoils of War: Prosecuting Rape as a War Crime in the International Criminal Tribunal for the Former Yugoslavia," *North Carolina Journal of International Law and Comparative Regulation* 26(2) (2000–2001): 183–237; Patricia Viseur Sellers and Kaoru Okuizumi, "Intentional Prosecution of Sexual Assaults," *Transnational Law and Contemporary Problems* 7(1) (1997): 45–80; Jocelyn Campanaro, "Women, War, and International Law: The Historical Treatment of Gender-Based War Crimes," *Georgetown Law Journal* 89(4) (2000–2001): 2557–2592.

82 Chinkin, "Rape and Sexual Abuse of Women," p.330.

83 Patricia Viseur Sellers, "Sexual Violence and Peremptory Norms: The Legal Value of Rape," *Case Western Reserve Law Review* 34(2) (2002): 287–303, discussed in David S. Mitchell, "The Prohibition of Rape in International Humanitarian Law as a Norm of *Jus Cogens*: Clarifying the Doctrine," *Duke Journal of Comparative and international Law* 15(2) (2005): 219–258, p.219.

84 E.g., Kathleen Daly and Brigette Bouhours, "Rape and Attrition in the Legal Process: A Comparative Analysis of Five Countries," *Crime and Justice* 39(1) (2010): 565–650.

85 Chinkin, "Rape and Sexual Abuse of Women," p.335.

86 Ibid.

87 Ibid., citing 28 USC para. 1350; 28 USC para. 1331 (Alien Tort Claims Act), Pub. L. No. 102-256, 106 Stat. 78 (1992) (Torture Victim Protection Act), and *Kadic v. Radovan Karadzic*, Civil Action No. 43, CN 1163, United States District Court, Southern District of New York; *Jane Doe I and Jane Doe II v. Radovan Karadzic*, Civil Action No. 93 Civ. 0878 PKL, United States District Court, Southern District of New York. In that case, a default judgment was issued against an absent defendant. A case from Bosnia also went to the International Court of Justice (see discussion in Elizabeth A. Kohn, "Rape as a Weapon of War: Women's Human Rights during the Dissolution of Yugoslavia," *Golden Gate University Law Review* 24[1] [1994]: 199–222).

88 Geneva Convention Relative to the Protection of Civilian Persons in Time of War (1949), pp.287–288, discussed in Nancy Farwell, "War Rape: New Conceptualizations and Responses," *Affilia* 19(4) (2004): 389–403, p.391. Relevant and related sections include Convention for the Amelioration of the Condition of the Wounded and Sick in Armed Forces in the Field, 75 UNTS 31; Convention for the Amelioration of the Condition of the Wounded, Sick and Shipwrecked Members of Armed Forces at Sea, 75 UNTS 85; Convention Relative to the Treatment of Prisoners of War, 75 UNTS 135; Convention Relative to the Protection of Civilian

Persons in Time of War, 75 UNTS 287, all at Geneva, 12 August 1949. Relevant updates include Protocol Additional to the Geneva Conventions of 12 August 1949, and Relating to the Protection of Victims of International Armed Conflicts (Protocol I); Protocol Additional to the Geneva Conventions of 12 August 1949, and Relating to the Protection of Victims of Non-International Armed Conflicts (Protocol 11), Geneva, 8 June 1977, Charter of the International Military Tribunal for the Far East, 19 January 1946, amended 26 April1946, TIAS 1589.

89 Chinkin, "Rape and Sexual Abuse of Women," pp.331–332, citing Natalie Kaufman Hevener, "An Analysis of Gender Based Treaty Law: Contemporary Developments in Historical Perspective," *Human Rights Quarterly* 8(1) (1986): 70–88. Hevener suggests that this provision is protective, when it should be enumerating rights, and suggests that the error is an active harm to women.

90 Gay McDougall, *Contemporary Forms of Slavery: Systematic Rape, Sexual Slavery, and Slavery-Like Practices in Armed Conflict* (E/CN.4/Sub.22/1993/13) (Geneva: UN Sub-Commission on Prevention of Discrimination and Protection of Minorities, 1998), pp.4–5.

91 Chinkin, "Rape and Sexual Abuse of Women," p.334.

92 Ibid., p.331, citing, for example, the Charter Annexed to the Agreement for the Establishment of an International Military Tribunal, 5 UNTS 251, Article 6 included "murder, ill-treatment or deportation to slave labour . . . of civilian population of or in occupied territory, . . . killing of hostages, plunder of public or private property, wanton destruction of cities, towns or villages, or devastation not justified by military necessity."

93 Chinkin, "Rape and Sexual Abuse of Women," p.332.

94 See, e.g., discussion of Nuremburg in Chinkin, "Rape and Sexual Abuse of Women," p.334, citing Jeri Laber, "Bosnia: Questions about Rape," *New York Review of Books* 40 (25 March 1993); Brownmiller, *Against Our Will*, pp.43–78.

95 Magdalini Karagiannakis, "Case Analysis: The Definition of Rape and Its Characterization as an Act of Genocide—A Review from the Jurisprudence of the International Criminal Tribunals for Rwanda and the Former Yugoslavia," *Leiden Journal of International Law* 12(2) (1999): 479–490, p.483, citing *Prosecutor v. Anto Furundzija*, Judgment, Case No. IT-95-17/1-T, T, ch.11, 10 December 1998, paras. 177–178.

96 Chinkin, "Rape and Sexual Abuse of Women," p.334.

97 UNSC Resolution 808 and 827 set up ICTY and UNSC Resolution 955 set up ICTR.

98 J. R. McHenry III, "The Prosecution of Rape under International Law: Justice That Is Long Overdue," *Vanderbilt Journal of Transnational Law* 35(4) (2002): 1249–1312.

99 Jennifer L. Green, "Uncovering Collective Rape: A Comparative Study of Political Sexual Violence," *International Journal of Sociology* 34(1) (2004): 97–116, p.100.

100 *Prosecutor v. Akayesu*, Case No. ICTR 96 4 T (1998).

101 *Akayesu*, ICTR 96 4 T, 694.

102 *Kadic v. Karadzic*, 70 F.3d 232 (2d Cir. 1995).

103 Catharine A. MacKinnon, "Rape, Genocide and Women's Human Rights," in Stiglmayer, *Mass Rape*, p. 190; discussed in Robin May Schott, "War Rape, Natality, and Genocide," *Journal of Genocide Research* 13(1–2) (2011): 5–21, p.8.

104 *Akayesu*, ICTR 96 4 T, 694, p.731.

105 Daniel Franklin, "Failed Rape Prosecutions at the International Criminal Tribunal for Rwanda," *Georgetown Journal of Gender and the Law* 9(1) (2008): 181–214, p.182.

106 Ibid., citing *Prosecutor v. Semanza*, Case No. ICTR-97–20-T, Judgment and Sentence (May 15, 2003). See also Kirsten Campbell, "Rape as a Crime against Humanity: Trauma and Justice in the International Criminal Tribunal for the former Yugoslavia," *Journal of Human Rights* 2(4) (2003): 507–515; Debra Bergoffen, "Toward a Politics of the Vulnerable Body," *Hypatia* 18(1) (2003): 116–134; Katie C. Richey, "Several Steps Sideways: International Legal Developments Concerning War Rape and the Human Rights of Women," *Texas Journal of Women and the Law* 17(1) (2007): 109–129, p.113; Obote-Odora, "Rape and Sexual Violence in International Law," p.152.

107 Ibid., p.188; Chiseche Salome Mibenge, *Sex and International Tribunals: The Erasure of Gender from the War Narrative* (Philadelphia: University of Pennsylvania Press, 2013).

108 See Franklin, "Failed Rape Prosecutions," for discussions of narrowed definitions of rape (p.194), burden of proof issues (p.192), issues with overgeneral allegations (pp.196, 207), issues with evidence of agency (p.196), discomfort with evidence of leadership (p.198), lack of eyewitnesses (p.199), witnesses that weren't credible (p.199), and pleas of guilt to other charges (p.207).

109 Richey, "Several Steps Sideways," p.117.

110 Ibid.

111 Ibid.

112 Ibid.

113 Doris E. Buss, "The Curious Visibility of Wartime Rape: Gender and Ethnicity in International Criminal Law," *Windsor Yearbook of Access to Justice* 25(1) (2007): 3–22, p.4, citing Hilary Charlesworth and Christine Chinkin, *The Boundaries of International Law: A Feminist Analysis* (Manchester, UK: Manchester University Press, 2000); Jutta Joachim, "Shaping the Human Rights Agenda: The Case of Violence Against Women," in Mary K. Meyer and Elisabeth Prugl, eds., *Gender Politics in Global Governance* (Lanham, MD: Rowman & Littlefield, 1999).

114 Chinkin, "Rape and Sexual Abuse of Women," p.337.

115 Ibid.

116 Ibid.

117 Ibid., p.326.

118 Rome Statute of the International Criminal Court, U. N. Doc A/CONF/183.9, 17 July 1998.

119 For a chronological list of state parties, see www.icc-cpi.int/en_menus/asp/
states%20parties/Pages/states%20parties%20_%20chronological%20list.aspx.

120 Preliminary investigations were opened, but concluded without full investigation,
into situations outside of Africa.

121 Kimberly E. Carson, "Reconsidering the Theoretical Accuracy and Prosecutorial
Effectiveness of International Tribunals' *Ad Hoc* Approaches to Conceptualizing
Crimes of Sexual Violence as War Crimes, Crimes Against Humanity, and Acts of
Genocide," *Fordham Urban Law Journal* 39(4) (2011–2012): 1249–1300, p.1274. See,
for a slightly more optimistic perspective, Rana Lehr–Lehnardt, "One Small Step for
Women: Female-Friendly Provisions of the Rome Statute of the International Crimi-
nal Court," *Brigham Young University Journal of Public Law* 16(2) (2002): 317–354.

122 Article 8(2)(b)(xxii) of *Elements of Crimes*. Here, the context of the existence
of armed conflict and the perpetrator's awareness together constitute the ICC's
subject-matter jurisdiction for sexual violence in war and conflict. See discussion
in Coan, "Rethinking the Spoils of War," p.204.

123 Carson, "Reconsidering the Theoretical Accuracy," p.1276, citing the *Women's
Initiative for Gender Justice ICC Gender Report Card 2011*, www.iccwomen.org.

124 Aditi Gorur, "Justice for Victims of Sexual Violence at the ICC?," *Stimson Center
Spotlight*, 5 March 2014, www.stimson.org; Kelly Dawn Askin, "Katanga Judgment
Underlines Need for Stronger ICC Focus on Sexual Violence," *Open Society Justice
Initiative*, 11 March 2014, www.opensocietyfoundations.org.

125 Askin, "Katanga Judgment Underlines Need."

126 Ibid., p.1277, citing Susana SaCouto and Katherine Cleary, "The Importance of
Effective Investigation of Sexual Violence and Gender-Based Crimes at the International Criminal Court," *American University Journal of Gender and Social Policy*
17 (2009): 339–359.

127 Patricia Viseur Sellers, "Gender Strategy Is Not Luxury for International Courts,"
American University Journal of Gender, Social Policy, and the Law 17(2) (2009):
301–326.

128 Buss, "Curious Visibility of Wartime Rape," p.12.

129 Ibid.

130 Ibid.

131 Ibid., p.4.

132 Ibid., p.10. For extended discussion of legal strategies, see Kelly Dawn Askin,
"Prosecuting Wartime Rape and Other Gender-Related Crimes under Inter-
national Law: Extraordinary Advances, Enduring Obstacles," *Berkeley Journal
International Law* 21(2) (2003): 288–349; Askin, "Gender Crimes Jurisprudence."

133 Buss, "Curious Visibility of Wartime Rape," p.10.

134 Ibid., p.22.

135 Ibid., citing Cynthia Enloe, *Maneuvers: The International Politics of Militarizing
Women's Lives* (Berkeley: University of California Press, 2000), p.109.

136 See discussion in Sherrie Russell-Brown, "Rape as an Act of Genocide," *Berkeley
Journal of International Law* 21(2) (2003): 350–374, p.363.

137 Chinkin, "Rape and Sexual Abuse of Women," p.338. She continues: "Suzanne Gibson discusses the examples of how rape of women in France during World War One became 'transformed into a representation of France as an innocent female nation assaulted by a barbaric and brutishly male Germany' and British military conscriptors used the image of 'the Hun' violating their sisters" (citing Gibson, "The Discourse of Sex/War: Thoughts on Catharine MacKinnon's 1993 Oxford Amnesty Lecture," *Feminist Legal Studies* 1[2] [1993]: 170–188).

138 Janet Halley, "Rape in Berlin: Reconsidering the Criminalisation of Rape in the International Law of Armed Conflict," *Melbourne Journal of International Law* 9(1) (2008): 78–124, p.118.

139 Julie Mertus, "Shouting from the Bottom of the Well: The Impact of International Trials for Wartime Rape on Women's Agency," *International Feminist Journal of Politics* 6(1) (2004): 110–128, p.111.

140 Chinkin, "Rape and Sexual Abuse of Women," p.328.

141 Butler, *Frames of War.*

142 "Rwanda: Ex-Women's Minister Guilty."

143 *Prosecutor v. Nyiramasuhuko et al.* decision, ICTR Case No. ICTR-98-42-T, decided 24 June 2011.

144 Ibid.

145 See discussion, e.g., in MacKenzie, "Securitization and Desecuritization," as well as Lauren Vogel, Louise Porter, and Mark Kebbell, "The Roles of Women in Contemporary Political and Revolutionary Conflict: A Thematic Model," *Studies in Conflict and Terrorism* 37(1) (2014): 91–114; Linda Ahall, "The Writing of Heroines: Motherhood and Female Agency in Political Violence," *Security Dialogue* 43(4) (2012): 287–303.

146 Louise du Toit, "Sex Specificity, Rape Law Reform, and the Feminist Quest for Justice," *South African Journal of Philosophy* 31(3) (2012): 465–483, p.465.

147 Mitchell, "The Prohibition of Rape," p.219.

148 Jean Seaton, "New 'Ethnic' Wars and the Media," in Tim Allen and Jean Seaton, eds., *The Media of Conflict: War Reporting and Representations of Ethnic Violence* (London: Zed Books, 1999), citing *Times*, 18 August 1994.

149 E.g., Janie Leatherman, *Sexual Violence in Armed Conflict* (London: Polity, 2011).

150 E.g. Augusta C. Del Zotto, "Weeping Women, Wringing Hands: How the Mainstream Media Stereotyped Women's Experiences in Kosovo," *Journal of Gender Studies* 11(2) (2002): 141–150.

151 Zarkov, *Body of War*, p.3.

152 Ibid.

153 Ibid., p.102.

154 Ibid. Wendy Bracewell (in "Rape in Kosovo: Masculinity and Serbian Nationalism," *Nations and Nationalism* 6[4] [2000]: 563–590) goes further to suggest that the Serbian media was a part of a political effort to use sexual violence to inspire Serbian nationalism when it was latent.

155 Zarkov, *Body of War*, p.3.

156 Ibid., p.125.

157 Hansen, "Gender, Nation, Rape," p.65, citing Beverly Allen, *Rape Warfare: The Hidden Genocide in Bosnia-Herzegovina and Croatia* (Minneapolis: University of Minnesota Press, 1996), pp.29–40; Pettman, *Worlding Women*.

158 Ibid., p.56, citing Allen, *Rape Warfare*; Mirjana Morokvasic, "The Logics of Exclusion: Nationalism, Sexism, and the Yugoslav War," in Nickie Charles and Helen Hintjens, eds., *Gender, Ethnicity, and Political Ideologies* (London: Routledge, 1998), pp.65–90; Penny Stanley, "Reporting of Mass Rape in the Balkans: *Plus Ca Change, Plus C'est Meme Chose?* From Bosnia to Kosovo," *Civil Wars* 2(2) (1999): 74–110.

159 Zarkov, *Body of War*, p.156.

160 Hansen, "Gender, Nation, Rape," p.65, citing Stanley, "Reporting of Mass Rape."

161 Ibid.

162 Zarkov, *Body of War*, p.156.

163 Ibid.

164 See, e.g., Nira Yuval-Davis, *Gender and Nation* (London: Sage, 1997).

165 Mibenge, *Sex and International Tribunals*.

166 The Hausa name for the Congregation of the People of Tradition for Proselytism and Jihad (Jama'atu Ahlis Sunna Lidda'awati Wal-Jihad), an organization established to end Westernization with the establishment of a pure Islamic state, classified by anyone who lists terrorist organizations as a terrorist organization, in Nigeria, Niger, and Cameroon.

167 Aminu Abubakar, "As Many as 200 Girls Abducted by Boko Haram, Nigerian Officials Say," *CNN News*, 16 April 2014, www.cnn.com.

168 Ibid.

169 Erin Conway-Smith, "Will Nigeria's Girls Be Recovered before They Have Been Hopelessly Brainwashed?," *Global Post*, 30 May 2014, www.dailynews.com.

170 Andy Kopsa, "We All Are the Kidnapped Nigerian Girls," *Ms.*, 1 May 2014, http://msmagazine.com.

171 Ibid.

172 See, e.g., coverage of the 2014 Isla Vista killings, or the shootings in Newtown, Connecticut. I realize I am using two American cases, where there would be less political complication in naming the victims—where in Nigeria, there are fears of reprisal from naming. Still, sex-neutral terms are available for (at least intermittent) use, and not used.

173 "Nigeria: Boko Haram Abducts Women, Recruits Children." *Human Rights Watch*, 29 November 2013, www.hrw.org. Human Rights Watch details that Boko Haram engages in "the killing and mutilation of ordinary Nigerians, the abduction and rape of women and girls, and the use of children for fighting" regularly.

174 Laura Sjoberg, "Whose Girls?," *RelationsInternational*, 13 May 2014, http://relationsinternational.com, citing Cynthia Enloe, "WomenandChildren: Making Feminist Sense of the Persian Gulf Crisis," *Village Voice*, 25 September 1990.

175 "Boko Haram Kidnaps More Girls in Nigeria," *Reuters/Australian News Network*, 7 May 2014, www.abc.net.au.

176 Ibid.

177 Nicholas Kristof, "'Bring Back Our Girls,'" *New York Times*, 3 May 2014, www. nytimes.com. Several other news articles mentioned the low price of the sale as an element of dehumanization. In reading those analyses, I wondered if it is considered more humane to sell someone into slavery for a significant sum?

178 E.g., Aminu Abubakar and Josh Levs, "'I Will Sell Them,' Boko Haram Leader Says of Kidnapped Nigerian Girls," *CNN World*, 6 May 2014, www.cnn.com.

179 Perry Chiaramonte, "Girls Held by Boko Haram Face Auction, Life as Sex Slaves If Rescue Fails," *Fox News.com*, 8 May 2014, www.foxnews.com.

180 Kopsa, "We All Are the Kidnapped Nigerian Girls."

181 Holly Yan and Vladimir Duthiers, "In Nigeria, the Mass Abduction of Schoolgirls Isn't Shocking," *CNN World*, 2 May 2014, www.cnn.com.

182 Chiaramonte, "Girls Held by Boko Haram."

183 Jina Moore, "Nigeria Prepares to Treat Rape, Sexual Trauma of Kidnapped School Girls," *Buzzfeed World*, 29 May 2014, www.buzzfeed.com.

184 Ibid.

185 Temitope Adefarakan, "To Bring Back Kidnapped Girls, Nigeria Should Negotiate with book Haram," *Toronto Star*, 27 May 2014, www.thestar.com.

186 Conway-Smith, "Will Nigeria's Girls Be Recovered?," quoting Shehu Sani, described as "a rights activist who in 2011 and 2012 served as a mediator in talks between Boko Haram and the Nigerian government."

187 E.g., "Nigeria Kidnapped Girls 'Shown in Boko Haram Video," *BBC News Africa*, 12 May 2014, www.bbc.com.

188 Felicity Morse, "The Bring Back Our Girls Campaign Is Working: Boko Haram Should Be Scared of a Hastag," *Independent*, 26 June 2014, www.independent.co.uk.

189 Ibid. See also Alyssa Litoff, "'Bring Back Our Girls' Becomes Rallying Cry for Kidnapped Nigerian Schoolgirls," *ABCNews.com*, 6 May 2014, http://abcnews.go.com.

190 Morse, "Campaign Is Working." The campaign originated on twitter, but moved to the web (bringbackourgirls.us), Facebook (facebook.com/bringbackourgirls), a Twitter account (twitter.com/rescueourgirls) and Instagram (instagram.com/ bringbackourgirls).

191 Ibid.

192 Bringbackourgirls.us, which may or may not be representative, has this text on its "About Us" page: "This website, our Facebook and Twitter pages are operated by a team of volunteers that started in California, but is now worldwide. We are students, mothers, and activists who are dedicated to the immediate rescue of the 230+ schoolgirls from Nigeria. We are here to share credible and vetted news stories, give people actions they can take and help the community around the world connect for rallies. We are a small part of the social awareness campaign on behalf of the girls. We are not an organization. We are individuals. This website and our facebook page was founded by Ramaa Mosley."

193 Morse, "The Bring Back Our Girls Campaign is Working"; Sam Jones and Emma Howard, "#BringBackOurGirls Focuses World's Eyes on Nigeria's Mass Kidnappings," *Guardian*, 7 May 2014, www.theguardian.com.

194 Megan MacKenzie, "Doing Nothing as Activism," *Duck of Minerva*, 12 May 2014, www.whiteoliphaunt.com. Others have called this sort of activism "slacktivism" (see, e.g., Laura Seay, "Does Slactivism Work?," *Monkey Cage/Washington Post*, 12 March 2014, www.washingtonpost.com).

195 Dan Hodges, "Boko Haram Didn't #bringbackourgirls. So What Are We Going to Do Now?," *Telegraph*, 26 June 2014, http://blogs.telegraph.co.uk.

196 Ibid.

197 Anne Look, "Both Sides Say 'Don't Play Politics' with Nigerian Girls," *Voice of America*, 20 May 2014, www.voanews.com.

198 Suman Varadani, "Nigeria's President Goodluck Jonathan Vows 'Total War' against Boko Haram on Democracy Day," *International Business Times*, 29 May 2014, www.ibtimes.com.

199 Samantha Nutt, "Nigeria's Conflict Won't Be Solved with Armed Intervention and Slogans," *Globe and Mail*, 28 May 2014, www.theglobeandmail.com. See also Mark Berman, "Here's What You Need to Know about the Kidnapped Nigerian Girls, Boko Haram, and How the U.S. Is Getting Involved," *Washington Post*, 13 May 2014, www.washingtonpost.com. In fact, a number of members of the US military have expressed concern about being asked to intervene in Nigeria. The concern, discussed in several news stories in the United States, is, "'We're being tweeted into combat,' an anonymous military official told NBC News. Senior Operations commanders for the Navy SEALs, Delta Force, and Rangers Regiment have warned their men that 'the hashtag will bring (them) out' to Northeast Nigeria to rescue the girls" (Richard Engel, "Nigeria Captives Could Get U. S. Troops 'Tweeted into Combat,'" *NBC News*, 27 May 2014, www.nbcnews.com).

200 Nutt, "Nigeria's Conflict Won't Be Solved."

201 See "Nigeria to Free Boko Haram Members," *Al Jazeera*, 21 May 2013, www.aljazeera.com; "Breaking: 486 Boko Haram Members, Including 8 Women, Arrested in Abia," *Gistmania: Nigerian Entertainment and Celebrity News*, 16 June 2014, www.gistmania.com; DPA, "Nigerian Army Arrested 486 Alleged Boko Haram Members," *Haaretz*, 17 June 2014, www.haaretz.com.

202 Mitchell, "The Prohibition of Rape," p.219.

203 Green, "Uncovering Collective Rape," p.108.

204 Ibid., p.107, citing Jennifer Early, Andrew Martin, John D. McCarthy, and Sara A. Soule, "The Use of Newspaper Data in the Study of Collective Action," *Annual Review of Sociology* 30 (2004): 65–80.

205 Robert M. Hayden, "Rape and Rape Avoidance in Ethno-National Conflicts: Sexual Violence in Liminalized States," *American Anthropologist* 102(1) (2000): 27–41, p.29.

206 del Zotto, "Weeping Women," p.141.

207 Yaschica Williams and Janine Bower, "Media Images of Wartime Sexual Violence," in Dew Humphries, ed., *Women, Violence, and the Media: Readings in Feminist Criminology* (Boston: University Press of New England, 2009), pp.156–174, p.156.

208 Patricia A. Weitsman, "The Discourse of Rape in Wartime: Sexual Violence, War Babies, and Identity," paper presented at the Annual Meeting of the International Studies Association, Portland, OR, 26 February–1 March 2003.

209 Gregory S. Gordon, "'A War of Media, Words, Newspapers, and Radio Stations': The ICTR Media Trial Verdict and a New Chapter in the International Law of Hate Speech," *Virginia Journal of International Law* 45(1) (2004–2005): 139–197, citing *Prosecutor v. Nahimana, Barayagwiza, & Ngeze*, Judgment and Sentence, ICTR Case No.99–52-T (3 December, 2003).

210 Tamara L. Tompkins, "Prosecuting Rape as a War Crime: Speaking the Unspeakable," *Notre Dame Law Review* 70(4) (1995): 845–890, p.847.

211 See, e.g., Cohen, Green, and Wood, "Wartime Sexual Violence: Misconceptions, Implications, and Ways Forward"; Cohen, "Explaining Rape During Civil War"; Cohen and Nordas, "Sexual Violence in Armed Conflict."

CHAPTER 3. THE UNFORGETTABLE WOUND

1 Patricia Pearson, *When She Was Bad: How and Why Women Get Away with Murder* (New York: Penguin Books, 1997), p.243.

2 Amnesty International, *Sudan: Darfur: Rape as a Weapon of War: Sexual Violence and Its Consequences*, 19 July 2004, www.amnesty.org/en/library/info/ AFR54/076/2004; see discussion in, for example, "Janjaweed Women Complicit in Genocide, Says Amnesty Report," *Sudanwatch.org*, 10 January 2006, www. sudanwatch.blogspot.com; Jeevan Vasagar and Ewen MacAskill, "Arab Women Singers Complicit in Rape," *Guardian*, 19 July 2004, www.theguardian.com. Information about the racialized sexual violence committed in Darfur can be found in Hale, "Rape as a Marker"; John Hagan, Wenona Rymond-Richmond, and Alberto Palloni, "Racial Targeting of Sexual Violence in Darfur," *American Journal of Public Health* 99(8) (2009): 1386–1392; Megan Bastick, Karin Grimm, and Rahel Kunz, *Sexual Violence and Armed Conflict: Global Overview and Implications for the Security Sector* (Geneva: Center for the Democratic Control of Armed Forces, 2007); Kelly Dawn Askin, "Prosecuting Gender Crimes Committed in Darfur: Holding Leaders Accountable for Sexual Violence," in Samuel Totten and Eric Markusen, eds., *Genocide in Darfur: Investigating the Atrocities in Sudan* (London: Routledge, 2006), pp.141–162.

3 Amnesty International, *Sudan: Darfur*.

4 Elsewhere, this is spelled *hakama, Hakama,* or *hakima*. It is spelled *Hakima* here not out of any certainty of correctness, but for internal consistency.

5 Isam Mohamed Ibrahim, "The Traditional Mechanisms of Conflict Resolution and Peace Building in Darfur: From an Anthropological Perspective," *Mediterranean Journal of Social Sciences* 4(9) (2013): 132–140, p.139; for other discussions of the role of *Hakima* traditional singers, see Jeffrey Kaplan, "Terrorism's Fifth Wave:

A Theory, a Conundrum, and a Dilemma," *Perspectives on Terrorism* 2(2) (2008), www.terrorismanalysts.com; Sondra Hale, "Memory Work as Resistance: Eritrean and Sudanese Women in Conflict Zones," *Comparative Studies of South Asia, Africa, and the Middle Eat* 32(2) (2012): 429–436.

6 Phyllis Chesler, "Feminism's Deafening Silence," *Frontpagemagazine.com*, 28 July 2004, http://archive.frontpagemag.com.

7 Ibid.

8 This should not be read as a claim to objective or unbiased knowledge or reporting of sexual violence in war and conflict—as such a thing does not exist. Instead, it is a suggestion that it is important to desconstruct and demystify some of the prevailing misconceptions and sensationalizations.

9 Bastick, Grimm, and Kunz, *Sexual Violence and Armed Conflict.*

10 Vahakn N. Dadrian, *The History of the Armenian Genocide: Ethnic Conflict from the Balkans to Anatolia to the Caucuses* (New York: Berghahn Books, 2003); Taner Akçam, *A Shameful Act: The Armenian Genocide and the Question of Turkish Responsibility* (London: Macmillan, 2006); Richard G. Hovannisian, ed., *Remembrance and Denial: The Case of the Armenian Genocide* (Detroit, MI: Wayne State University Press, 1998); Richard G. Hovannisian, ed., *The Armenian Genocide in Perspective* (New Brunswick, NJ, and London: Transaction Publishers, 2009).

11 The list of countries formally recognizing that what happened to the Armenians in 1915–1916 constituted genocide can be found at www.armenian-genocide.org/recognition_countries.html, with references to specific laws and resolutions. There has been significant discussion of the Turkish refusal to acknowledge it as genocide, including but not limited to Vahakn N. Dadrian, "The Historical and Legal Interconnections between the Armenian Genocide and the Jewish Holocaust: From Impunity to Retributive Justice," *Yale Journal of International Law* 23(2) (1998): 503–560; Akçam, *A Shameful Act*; Guenter Lewy, *The Armenian Massacres in Ottoman Turkey: A Disputed Genocide* (Salt Lake City: University of Utah Press, 2005).

12 Helen Fein, "Genocide and Gender: The Uses of Women and Group Destiny," *Journal of Genocide Research* 1(1) (1999): 43–63, p.50. See also Donald Bloxham, *The Great Game of Genocide: Imperialism, Nationalism, and the Destruction of Ottoman Armenians* (Oxford: Oxford University Press, 2005); Samuel Totten, William S. Parsons, and Israel W. Charny, eds., *Century of Genocide: Critical Essays and Eyewitness Accounts* (New York: Routledge, 2004), especially Rouben Paul Adalian's chapter on the Armenian genocide (ch.2, pp.53–92).

13 See, e.g., Yair Auron, *The Banality of Indifference: Zionism and the Armenian Genocide* (New Brunswick, NJ, and London: Transaction, 2000), p.44; Richard G. Hovannisian, "The Historical Dimensions of the Armenian Question, 1878–1923," and Robert Melson, "Provocation or Nationalism?," in Frank Robert Chalk, ed., *The History and Sociology of Genocide: Analyses and Case Studies* (New Haven, CT: Yale University Press, 1990), pp.249–289.

14 Katharine Derderian, "Common Fate, Different Experience: Gender-Specific Aspects of the Armenian Genocide, 1915–1917," *Holocaust and Genocide Studies* 19(1) (2005): 1–25, p.1.

15 See, e.g., Peter Balakian, *The Burning Tigris: The Armenian Genocide and America's Response* (New York: HarperCollins, 2003); Donald Earl Miller and Lorna Touryan Miller, *Survivors: An Oral History of the Armenian Genocide* (Berkeley: University of California Press, 1993); Tessa Hoffman, "German Eyewitness Reports of the Genocide of the Armenians, 1915–1916," in Permanent People's Tribunal, *A Crime of Silence: The Armenian Genocide* (London: Zed Books, 1985), pp. 61–92; Jay Winter, ed. *America and the Armenian Genocide of 1915* (Cambridge, UK: Cambridge University Press, 2004); Raymond Kévorkian, *The Armenian Genocide: A Complete History* (London: I. B. Tauris, 2011).

16 Hoffman, "German Eyewitness Reports"; Vahakn N. Dadrian, "Documentation of the Armenian Genocide in German and Austrian Sources," in Israel W. Charney, ed., *The Widening Circle of Genocide* (London: Transaction, 1994), pp.77–126; Fein, "Genocide and Gender."

17 E.g., Raphael Lemkin, "Genocide as a Crime under International Law," *American Journal of International Law* 41(1) (1947): 145–151; Chalk, *The History and Sociology of Genocide*; Ben Kiernan, *Blood and Soil: A World History of Genocide and Extermination from Sparta to Darfur* (Melbourne: Melbourne University Publishing, 2008). See also the United States Holocaust Memorial Museum's Holocaust Encyclopedia, which provides an accessible account of the origin of the word "genocide" (www.ushmm.org/wlc/en/article.php?ModuleId=10007043).

18 E.g., Totten, Parsons, and Charny, *Century of Genocide*; Charny, *Widening Circle of Genocide*; Chalk, *History and Sociology of Genocide*; Samantha Power, *"A Problem from Hell"*; Benjamin A. Valentino, *Final Solutions: Mass Killing and Genocide in the 20th Century* (Ithaca, NY: Cornell University Press, 2013); Eric D. Waltz, *A Century of Genocide: Utopias of Race and Nation* (Princeton, NJ: Princeton University Press, 2009).

19 Council of Europe Parliamentary Assembly Resolution, "Commemoration of the Armenian Genocide of 1915," Written Declaration No.275, 24 April 1998, www.armenian-genocide.org.

20 "Federal Senate of Brazil Recognizes Armenian Genocide," *Armenian Weekly*, 3 June 2015, http://armenianweekly.com.

21 Jake Tapper, "For the 7th Year in a Row, Obama Breaks Promise to Acknowledge Armenian Genocide," *CNN*, 24 April 2015, www.cnn.com.

22 Derderian, "Common Fate, Different Experience," p.3. For discussions of the relationship between gender ideologies and genocide in other conflicts, see, e.g., Janet Jacobs, *Memorializing the Holocaust: Gender, Genocide, and Collective Memory* (London: I. B. Tauris, 2010); Andrea Smith, *Conquest: Sexual Violence and the American Indian Genocide* (Cambridge, MA: South End Press, 2005); Ronit Lentin, "The Rape of the Nation: Women Narrativising Genocide," *Sociologi-*

cal Research Online 4(2) (1999), http://socresonline.org.uk; Copelon, "Surfacing Gender."

23 S. D. Stein, "The Armenian and Roma Genocides," *"Remember"—The Armenian Genocide*, 19 November 2001, www.wbarrow.co.uk/rememberarmenia.

24 See, e.g., Miller and Miller, *Survivors*; Vahe Tachjian, "Gender, Nationalism, and Exclusion: The Reintegration Process of Female Survivors of the Armenian Genocide," *Nations and Nationalism* 15(1) (2009): 60–80; Fein, "Genocide and Gender"; Rubina Peroomian, "Women and the Armenian Genocide: The Victim, the Living Martyr," in Samuel Totten, ed., *The Plight and Fate of Women During and Following Genocide* (New Brunswick, NJ, and London: Transaction, 2011), pp.7–24; Uğur Ümit Üngör, "Orphans, Converts, and Prostitutes: Social Consequences of War and Persecution in the Ottoman Empire: 1914–1923," *War in History* 19(2) (2012): 173–192. See also media and popular accounts, like Lyz Anzia, "100 Years Later Armenian Women Continue to be Haunted by Genocide," *Women's News Network*, 19 October 2012, http://womennewsnetwork.net; Müjan Halis, "Armenian Genocide and Women's Double Pain," *Demokrat Haber*, 19 March 2014, www.tert.am.

25 Derderian, "Common Fate, Different Experience."

26 Ibid., p.3. See also Ayse Gul Altinay, "Gendered Silences, Gendered Memories," *L'Homme* 2 (2013): 1–15.

27 See, e.g., Robert Melson, *Revolution and Genocide: On the Origins of the Armenian Genocide and the Holocaust* (Chicago: University of Chicago Press, 1992); Dadrian, *The History of the Armenian Genocide*; Vahakn N. Dadrian, "The Secret Young-Turk Ittihadist Conference and the Decision for the World War I Genocide of the Armenians," *Holocaust Genocide Studies* 7(2) (1993): 173–201; Taner Akcam, *The Young Turks' Crimes Against Humanity: The Armenian Genocide and Cleansing the Ottoman Empire* (Princeton, NJ: Princeton University Press, 2012).

28 Stein, "The Armenian and Roma Genocides," p.4.

29 Ibid.

30 Eliz Sanasarian, "Gender Distinction in the Genocidal Process: A Preliminary Study of the Armenian Case," *Holocaust and Genocide Studies* 4(4) (1989): 449–461.

31 Ibid.

32 Ibid., p.453.

33 Ibid., p.454.

34 Ibid.

35 Ibid., p.456.

36 Ibid., p.459. While she expected to find women less likely to be perpetrators and more likely to be peacemakers, Sanasarian did not, and suggested that the Armenian genocide evidence seems "to corroborate Israel W. Charny's thesis that 'all "normal" people are capable of being genociders, accomplices, or bystanders'" (quoting Israel W. Charny, *How Can We Commit the Unthinkable? Genocide: The Human Cancer* [Boulder, CO: Westview Press, 1982], p.10).

37 For histories of the Nazi genocide, see, e.g., Henry Friedländer, *The Origins of Nazi Genocide* (Chapel Hill: University of North Carolina Press, 1997); Dominick LaCapra, *Representing the Holocaust: History, Theory, Trauma* (Ithaca, NY: Cornell University Press, 1996); Doris L. Bergen, *War and Genocide: A Concise History of the Holocaust*, 2d ed. (New York: Rowman & Littlefield, 2009); Raul Hilberg, *The Destruction of the European Jews* (New Haven, CT: Yale University Press, 2003 [1961]); Michael Berenbaum, *The World Must Know: The History of the Holocaust as Told in the United States Holocaust Memorial Museum* (Baltimore: Johns Hopkins University Press, 2005); Yehuda Bauer, *Rethinking the Holocaust* (New Haven, CT: Yale University Press).

38 For discussion of Jewish victims specifically, see, e.g., Saul Friedländer, *Nazi Germany and the Jews* (New York: HarperCollins, 2009); of Roma, see, e.g., Donald Kenrick, *In the Shadow of the Swastika: The Gypsies during the Second World War* (Hertfordshire: University of Hertfordshire Press, 1999), part of a three-volume series on theories that have led to persecution of Roma; of Slavs, see, e.g., John Connelly, "Nazis and Slavs: From Racial Theory to Racist Practice," *Central European History* 32(1) (1999): 1–33); of communists, see, e.g., Friedländer, *Origins of Nazi Genocide*; of homosexuals, see, e.g., Frank Rector, *The Nazi Extermination of Homosexuals* (New York: Stein and Day, 1981); Pierre Seel, *I, Pierre Seel, Deported Homosexual: A Memoir of Nazi Terror* (New York: Basic Books, 2011); of Jehovah's Witnesses, see, e.g., Detlef Garbe, *Between Resistance and Martyrdom: Jehovah's Witnesses in the Third Reich*, trans. Dagman C. Grimm (Madison: University of Wisconsin Press, 2008).

39 See discussion in the United States Holocaust Memorial Museum's Holocaust Encyclopedia, www.ushmm.org/wlc/en/article.php?ModuleId=10005687, for calculation of the death toll. For discussion of the Nazi camp sysem, see Konnilyn G. Feig, *Hitler's Death Camps: The Sanity of Madness* (Boulder, CO: Lynne Rienner, 1981); Nikolaus Wachsmann and Jane Caplan, *Concentration Camps in Nazi Germany: The New Histories* (New York: Routledge, 2009).

40 See, e.g., discussions in Christopher R. Browning, *Nazi Policy, Jewish Workers, German Killers* (Cambridge, UK: Cambridge University Press, 2000); Goldhagen, *Hitler's Willing Executioners.*

41 See, e.g., discussions in Avishai Margalit and Gabriel Motzkin, "The Uniqueness of the Holocaust," *Philosophy and Public Affairs* 25(1) (1996): 65–83; Michael Berenbaum and Abraham J. Peck, *The Holocaust and History: The Known, the Unknown, the Disputed, and the Reexamined* (Bloomington: Indiana University Press, 2002).

42 See, e.g., Lemkin, "Genocide as a Crime"; William Schabas, *Genocide in International Law: The Crime of Crimes* (Cambridge, UK: Cambridge University Press, 2000); Lori Lyman Bruun, "Beyond the 1948 Genocide Convention—Emerging Principles of Genocide in Customary International Law," *Maryland Journal of International Law and Trace* 17(1) (1993): 193–226; Steven R. Ratner, Jason S.

Abrams, and James L. Bischoff, *Accountability for Human Rights Atrocities in International Law: Beyond the Nuremburg Legacy* (Oxford: Oxford University Press, 2009).

43 On sexual violence, see, e.g., MacKinnon, "Rape, Genocide, and Women's Human Rights"; on enslavement, see, e.g., William L. Sauders, Jr., and Yuri G. Mantilla, "Human Dignity Denied: Slavery, Genocide, and Crimes against Humanity in Sudan," *Catholic University Law Review* 51(3) (2002): 715–739; on forced impregnation, see, e.g., Siobhan K. Fisher, "Occupation of the Womb: Forced Impregnation as Genocide," *Duke Law Journal* 46(1) (1996): 91–133; on forced migration, see, e.g., Kathleen Sara Galbraith, "Moving People: Forced Migration and International Law," *Georgetown Immigration Law Journal* 13(4) (1999): 597–616.

44 For example, Rhonda Copelon explains that "the maintenance of concentration camp brothels for the rape of Jewish and Aryan women as well as rape in the course of conquest did not figure in the proceedings against high-level Nazis in the International Military Tribunal at Nuremberg" but that its failure to be addressed does not mean that it did not happen ("Surfacing Gender," pp.243–244). There is an evolving literature in the discipline of history about Wehrmacht sex crimes jurisprudence that discusses the ways in which different sex crimes were treated differently by different courts (e.g., David Raub Snyder, *Sex Crimes under the Wehrmacht* [Lincoln: University of Nebraska Press, 2007]).

45 This is even though Elisa von Joeden-Forgey (in "Gender and the Future of Genocide Studies and Prevention," *Genocide Studies and Prevention: An International Journal* 7[1] [2014]: 89–107, p.104) suggests that "the study of women perpetrators is most developed for the Holocaust," citing Claudia Koonz, *Mothers in the Fatherland: Women, the Family, and Nazi Politics* (New York: St. Martin's Press, 1987); Roger Smith, "Women and Genocide: Notes on an Unwritten History," *Holocaust and Genocide Studies* 8(3) (1994): 215–334; Christina Herkommer, "Women under National Socialism: Women's Scope for Action and the Issue of Gender," in Olaf Jensen and Claus-Christian W. Szejnmann, eds., *Ordinary People as Mass Murderers*, (New York: Palgrave Macmillan, 2008), pp.99–119; Irmtaud Heike, "Female Concentration Camp Guards as Perpetrators: Three Case Studies," in Jensen and Szejnmann, *Ordinary People*, pp.120–144; Wendy Adele-Marie Sarti, *Women and Nazis: Perpetrators of Genocide and Other Crimes During Hitler's Regime, 1933–1945* (Palo Alto, CA: Academica, 2010).

46 See, e.g., Alexandra Przyrembel, "Transfixed by an Image," p.396; Egon W. Fleck and Edward A. Tenenbaum. "Buchenwald: ein vorläufiger Bericht vom 24.4.1945," in Lutz Niethammer, ed., *Der gesäuberte Antifaschismus. Die SED und die roten Kapos von Buchenwald* (Berlin: Akademic Verlag, 1994), pp.180–198; Smith, *Die Hexe von Buchenwald*.

47 See, e.g., Sarti, *Women and Nazis*; Sjoberg and Gentry, *Mothers, Monsters, Whores*; Koonz, *Mothers in the Fatherland*.

48 See discussions in Koonz, *Mothers in the Fatherland*; Sjoberg and Gentry, *Mothers, Monsters, Whores*; Gentry and Sjoberg, *Beyond Mothers, Monsters, Whores*.

49 Discussions of men's perpetration of sexual violence include Copelon, "Surfacing Gender"; Jacobs, *Memorializing the Holocaust*; Carol Harrington, *Politicization of Sexual Violence: From Abolitionism to Peacekeeping* (London: Ashgate, 2010), p.79; Jessica R. Anderson Hughes, *Forced Prostitution: The Competing and Contested Uses of the Concentration Camp Brothel* (dissertation at Rutgers, the State University of New Jersey—New Brunswick, 2011), http://gradworks.umi.com/34/74/3474863.html; discussions of women's perpetration of other sorts of crimes can be seen in, e.g., the sources cited in notes 46 and 47, above.

50 See, e.g., Daniel Patrick Brown, *The Camp Women: The Female Auxiliaries Who Assisted the SS in Running the Nazi Concentration Camp System* (Atglen, PA: Schiffer Military History, 2002), p.25; Jack G. Morrison, *Ravensbruck: Everyday Life in a Women's Concentration Camp: 1939–1945* (Princeton, NJ: Princeton University Press, 2000), p.16; Goldhagen, *Hitler's Willing Executioners*; Dalia Ofer and Lenore J. Weitzman, *Women in the Holocaust* (New Haven, CT: Yale University Press, 1998); Carol Rittner and John K. Roth, *Different Voices: Women and the Holocaust* (New York: Paragon House, 1993); Charlotte Delbo, *Auschwitz and After*, trans. Rosette C. Lamont (New Haven, CT: Yale University Press, 1995); Wendy Lower, *Hitler's Furies: German Women in the Nazi Killing Fields* (New York: Houghton Mifflin Harcourt, 2013); Bronwyn Rebekah McFarland-Icke, *Nurses in Nazi Germany: Moral Choice in History* (Princeton, NJ: Princeton University Press, 1999); Victor W. Sidel, "The Social Responsibilities of Health Professionals: Lessons from their Role in Nazi Germany," *Journal of the American Medical Association* 276(20) (1996): 1679–1681; Paul Weindling, *Health, Race, and German Politics Between National Unification and Nazism* (Cambridge, UK: Cambridge University Press, 1993).

51 See, e.g., discussion in Lower, *Hitler's Furies*.

52 Everette Lemons, *The Third Reich: A Revolution of Ideological Inhumanity, Volume I: The Power of Perception* (Raleigh, NC: Lulu.com, 2005).

53 Brown, *The Camp Women*.

54 See, e.g., discussions in Wolfgang Weyers, *The Abuse of Man: An Illustrated History of Dubious Medical Experimentation* (New York: Ardor Scribendi, 2007); Horst Freyhofer, *The Nuremberg Medical Trial: The Holocaust and the Origin of the Nuremberg Medical Code* (New York: Peter Lang, 2004); M. H. Armstrong Davison, "Medical War Crimes," *British Medical Journal* 1(5079) (10 May 1958): 1121; Vivien Spitz, *Doctors from Hell: The Horrific Account of Nazi Experiments on Humans* (Boulder, CO: Sentient Publications, 2005); George J. Annas and Michael A. Grodin, *The Nazi Doctors and the Nuremberg Code: Human Rights in Human Experimentation* (New York: Oxford University Press, 1992); Morrison, *Ravensbruck*; Francis R. Nicosia and Jonathan Huener, eds., *Medicine and Medical Ethics in Nazi Germany, Origins, Practices, and Legacies* (New York: Berghahn Books, 2002); Alexander Mikaberidze, *Atrocities, Massacres, and*

War Crimes: An Encyclopedia, 2 vols. (Santa Barbara, CA: ABC-CLIO, 2013), pp.501–502.

55 Lemons, *The Third Reich*; Michael H. Kater, *Doctors Under Hitler* (Raleigh: University of North Carolina Press Books, 1990), p.110; Eric W. Hickey, *Serial Murderers and Their Victims*, 5th ed. (New York: Wadsworth/CENGAGE, 2010), p.253.

56 Przyrembel, "Transfixed by an Image"; Sarti, *Women and Nazis*; Andrea S. Dauber, "Not All Nazis are Men: Women's Underestimated Potential for Violence in German Neo-Nazism. Continuation of the Past or Novel Phenomenon?" in Marcia Texler Segal and Vasikikie Demos, eds. *Gendered Perspectives on Conflict and Violence: Part B (Advances in Gender Research, Volume 18)* (Bradford, UK: Emerald Publishing Group Limited, 2014), pp.171–194; Felicia Morris, "Beautiful Monsters," *Legacy* 11(1) (2012): 59–70; Margaret-Anne Hutton, *Testimony from the Nazi Camps: French Women's Voices* (New York: Routledge, 2005); Lord Russell of Liverpool, *The Scourge of the Swastika* (London: Cassell, 1954); Sarah Helm, *A Life in Secrets: Vera Atkins and the Missing Agents of WWII* (New York: Knopf Doubleday Publishing Group, 2008).

57 Alix Christie, "Guarding the Truth," *Washington Post*, 26 February 2006, p.W08.

58 Brown, *The Camp Women*.

59 Christie, "Guarding the Truth."

60 Sarti, *Women and Nazis*, pp.60–61.

61 James Waller, *Becoming Evil: How Ordinary People Commit Genocide and Mass Killing*, 2d ed. (Oxford: Oxford University Press, 2007), p.267.

62 E.g., discussions of Dorothea Binz and Ilse Koch's relationships with male guards in Sjoberg, "Women and the Genocidal Rape of Women."

63 Waller, *Becoming Evil*, p.266; McFarland-Icke, *Nurses in Nazi Germany*. For discussions of the Nazi forced sterilization programs, see George Annas, Edward Utley, and Michael Grodin, *Nazi Doctors and the Nuremberg Code: Human Rights in Human Experimentation* (New York: Oxford University Press, 1992); Patricia Heberer, "Targeting the 'Unfit' and Radical Public Health Strategies in Nazi Germany," in Donna F. Ryan and John S. Schuchman, eds., *Deaf People in Hitler's Europe* (Washington, DC: Galludet University Press, 2002), pp.49–73; Naomi Baumslag, *Murderous Medicine: Nazi Doctors, Human Experimentation, and Typhus* (Westport, CT: Greenwood, 2005).

64 See, e.g., Robert Jay Lifton, *The Nazi Doctors: Medical Killing and the Psychology of Genocide* (New York: Basic Books, 2000); Karl A Schleunes, *The Twisted Road to Auschwitz: Nazi Policy toward German Jews, 1933–1939* (Urbana-Champaign: University of Illinois Press, 1970); Gotz Aly, Peter Chroust, and Christian Pross, *Cleansing the Fatherland: Nazi Medicine and Racial Hygiene* (Baltimore: Johns Hopkins University Press, 1994).

65 Gisela Bock, "Racism and Sexism in Nazi Germany: Motherhood, Compulsory Sterilization, and the State," *Signs: Journal of Women in Culture and Society* 8(3) (1983): 400–421; Kate Lacey, "Driving the Message Home: Nazi Propaganda in the Private Sphere," in Lynn Abrams and Elizabeth Harvey, eds.,

Gender Relations and German History: Power, Agency, and Experience from the Sixteenth to the Twentieth Century (Durham, NC: Duke University Press, 1997), pp.180–211; Herbert F. Ziegler, "Fight against the Empty Cradle: Nazi Pronatal Policies and the SS-Fuhrerkorps," *Historical Social Research* 38 (April 1996): 25–40.

66 Herberer, "Targeting the 'Unfit'"; Baumslag, *Murderous Medicine*; Elizabeth D. Heineman, "Sexuality and Nazism: The Doubly Unspeakable?," *Journal of the History of Sexuality* 11(1–2) (2002): 22–66.

67 Fisher, "Occupation of the Womb"; Skjelsbaek, "Sexual Violence and War"; Kristen Boon, "Rape and Forced Pregnancy under the ICC Statute: Human Dignity, Autonomy, and Consent," *Columbia Human Rights Law Review* 32(2) (2000): 625–676; Lisa Sharlach, "Rape as Genocide: Bangladesh, the Former Yugoslavia, and Rwanda," *New Political Science* 22(1) (2000): 89–102; R. Charli Carpenter, "Forced Maternity, Children's Rights, and the Genocide Convention: A Theoretical Analysis," *Journal of Genocide Research* 2(2) (2000): 213–244.

68 See, e.g., Lifton, *The Nazi Doctors*; Friedländer, *Origins of Nazi Genocide*; Michael Burleigh, "Racism as Social Policy: The Nazi 'Euthanasia' Programme, 1939–1945," *Ethnic and Racial Studies* 14(4) (1991): 453–473; Roger W. Smith, "Genocide and the Politics of Rape: Historical and Psychological Perspectives," in Joyce Apsel and Ernesto Verdeja, eds., *Genocide Matters: Ongoing Issues and Emerging Perspectives* (New York: Routledge, 2013), pp.82–105; Patricia Weitsman, "Children Born of War and the Politics of Identity," in R. Charli Carpenter, ed. *Born of War: Protecting Children of Sexual Violence Survivors in Conflict Zones* (Bloomfield, CT: Kumarian Press, 2007), pp.110–127.

69 See, e.g., discussion in Snyder, *Sex Crimes under the Wehrmacht*, about Nazi soldiers being punished for raping women classified as genetically undesirable.

70 I was able to find no such accounts in an extensive review of primary and secondary sources. While that doesn't mean it never happened, it suggests that it was rare, quiet, or both.

71 On beating women's breasts, see, e.g., Hutton, *Testimony from the Nazi Camps*; Donald McKale, *Nazis after Hitler: How the Perpetrators of the Holocaust Cheated Justice and Truth* (New York: Rowman & Littlefield, 2012), p.43; Alana Fangrad, *Wartime Rape and Sexual Violence: An Examination of the Perpetrators, Motivations, and Functions of Sexual Violence against Jewish Women during the Holocaust* (Bloomington, IN: AuthorHouse, 2013), p.57, Sarti, *Women and Nazis*, p.119; on medical experimentation on pregnant women, see, e.g., discussion in Sonja Maria Hedgepeth and Rochelle G. Saidel, *Sexual Violence Against Jewish Women during the Holocaust* (Hanover: University Press of New England, 2010); on sterilization, see sources cited in note 66, above.

72 McFarland-Icke, *Nurses in Nazi Germany*; Susan Benedict and Jochen Kuhla, "Nurses' Participation in the Euthanasia Programs of Nazi Germany," *Western Journal of Nursing Research* 21(2) (1999): 246–263.

73 Ibid., p.147; Lifton, *The Nazi Doctors*, p.25; Joachim-Ernst Meyer, "The Fate of the Mentally Ill in Germany during the Third Reich," *Psychological Medicine* 18(3) (1988): 575–581; Michael Dudley and Fran Gale, "Psychiatrists as a Moral Community? Psychiatry under the Nazis and its Contemporary Relevance," *Australian and New Zealand Journal of Psychiatry* 36(4) (2002): 585–594; Benedict and Kuhla, "Nurses' Participation."

74 McFarland-Icke, *Nurses in Nazi Germany*, p.147.

75 Ibid.

76 Ibid., p.148; Hans Hoffmann, "Die Sterilisierung (Unfrucbarmachung) Minderwertiger aus eugenischen Günden," *Geisteskrankenpfledge* 37 (October 1933): 148.

77 McFarland-Icke, *Nurses in Nazi Germany*, p.148.

78 Ibid., pp.148–149.

79 Ibid., pp.149–150, citing Hoffman, "Die Sterilisierung," pp.150–151; R. Herrmann, "Geisteskrankenpfleger und Erbkunde," *Geisteskrankenpfledge* 38 (February 1934): 22.

80 McFarland-Icke, *Nurses in Nazi Germany*, p.150.

81 Ibid., p.151.

82 Ibid., p.133, citing Michael Burleigh, *Death and Deliverance: "Euthanasia" in Germany, c.1900–1945* (Cambridge, UK: Cambridge University Press, 1994), p.61; Gisele Bock, *Zwangssterilisation im Nationalsozialismus: Studién zué Rassenpolitik und Frauenpolitik* (Opladen: Westdeutscher Verlag, 1986), pp.252, 262; Hans Ludwig Siemen, *Menschen blieben auf der Strecke . . . : Psychiatrie zwischen Reform und Nationalsozialismus* (Gütersloh: Van Hoddis, 1987), p.143.

83 Benedict and Kuhla, "Nurses' Participation"; McFarland-Icke, *Nurses in Nazi Germany.*

84 See discussion in McFarland-Icke, *Nurses in Nazi Germany*, pp.133–135, 147–151.

85 See discussion in Lower, *Hitler's Furies*; see also Thomas Foth, Jochen Kuhla, and Susan Benedict, "Nursing during National Socialism," in Susan Benedict and Linda Shields, eds., *Nurses and Midwives in Nazi Germany: The "Euthanasia Programs"* (New York: Routledge, 2014), pp.27–47.

86 Benedict and Kuhla, "Nurses' Participation"; Susan Benedict, Arthur Caplan, Traute Lafrenz Page, "Duty and 'Euthanasia': The Nurses of Meseritz-Obrawalde," *Nursing Ethics* 14(6) (2007): 781–794.

87 See, e.g., Maria Berghs, Bernadette Dierckx de Casterlé, and Chris Gastmans, "Practices of Responsibility and Nurses during the Euthanasia Programs of Nazi Germany: A Discussion Paper," *International Journal of Nursing Studies* 44(5) (2007): 845–854.

88 Robert Proctor, *Racial Hygiene: Medicine under the Nazis* (Cambridge, MA: Harvard University Press, 1988); James Watson, "The Connection between American Eugenics and Nazi Germany," interview at the DNA Learning Center, www.dnalc.org.

89 New accounts that have gotten some attention include Lower's *Hitler's Furies* and related publications (e.g., Tony Rennell, "The Nazi Women Who Were Every Bit

as Evil as the Men," *MailOnline*, 25 September 2013, www.dailymail.co.uk; Jacob Sugarman, "In Nazi Germany, Women Were Killers Too," *Salon.com*, 27 October 2013, www.salon.com).

90 For discussions of the history of the conflict, see, e.g., Carole Rogel, *The Breakup of Yugoslavia and Its Aftermath* (Westport, CT: Greenwood, 2004); Sonia Lucarelli, *Europe and the Breakup of Yugoslavia: A Political Failure in Search of a Scholarly Explanation* (Leiden: Martinus Nijhoff Publishers, 2000); Sabrina P. Ramet, *Thinking about Yugoslavia: Scholarly Debates about the Yugoslav Breakup and the Wars in Bosnia and Kosovo* (Cambridge, UK: Cambridge University Press, 2005); Misha Glenny, *The Fall of Yugoslavia: The Third Balkan War* (New York: Penguin Books, 1996).

91 The discussion of the historical composition of Yugoslavia in John R. Lampe's *Yugoslavia as History: Twice There Was a Country* (Cambridge, UK: Cambridge University Press) is an accessible one for those not well-versed in the conflict. See also Ivo Banac, *The National Question in Yugoslavia: Origins, History, and Politics* (Ithaca, NY: Cornell University Press, 1988), which focuses on the World War I era, for the development of the underlying tensions between the component republics; Viktor Meier, *Yugoslavia: A History of Its Demise* (New York: Routledge, 2014), which focuses on the post-Tito era to understand the pressures on Yugoslav unification; Duško Sekulić, Garth Massey, and Randy Hodson, "Who Were the Yugoslavs? Failed Sources of Common Identity in the Former Yugoslavia," *American Sociological Review* 59(1) (1994): 83–97, which focuses on the perception that the Yugoslav republics never developed a common identity; Josef Joffe, "The New Europe: Yesterday's Ghosts," *Foreign Affairs* 72(1) (1992/1993): 29–43, which focuses on the interaction of Cold War history and Yugoslav history.

92 For discussion of the influence of Tito's presidency-for-life on the structure of Yugoslavia and Yugoslav foreign policy, see, e.g., Aleksa Djilas, "The Academic West and the Balkan Test," *Journal of Southern Europe and the Balkans Online* 9(3) (2007): 323–332; Susan L. Woodward, "Violence-Prone Area or International Transition? Adding the Role of Outsiders in Balkan Violence," in Veena Das, ed., *Violence and Subjectivity* (Berkeley: University of California Press, 2000), pp.19–45.

93 For the question of the role of the death of Tito in the conflict, see Meier, *Yugoslavia*; Tone Bringa, "The Peaceful Death of Tito and the Violent End of Yugoslavia," in John Borneman, ed., *Death of the Father: An Anthropology of the End of Political Authority* (New York: Berghahn Books, 2004), pp.148–200; Richard West, *Tito and the Rise and Fall of Yugoslavia*, 3d ed. (New York: Faber & Faber, 2012); Steven L. Burg, "Elite Conflict in post-Tito Yugoslavia," *Soviet Studies* 38(2) (1986): 170–193.

94 See, e.g., discussions in Louis Sell, *Slobodan Milošević and the Destruction of Yugoslavia* (Durham, NC: Duke University Press, 2002); Lenard J. Cohen, *Serpent in the Bosom: The Rise and Fall of Slobodan Milošević* (Boulder, CO: Westview Press, 2002), especially part I, which discusses the rise of Milošević and the relevance of

Kosovo; Nebojsa Vladisavjević, *Serbia's Antibureaucratic Revolution: Milošević, the Fall of Communism, and Nationalist Mobilization* (Basingstoke: Palgrave Macmillan, 2008); Takis S. Pappas, "Shared Culture, Individual Strategy, and Collective Action: Explaining Slobodan Milošević's Charismatic Rise to Power," *Southeast European and Black Sea Studies* 5(2) (2005): 191–211; Philip Auerswald and David Auerswald, eds., *The Kosovo Conflict: A Diplomatic History through Documents* (The Hague: Kluwer Law International, 2000); V. P. Gagnon, Jr., "Yugoslavia: Prospects for Stability," *Foreign Affairs* 70(3) (1991): 17–35.

95 See, e.g., the discussion in Bogdan Denis Denitch, *Ethnic Nationalism: The Tragic Death of Yugoslavia* (Minneapolis: University of Minnesota Press, 1996); Vladislavjević, *Serbia's Antibureaucratic Revolution;* Gale Stokes, *The Walls Came Tumbling Down: The Collapse of Communism in Eastern Europe* (Oxford: Oxford University Press, 1993), particularly ch.7, "The Devil's Finger: The Disintegration of Yugoslavia," pp.218–252.

96 For a timeline, see https://history.state.gov/milestones/1989–1992/breakup-yugoslavia, which chronicles the Croatian and Slovenian declarations of independence on June 25, 1991, the Bosnian declaration in May 1992, and the Macedonian declaration in the fall of 1991.

97 See, e.g., discussion of Serbs in Bosnia by Steven L. Burg and Paul S. Shoup, *The War in Bosnia-Herzegovina: Ethnic Conflict and International Intervention* (London: M. E. Sharpe, 1999). Ethnic minorities across the former Yugoslav republics were featured prominently in the political claims of the new states against each other during the breakup and ensuing conflict.

98 Lucarelli, *Europe and the Breakup of Yugoslavia*; Richard Ullman, ed., *The World and Yugoslavia's Wars* (New York: Council on Foreign Relations, 1996); Cushman and Meštrović, *This Time We Knew*; James Gow, *The Triumph of the Lack of Will: International Diplomacy and the Yugoslav War* (New York: Columbia University Press, 1997).

99 Glenny, *The Fall of Yugoslavia*; for a detailed analysis of Serbian motivations, see Tim Judah, *The Serbs: History, Myth, and the Destruction of Yugoslavia* (New Haven, CT: Yale University Press, 2000); Eric D. Gordy, *The Culture of Power in Serbia: Nationalism and the Destruction of Alternatives* (University Park: Penn State University Press, 2010); Bette Denich, "Dismembering Yugoslavia: Nationalist Ideologies and the Symbolic Revival of Genocide," *American Ethnologist* 21(2) (1994): 367–390.

100 Roland Rich, "Recognition of States: The Collapse of Yugoslavia and the Soviet Union," *European Journal of International Law* 4(1) (1993): 36–65.

101 For detail, see Burg and Shoup, *The War in Bosnia-Herzegovina*. A question of the degree to which ethnicity was actually a motivation for some of the leaders has become a controversy in the scholarly literature, e.g., V. P. Gagnon, *The Myth of Ethnic War: Serbia and Croatia in the 1990s* (Ithaca, NY: Cornell University Press, 2006). Several discourse analysts have engaged the conflict in Bosnia, including Hansen, *Security as Practice*.

102 See, e.g., discussion in John Webb, "Genocide Treaty—Ethnic Cleansing—Substantive and Procedural Hurdles in the Application of the Genocide Convention to Alleged Crimes in the Former Yugoslavia," *Georgia Journal of International and Comparative Law* 23(2) (1993): 377–408; Damir Mirković, "Ethnic Conflict and Genocide: Reflections on Ethnic Cleansing in the Former Yugoslavia," *Annals of the American Academy of Political and Social Science* 48 (The Holocaust: Remembering for the Future) (November 1996): 191–199; Human Rights Watch, *Genocide, War Crimes, and Crimes Against Humanity: A Topical Digest of the Case Law of the International Criminal Tribunal for the Former Yugoslavia* (New York: Human Rights Watch, 2006).

103 Milton Leitenberg, "Deaths in Wars and Conflicts in the 20th Century" (2006), suggests that the death toll neared 200,000 (www.cissm.umd.edu); other estimations range between 104,732 (from the ICTY, Jan Zwierzchowski and Ewa Tabeau, only counting the 1992–1995 war in Bosnia and Herzegovina, www.icty.org) to around 150,000 (Nedim Dervibegovic, "Revised Death Toll for Bosnian War," Bosnian Institute, 23 December 2004, www.bosnia.org.uk).

104 See, e.g., Jennifer Hyndman, "Preventive, Palliative, or Punitive? Safe Spaces in Bosnia-Herzegovina, Somalia, and Sri Lanka," *Journal of Refugee Studies* 16(2) (2003): 162–185.

105 See discussions in, e.g., David Rohde, *Endgame: The Betrayal and Fall of Srebrenica, Europe's Worst Massacre since World War II* (New York: Penguin, 2012); Helge Brunborg, Torkild Hovde Lyngstad, and Henrik Urdal, "Accounting for Genocide: How Many Were Killed in Srebrenica?," *European Journal of Population* 19(3) (2003): 229–248; Katherine G. Southwick, "Srebrenica as Genocide? The *Krstić* Decision and the Language of the Unspeakable," *Yale Human Rights and Development Law Journal* 8(1) (2005): 188–227; Selma Leydesdorff, *Surviving the Bosnian Genocide: The Women of Srebrenica Speak* (Bloomington: Indiana University Press, 2011); Mark Drumbl, "Prosecutor vs. Radislav Krstić: ICTY Authenticates Genocide at Srebrenica and Convicts for Aiding and Abetting," *Melbourne Journal of International Law* 5(2) (2004): 454–449.

106 For discussions of sexual violence against women, see, e.g., Leydesdorff, *Surviving the Bosnian Genocide*; Catharine A. MacKinnon, "Defining Rape Internationally: A Comment on *Akayesu*," *Columbia Journal of Transnational Law* 44(3) (2006): 940–958; Southwick, "Srebrenica as Genocide." For discussion of the killing of men, see, e.g., R. Charli Carpenter, "Beyond 'Gendercide': Incoporating Gender into Comparative Genocide Studies," *International Journal of Human Rights* 6(4) (2002): 77–101.

107 Drumbl, "Prosecutor vs. Radislav Krstić"; for coverage of the death toll, see, e.g., "Timeline: The Siege of Srebrenica," *BBCNews*, 17 May 2012, www.bbc.com; Graham Jones, "Srebrenica: Worst European Atrocity since WWII," *CNNWorld*, 2006, www.cnn.com.

108 For discussions of displacement, see, e.g., discussions in Nicklaus Steiner, Mark Gibney, and Gil Loescher, eds., *Problems of Protection: the UNHCR, Refugees, and*

Human Rights (New York: Routledge, 2003), especially p.213; Berg and Shoup, *The War in Bosnia-Herzegovina*, p.171; Susan L. Woodward, *Balkan Tragedy: Chaos and Dissolution after the Cold War* (Washington, DC: Brookings Institution Press, 1995), p.364.

109 See, e.g., discussions in Robert M. Hayden, "Imagined Communities and Real Victims: Self-Determination and Ethnic Cleansing in Yugoslavia," *American Ethnologist* 23(4) (1996): 783–801; Stevan M. Weine, *When History Is a Nightmare: Lives and Memories of Ethnic Cleansing in Bosnia-Herzegovina* (New Brunswick, NJ: Rutgers University Press, 1999); Norman M. Naimark, *Fires of Hatred: Ethnic Cleansing in Twentieth-Century Europe* (Cambridge, MA: Harvard University Press, 2002).

110 Daniel Jonah Goldhagen, *Worse than War: Genocide, Eliminationism and the On-going Assault on Humanity* (New York: PublicAffairs, 2009); Sergey Y. Marochkin and Galina A. Nelaeva, "*Human Rights Review* 15(4) (2014): 473–488; Johanna Bond, "Victimization, Mainstreaming, and the Complexity of Gender in Armed Conflict," *Santa Clara Journal of International Law* 225 (2012): 227–235.

111 Rogel, *The Breakup of Yugoslavia and Its Aftermath*, pp.134, 136. Daryl A. Mundis, "Current Developments and the Ad Hoc International Criminal Tribunals," *Journal of International Criminal Justice* 1(3) (2003): 703–727.

112 "Biljana Plavšić: Serbian Iron Lady," BBCNews, 27 February 2003, news.bbc. co.uk; *Plavšić Sentencing Judgment*, para. 108, notes that she was once the Dean of Sciences at Sarajevo University; Jelena Subotic (in "The Cruelty of False Remorse: Bijana Plavšić at the Hague," *Southeastern Europe* 36[1] [2012]: 39–59, p.41) notes that she was once in the United States as a Fulbright scholar. Many sources suggest that her work was well-respected and well-cited; indeed much of her work can still be found through Google Scholar, published in journals like *Phytopathology, Journal of Phytopathology, Protoplasma,* and *Biologia Plantarum.*

113 Patrick FitzPatrick, "It Isn't Easy Being Biljana," *Central Europe Review* 22(2) (2000), www.ce-review.org. Another source suggested she called Muslims in Bosnia "a genetic mistake on the Serbian body" such that "to eliminate the was a 'natural phenomenon,' not a war crime" (Salvenka Drakulić, *They Would Never Hurt a Fly: War Criminals on Trial in The Hague* [New York: Viking Press, 2004], ch.12). She is said to have refused to negotiate with Bosnian Muslims due to genetics, saying, "it was genetically deformed material that embraced Islam. And now, of course, with each successive generation it simply becomes concentrated. It gets worse and worse" (Maya Shatzmiller, *Islam and Bosnia: Conflict Resolutions and Foreign Policy in Multi-Ethnic States* [Montreal: McGill-Queen's University Press, 2002], p.58). She is known for complaining that "they have introduced the term 'ethnic cleansing' to denote a perfectly natural phenomenon and qualified it as a war crime" on more than one occasion (John Hagan, *Justice in the Balkans: Prosecuting War Crimes in the Hague* Tribunal [Chicago: University of Chicago Press, 2010], p.11).

114 FitzPatrick, "It Isn't Easy Being Biljana," notes that she characterized Arkan, a noted rapist and war criminal as "the kind of man that we need" after the massacre at Bijeljina, which was one of the more sexually violent attacks during the conflict, and after her 'conversion' to being willing to cooperate with the West; see also "Biljana Plavšić: Serbian Iron Lady"; Gabrielle Ferrales and Suzy Maves McElrath, "Beyond Rape: Reconceptualizing Gender-Based Violence During Warfare," in Rosemay Gartner and Bill McCarthy, eds., *The Oxford Handbook of Gender, Sex, and Crime* (New York: Oxford University Press, 2014), pp.671–689, p.684.

115 E.g., "we are upset by a rising number of mixed marriages between Serbs and Muslims, for they allow genes to be exchanged between ethnic groups, and lead subsequently to the degeneration of Serb nationality," cited in Subotić, "The Cruelty of False Remorse," p.42.

116 Askin, "Quest for Post-Conflict Gender Justice"; Anne-Marie de Brouwer, *Supranational Criminal Prosecution of Sexual Violence: The ICC and the Practice of the ICTY and the ICTR* (Mortsel: Intersentia NV, 2005), p.490.

117 ICTY Sentencing Hearing, 16 and 18 December 2002, pp.395, 625, www.icty. org/x/cases/plavsic/trans/en/021216IT.htm and www.icty.org/x/cases/plavsic/ trans/en/021218IT.htm. See also Robin May Schott, "War Rape, Natality, and Genocide," *Journal of Genocide Research* 13(1–2) (2011): 5–21; Kelly Dawn Askin, "Holding Leaders Accountable in the International Criminal Court for Gender Crimes Committed in Darfur," *Genocide Studies and Prevention* 1(1) (2006): 13–28, p.24; Biljana Plavšić, *Svet*, Novi Sad, September 1993, translated and cited in Slobodan Inic, "Biljana Plavšić: Geneticist in Service of a Great Crime," *Bosnia Report: Newsletter of the Alliance to Defend Bosnia-Herzegovina* (June–August 1997); Askin, "Quest for Post-Conflict Gender Justice"; De Brouwer, *Supranational Criminal Prosecution.*

118 Information can be found at www.icty.org/case/plavsic/4.

119 See passages from ICTY sentencing hearing cited in note 117.

120 For discussions of the plea bargain in this case, see, e.g., Mark B. Harmon and Fergal Gaynor, "Ordinary Sentences for Extraordinary Crimes," *Journal of International Criminal Justice* 5(3) (2007): 683–712; Janine Natalya Clark, "Plea Bargaining and the ICTY: Guilty Pleas and Reconciliation," *European Journal of International Law* 20(2) (2009): 415–436; Alan Tieger and Milbert Shin, "Plea Agreements and the ICTY: Purpose, Effects, and Propriety," *Journal of International Criminal Justice* 3(3) (2005): 666–679; Regina E. Rauxloh, "Negotiated History: The Historical Record in International Criminal Law and Plea Bargaining," *International Criminal Law Review* 10(5) (2010): 739–770; Nancy Amoury Combs, *Guilty Pleas in International Criminal Law: Creating a Restorative Justice Approach* (Palo Alto, CA: Stanford University Press, 2007), pp.73–74, 145.

121 De Brouwer, *Supranational Criminal Prosecution*, p.490; Askin, "Quest for Post-Conflict Gender Justice."

122 Mundis, "Current Developments and the Ad Hoc International Criminal Tribunals," p.718, lists the mitigating factors (from para. 110 of the Sentencing Judgment) as the guilty plea, voluntary surrender, age, and post-conflict conduct (her support for the Dayton Agreement).

123 Subotic, "The Cruelty of False Remorse," p.46, citing a March 12, 2005, interview with Banjaluka-based Alternative TV, as well as another interview in January 2009, where she argued that "I sacrificed myself. I have done nothing wrong." Subotic suggests that Plavšić's 2005 memoirs, which were not published in English and have not received a significant amount of attention from English-language analysts, show "a remarkably clear worldview of an unrepentant nationalist, whose collectivist understanding of ethnicity, race, and politics demonstrates a profound lack of rehabilitation" (p.50).

124 The ICTY decision granting her early release can be found at www.icty.org/x/cases/plavsic/presdec/en/090914.pdf.

125 See e.g., "Biljana Plavšić: Serbian Iron Lady"; Emir Suljagic "Kisses as Bosnian War Kicked Off," Institute for War and Peace Reporting, 29 April 2005, http://iwpr.net.

126 Tawia Ansah, "Genocide and the Eroticization of Death: Law, Violence, and Moral Purity," Southern California Interdisciplinary Law Journal 14(2) (2005): 181–236.

127 A number of sources suggest that Milosevic saw her as an extremist, e.g., "Biljana Plavšić: Serbian Iron Lady"; Drakulic, They Would Never Hurt a Fly, ch.12 ("Even Slobodan Milosevic considered her too radical, deeming her qualified for the madhouse.")

128 Mundis, "Current Developments," p.717; Joshua Hammer, "'The Empress' Deposed," Newsweek, 21 January 2001, updated 13 March 2013, www.newsweek.com.

129 Ibid.

130 Ibid., p.718. Witnesses who came to her defense included Madeline Albright (then US secretary of state), Alex Boraine (then deputy chairperson of the South African Truth and Reconciliation Commission), Elie Wiesel (recipient of the 1986 Nobel Peace Prize), Carl Bildt (co-chairman of the Dayton Conference and former prime minister of Sweden), and Robert Frowick (head of the OSCE mission in Bosnia and Herzegovina during the conflict).

131 See testimony transcripts. Specifically, Albright testified December 17, 2002, and Wiesel December 16, 2002.

132 See, e.g., accounts of the violence advocated for and committed by Mira Markovic, Slobodon Milošević's wife ("Mira Marovic: Slobodan Milosevic's Lady Macbeth," Independent, 13 March 2006, www.independent.co.uk; Ed Vulliamy, "Mira Cracked," Observer, 7 July 2001, www.theguardian.com; Bojana Balovac, "Milosevic's Widow Accused Over Serbian Journalist's Slaying," BIRN Belgrade, 16 January 2014, www.balkaninsight.com; Misha Savic, "Warrant Out for Arrest of Milosevic's Wife in Two Political Killinds," Seattle Times, 5 April 2003, http://community.seattletimes.nwsource.com; for accounts of Rasema Handanovic, who emigrated to the United States after killing six Bosnian Croats, see Amy Oli-

ver, "The US Single Mother Who Was Actually a War Criminal: Killer Becomes First Woman to Be Convicted of Bosnian War Crimes," *MailOnline*, 1 May 2012, www.dailymail.co.uk; Aida Cerkez, "US Extradites War Crimes Suspect to Bosnia," *NBCNews*, 27 December 2011, www.nbcnews.com; "Bosnian War Crimes Court Jails First Woman," *Reuters*, 30 April 2012, www.reuters.com. While few of these stories explicitly mention or even imply the perpetrators being discussed committed acts of sexual violence, the prevalence of women perpetrators and the prevalence of sexual violence in war and conflict suggest there was probably some overlap.

133 See notes 114–117.
134 Subotic, "The Cruelty of False Remorse."
135 Some useful histories include J. J. Carney, *Rwanda before the Genocide: Catholic Politics and Ethnic Discourse in the Late Colonial Era* (Oxford: Oxford University Press, 2013); Jan Vasina, *Antecedents to Modern Rwanda: The Nyiginya Kingdom* (Madison: University of Wisconsin Press, 2005); Prunier, *The Rwanda Crisis*; Catharine Newbury, "Ethnicity and the Politics of History in Rwanda," *Africa Today* 45(1) (1998): 7–24; Jean-Pierre Chrétien, *The Great Lakes of Africa: Two Thousand Years of History*, trans. Scott Straus (Cambridge, MA: MIT Press, 2003).
136 Richard Sigwalt, "Early Rwandan History: The Contribution of Comparative Ethnography," *History in Africa* 2(1) (1975): 137–146; Mahmood Mamdani, *When Victims Become Killers: Colonialism, Nativism, and Genocide in Rwanda* (Princeton, NJ: Princeton University Press, 2001); Christopher C. Taylor, "Dual Systems in Rwanda: Have They Ever Really Existed," *Anthropological Theory* 4(3) (2004): 353–371; Paul J. Magnarella, "The Background and Causes of the Genocide in Rwanda," *Journal of International Criminal Justice* 3(4) (2005): 801–822.
137 Kennedy Ndahiro, "Where Slave Traders Failed, Bagosora Could Not Succeed," *New Times*, 8 April 2014, www.newtimes.co.rw. It is estimated that very few Rwandans ended up being a part of the global slave trade, with the majority of the victims being from (in descending order of percentage) Nigeria, Angola, Ghana, Senegal/Gambia, Guinea-Bissau, and Sierra Leone (Arthur Lewin, *Africa Is Not a Country, It Is a Continent* [London: Clarendon, 1990]).
138 Mamdani, *When Victims Become Killers*, ch.3; Chrétien, *The Great Lakes of Africa*; Catharine Newbury, *The Cohesion of Oppression: Clientship and Ethnicity in Rwanda, 1860–1960* (New York: Columbia University Press, 1988); Carney, *Rwanda before the Genocide*.
139 Chrétien, *The Great Lakes of Africa*, pp.69, 88–89; Philip Gourevitch, *We Wish to Inform You That Tomorrow We Will Be Killed with Our Families: Stories from Rwanda* (Basingstoke: Macmillan, 1998), pp.56–57; Mamdani, *When Victims Become Killers*, p.61.
140 Benson Okello, *A History of East Africa* (Kampala: Fountain Publishers, 2002); Chrétien, *The Great Lakes of Africa*, p.217; Prunier, *The Rwanda Crisis*, p.9.
141 Prunier, *The Rwanda Crisis*, p.25.

142 There is evidence that this started in the German era and worsened in the Belgian era. See, e.g., Prunier, *The Rwanda Crisis*; Chrétien, *The Great Lakes of Africa*; Paul Kerstens, "'Deliver Us from Original Sin: Belgian Apologies to Rwanda and the Congo," in Mark Gibney, ed., *The Age of Apology: Facing Up to the Past* (Philadelphia: University of Pennsylvania Press, 2008), pp.187–202; Mamdani, *When Victims Become Killers*, ch.3; John Rucyahana, *The Bishop of Rwanda* (Nashville: Thomas Nelson, 2007).

143 Johan Pottier, *Re-Imagining Rwanda: Conflict, Survival, and Disinformation in the Late Twentieth Century* (New York: Cambridge University Press, 2002).

144 Ibid.; Helen M. Hintjens, "Explaining the 1994 Genocide in Rwanda," *Journal of Modern African Studies* 37(2) (1999): 241–286; Robert Block, "The Tragedy of Rwanda," *New York Review of Books* 41(17) (1994): 3–8; Nigel Eltringham, "'Invaders Who Have Stolen the Country': The Hamitic Hypothesis, Race, and the Rwandan Genocide," *Social Identities: Journal for the Study of Race, Nation, and Culture* 12(4) (2006): 425–446; Prunier, *The Rwanda Crisis*, p.8.

145 In 1919, Belgium accepted a League of Nations mandate to govern the territory that had been proposed in 1916, and received the right to govern the territory in August of 1923.

146 Prunier, *The Rwanda Crisis*. Belgian active involvement included attempts to harvest crops for a profit and a system of forced labor to increase the efficiency of that effort. See, e.g., discussions in Arthur Blouin, "Culture and Contracts: The Historical Legacy of Forced Labour," unpublished paper, November 2013, www2. warwick.ac.uk/fac/soc/economics/staff/atblouin/research/culturecontracts11.pdf; Newbury, *The Cohesion of Oppression*; Pierre Erny, *L'Enseignment au Rwanda après l'indépendance* (Paris: L'Harmattan, 2005); Alain Destexhe, *Rwanda and Genocide in the Twentieth Century* (London: Pluto Press, 1995); Peter Uvin, "Tragedy in Rwanda: The Political Ecology of Conflict," *Environment: Science and Policy for Sustainable Development* 38(3) (1996): 7–29.

147 Gourevitch, *We Wish to Inform You*, pp.56–57. See discussion in Timothy Longman, "Identity Cards, Ethnic Self-Perception, and Genocide in Rwanda," in Jane Caplan and John C. Torpey, eds., *Documenting Individual Identity: The Development of State Practices in the Modern World* (Princeton, NJ: Princeton University Press, 2001), pp.345–358.

148 See, e.g., discussions in Helen M. Hintjens, "When Identity Becomes a Knife: Reflecting on the Genocide in Rwanda," *Ethnicities* 1(1) (2001): 25–55; Said Adejumobi, "Citizenship, Rights, and the Problem of Conflicts and Civil Wars in Africa," *Human Rights Quarterly* 23(1) (2001): 148–170, pp.163–169.

149 For general discussions of ethnic segregation, see, e.g., Regine Andersen, "How Multilateral Development Assistance Triggered the Conflict in Rwanda," *Third World Quarterly* 21(3) (2000): 441–456; Ravi Bhavnani, "Ethnic Norms and Interethnic Violence: Accounting for Mass Participation in the Rwandan Genocide," *Journal of Peace Research* 43(6) (2006): 651–659; Newbury, "Ethnicity and the Politics of History"; Mamdani, *When Victims Become Killers*; for discussion of the

church specifically, see, e.g., extensive discussion in Carney, *Rwanda before the Genocide*; Carol Ritter, John K. Roth, and Wendy Whitworth, eds., *Genocide in Rwanda: Complicity of the Churches?* (St. Paul, Minnesota: Aegis, 2004); Timothy Longman, "Church Politics and the Genocide in Rwanda," *Journal of Religion in Africa* 31(2) (2001): 163–186.

150 Prunier, *The Rwanda Crisis*, p.51. For extensive discussion, see L. Christian Marlin, "A Lesson Unlearned: The Unjust Revolution in Rwanda, 1959–1961," *Emory International Law Review* 12(3) (1998): 1271–1330; Peter Uvin, "Prejudice, Crisis, and Genocide in Rwanda," *African Studies Review* 40(2) (1997): 91–115.

151 Gourevitch, *We Wish to Tell You*, pp.58–59; Mamdani, *When Victims Become Killers*, ch.4; Christopher Clapham, "Rwanda: The Perils of Peacemaking," *Journal of Peace Research* 35(2) (1998): 193–210.

152 Prunier, *The Rwanda Crisis*, p.53; Mamdani, *When Victims Become Killers*; Alan J. Kuperman, "The Other Lesson of Rwanda: Mediators Sometimes Do More Damage than Good," *SAIS Review* 16(1) (1996): 221–240. The colonization-era territory was actually Ruanda-Urundi (see, e.g., A. L. Latham-Koenig, "Ruanda-Urundi on the Threshold of Independence," *The World Today* 18[7] [July 1962]: 288–295), but Belgian efforts to create an independent Ruanda-Urundi with ethnic power-sharing failed, and two countries, Rwanda and Burundi, were established. See, e.g., Peter Uvin, "Ethnicity and Power in Burundi and Rwanda: Different Paths to Mass Violence," *Comparative Politics* 31(3) (1999): 253–271, for a discussion of the postcolonial differences in the two countries.

153 Magnarella, "The Background and Causes of the Genocide in Rwanda"; Philip Verwimp, "The Political Economy of Coffee, Dictatorship, and Genocide," *European Journal of Political Economy* 19(2) (2003): 161–181; Edmund Abaka and J.B. Gashugi, "Forced Migration from Rwanda: Myths and Realities," *Refuge* 14(5) (1994): 9–12; Samuel Totten and Rafiki Ubaldo, "Introduction," in Samuel Totten and Rafiki Ubaldo, eds., *We Cannot Forget: Interviews with Survivors of the 1994 Genocide in Rwanda* (New Brunswick, NJ: Rutgers University Press, 2011), pp.1–22, p.6; A. Walter Dorn and Jonathan Matloff, "Preventing the Bloodbath: Could the UN Have Predicted and Prevented the Rwandan Genocide," *Journal of Conflict Studies* XX(1) (2000), https://journals.lib.unb.ca/index.php/JCS.

154 Prunier, *The Rwanda Crisis*, pp.74–76; see discussion in René Lemarchand, "Managing Transition Anarchies: Rwanda, Burundi, and South Africa in Comparative Perspective," *The Journal of Modern African Studies* 32(4) (1994): 581–604.

155 For characterizations of Juvénal Habyarimana as a moderate, see, e.g., Sadye Logan, "Remembering the Women in Rwanda: When Humans Rely on Old Concepts of War to Resolve Conflict," *Affilia* 21(2) (2006): 234–239; Des Forges, *Leave None to Tell the Story*; Scott Straus, *The Order of Genocide: Race, Power, and War in Rwanda* (Ithaca, NY: Cornell University Press, 2006).

156 A 1991 constitution permitted the opening of cabinet posts and parliamentary seats to other parties, though implementation was slow and often limited to other parties that were allies of the Habyarimana administration. See, e.g., discussions in Straus, *The Order of Genocide*; Learthen Dorsey, *Historical Dictionary of Rwanda* (Lanham, MD: Scarecrow Press, 1994), pp.119–120; Peter Uvin, *L'Aide Complice? Cooperation Internationale et Violence au Rwanda* (Paris: L'Harmattan, 1999), pp.64–65; Emmanuel Viret, "Rwanda—A Chronology (1867–1994)," *Online Encyclopedia of Mass Violence*, 1 March 2010, www.massviolence.org.

157 Bruce D. Jones, *Peacemaking in Rwanda: The Dynamics of Failure* (Boulder, CO: Lynne Rienner, 2001); Prunier, *The Rwanda Crisis*, p.93. There is some debate about whether the RPF invasion was looking for concessions for joint governance or a full-scale takeover attempt; the RPF claimed the former and many Rwandese Hutu were concerned about the latter.

158 Prunier, *The Rwanda Crisis*, pp.190–191; Magnarella, "The Background and Causes of the Genocide"; Timothy Longman, "Obstacles to Peacebuilding in Rwanda," in Taiser Mohamed Ahmed Ali and Robert O. Matthews, eds., *Durable Peace: Challenges for Peacebuilding in Africa* (Toronto: University of Toronto Press), pp.61–85, p.67; Linda Melvern, *A People Betrayed: The Role of the West in Rwanda's Genocide* (London: Zed Books, 2000), ch.5; Barbara F. Walter, *Committing to Peace: The Successful Settlement of Civil Wars* (Princeton, NJ: Princeton University Press, 2002), p.146.

159 Gourevitch, *We Wish to Inform You*, p.26; Alan Kuperman, "Rwanda in Retrospect," *Foreign Affairs* 79(1) (2000): 94–118.

160 "Hutus Killed Rwanda President Juvénal Habyaimana,'" *BBCNews*, 12 January 2010, http://news.bbc.co.uk; Pierre-Antoine Souchard, "Juvenal Habyaimana, Former Rwanda President, Killed by Military Fire, Not Rebels, French Investigation Finds," *Huffington Post*, 10 January 2012, www.huffingtonpost.com; "Rwanda Inquiry Concludes Hutus Shot Down President's Plane," *Associated Press/Guardian*, 12 January 2010, www.theguardian.com; "Report: Rebels Cleared in Plane Crash that Sparked the Rwandan Genocide," *CNN.com*, 11 January 2012, www.cnn.com.

161 Prunier, *The Rwanda Crisis*, pp.182, 230; Roméo Dallaire, *Shake Hands with the Devil: The Failure of Humanity in Rwanda* (London: Arrow Books, 2005), p.231; Des Forges, *Leave None to Tell the Story*, tells at least fifteen separate stories of different people having lists of those to be killed.

162 See, e.g., Michele Schweisfurth, "Global and Cross-National Influences on Education in Post-Genocide Rwanda," *Oxford Review of Education* 32(5) (2006): 697–709, p.699, citing Melvern, *A People Betrayed*; Frank Moller, "Rwanda Revisualized: Genocide, Photography, and the Era of the Witness," *Alternatives: Global, Local, Political* 35(1) (2010): 113–136, p.119; Lt. Col. Keith Reeves, USAF, "Defeating Genocide: An Operational Concept Based on the Rwandan Experiment," in Douglas Carl Peifer, ed., *Stopping Mass Killings in Africa: Genocide, Airpower, and Intervention* (Darby, PA: DIANE Publishing, 2009), pp.77–100, p.78.

163 The Human Rights Council estimates 800,000 deaths (www.unitedhumanrights. org); a Rwandan Youth Ministry Census estimates 937,000 (www.irinnews.org); estimates as high as 1.17 million have been published in news outlets and by parts of the Rwandan government.

164 Calculated using raw population data before and after the summer of 1994.

165 Des Forges, *Leave None To Tell the Story*, p.2; Mamdani, *When Victims Become Killers*; Waller, *Becoming Evil*, p.67. The most detailed calculation of the number of perpetrators who had a role in the genocide that I have seen is by Scott Straus, in *The Order of Genocide*, p.117.

166 Adler, Loyle, and Globerman, "Calamity in the Neighborhood," p.212.

167 African Rights, *Rwanda—Not So Innocent: When Women Become Killers* (London: African Rights, 1995), p.5.

168 Donna J. Maier, "Women Leaders in the Rwandan Genocide: When Women Choose to Kill," *Universitas* 8 (2012–2013), www.uni.edu/universitas.

169 Adler, Loyle, and Globerman, "Calamity in the Neighborhood," p.212, citing African Rights, *Rwanda—Not So Innocent*; Lisa Sharlach, "Gender and Genocide in Rwanda: Women as Agents and Objects of Genocide," *Journal of Genocide Research* 1 (1999): 387–399.

170 Adler, Loyle, and Globerman, "Calamity in the Neighborhood," p.212.

171 Ibid., p.211.

172 Ibid., p.212.

173 See, e.g., Philip Gourevitch, "The Arrest of Madame Agathe," *New Yorker*, 2 March 2010, www.newyorker.com; Chris McGreal, "Profile: Agathe Habyarimana, The Power Behind the Hutu Presidency," *Guardian*, 2 March 2010, www.theguardian. com; "Rwandan Ex-Leader's Widow Arrested," *Al Jazeera*, 2 March 2010, www. aljazeera.com.

174 African Rights, *Rwanda—Not So Innocent*, p.58; Ruth Jamieson, "Genocide and the Social Production of Immorality," *Theoretical Criminology* 3(2) (1999): 131–146; Melynda J. Price, "Balancing Lives: Individual Accountability and the Death Penalty as Punishment for Genocide, Lessons from Rwanda," *Emory International Law Review* 21(2) (2007): 563–600; Edmund Kagire, "Sentenced to Life in 2009, Former Rwandan Justice Minister Appeals," *East African*, 20 January 2014, www. theeastafrican.co.ke.

175 African Rights, *Rwanda—Not So Innocent*, pp.80–82; Darryl Li, "Echoes of Violence: Considerations on Radio and Genocide in Rwanda," *Journal of Genocide Research* 6(1) (2004): 9–27; Alison Des Forges, "Silencing the Voices of Hate in Rwanda," in Monroe Edwin Price and Mark Thompson, eds., *Forging Peace: Intervention, Human Rights, and the Management of Media Space* (Bloomington: Indiana University Press, 2002), pp.236–258, p.236; "Rwanda Jails Journalist Valérie Bermeriki for Genocide," *BBCNews*, 14 December 2009, news.bbc.co.uk.

176 African Rights, *Rwanda—Not So Innocent*, pp.60–67 (Rose Karushara), 67–72 (Odette Nyirabegenzi), 72–77 (Euphrasie Kamatamu).

177 Ivan R. Mugisha, "Women's Roles Have Evolved—First Lady," *New Times*, 17 April 2014, www.newtimes.co.rw.

178 African Rights, *Rwanda—Not So Innocent*, pp.4, 19–20.

179 Adler, Loyle, and Globerman, "Calamity in the Neighborhood."

180 Ibid., p.212.

181 Ibid., pp.215–216.

182 Ibid.

183 Ibid., p.221. In fact, as the authors recount, "some women who agreed to join the militias had reputations for challenging limits in other spheres and may have become involved precisely because of their familiarity with crossing social boundaries" (p.223).

184 Ibid., p.226.

185 Mamdani, *When Victims Become Killers*, p.225, citing personal interviews. In the next sentence, though, Mamdani compares women to children.

186 Ibid.

187 See, e.g., discussion in Adler, Loyle, and Globerman, "Calamity in the Neighborhood."

188 Ibid., p.212.

189 Ibid., citing Nicole Hogg, *"I Never Poured Blood": Women Accused of Genocide in Rwanda* (Montreal: McGill-Queens University Press, 2001).

190 Adler, Loyle, and Globerman, "Calamity in the Neighborhood," p.212, citing Ligue Rwandaise, pour le promotion et la defense des droits de l'homme, *Situation des droits de la personne au Rwanda en 2002: rapport annuel de la Liprodhor* (Kigali: Ligue Rwandaise, 2003).

191 Adler, Loyle, and Globerman, "Calamity in the Neighborhood," p.212.

192 Mamdani, *When Victims Become Killers*, p.225.

193 Ibid.

194 See extensive discussion of the case of Pauline Nyiramasuhuko as an example in chapter 2; because it was discussed there, other cases will be focused on in this chapter.

195 E.g., the testimony of Liberee Mukarugwiza, in African Rights, *Rwanda—Not So Innocent*, p.54.

196 African Rights, *Rwanda—Not So Innocent*, p.21.

197 Ibid., p.22.

198 Ibid., p.20, quoting a story of Lindsey Hilsum in *The Observer*. The account continues to suggest that, after the committed rape, Aline went on to direct the killing of the victim.

199 Megan Gerecke, "Explaining Sexual Violence in Conflict Situations" (unpublished master's thesis at McGill University), http://s3.amazonaws.com/zanran_storage/zunia.org/ContentPages/1289436607.pdf, p.19n20, citing Luke Fletcher, "Turning Interahamwe: Individual and Community Choices in the Rwandan Genocide," *Journal of Genocide Research* 9(1) (2007): 25–48.

200 African Rights, *Rwanda—Not So Innocent*, p.15.

201 Ibid., p.16.

202 Ibid., p.39.

203 As African Rights describes, "very often, groups of women ululated their men into the 'action' that would result in the deaths of thousands" (*Rwanda—Not So Innocent*, p.39).

204 This is the story of Zakia Uwamugira, in an interview with African Rights on January 30, 1995, recounted in *Rwanda—Not So Innocent*, p.39.

205 Janie Leatherman, *Sexual Violence and Armed Conflict* (London: Polity, 2011), p.44, citing De Brouwer, *Supranational Criminal Practice*, p.13.

206 Prunier, *The Rwanda Crisis*, pp.4, 24. There was also a parallel in-migration to Rwanda of Tutsis who had been outside of Rwanda for much or even all of the preceding thirty years of Hutu rule (p.5).

207 For discussion, see, e.g., Lea-Lisa Westerhoff and Medhi Meddeb, "Rwandan Genocide: What Future for Hutu Refugees?," *Focus*, 8 April 2014, www.france24. comMichelle Faul, "Second Rwanda Genocide Is Revealed in Congo," *NBCNews. com*, 10 October 2010, www.nbcnews.com; "Rwanda Genocide: 'Domino Effect' in DR Congo," *BBCNews Africa*, 10 April 2014, www.bbc.com.

208 UNHCR suggests that, with movement across the border, it is sometimes hard to tell which refugees are from Rwanda and which are from the DRC. Between external refugees and internally displaced persons, UNHCR's December 2013 estimate was that there were almost 2.9 million people in the Democratic Republic of Congo (mostly in the Eastern DRC) who are in transitory status and classified as under UNHCR coverage (www.unhcr.org). See also Prunier, *Rwanda in Crisis*, pp.24–26.

209 Filip Reyntjens, *The Great African War: Congo and Regional Geopolitics, 1996–2006* (Cambridge, UK: Cambridge University Press, 2009), p.45. The Eastern Congo Initiative estimates that it was 7 percent of the 1.5 million refugees to the Eastern DRC in 1994 who had actually been perpetrators ("History of the Conflict," www.easterncongo.org).

210 Craig Timberg, "Rwanda's Tormenters Emerge from the Forest to Haunt Congo," *Washington Post*, 10 February 2005, www.washingtonpost.com; Chris Simpson, "Interahamwe: A Serious Military Threat," *BBCNews*, 2 March 1999, http://news. bbc.co.uk; "Democratic Republic of Congo Casualties of War: Civilians, Rule of Law, and Democratic Freedom," *Human Rights Watch Reports* 11(1) (1999), www. hrw.org.

211 John Pomfret, "Rwandans Led Revolt in Congo; Defense Minister Says Arms, Troops Supplied for Anti-Mobutu Drive," *Washington Post*, 9 July 1997, www. highbeam.com/doc; Timothy Longman, "The Complex Reasons for Rwanda's Engagement in Congo," in John F. Clark, ed., *The African Stakes of the Congo War* (New York: Palgrave Macmillan, 2002), pp.129–144, p.131; Eastern Congo Initiative, "History of the Conflict"; Max Fisher, "UN Report on Rwanda Genocide Shakes Africa," *Wire*, 10 August 2010, www.thewire.com.

212 Eastern Congo Initiative, "History of the Conflict"; Reyntjens, *The Great African War.*

213 See, e.g., Jeffrey Gettleman, "The World's Worst War," *New York Times*, 15 December 2012, www.nytimes.com ; Gérard Prunier, *Africa's World War: Congo, the Rwandan Genocide, and the Making of a Continental Catastrophe* (New York: Oxford University Press, 2008); Jason Steams, *Dancing in the Glory of Monsters: The Collapse of the Congo and the Great War of Africa* (New York: PublicAffairs, 2011); Michael Deibert, *The Democratic Republic of Congo: Between Hope and Despair* (London: Zed Books, 2013).

214 For discussions of Kabila's assassination, see, e.g., Stuart Jeffries, "Revealed: How Africa's Dictator Died at the Hands of His Boy Soldiers," *Guardian*, 10 February 2001, www.theguardian.com; "Kabila Death Confirmed," *BBCNews*, 18 January 2001, news.bbc.co.uk. Different accounts of his death suggest that he was killed by his son, by his soldiers, or by the Rwandan president. While any co-conspirators have not been identified, it has been confirmed that it was one of his bodyguards who actually killed him.

215 See, e.g., discussions by the UN ("2006: A Year of Hope for the Congolese People," www.un.org), the British Department for International Development ("Elections in the Democratic Republic of Congo in 2006," www.gov.uk); and the United States Institute of Peace (Tatiana Carayannis, "Elections in the DRC: The Bemba Surprise," Special Report 200, February 2008, www.usip.org).

216 "DRC: Cautious Welcome for Kivu Peace Deal," *IRIN News*, 29 January 2008, www.irinnews.org; Koen Vlassenroot and Timoth Raeymaekers, "Kivu's Intractable Security Conundrum," *African Affairs*, 29 May 2009: 1–10; Denis M. Tull, "Peacekeeping in the Democratic Republic of Congo: Waging Peace and Fighting War," *International Peacekeeping* 16(2) (2009): 215–230.

217 "Rwanda-DRC: Kagame Seeks Co-Operation on Rebels," *IRIN News*, 7 May 2007, www.irinnews.org; "UN Chief Praises Improved Rwanda-DRC Relations," *New Times*, January 2009, www.newtimes.co.rw; "Congo: Five Priorities for Peacebuilding Strategy," Africa Report #150, *Crisis Group*, 11 May 2009, www.crisisgroup.org.

218 For instability in the summer of 2014, see, e.g., "Rwanda-Congo Border Tense after Gun Battle," *Independent*, 22 June 2014, www.independent.co.uk; "Dozens Die as Ugandan Soldiers Fight 'Tribal Gunmen' Near DR Congo Borders," *ABC Online*, 7 July 2014, www.independent.co.uk; Andrew Siddons, "U.S. Will Broaden Sanctions to Deter Violence in Congo," *New York Times*, 9 July 2014, www.nytimes.com.

219 This estimate is widely agreed on, and can be found in a number of news and scholarly outlets, e.g., Gettleman, "The World's Worst War"; "Congo Crisis," International Rescue Committee, 2007, www.rescue.org. The original source of the estimate of 5.4 million deaths is the Human Security Report Project at Simon Fraser University ("Human Security Report 2009: The Shrinking Costs of War," Human Security Report Project at the School for International Studies, Simon Fraser University, 20 January 2010, ch.7, pp.123–131, www.hsrgroup.org).

220 E.g., Gettleman, "The World's Worst War"; John Predergast, "Hope for an End to the World's Deadliest War," *CNN*, 22 February 2013, www.cnn.com/; Peter Eichstaedt, *Consuming the Congo: War and Conflict Minerals in the World's Deadliest Place* (Chicago: Chicago Review Press, 2011); "DR Congo: Africa's Worst War," *BBC News*, 8 April 2003, http://news.bbc.co.uk.

221 E.g., Robert I. Rotberg, "The New Nature of Nation-State Failure," *Washington Quarterly* 25(3) (2002): 83–96; Pierre Englebert and Denis M. Tull, "Postconflict Reconstruction in Africa: Flawed Ideas about Failed States," *International Security* 32(4) (2008): 106–139; Georgianne Nienaber, "Why the Democratic Republic of Congo Is a Failed State," *World Post*, 23 July 2012, www.huffingtonpost.com; J. J. Messner and Kendall Lawrence, "Failed States Index 2013: The Troubled Ten," *Fund for Peace*, 24 June 2013, http://library.fundforpeace.org.

222 E.g., Abiodun Alao, *Natural Resources and Conflict in Africa: The Tragedy of Endowment* (Rochester, NY: University of Rochester Press, 2007); Gettleman, "The World's Worst War."

223 Stephanie McCrummen, "Prevalence of Rape in E. Congo Described as Worst in World," *Washington Post*, 9 September 2007, www.washingtonpost.com. See also Desiree Lwambo, "'Before the War, I Was a Man': Men and Masculinities in the Eastern Democratic Republic of Congo," *Gender and Development* 21(1) (2013): 47–66.

224 McCrummen, "Prevalence of Rape," quoting John Holmes, then coordinator of UN emergency relief operations.

225 Joe Bavier, "Congo War-Driven Crisis Kills 45,000 a Month: Study," *Reuters*, 22 January 2008, http://mobile.reuters.com.

226 Simon Robinson and Vivenne Walt, "The Deadliest War in the World," *Time*, 28 May 2006, http://content.time.com.

227 Kristen Johnson, Jennifer Scott, Bigy Rughita, Michael Kisielewski, Jana Asher, Ricardo Ong, and Lynn Lawry, "Association of Sexual Violence and Human Rights Violations with Physical and Mental Health in Territories of the Eastern Democratic Republic of Congo," *Journal of the American Medical Association* 4(5) (4 August 2010): 553–562.

228 Ibid., p.553.

229 Ibid., p.558.

230 Ibid. See also discussion in Lara Stemple, "Human Rights, Sex, and Gender: Limits in Theory and Practice," *Pace Law Review* 31(3) (2011): 824–836, p.833.

231 E.g., Jocelyn Kelly, Justin Kabanga, Will Cragin, Lys Alcayna-Stevens, Sadia Haider, and Michael Vanrooyen, "If Your Husband Doesn't Humiliate You, Other People Won't': Gendered Attitudes toward Sexual Violence in the Eastern DRC," *Global Public Health: An International journal for Research, Policy, and Practice* 7(3) (2003): 285–298.

232 Quoted in Jessica Hatcher, "Congo's Forgotten Curse: Epidemic of Female-on-Female Rape," *Time*, 3 December 2013, http://world.time.com.

233 Ibid.

234 Ibid.

235 Waller, *Becoming Evil*, p.267.

236 See, e.g., Cohen, "Female Combatants and the Perpetration of Violence."

237 See, e.g., "British Female Jihadists 'Are Running Brothels Full of Captured Sex Slaves for Islamic State Militants," *Huffington Post UK*, 11 September 2014, www. huffingtonpost.co.uk; Jay Akbar, "'I Rejoiced When We Had Our First Sex Slave, Forced Sex ISN'T Rape and They Should Be Thankful': Chilling Rant of Twisted ISIS Jihadi Bride Who Justifies Kidnapping and Abusing Yazidi Girls," *Daily Mail*, 22 May 2015, www.dailymail.co.uk; Russell Myers, "British Female Jihadis Running ISIS 'Brothels' Allowing Killers to Rape Kidnapped Yazidi Women," *Mirror*, 10 September 2014, www.mirror.co.uk.

238 Johnson et al., "Association of Sexual Violence," p.553.

239 Hatcher, "Congo's Forgotten Curse."

240 Ibid.

CHAPTER 4. THERE'S NO EVIDENCE WOMEN ARE ANY WORSE AT RAPE THAN MEN ARE

1 Andy Park, "Female Rapists: 'You Don't Really Expect It From a Woman Because They're Meant to Be on Your Side," *News.com.au*, 28 August 2014, www.news.com.au.

2 Waller, *Becoming Evil*, p.266.

3 Desiree Lwambo, "'Before the War, I Was a Man': Men and Masculinities in the Eastern DRC," *Gender and Development* 21(1) (2013): 47–66.

4 Mibenge, *Sex and International Tribunals*, p.164.

5 Tickner, *Gender in International Relations*, p.141.

6 Adler, Loyle, and Globerman, "Calamity in the Neighborhood," p.211, citing Graeme R. Newman, ed., *Global Report on Crime and Justice* (New York: Oxford University Press/United Nations Centre for International Crime Prevention, 1999).

7 Adler, Loyle, and Globerman, "Calamity in the Neighborhood," p.211, citing Christopher Browning, *Ordinary Men: Reserve Police Battalion 101 and the Final Solution in Poland* (New York: Harper Perennial, 1993).

8 Adler, Loyle, and Globerman, "Calamity in the Neighborhood," p.228.

9 For discussions of the idea that women's violence might be more scary, see, e.g., Elshtain, *Women and War*; Waller, *Becoming Evil*, p.266.

10 Johnson et al., "Association of Sexual Violence." See discussion of this in Stemple, "Human Rights, Sex."

11 Johnson et al., "Association of Sexual Violence," p.554. reports: "Senior author Lynn Lawry tells me that the change was at the behest of JAMA who removed the term 'sexual gender based violence' during its edits, due to the confusion between the terms sex and gender. The authors then objected in writing, explaining that gender-based violence, an internationally accepted phenomenon, 'occurs to either men or women' . . . nevertheless, the neutered term 'interpersonal violence was ultimately used. Lawry concludes that the term 'gender-based violence' has

been 'overtaken by advocacy groups to push agendas' focused only on male violence against women'" ("Human Rights, Sex," p.834). I know that this is quoting at length, but I think that the discussion crystallizes the issues this chapter discusses—the ability to use the term "gender-based" in complex ways that does not rely on sex specificity but can deal with it.

12 Stemple, "Human Rights, Sex," p.825.

13 Ibid.

14 Ibid.

15 Ibid.

16 Ibid., pp.825–826.

17 Ibid., p.826.

18 Ibid, p.827. Stemple points out the example of the clumsy definition of gender within the Rome Statute of the International Criminal Court, which explicitly references the existence of two sexes—male and female—and their coexistence "within the context of society" (p.828).

19 Ibid., p.829.

20 Ibid., p.830. She suggests that the biggest hurdle that such an approach has to tackle is "discomfort with male vulnerability"—I disagree. As will be discussed below, I think that the biggest hurdle such an approach has to surmount is the victim/perpetrator dichotomy—where people (both individually and in collective groups of *sorts* of people) who are victimized are excluded from the class of perpetrators, and people who are perpetrators (both individually and in collective groups of *sorts* of people) are excluded from the class of (actual or potential) victims. I also suggest that the flip side of male vulnerability—female *power*—is equally if not more difficult to deal with in the context of the analysis of sexual violence in war and conflict.

21 Ibid., p.833, citing Jamie R. Abrams, "The Collateral Consequences of Masculinizing Violence," *William and Mary Journal of Women and the Law* 16(3) (2010): 703–752, p.704. Stemple argues that "female perpetration of conflict sexual violence is a particularly thorny issue for women's rights advocates to confront, as it runs counter to the well-established and politically-potent feminist narrative about men's use of violence to subordinate women." I think that is true, and look to reconcile it.

22 Ibid., p.835.

23 Ibid., p.836.

24 Rosemary Grey and Laura J. Shepherd, "'Stop Rape Now?': Masculinity, Responsibility, and Conflict-Related Sexual Violence," *Men and Masculinities* 16(1) (2013): 115–135, p.116.

25 Ibid., p.119. Grey and Shepherd's article is about the recognition of male victims, though similar logic could be applied to the recognition of female perpetrators (and their omission from the article is a matter of interest to me). The authors argue that "it is understandable that the literature has focused on sexual violence against women, given the gravity and assumed scale of the problem," paired with

the majority of the scholarship being written by feminists with an interest in improving women's lives and (relative and absolute) positionalities—while I don't think that's untrue, I think it might ultimately be counterproductive to the goals of the scholarship in even more ways than Grey and Shepherd point out.

26 Ibid., p.129. The implication therein, to the authors, is that "the literature . . . not only fails to envision sexual violence against a male body, it is also fairly disinterested in the politics of sexual violence against men." Still, while this piece is explicitly arguing for the visibility of those who play sex-non-traditional roles in sexual violence in war and conflict, it focuses on male victims, and, in my view, is missing an understanding that those very same assumptions make women perpetrators invisible and of the article's complicity in that invisibility.

27 Ibid., p.122.

28 Johanna Bond, "Victimization, Mainstreaming, and the Complexity of Gender in Armed Conflict," *Santa Clara Journal of International Law* 11(2) (2012): 225–235, p.232.

29 Debra Bergoffen, in "Toward a Politics of the Vulnerable Body," suggests that sexual violence in war and conflict be framed as heterosexual and non-heterosexual. While I find there to be significant problems with that formulation, I do think it describes (yet another group of) blindnesses in the male perpetrator/female victim dichotomy).

30 Arden B. Levy, "International Prosecution of Rape in Warfare: Nondiscriminatory Recognition and Enforcement," *University of California-Los Angeles Women's Law Journal* 4(2) (1993): 255–297.

31 Mibenge, *Sex and International Tribunals*, pp.10–11.

32 Ibid., p.62.

33 Ibid., p.42.

34 Ibid., p.7.

35 Butler, *Bodies That Matter*, p.27.

36 Ibid., p.64.

37 Enloe, *Bananas, Beaches, and Bases*.

38 Butler, *Bodies That Matter*, p.181.

39 Mibenge, *Sex and International Tribunals*, p.158.

40 Butler, *Bodies That Matter*, p.181. As Obote-Odora explains, though, "the development of international criminal law in the area of sex-based crimes is only the beginning of the process of international prosecution of these crimes" ("Rape and Sexual Violence in International Law," p.158)—it is also important to understand both structural and procedural barriers, which will be discussed in more detail in chapter 6.

41 Maria Ericksson Baaz and Maria Stern, *Sexual Violence as a Weapon of War?* (London: Zed Books, 2013), p.3.

42 Ibid., p.4.

43 Ibid. As I will discuss below and in chapter 6, I do not think that the "gender story" necessarily includes the sex-essentialist holdovers of the sexed story.

44 Ibid, p.30.

45 Ibid., p.35, citing Gerard J. deGroot, "Introduction to Part I: Arms and the Woman," in Gerard. J. DeGroot and Corinne Peniston-Bird, eds., *A Soldier and a Woman: Sexual Integration in the Military* (Harlow: Pearson Education, 2000), pp.3–17.

46 Ibid., p.4.

47 Ibid., p.3.

48 See, e.g., discussions in Anne Sisson Runyan and V. Spike Peterson, *Global Gender Issues in the New Millennium*, 4th ed. (Boulder, CO: Westview Press, 2013); Laura Sjoberg, "Gender/Violence in a Gendered/Violent World," *Millennium Journal of International Studies* 42(2) (2014): 532–542; Eric M. Blanchard, "Gender, International Relations, and the Development of Feminist Security Theory," *Signs: Journal of Women in Culture and Society* 28(4) (2003): 1289–1312.

49 E.g., United Nations Security Council Resolution 1325. See discussion in Shepherd, "Power and Authority."

50 Mibenge, *Sex and International Tribunals*.

51 Sjoberg, "Gender/Violence."

52 See a significantly more sophisticated understanding in Connell, *Masculinities*; Charlotte Hooper, *Manly States: Masculinities, International Relations, and Gender Politics* (New York: Columbia University Press, 2001). There are explicit discussions of how this translates into expectations in politics in the leadership literature, e.g., Leonie Huddy and Nayda Terkildsen, "The Consequences of Gender Stereotypes for Women Candidates at Different Levels and Types of Public Office," *Political Research Quarterly* 46(3) (1993): 503–525.

53 See, e.g., discussions in Joan Acker, "From Sex Roles to Gendered Institutions," *Contemporary Sociology* 21 (1992): 565–569; Butler, *Gender Trouble*; Heyes, "Feminist Solidarity"; Gayle Rubin, "The Traffic in Women: Notes on the 'Political Economy' of Sex," in Rayna R. Reiter, ed., *Toward an Anthropology of Women* (New York: Monthly Review Press, 1975), pp.157–210.

54 See, e.g., Tickner, *Gender in International Relations*; Peterson and Runyan, *Global Gender Issues*.

55 Sjoberg, "Women and the Genocidal Rape of Other Women," p.30. In 2008, I explained that this was related to "ideal-types of masculinity and femininity based on class, culture, religion, race, ethnicity, and time—and other masculinities and femininities related to those ideal-types. Those multiple masculinities and femininities come together to set boundaries for what women should be and what men should be, situated in sociocultural contexts. These boundaries provide the content of perceived membership in sex classes" (ibid.). As discussed in this section, while I maintain that basic understanding, I have come to see it as more complicated.

56 For discussions of the complexity of these issues, see, e.g., Butler, *Bodies That Matter*; Anne Fausto-Sterling, *Myths of Gender: Biological Theories about Women and Men* (New York: Basic Books, 2008); Anne Fausto-Sterling, *Sexing the Body: Gender Politics and the Construction of Sexuality* (New York: Basic Books, 2000);

John H. Gagnon and William Simon, *Sexual Conduct: The Social Sources of Human Sexuality* (New York: Transaction Publishers, 2011); Mary-Lou Pardue and Theresa M. Wizemann, eds., *Exploring the Biological Contributions to Human Health: Does Sex Matter?* (Washington, DC: National Academies Press, 2001).

57 I rely on the explanation of these dynamics in the new edition of Anne McClintock's *Imperial Leather: Race, Gender and Sexuality in the Colonial Contest* (New York: Routledge, 2013).

58 Sjoberg, *Gender, War, and Conflict*, p.17.

59 This idea builds on a combination of Joan Acker's understanding of the gendered dynamics of organizations (in "Hierarchies, Jobs, Bodies: A Theory of Gendered Organizations," *Gender & Society* 4[2] [1990]: 139–158) and Nicholas Greenwood Onuf's notion of rules in global politics which create states of rule (in *Worlds of Our Making* [Columbia: University of South Carolina Press, 1988]). In my view, *orders* are broader than organizations, per se, though composed of them, and identifiable, influential tracks within "states of rule," which may endure across multiple states of rule and morph to adapt to them.

60 Sjoberg, *Gender, War, and Conflict*, p.101.

61 See discussions, e.g., in L. H. M. Ling, "Cultural Chauvinism and the Liberal International Order," in Geeta Chowdhry and Sheila Nair, eds., *Power in a Postcolonial World: Race, Gender, and Class in International Relations* (New York: Routledge, 2004), pp.115–140; Jane L. Parpart and Marysia Zalewski, eds. *Rethinking the Man Question: Sex, Gender, and Violence in International Relations* (London: Zed Books, 2008); Meghana Nayak, "Orientalism and 'Saving' US State Identity after 9/11," *International Feminist Journal of Politics* 8(1) (2006): 42–61; Janie Leatherman, *Sexual Violence and Armed Conflict* (London: Polity Press, 2011).

62 Peterson, "Gendered Identities, Ideologies, and Practices."

63 Ibid.; V. Spike Peterson, "The Intended and Unintended Queering of States/Nations," *Studies in Ethnicity and Nationalism* 13(1) (2013): 57–68; V. Spike Peterson, "Informalization, Inequalities, and Global Insecurities," *International Studies Review* 12(2) (2010): 244–270.

64 See, e.g., discussion in Jane Flax, "Postmodernism and Gender Relations in Feminist Theory," *Signs: Journal of Women in Culture and Society* 12(4) (1987): 621–643; Judith Butler, *Undoing Gender* (New York: Psychology Press, 2004); Schippers, "Recovering the Feminine Other"; Shepherd, *Gender, Violence and Security*.

65 Sjoberg, "Women and the Genocidal Rape of Women," p.30.

66 Ibid., p.32.

67 Sjoberg, *Gender, War, and Conflict*, p.101.

68 Sjoberg, "Women and the Genocidal Rape of Women," p.32.

69 I am thinking of gender disempowerment in the senses used in S. J. Creek and Jennifer L. Dunn, "Rethinking Gender and Violence: Agency, Heterogeneity, and Intersectionality," *Sociology Compass* 5(5) (2011): 311–322; Marie-Helene Bourcier,

"Cultural Translation, Politics of Disempowerment, and the Reinvention of Queer Power and Politics," *Sexualities* 15(1) (2012): 93–109.

70 See extensive discussion in Laura Sjoberg, "Gender, Structure, and War: What Waltz Couldn't See," *International Theory* 4(1) (2012): 1–38.

71 Peterson, "Gendered Identities, Ideologies, and Practices;" Sjoberg, "Gender, Structure, and War;" Sjoberg, *Gendering Global Conflict*; Runyan and Peterson, *Global Gender Issues*, 4th ed.

72 Sjoberg, *Gender, War, and Conflict*, p.17.

73 Enloe, *Nimo's War, Emma's War*, preface/introduction.

74 In making this distinction, I am not suggesting that there are times of "war" and times of "peace" that have distinguishable features and can be separated. Instead, I use a continuum approach to war and violence (e.g., Cuomo, "Not Just an Event").

75 Sjoberg, *Gender, War, and Conflict*, p.90; Enloe, *Does Khaki Become You?*; Goldstein, *War and Gender*; Fionnuala Ní Aoláin, Dina Francesca Haynes, and Naomi Cahn, *On the Frontlines: Gender, War, and Post-Conflict Processes* (New York: Oxford University Press, 2011); Cohn, *Women and Wars*.

76 See discussions in the various subject-disaggregated chapters in Cohn, *Women and Wars*, on the political economy of war, sexual violence in war, women's health in war, women forced to flee, women in/and state and non-state opposition groups, and women after wars.

77 For discussions of wartime masculinities, see, e.g., Goldstein, *War and Gender*; Alison, "Wartime Sexual Violence"; Jessica Meyer, *Men of War: Masculinity and the First World War in Britain* (London: Palgrave Macmillan, 2009); Paul Higate, *Military Masculinities: Identity and the State* (Santa Barbara, CA: Praeger, 2003); Higate and Hopton, "War, Militarism, and Masculinities."

78 For discussions, see, e.g., Enloe, *Does Khaki Become You?*; Sjoberg, "Agency, Militarized Femininity,"; Enloe, *Maneuvers*; Cynthia Cockburn, "Gender Relations as Causal in Militarization and War: A Feminist Standpoint," *International Feminist Journal of Politics* 12(2) (2010): 139–157; Maria Eriksson Baaz and Maria Stern, "Whores, Men, and Other Misfits: Undoing 'Feminization' in the Armed Forces in the DRC," *African Affairs* 110(441) (2011): 563–585; Melissa T. Brown, "'A Woman in the Army Is Still a Woman': Representations of Women in US Military Recruiting Advertisements for the All-Volunteer Force," *Journal of Women, Politics, and Policy* 33(2) (2012): 151–175.

79 Sjoberg, *Gender, War, and Conflict*, p.94.

80 It is not only sexism and gender subordination that impact access to fluidity along gender hierarchies, but culture, heteronormativity, class, nationality, religion, and a host of other factors.

81 See Sjoberg, "Gender, Structure, and War"; Sjoberg, *Gendering Global Conflict*, ch.3.

82 In fact, a number of discussions have suggested that there is additional feminization in the performance of feminization of the enemy *by a woman*, e.g., Sjoberg and Gentry, *Mothers, Monsters, Whores*; Sjoberg, "Agency, Militarized Feminin-

ity"; Jennifer K. Lobasz, "The Woman in Peril and the Ruined Woman: Representations of Female Soldiers in the Iraq War," *Journal of Women, Politics, & Policy* 29(3) (2008): 305–344.

83 See Sjoberg, "Women and the Genocidal Rape of Women," p.33.

84 Sjoberg and Gentry, *Mothers, Monsters, Whores*; Gentry and Sjoberg, *Beyond Mothers, Monsters, Whores*.

85 I wrote an in-depth discussion of this dynamic (as relates to disciplinary international relations) in "The Norm of Tradition."

86 Gentry and Sjoberg, *Beyond Mothers, Monsters, Whores*.

87 See discussions of the shortfalls of such an approach, e.g., Christine Chinkin, "Feminist Interventions in International Law," *Adelaide Law Review* 19 (1997): 13–24; Marysia Zalewski, "Well, What Is the Feminist Perspective on Bosnia?," *International Affairs* 71(2) (1995): 339–356; Terrell Carver, "Gender and International Relations," *International Studies Review* 5(2) (2003): 287–302; Julie Mertus, "Teaching Gender in International Relations," *International Studies Perspectives* 8(3) (2007): 323–325; Carol Cohn, Helen Kinsella, and Sheri Gibbings, "Women, Peace, and Security: Resolution 1325," *International Feminist Journal of Politics* 6(1) (2004): 130–140.

88 See extended discussion in Gentry and Sjoberg, *Beyond Mothers, Monsters, Whores*.

89 E.g., Mia Bloom, *Dying to Kill: The Allure of Suicide Terror* (New York: Columbia University Press, 2005); Mia Bloom, "Female Suicide Bombers: A Global Trend," *Daedalus* 136(1) (2007): 94–102; Bloom, *Bombshell*; Anat Berko and Edna Erez, "Gender, Palestinian Women, and Terrorism: Women's Liberation or Oppression?," *Studies in Conflict and Terrorism* 30(6) (2007): 493–519; Jessica Davis, "Gendered Terrorism: Women in the Liberation Tamil Tigers of Eelam (LTTE)," *Minerva: Journal of Women and War* 2(1) (2008): 22–38; Lori Poloni-Staudinger and Candice D. Ortbals, *Terrorism and Violent Conflict: Women's Agency, Leadership, and Responses* (New York: Springer, 2013); Bradley A. Thayer and Valerie M. Hudson, "Sex and the Shaheed: Insights from the Life Sciences on Terrorism," *International Security* 34(4) (2010): 37–62; Alessandra L. González, Joshua D. Freilich, and Steven M. Chermak, "How Women Engage Homegrown Terrorism," *Feminist Criminology* 9(4) (2014): 344–366; Jessica Davis, "Evolution of Global Jihad: Female Suicide Bombers in Iraq," *Studies in Conflict and Terrorism* 36(4) (2013): 279–291; Dagmar Hellmann-Rajanyagam, "Female Warriors, Martyrs, and Suicide Attackers: Women in the LTTE," *International Review of Modern Sociology* 34(1) (2008): 1–25; Karla Cunningham, "Cross-Regional Trends in Female Terrorism," *Studies in Conflict and Terrorism* 26(3) (2003): 171–195; Karla Cunningham, "Countering Female Terrorism," *Studies in Conflict and Terrorism* 30(2) (2007): 113–129; Karla Cunningham, "Female Survival Calculations in Politically Violent Settings: How Political Violence and Terrorism Are Viewed as Pathways to Life," *Studies in Conflict and Terrorism* 32(7) (2009): 561–575.

90 Bloom, "Female Suicide Bombers," p.96.

91 Gentry and Sjoberg, *Beyond Mothers, Monsters, Whores.*

92 Ibid.

93 Ibid.

94 Ibid.

95 See discussion of agency as a term in note 107, below.

96 See, e.g., discussion in Nancy J. Hirschmann, "Freedom, Recognition, and
    Obligation: A Feminist Approach to Political Theory," *American Political Science
    Review* 83(4) (1989): 1227–1244; Nancy J. Hirschmann, *Rethinking Obligation: A
    Feminist Method for Political Theory* (Ithaca, NY: Cornell University Press, 1992);
    Hirschmann, *The Subject of Liberty*; Carole Pateman and Nancy J. Hirschmann,
    "Political Obligation, Freedom, and Feminism," *American Political Science Review*
    86(1) (1992): 179–188; Catia C. Confortini and Abigail E. Ruane, "Sara Ruddick's
    Maternal Thinking as Weaving Epistemology for Just Peace," *Journal of Interna-
    tional Political Theory* 10(1) (2014): 70–93. For example, Nancy Hirschmann uses
    the example of pregnancy resulting from rape. A pregnancy resulting from rape
    limits the freedom of, and puts obligation on, the pregnant rape victim, whether
    that obligation is to terminate or follow through with the pregnancy. The only
    way that such a pregnancy could be a voluntary limit on women's freedom is if
    women had somehow agreed to live in rape culture in exchange for some benefit
    to them—a construction that is deeply problematic.

97 E.g., Sjoberg and Gentry, *Mothers, Monsters, Whores*; Francis Beer, Grant P. Sin-
    clar, Alice F. Healy and Lyle E. Bourne, Jr., "Peace Agreement Intractable Conflict,
    Escalation Trajectory: A Psychological Laboratory Experiment," *International
    Studies Quarterly* 39(3) (1995): 297–312; Iris Marion Young, "Modest Reflections
    on Hegemony and Global Democracy," *Theoria: A Journal of Social and Political
    Theory* 103 (2004): 1–14; Joan C. Tronto, "Partiality Based on Relation Responsi-
    bilities: Another Approach to Global Ethics," *Ethics and Social Welfare* 6(2) (2012):
    303–316.

98 See, e.g., the works cited in note 89, above. See also discussion in Sjoberg and
    Gentry, *Mothers, Monsters, Whores*; Claudia Brunner, "Occidentalism Meets the
    Female Suicide Bomber: A Critical Reflection on Recent Terrorism Debates,"
    Signs: Journal of Women in Culture and Society 32(4) (2007): 957–971; Laura Sjo-
    berg, "Conclusion: The Study of Women, Gender, and Terrorism," in Sjoberg and
    Gentry, *Women, Gender, and Terrorism*, pp.227–240.

99 See, e.g., discussion in Sjoberg and Gentry, "Reduced to Bad Sex." For examples of
    work that take this sort of position, see, e.g., Morgan, *The Demon Lover*; W. Andy
    Knight and Tanya Narozhna, "Social Contagion and the Female Face of Terror:
    New Trends in the Culture of Political Violence," *Canadian Foreign Policy Journal*
    12(1) (2005): 141–166; R. Kim Cragin and Sara A. Daly, *Women as Terrorists: Moth-
    ers, Recruiters, and Martyrs* (Santa Barbara, CA: ABC-CLIO, 2009).

100 See discussions in Sjoberg and Gentry, *Mothers, Monsters, Whores*; Gentry and
    Sjoberg, *Beyond Mothers, Monsters, Whores*; Chimène I. Keitner, "Victim or

Vamp—Images of Violent Women in the Criminal Justice System," *Columbia Journal of Gender and the Law* 11(1) (2002): 38–87.

101 This is the basic argument in Sjoberg and Gentry, *Mothers, Monsters, Whores.*

102 Gentry and Sjoberg, *Beyond Mothers, Monsters, Whores.* We first encountered the term "reactive autonomy" in Christine Sylvester's "Feminists and Realists View Autonomy and Obligation in International Relations," in V. Spike Peterson, ed., *Gendered States: Feminist (Re)Visions of International Relations Theory* (Boulder, CO: Westview Press, 1992), pp.155–178.

103 Hirschmann, "Freedom, Autonomy, and Obligation," p.1228.

104 Ibid., pp.1228–1229. See also discussions in MacKinnon, *Sex Equality*; Sjoberg, *Gender, Justice, and the Wars in Iraq*, p.124.

105 Gentry and Sjoberg, *Beyond Mothers, Monsters, Whores*, p.44, citing Hirschmann, "Freedom, Autonomy, and Obligation."

106 Hirschmann, *The Subject of Liberty*, p.ix. See also Sylvester, "Feminists and Realists View Autonomy and Obligation."

107 Ibid., p.204.

108 Ibid.

109 Hirschmann, "Freedom, Autonomy, and Obligation"; Sjoberg, *Gender, Justice, and the Wars in Iraq*; Christine Sylvester, *Feminist International Relations: An Unfinished Journey* (Cambridge, UK: Cambridge University Press, 2002), p.219; Sylvester, "Feminists and Realists View Autonomy and Obligation"; Catriona Mackenzie and Natalie Stoljar, eds., *Relational Autonomy: Feminist Perspectives on Autonomy, Agency, and the Social Self* (New York: Oxford University Press, 2000).

110 For a sense of what decision-making with fellow constrainees looks like, see Amy Allen, *The Power of Feminist Theory: Domination, Resistance, and Solidarity* (Boulder, CO: Westview Press, 1999), particularly the discussion of the ideas of power-to and power-with.

111 This is following the "practice turn" in international relations scholarship, e.g., Iver B. Neumann, "Returning Practice to the Linguistic Turn: The Case of Diplomacy," *Millennium: Journal of International Studies* 31(3) (2002): 627–651; Emanuel Adler, *Communitarian International Relations: The Epistemic Foundations of International Relations* (New York: Psychology Press, 2005); Vincent Pouliot, *International Security in Practice* (Cambridge, UK: Cambridge University Press, 2010); Vincent Pouliot, "The Logic of Practicality: A Theory of Practice of Security Communities," *International Organization* 62(2) (2008): 257–288; Emanuel Adler and Vincent Pouliot, "International Practices," *International Theory* 3(1) (2011): 1–36; Emanuel Adler and Vincent Pouliot, eds., *International Practices* (Cambridge, UK: Cambridge University Press, 2011); Christian Buger and Frank Gadinger, "The Play of International Practice," *International Studies Quarterly* (2015) (early view).

112 Adler and Pouliot, *International Practices*, p.6.

113 Ibid.

114 Ibid., p.7.

115 Ibid., citing Judith Butler's (*Gender Trouble*) notion of performativity and Patrick Thaddeus Jackson and Dan Nexon's ("Relations Before States: Substance, Process, and the Study of World Politics," *European Journal of International Relations* 5[3] [1999]: 291–332) understanding of how performance exists and works.

116 Adler and Pouliot, *International Practices*, p.7.

117 Ibid.

118 Ibid., p.8, emphasis in the original.

119 Ibid., emphasis in the original.

120 Rebecca Adler-Nissen, "Why International Relations Theory Needs Bourdieu," *e-IR*, 23 October 2012, www.e-ir.info.

121 Ibid.

122 For example, Lauren Wilcox, though addressing a different subject matter, lays the foundation for such an approach in "Explosive Bodies and Bounded States: Abjection and the Embodied Practice of Suicide Bombing," *International Feminist Journal of Politics* 16(1) (2014): 66–85.

123 Buss, "Rethinking 'Rape as a Weapon of War.'"

124 For discussions of the normalization of rape, see, e.g., Buss, "Rethinking 'Rape as a Weapon of War'"; Baaz and Stern, "Why Do Soldiers Rape?"; Aaron Belkin, "Spam Filter: Gay Rights and the Normalization of Male-Male Rape in the U.S. Military," *Radical History Review* 100 (2008): 180–185; Shelley Young, "The Use of Normalization as a Strategy in the Sexual Exploitation of Children by Adult Offenders," *Canadian Journal of Human Sexuality* 6 (1997): 285–296; Julia T. Wood, "The Normalization of Violence in Heterosexual Romantic Relationships: Women's Narratives of Love and Violence," *Journal of Social and Personal Relationships* 18(2) (2001): 239–261.

125 Copelon, "Surfacing Gender," p.257; Mibenge, *Sex and International Tribunals*, pp.112–113.

126 See, e.g., Cohn, *Women and Wars*; Betty Reardon, *Sexism and the War System* (New York: Teachers College Press, 1985); Sjoberg, *Gendering Global Conflict*, ch.9.

127 Copelon, "Surfacing Gender," p.265.

128 Ibid.

129 A recent proliferation of work has been interested in crossing the conceptual lines between war/violence and everyday violence, e.g., Rachel Pain, "Everyday Terrorism: Connecting Domestic Violence and Global Terrorism," *Progress in Human Geography* 38(4) (2014): 531–550; Rachel Pain, "Intimate War," *Political Geography* 44(2) (2015): 64–73; Laura Sjoberg, "Intimacy, Warfare, and Gender Hierarchy," *Political Geography* 44(2) (2014): 74–76.

130 See contents of footnote 134, below, as well as discussions of rape culture in popular media (e.g., Zerlina Maxwell, "Rape Culture Is Real," *Time*, 27 March 2014, http://time.com) and scholarly work (Brownmiller, *Against Our Will*; Andrea Dworkin, *Mercy* [New York: Four Walls Eight Windows, 1991]).

131 Copelon, "Surfacing Gender," p.263.

132 I am thinking here of accounts that attribute motivation for the perpetration of sexual violence in war and conflict to group cohesion, e.g., Cohen, "Explaining Rape during Civil War."

133 Copelon, "Surfacing Gender," p.253.

134 See, e.g., MacKenzie, "Securitization and Desecuritization"; MacKenzie, *Female Soldiers*. There is also evidence of this in the Rwandan genocide, as discussed, e.g., in African Rights, *Rwanda—Not So Innocent*.

135 Mibenge, *Sex and International Tribunals*, p.141.

136 Sjoberg, "Women and the Genocidal Rape of Women," p.31.

137 Sjoberg and Gentry, *Mothers, Monsters, Whores*, p.189.

138 Mibenge, *Sex and International Tribunals*.

139 Ibid., p.181.

CHAPTER 5. THE WRONG OF RAPE

1 Mark Tran, "Woman Alegedly Raped by Militia Has Been Freed, Regime Says," *Guardian*, 27 March 2011, www.theguardian.com.

2 E.g., Mark Phillips, "The Qaddafi Regime and a Woman Violated," *CBS News*, 28 March 2011, www.cbsnews.com ; Mark Colvin, "Foreign Journalists in Libya Say They Are under House Arrest," *ABC News*, 28 March 2011, www.abc.net.au; Rana Jawad, "Tripoli Witness: Humour amid the Fear," *BBC News Africa*, 31 March 2011, www.bbc.co.uk; Tim Shipman, "Gaddafi Must Face a War Crime Trial Not Exile, Insists Cameron," *Mail Online*, 29 March 2011, www.dailymail.co.uk. There will be some who suggest that the use of this case in this context is inappropriate, given that, since that day in 2011, significant doubts have been cast on al-Obeidi's credibility, given her criminal trouble since she entered the United States (e.g., Mitchell Byars, "Libyan Refugee Arrested in Boulder Again on Suspicion of Violating Bond, Probation," *Boulder DailyCamera*, 19 November 2014, www.beaumontenterprise.com). I think three things: (1) that there remains significant credibility to al-Obeidi's account of what happened in Libya (e.g., Moni Basu, "A Symbol of Defiance in Gadhafi's Libya, Eman al-Obeidi Just Wants to Be Left Alone," *CNN News*, 9 April 2012, http://edition.cnn.com); (2) that I remain worried about judgments of incidences of sexual violence in war and conflict that tend to turn on the perceived credibility of the victim, especially in terms of post-assault mental health; (3) that the whole point of the utilization of this example is to suggest the inherent *believability* of the story in the international media and to many power players in international law *regardless of its truth* because it fits within the expected parameters of preconceived notions of what wartime sexual violence is and who commits it.

3 See, e.g., Allan Little, "Libya: US, UK and France Attack Gaddafi Forces," *BBC News Africa*, 20 March 2011, www.bbc.co.uk; "Obama: Not Acting in Libya 'Would Have Been a Betrayal of Who We Are,'" *CNN*, 29 March 2011, http://edition.cnn.

com; Alan Cowell and Steven Erlanger, "France Becomes First Country to Recognize Libyan Rebels," *New York Times*, 10 March 2011, www.nytimes.com.

4 E.g., Juan Cole and Shahin Cole, "An Arab Spring for Women," *Nation*, 26 April 2011, www.thenation.com; Carla Power, "Silent No More: The Women of the Arab Revolutions," *Time*, 24 March 2011, http://content.time.com; "Women on the Back Foot in the Arab Spring," *Agence France Presse/Al Arabiya News*, 7 March 2012, http://english.alarabiya.net; Shirin Ebadi, "A Warning for Women of the Arab Spring," *Wall Street Journal*, 14 March 2012, http://online.wsj.com/article. See theoretical discussions of the complexities of these significations in Nadje Al-Ali, "Gendering the Arab Spring," *Middle East Journal of Culture and Communications* 5(1) (2012): 26–31; Laura Sjoberg and Jonathon Whooley, "The Arab Spring for Women? Representations of Women in Middle East Politics in 2011," *Journal of Women, Politics, & Policy*, forthcoming; Valentine Moghadam, "Modernising Women and Democratisation after the Arab Spring," *Journal of North African Studies* 19(2) (2014): 137–142.

5 As al-Obeidi's case and countless others demonstrate, however, attention to a case of sexual violence does not always produce justice for either the victims or the perpetrators. Initially, al-Obeidi was detained on criminal charges after being raped (see Ian Black, "Iman al-Obeidi Faces Criminal Charges over Libya Rape Claim," *Guardian*, 29 March 2011, www.theguardian.com) and there is no evidence that anyone was ever prosecuted or punished for the assault on her.

6 Mibenge, *Sex and International Tribunals*.

7 In reference to Libya, see discussion in Heidi Hudson, "Gendercidal Violence and the Technologies of Othering in Libya and Rwanda," *Africa Insight* 44(1) (2014): 103–120. For more general theoretical framings, see, e.g., Catherine N. Niarchos, "Women, War, Rape: Challenges Facing the International Tribunal for the Former Yugoslavia," *Human Rights Quarterly* 17(4) (1995): 649–690; Carolyn Nordstrom, "Rape: Politics and Theory in War and Peace," *Australian Feminist Studies* 11(23) (1996): 147–162.

8 See, e.g., Niarchos, "Women, War, Rape"; Kelly D. Askin, "Prosecuting Wartime Rape."

9 For discussion, see Sjoberg and Peet, "A(nother) Dark Side," citing and building on Hansen, "Gender, Nation, Rape"); Young, "The Logic of Masculinist Protection."

10 Mibenge, *Sex and International Tribunals*, p.224.

11 Ibid., pp.224–225. See also David S. Mitchell, "The Prohibition of Rape in International Humanitarian Law as a Norm of *Jus Cogens*: Clarifying the Doctrine," *Duke Journal of Comparative and International Law* 15 (2004–2005): 219–259; Dean Adams, "The Prohibition of Widespread Rape as a *Jus Cogens*," *San Diego International Law Journal* 6 (2004–2005): 357–399; MacKinnon, "Rape, Genocide, and Women's Human Rights"; Nicola Henry, "The Fixation on Wartime Rape: Feminist Critique and International Criminal Law," *Social Legal Studies* 23(1) (2014): 93–111.

12 See, e.g., explanations in Alfred Verdoss, "Jus Dispositivum and Jus Cogens in International Law," *American Journal of International Law* 60(1) (1966): 55–63. For a feminist critique of the gender bias inherent in the idea of *jus cogens*, see Hilary Charlesworth and Christine Chinkin, "The Gender of *Jus Cogens*," *Human Rights Quarterly* 15(1) (1993): 63–76.

13 See, e.g., discussion in MacKinnon, "Rape, Genocide, and Women's Human Rights"; Catharine A. MacKinnon, *Are Women Human?* (Cambridge, MA: Harvard University Press, 2006); Niarchos, "Women, War, Rape"; Stiglmayer, *Mass Rape*; Dorothy Q. Thomas and Regan E. Ralph, "Rape in War: Challenging the Tradition of Impunity," *SAIS Review* 14(1) (1994): 81–99.

14 Bergoffen, "Toward a Politics," p.117; Kelly D. Askin, *War Crimes against Women: Prosecution in International War Crimes Tribunals* (Amsterdam: Martinus Nijhoff Publishers, 1997); Katrina Lee-Koo, "Confronting a Disciplinary Blindness: Women, War, and Rape in the International Politics of Security," *Australian Journal of Political Science* 37(3) (2002): 525–536.

15 Bergoffen, "February 22, 2001"; Doris Buss, "Prosecuting Mass Rape: Prosecutor v. Dragoljub Kunarac, Radomir Kovac and Zoran Vukovic," *Feminist Legal Studies* 10(1) (2002): 91–99; MacKinnon, "Defining Rape Internationally," p.940. See court proceeding Kunarac et al. (IT-96-23 & 23/1), www.icty.org/case/kunarac/4.

16 Bergoffen, "February 22, 2001," p.116.

17 Mibenge, *Sex and International Tribunals*.

18 Copelon, "Surfacing Gender," p.244; see also discussion in Heidi Nichols Haddad, "Mobilizing the Will to Prosecute: Crimes of Rape at the Yugoslav and Rwandan Tribunals," *Human Rights Review* 12(1) (2011): 109–132.

19 Copelon, "Surfacing Gender," p.245. This lack of jurisprudence is mirrored, constitutes, and is constituted by lesser media and activist coverage in these areas as well, with the exception of the discussion of Ecuador linked to Julian Assange (e.g., Tim Padgett, "Defending Assange, Ecuador's President Kindles a Controversy over Defining Rape," *Time*, 23 August 2012, http://world.time.com).

20 For earlier forms of this argument, see, e.g., Chinkin, "Rape and Sexual Abuse of Women in International Law"; MacKinnon, *Are Women Human?*; Askin, "Prosecuting Wartime Rape"; Copelon, "Gender Crimes as War Crimes."

21 Mibenge, *Sex and International Tribunals*, p.135; see also Nicola Henry, "The Impossibility of Bearing Witness: Wartime Rape and the Promise of Justice," *Violence against Women* 16(10) (2010): 1098–1119; Doris E. Buss, "Knowing Women: Translating Patriarchy in International Criminal Law," *Social Legal Studies* 23(1) (2014): 73–92; Sara Sharratt, *Gender, Shame and Sexual Violence: The Voices of Witnesses and Court Members at War Crimes Tribunals* (Aldershot: Ashgate, 2011).

22 Bergoffen, "February 22, 2001," p.118, discussing an instance where the court "identified an act as rape, a crime against humanity, whether or not there was evidence of violence or physical pain or injury." For discussions of definition problems, see also Kimberly E. Carson, "Reconsidering the Theoretical Accuracy and Prosecutorial Effectiveness of International Tribunals' *Ad Hoc* Ap-

proaches to Conceptualizing Crimes of Conflict Sexual Violence as War Crimes, Crimes against Humanity, and Acts of Genocide," *Fordham Urban Law Journal* 39(4) (2012): 1249–1300; Kiran Grewal, "The Protection of Sexual Autonomy under International Criminal Law: The International Criminal Court and the Challenge of Defining Rape," *Journal of International Criminal Justice* 10(2) (2012): 373–396.

23 Girshick, *Woman-to-Woman Sexual Violence*, p.22.

24 See discussions in Sjoberg, "Women and the Genocidal Rape of Women," p.31; Dubravka Zarkov, "Exposures and Invisibilities: Media, Masculinities, and the Narratives of War in an Intersectional Perspective," in Helma Lutz, Maria Teresa Herrera Vivar, and Linda Supik, eds., *Framing Intersectionality: Debates on a Multi-Faceted Concept in Gender Studies* (Aldershot: Ashgate, 2012), pp.105–120.

25 Sjoberg, "Women and the Genocidal Rape of Women," p.31.

26 See discussion in Stemple, "Human Rights, Sex," p.825.

27 Joanna Bourke, *Rape: A History from 1860 to Present* (London: Virago, 2007), p.8; see also the works cited in note 22, above.

28 Bourke, *Rape*, p.8; Copelon, "Gender Crimes as War Crimes"; Buss, "Prosecuting Mass Rape"; Rebecca J. Haffajee, "Prosecuting Crimes of Rape and Sexual Violence at the ICTR: The Application of Joint Criminal Enterprise Theory," *Harvard Journal of Law and Gender* 29(1): 201–222.

29 Mibenge, *Sex and International Tribunals*, p.57. For analysis of the penetration of wars into households, see, e.g., Cynthia Enloe, *Bananas, Beaches, and Bases*; Enloe, *Nimo's War, Emma's War*; Greg Castillo, "Domesticating the Cold War: Household Consumption as Propaganda in Marshall Plan Germany," *Journal of Contemporary History* 40(2) (2005): 261–288; Sjoberg, *Gendering Global Conflict*, ch.9.

30 Katie C. Richey, "Several Steps Sideways: International Legal Developments Concerning War Rape and the Human Rights of Women," *Texas Journal of Women and the Law* 17(1) (2007–2008): 109–129, p.117.

31 African Rights, *Rwanda—Not So Innocent*, p.2.

32 See, e.g., Grey and Shepherd, "'Stop Rape Now?'"; Alison, "Wartime Sexual Violence"; Kelly Askin, "Sexual Violence in Decisions and Indictments of the Yugoslav and Rwandan Tribunals: Current Status," *American Journal of International Law* 93(1) (1999): 97–123; Askin, "Prosecuting Wartime Rape"; Buss, "Rethinking 'Rape as a Weapon of War'"; Valerie Oosterveld, "The Gender Jurisprudence of the Special Court for Sierra Leone: Progress in the Revolutionary United Front Judgments," *Cornell International Law Journal* 441(1) (2011): 49–74; Lara Stemple, "Male Rape and Human Rights," *Hastings Law Journal* 60(4) (2009): 605–646.

33 See discussion in Stemple, "Human Rights, Sex," p.825.

34 Ibid.

35 Ibid. This dovetails well with Marysia Zalewski's understanding of the disposition of feminist research in global politics, where "the driving force of feminism is its

attention to gender, and not simply women . . . the concept, nature, and practice of gender are key" (in "Well, What Is the Feminist Perspective on Bosnia?" *International Affairs* 71[2] [1995]: 339–356).

36 Copelon, "Surfacing Gender," p.253. This discussion has interesting parallels to Rachel Pain's work on intimate warfare ("Intimate War").

37 Stemple, "Human Rights, Sex," p.825.

38 Ibid.

39 Ibid., p.826. This problem has been considered extensively outside of the specific context of sexual violence in war and conflict in several contexts, e.g., Anne McLeer, "Saving the Victim: Recuperating the Language of the Victim and Reassessing Global Feminism," *Hypatia* 13(1) (1998): 41–55; Amy Leisenring, "Confronting 'Victim' Discourses: The Identity Work of Battered Women," *Symbolic Interaction* 29(3) (2006): 307–330; Rebecca Stringer, *Knowing Victims: Feminism and Victim Politics in Neoliberal Times* (New York: Routledge, 2014).

40 Anne Marie Goetz, "Gender Justice, Citizenship, and Entitlements: Core Concepts, Debates, and New Directions for Research," in Maitrayee Mukhopadhyay and Navsharan Singh, eds., *Gender Justice, Citizenship, and Development* (Geneva: Zubaan/IDRC, 2007), http://198.62.158.214/geh/ev-111764-201-1-DO_TOPIC.html.

41 See, e.g., Sellers, "Sexual Violence and Peremptory Norms"; Patricia Viseur Sellers, "The Cultural Value of Sexual Violence," *American Society of International Law Proceedings* 93 (1999): 312–324; Tamara L. Tompkins, "Prosecuting Rape as a War Crime: Speaking the Unspeakable," *Notre Dame Law Review* 70(4) (1995): 845–890.

42 This is one of the descriptions of gender-justice approaches outlined in Goetz, "Gender Justice."

43 Ibid.

44 Doris Buss, "Seeing Sexual Violence in Conflict and Post-Conflict Societies: The Limits of Visibility," in Doris Buss, Joanne Lebert, Blair Rutherford, Donna Sharkey, and Obijiofor Aginam, eds., *Sexual Violence in Conflict and Post-Conflict Societies: International Agendas and African Contexts* (New York and London: Routledge), pp. 3–27, p.11.

45 See, e.g., Rebecca J. Cook, ed., *Human Rights of Women: National and International Perspectives* (Philadelphia: University of Pennsylvania Press, 2011); MacKinnon, *Are Women Human?*; Susan Moller Okin, "Feminism, Women's Human Rights, and Cultural Differences," *Hypatia* 13(2) (1998): 32–52; Brooke A. Ackerly, *Universal Human Rights in a World of Difference* (Cambridge, UK: Cambridge University Press, 2008).

46 Goetz, "Gender Justice."

47 Catharine MacKinnon, *Are Women Human?*

48 Goetz, "Gender Justice."

49 Ibid. For information about the Convention on the Elimination of Discrimination against Women, see www.un.org/womenwatch/daw/cedaw.

50 See, e.g., discussion in Copelon, "Gender Crimes as War Crimes"; Joanne Barkan, "As Old as War Itself: Rape in Foca," *Dissent* 49(1) (2002): 60–66, p.62. Diana Elizabeth Anders characterizes the gender-justice paradigm as "self-congratulatory" in "character," and expresses concern that the celebration of both the volume of prosecutions and the equal-access approach that produced them may be premature (*The Therapeutic Turn in International Humanitarian Law: War Crimes as Sites of "Healing"?* [dissertation at the University of California, Berkeley, 2012], https://escholarship.org/uc/item/0vc1f4gc).

51 Goetz, "Gender Justice." As I will discuss below, I think that the majority of "gender justice" jurisprudence and advocacy in global politics is committed to ending *women's subordination* without seeing that women's subordination is a part of a broader paradigm of *gender subordination* that indeed exists as a condition of possibility of *women's subordination* not least because it creates and constitutes the subject of woman to be subordinated.

52 Maxine Molyneux and Shahra Razavi, "Beijing Plus Ten: An Ambivalent Record on Gender Justice," *Development and Change* 36(3) (2005): 983–1010; Martha I. Morgan, "Taking Machismo to Court: The Gender Jurisprudence of the Colombian Constitutional Court," *University of Miami Inter-American Law Review* 30(2) (1999): 253–342.

53 See, e.g., discussion in Karen L. Baird, *Gender Justice and the Health Care System* (New York: Taylor & Fancis, 1998), ch.5.

54 Goetz, "Gender Justice."

55 Either explicitly or implicitly. See, e.g., Copelon, "Gender Crimes as War Crimes"; Kelly Askin, "Quest for Post-Conflict Gender Justice"; Campanaro, "Women, War, and International Law."

56 Sienna Merope, "Recharacterizing the Lubanga Case: Regulation 55 and the Consequences for Gender Justice at the ICC," *Criminal Law Forum* 22 (2011): 311–346; Valerie Oosterveld, "The Definition of 'Gender' in the Rome Statute of the International Criminal Court: A Step Forward or Back for International Criminal Justice?," *Harvard Human Rights Journal* 18(1) (2005): 55–84.

57 Beth Van Schaack, "Obstacles on the Road to Gender Justice: The International Criminal Tribunal for Rwanda as Object Lesson," *American University Journal of Gender, Social Policy, & the Law* 17(2) (2009): 361–406.

58 See, e.g., Mary Joe Flug, *Postmodern Legal Feminism* (New York: Routledge, 1993, 2014); Fionnuala Ní Aoláin, "Advancing Feminist Positioning in the Field of Transitional Justice," *International Journal of Transitional Justice* 6(2) (2012): 205–228; Nikol G. Alexander-Floyd, "Critical Race Black Feminism: A 'Jurisprudence of Resistance' and the Transformation of the Academy," *Signs: Journal of Women in Culture and Society* 35(4) (2010): 810–820.

59 Van Shaack, "Obstacles on the Road."

60 Nicola Henry, *War and Rape: Law, Memory, and Justice* (London: Routledge, 2011), p. 2, citing Inga Markovits, "Selective Memory: How the Law Affects What

We Remember and What We Forget about the Past—The Case of East Germany," *Law & Society Review* 35(3) (2001): 513–563.

61 Ibid., p.118, citing Joachim Savelsberg and Ryan King, "Law and Collective Memory," *Annual Review of Law and Social Science* 3 (2007): 189–211.

62 Ibid., p.21, citing Mark Osiel, *Mass Atrocity, Collective Memory, and the Law* (New Brunswick, NJ: Transaction Publishers, 1999).

63 Ibid., pp.111–112. See also Mibenge, *Sex and International Tribunals*, p.135; Henry, "The Impossibility of Bearing Witness"; Buss, "Knowing Women"; Sharratt, *Gender, Shame and Sexual Violence*.

64 Henry, *War and Rape*, p.123. See also discussion in Donna Pankhurst, "Issues of Justice and Reconciliation in Complex Political Emergencies: Conceptualising Reconciliation, Justice, and Peace," *Third World Quarterly* 20(1) (1999): 239–255.

65 Henry, *War and Rape*, p.123. For discussions of this dynamic, see, e.g., G. P. Fletcher, *With Justice for Some: Victims' Rights in Criminal Trials* (Boston, MA: Addison-Wesley, 1995); Lisa Marie De Sanctis, "Bridging the Gap Between Rules of Evidence and Justice for Victims of Domestic Violence," *Yale Journal of Law and Feminism* 8(1) (1996): 359–408; Jonathan Doak, "The Therapeutic Dimension of Transitional Justice: Emotional Repair and Victim Satisfaction in International Trials and Truth Commissions," *International Criminal Law Review* 11(2) (2011): 263–298; Henry, "The Impossibility of Bearing Witness."

66 Henry, *War and Rape*, p.26. See discussions of this as an evidentiary problem in Nancy A. Combs, *Fact-Finding without Facts: The Uncertain Evidentiary Foundation of International Criminal Convictions* (Cambridge, UK: Cambridge University Press, 2010), who argues (generally) that victim eyewitness testimony should be valued *less* than it is (and therefore that international courts are failing at their fact-finding missions), contra Godfrey M. Musila, *Rethinking International Criminal Law: Restorative Justice and the Rights of Victims in the International Criminal Court* (Location: LAP Lampert Academic Publishing, 2010), who argues (generally) that victim testimony should be taken more seriously.

67 Henry, *War and Rape*, p.115. See discussions in Donna Pankhurst, ed., *Gendered Peace: Struggles for Post-War Justice and Reconciliation* (London: Routledge, 2012); Elaine Zuckerman and Marcia Greenberg, "The Gender Dimensions of Post-Conflict Reconstruction: An Analytical Framework for Policymakers," *Gender & Development* 12(3) (2004): 70–82.

68 Hilary Charlesworth, Christine Chinkin, and Shelley Wright, "Feminist Approaches to International Law," *American Journal of International Law* 85(4) (1991): 613–645, p.627. Henry makes the point differently, citing Giorgio Agamben (*The Remnants of Auschwitz: The Witness and the Archive.* trans D. Heller-Roazen [New York: Zone Books, 2002], p.18), "law, by its nature 'is solely directed towards judgment, independent of truth and justice'" (*War and Rape*, p.111).

69 Henry, *War and Rape*, p.119.

70 Ibid., pp.119, 125. Analysts have also suggested that the adversarial nature of the legal process creates a problem here, where defenses have an incentive to dis-

credit victim-witnesses, and sometimes capitalize on gender-based assumptions in order to do so. A victim's testimony being attacked in court has been discussed as problematic both for healing purposes and for the outcomes of conflict sexual violence trials.

71 E.g., Anna Agathangelou and L. H. M. Ling, "The House of IR: From Family Power Politics to the Poisies of Worldism," *International Studies Review* 6(4) (2004): 21–50.

72 For a more sophisticated discussion, see Rosemary Hunter, "Law's (Masculine) Violence: Reshaping Jurisprudence," *Law and Critique* 17(1) (2006): 27–46.

73 See, e.g., discussion in Skjelsbaek, "Sexual Violence and War"; Lynda E. Boose, "Crossing the River Drina: Bosnian Rape Camps, Turkish Impalement, and Serb Cultural Memory," *Signs: Journal of Women in Culture and Society* 28(1) (2002): 71–96; Jan Jindy Pettman, "Boundary Politics: Women, Nationalism, and Danger," in Mary Maynard and June Purvis, eds., *New Frontiers in Women's Studies: Knowledge, Identity, and Nationalism* (New York: Taylor & Francis, 2005), ch.1.

74 Buss, "Seeing Sexual Violence," p.9.

75 See discussions in Tony Ward and Richard Siegert, "Rape and Evolutionary Psychology: A Critique of Thornhill and Palmer's Theory," *Aggression and Violent Behavior* 7(2) (2002): 145–168; Susan G. Cole, *Power Surge: Sex, Violence, and Pornography* (New York: Second Story Press, 1995), p.218. Most work citing this understanding cites Brownmiller's *Against Our Will*.

76 This response has been multiply attributed to Catharine MacKinnon, though I cannot find it anywhere in her written work.

77 Older discussions deal with this a little bit, though newer ones tend to shy away from it. See, e.g., Rosalind Coward, "Sexual Violence and Sexuality," *Feminist Review* 11(1) (1982): 9–22.

78 See discussion in Baaz and Stern, *Sexual Violence as a Weapon of War?*, ch.2.

79 Nira Yuval-Davis, *Gender and Nation* (London: Sage, 1997); V. Spike Peterson, "Sexing Political Identities"; Pettman, "Boundary Politics"; Anne McClintock, "Family Feuds: Gender, Nationalism, and the Family," *Feminist Review* 44 (1993): 61–80. A number of authors suggest that there is a racial dynamic to this, where acts of sexual violence in conflict are performances of "producing a racially inferior and disempowered subject" (Tshepo Madlingozi, "On Transitional Justice Entrepreneurs and the Production of Victims," in Buss et al., *Sexual Violence in Conflict*, pp.169–189, p.173).

80 Ibid. See also Brownmiller, "Making Female Bodies the Battlefield."

81 Enloe, *The Curious Feminist*, p.6.

82 Peterson, "Gendered Identities, Ideologies, and Practices"; Hawkesworth, "Feminists v. Feminization."

83 Madlingozi, "On Transnational Justice Entrepreneurs," p.169.

84 Tami Amanda Jacoby, "A Theory of Victimhood: Politics, Conflict, and the Construction of Victim-Based Identity," *Millennium: Journal of International Studies* 43(2) (2015): 511–530.

85 Ibid., p.512.

86 Ibid., p.516. This is why "contemporary feminist and post-colonial scholars have expressed serious reservations about framing women's identities and other identities based on race, class, religion, ethnicity, and so on, exclusively in terms of oppression. This anti-victim sentiment seeks to retrieve the voice and agency of oppressed groups by deconstructing categories such as 'woman,' 'nation,' and 'other'" (ibid.).

87 Ibid. In this way "the potential *violence* of victimhood challenges well-intentioned social scientists whose activism risks recreating the kind of politics that bore victimhood to begin with" (ibid., p.529).

88 Ibid, p. 512. According to Jacoby, this contestation is in the courts, but not only in the courts, since "the construction of a grievance-based identity is a fundamentally contested process as the lines between victim and perpetrator are blurred by ongoing cycles of belligerence and retribution" (ibid.).

89 Mibenge, *Sex and International Tribunals*; Henry, *War and Rape*.

90 Jacoby, "A Theory of Victimhood." See also Vlasta Jalūsić, "Gender and Victimization of the Nation and Pre- and Post-War Identity Discourse," in Miroslav Hadžić, ed., *The Violent Dissolution of Yugoslavia: Causes, Dynamics, and Effects* (OSCE: Belgrade, 2004), pp.145–166; Dawn McCaffrey, "Victim Feminism/Victim Activism," *Sociological Spectrum* 18(3) (1998): 263–284.

91 Peace studies discusses this in some detail. See, e.g., Trudy Govier and Wilhellm Verwoerd, "How Not to Polarize 'Victims' and 'Perpetrators," *Peace Review* 16(3) (2004): 371–377; Chris Coulter, "Female Fighters in the Sierra Leone War: Challenging the Assumptions?," *Feminist Review* 88 (2008): 54–73; Nneoma Nwogu, "When and Why It Started: Deconstructing Victim-Centered Truth Commissions in the Context of Ethnicity-Based Conflict," *International Journal of Transitional Justice* 4(2) (2010): 275–289.

92 Jacoby, A Theory of Victimhood," p.5.

93 Sjoberg, "Women and the Genocidal Rape of Women," p.31.

94 See, e.g., discussions in Mertus, "Shouting from the Bottom of the Well." Thinking more broadly about the adversarial system, see, e.g., Kathleen E. Hull and Robert L. Nelson, "Gender Inequality and the Law: Problems of Structure and Agency in Recent Studies of Gender in Anglo-American Legal Professions," *Law & Social Inquiry* 23(3) (1998): 681–705.

95 Phrasing taken from Henry, *War and Rape*, p.115.

96 Henry suggests that it is possible to make testimony "not futile"—my goal is to shift the spectrum of possible readings (or, as Baaz and Stern call it, "grids of intelligibility") of sexual violence in war and conflict.

97 Sjoberg, "Women and the Genocidal Rape of Women."

98 See extensive discussions of civilian immunity in Michael Walzer, *Just and Unjust Wars* (New York: Basic Books, 1997); Michael Walzer, *Arguing about War* (New Haven, CT: Yale University Press, 2008); Igor Primoratz, *Civilian Immunity in War: Its Grounds, Scope, and Weight* (Oxford: Oxford University Press, 2010). Ap-

plied to gender-based violence, see, e.g., Sjoberg, "The Gendered Realities of the Immunity Principle."

99 See extensive discussions of torture in Kim Lane Scheppele, "Hypothetical Torture in the 'War on Terrorism,'" *Journal of National Security Law and Policy* 1(2) (2005): 285–340; Alfred McCoy, *A Question of Torture: CIA Interrogation, from the Cold War to the War on Terror* (New York: Macmillan, 2007); Gerry J. Simpson, *Law, War, & Crime: War Crimes, Trials and the Reinvention of International Law* (London: Polity, 2007); Florian Jessberger, "Bad Torture—Good Torture? What International Criminal Lawyers May Learn from the Recent Trial of Police Officers in Germany," *Journal of International Criminal Justice* 3(5) (2005): 1059–1073. Discussing war rape, see, e.g., Copelon, "Gender Crimes as War Crimes"; Christopher Scott Maravilla, "Rape as a War Crime: The Implications of the International Criminal Tribunal for the Former Yugoslavia's Decision in *Prosecutor v. Kunarač, Kovač & Vuković* on International Humanitarian Law," *Florida International Law Journal* 13(3) (2001): 321–342; Clare McGlynn, "Rape as 'Torture'? Catharine MacKinnon and Questions of Feminist Strategy," *Feminist Legal Studies* 16(1) (2008): 71–85.

100 See extensive discussions of crimes against humanity in Geoffrey Robertson, *Crimes against Humanity: The Struggle for Global Justice*, 4th ed. (New York: New Press, 2013); Larry May, "Crimes against Humanity," *Ethics & International Affairs* 20(3) (2006): 349–352; David Luban, "A Theory of Crimes against Humanity," *Yale Law Journal* 29(1) (2004): 85–164. For explicit discussions of sexual violence, see Margaret McAuliffe deGuzman, "The Road from Rome: The Developing Law of Crimes against Humanity," *Human Rights Quarterly* 22(2) (2000): 335–403; Mohamed Elewa Badar, "From Nuremberg Charter to the Rome Statute: Defining the Elements of Crimes Against Humanity," *San Diego International Law Journal* 5(1) (2004): 73–144; Buss, "Prosecuting Mass Rape"; Balthazar, "Gender Crimes."

101 Discussing war rape as violation of women's human rights, see, e.g., Sylvanna Falcon, "Rape as a Weapon of War: Advancing Human Rights for Women at the US-Mexico Border," *Social Justice* 28(2) (2001): 31–60; Sally Engle Marry, *Human Rights and Gender Violence: Translating International Law into Local Justice* (Chicago: University of Chicago Press, 2009); Rhonda Copelon, "International Human Rights Dimensions of Intimate Violence: Another Strand in the Dialectic of Feminist Lawmaking," *American University Journal of Gender, Social Policy, and the Law* 11(2) (2003): 865–876.

102 Baaz and Stern, *Sexual Violence as a Weapon of War?*, ch.3. Baaz and Stern argue that much of the literature treats all of sexual violence in war and conflict as if it is strategic, when there is evidence that some parties to some conflicts do use it as strategic, but evidence that, in other conflicts and with other parties, the commission of sexual violence is the result of the breakdown of troop order.

103 See, e.g., discussions in Runyan and Peterson, *Global Gender Issues*, 4th ed.; Sjoberg, *Gendering Global Conflict*; Sjoberg, "Gender/Violence"; Blanchard, "Gender, International Relations."

104 Sjoberg, "Gender/Violence."

105 Baaz and Stern, *Sexual Violence as a Weapon of War?*, pp.3–4. The authors suggest (and I agree) that this is especially true when it becomes politically incorrect to directly frame sexual violence in war and conflict as the sex-specific fulfillment of men's sex-specific sexual needs, which is an underlying implication of the "sex story" of sexual violence in war and conflict.

106 Ibid., ch.3.

107 Which is not to say that a bunch of good work has not been done on these issues; just that it is not fully being captured by the individual legal grounds employed in international criminal jurisprudence for sexual violence in war and conflict.

108 Baaz and Stern, *Sexual Violence as a Weapon of War?*, pp.2–3. For analysis suggesting that rape is a weapon of war, see, e.g., Card, "Rape as a Weapon of War"; Bulent Diken and Carsten Bagge Laustsen, "Becoming Abject: Rape as a Weapon of War," *Body & Society* 11(1) (2005): 111–128; Stephen Schwartz, "Rape as a Weapon of War in the Former Yugoslavia," *Hastings Women's Law Journal* 5(1) (1994): 69–88.

109 Sjoberg, *Gender, War, and Conflict*.

110 See discussions in Sjoberg, *Gendering Global Conflict*; Sjoberg, *Gender, War, and Conflict*; Sjoberg, "Gender, Structure, and War."

111 Sjoberg, *Gender, War, and Conflict*.

112 Mibenge, *Sex and International Tribunals*.

113 Baaz and Stern, *Sexual Violence as a Weapon of War?*

114 For discussion of the different frequencies of sexual violence in war and conflict, see, e.g., Elisabeth Jean Wood, "Variation in Sexual Violence during War," *Politics & Society* 34(3) (2006): 307–342; Cohen, "Explaining Rape during Civil War."

115 See, e.g., the discussion of the "tough but tender" masculinity rather than hyper-masculinity on display by the United States in the first Gulf War in Steve Niva, "Tough and Tender: New World Order Masculinity and the Gulf War," in Marysia Zalewski and Jane Parpart, eds., *The "Man" Question in International Relations* (Boulder, CO: Westview Press, 1998). For a broader discussion, see Hooper, *Manly States*; Connell, *Masculinities*.

116 As if that were a useful distinction, and the barriers between "conflict" and "not conflict" were clear. See, e.g., Betty Reardon, *Sexism and the War System* (New York: Teachers College Press, 1985); Cuomo, "Not Just an Event"; Pain, "Everyday Terrorism"; Pain, "Intimate War."

117 See, e.g., Cuomo, "Not Just an Event"; Sjoberg, *Gendering Global Conflict*, ch.10.

118 Sjoberg, *Gendering Global Conflict*.

119 Goetz, "Gender Justice."

120 Ibid., citing Suad Joseph, "Gender and Citizenship in the Arab World," paper at the UNDP Mediterranean Development Forum, Amman, April 8, 2002; Will Kymlicka, *The Rights of Minority Cultures* (Oxford: Oxford University Press, 1995).

121 See, e.g., discussion in Rosalind Shaw, "Memory Frictions: Localizing the Truth and Reconciliation Commission in Sierra Leone," *International Journal of Transitional Justice* 1(2) (2007): 183–207.

122 Defining what justice might look like is beyond the scope of this book, but this estimation is in my view easier to make in the negative (x is not enough) than in the positive (what would justice be?).

123 The distinction made by Baaz and Stern, *Sexual Violence as a Weapon of War?*

124 See discussion of Srebrenica in chapter 3.

125 See, e.g., discussion in Jennifer Green, Rhonda Copelon, Patrick Cotter, and Beth Stevens, "Affecting the Rules for Prosecution of Rape and Other Gender-Based Violence before the International Criminal Tribunal for the Former Yugoslavia: A Feminist Proposal and Critique," *Hastings Women's Law Journal* 5(2) (1994): 171–242; Rebecca Haffajee, "Prosecuting Crimes of Rape and Sexual Violence at the ICTR: The Application of Joint Criminal Enterprise Theory," *Harvard Journal of Law and Gender* 29(1) (2006): 201–222.

126 Sjoberg, "Women and the Genocidal Rape of Women," p.31.

CHAPTER 6. ONE OF THE MOST ABIDING MYTHS OF OUR TIME

1 Pearson, *When She Was Bad . . . ,*" p.7. Pearson notes this after observing the incorrectness of this myth in a wide variety of circumstances ("ordinary women have proven to be just as militaristic, supporting the continuance of war, shaming men who would dodge the draft, screaming for blood in mob, fighting alongside their brothers and sons when they could, acting as snipers, as fighter pilot, as guerrilla soldiers and terrorists" [ibid., p.5]).

2 See discussion in chapter 5, as well as in Baaz and Stern, *Sexual Violence as a Weapon of War?*; see similar discussions applied elsewhere in Christine Sylvester, "TerrorWars: Boston, Iraq," *Critical Studies on Terrorism* 7(1) (2014): 11–23; Sabine Hirschauer, "Rape and State-Sexual Violence and Its Political Narrative and Othering in 21st-Century South Africa," *Africa Insight* 44(1) (2014): 84–102.

3 Discussed in Baaz and Stern, *Sexual Violence as a Weapon of War?*, ch.2; Baaz and Stern, "Why Do Soldiers Rape?"; Cynthia Enloe, *The Morning After: Sexual Politics at the End of the Cold War* (Berkeley, CA: University of California Press, 1990), pp.64, 97, 118; Rhonda Copelon, "Women and War Crimes," *St. Johns Law Review* 69(1): 61–68, p.65; Campanaro, "Women, War, and International Law."

4 Baaz and Stern, *Sexual Violence as a Weapon of War?*, pp.3, 5.

5 Balthazar, "Gender Crimes."

6 E.g., Landesman, "A Woman's Work"; Sperling, "Mother of All Atrocities," p.102; discussions in Sjoberg and Gentry, *Mothers, Monsters, Whores*; Drumbl, "She Makes Me Ashamed."

7 See, e.g., discussions in Sjoberg and Gentry, *Mothers, Monsters, Whores*; Drumbl, "She Makes Me Ashamed," and dozens if not hundreds of examples of news cov-

erage, e.g., Josephine Hazeley, "Profile: Female Rwandan Killer Pauline Nyirama-suhuko," *BBC News Africa*, 24 June 2011, www.bbc.com.

8 Balthazar, "Gender Crimes"; Harman, "A Woman on Trial for Rwanda's Massacre"; *Prosecutor v. Nyiramasuhuko et al.* decision, ICTR Case No. ICTR-98–42-T, decided 24 June 2011, indictment, the relevant parts of which are on pp.11–13.

9 Balthazar, "Gender Crimes," p.47.

10 Melvern, *Conspiracy to Murder*; see also Wood, "A Woman Scorned for the 'Least Condemned' War Crime."

11 Landesman, "A Woman's Work."

12 Drumbl, "She Makes Me Ashamed."

13 As we are reminded by Drumbl, "Nyiramasuhuko may reflect a new kind of international convict, but she is far from a new kind of perpetrator, whether in Rwanda or wherever episodes of mass atrocity erupt" ("She Makes Me Ashamed," p.563). For extensive discussion of women perpetrators in Rwanda specifically, see African Rights, *Rwanda—Not So Innocent*.

14 "Rwanda: Ex-Women's Minister Guilty"; *Prosecutor v. Nyiramasuhuko et al.* decision, para. 6200.

15 See *Prosecutor v. Nyiramasuhuko et al.* decision.

16 See discussion of prosecution strategy in para. 2165 of *Prosecutor v. Nyiramasuhuko et al.* decision, esp. FN5754; for discussion of defense strategy, see para. 2153 of *Prosecutor v. Nyiramasuhuko et al.* decision.

17 *Prosecutor v. Nyiramasuhuko et al.*, Prosecution Opening Statement, T. 12 June 2001, p. 92.

18 *Prosecutor v. Nyiramasuhuko et al.* decision, para. 2153.

19 Ibid., citing Nyiramasuhuko Closing Argument, T. 22 April 2009 p. 5; Nyiramasuhuko Closing Brief, paras. 617, 696, 698, 725, 796, 834, 857.

20 Ibid. See, e.g., discussions in paras. 10, 2113, 2159 FN5746, 2165 FN5754, 2178, 2233, 2633, 5883.

21 Ibid., see esp. paras. 5883, 2239, 2480.

22 Ibid., para. 4915.

23 Ibid., para. 6093. Nyiramasuhuko was also held responsible for killing Tutsis (para. 5678), conspiracy to commit genocide (para. 5737), genocide (para. 5873), and outrages on personal dignity (para. 6187).

24 Ibid., para, 6207.

25 Ibid.

26 Ibid.

27 Ibid., see, e.g., discussion in section 4.2.1.4.1.

28 Ibid., para. 4917, citing prosecution relying on the testimony of prosecution witness FAE. 12992 Prosecution Closing Brief, pp.109, 121–122, paras. 280, 322.

29 These scare quotes are there because I am skeptical of the notion of the "normal" or "non-sexual" here—see, e.g., Michael Warner, *The Trouble with Normal: Sex, Politics, and the Ethics of Queer Life* (Cambridge, MA: Harvard University Press, 2000).

30 See, e.g., discussion in *Prosecutor v. Nyiramasuhuko et al.* decision, para. 2159 FN5744; 5612 FN14558, citing Prosecution Pre-Trial Brief Appendix.
31 See, e.g., discussion in Baines, "Body Politics and the Rwandan Crisis," p.488; *Prosecutor v. Nyiramasuhuko et al.* decision, paras. 2268 and 2605, citing T. 24 October 2002, p.85; T. 28 October 2002, pp.81, 88, 99; T. 29 October 2002, p.21 (all witness QBP); T. March 2003 pp.52, 54 (witness SS), T. 11 March 2003 p.54 (witness FAP), T. 3 February 2004, pp.10, 12, 61 (witness QBQ).
32 *Prosecutor v. Nyiramasuhuko et al.* decision, para. 4915.
33 See, e.g., discussions in Sharlach, "Rape as Genocide," pp.89–102; Margaret A. Lyons, "Hearing the Cry without Answering the Call: Rape, Genocide, and the Rwandan Tribunal," *Syracuse Journal of International Law and Commerce* 28(1) (2011): 99–124; Binaifer Nowrojee, *Shattered Lives: Sexual Violence during the Rwandan Genocide and Its Aftermath* (New York: Human Rights Watch, 1996).
34 See, e.g., extensive discussions of the significations of strategic war rape in Sjoberg, *Gendering Global Conflict*, chs.7, 8.
35 Butler, *Bodies That Matter*; Baaz and Stern, *Sexual Violence as a Weapon of War?*
36 See, e.g., the discussion below of *Prosecutor versus Jean-Paul Akayesu*, Case No. ICTR-96-4-T, decision of 2 September 1998.
37 See, e.g., discussions in Llezlie L. Green, "Gender Hate Propaganda and Sexual Violence in the Rwandan Genocide: An Argument for Intersectionality in International Law," *Columbia Human Rights Law Review* 33(2) (2002): 733–776; Christopher C. Taylor, "A Gendered Genocide: Tutsi Women and Hutu Extremists in the 1994 Rwanda Genocide," *PoLAR: Political and Legal Anthropology Review* 22(1) (1999): 42–54; Baines, "Body Politics and the Rwandan Crisis"; Alison, "Wartime Sexual Violence."
38 And with significantly less to-do about it in the media, despite it being the first conviction for genocide and the first conviction for rape as genocide in an international criminal tribunal. See discussion in Paul J. Magnarella, "Some Milestones and Achievements at the International Criminal Tribunal for Rwanda: The 1998 *Kambanda* and *Akayesu* Cases," *Florida Journal of International Law* 11(3) (1997): 517–538.
39 See *Prosecutor v. Akayesu* decision, para. 694.
40 Ibid., paras. 694, 731.
41 Ibid., Count 12, p.1, under article 3(g) of the ICTR statutes (discussion on p.13).
42 Ibid., para. 12a indictment, reprinted on p.7 of the decision.
43 Ibid., para. 12b indictment, reprinted on p.7 of the decision.
44 Ibid., para. 450.
45 Ibid., para. 416.
46 Ibid., para. 417.
47 Ibid., para. 421.
48 Ibid., para. 422.
49 Ibid., para. 421.
50 Ibid., para. 429.

51 Ibid., para. 449.
52 Ibid., para. 452.
53 Ibid., paras. 685–696, 731–734.
54 Ibid., para. 597.
55 Ibid.
56 Ibid.
57 Ibid., para. 598.
58 Ibid.
59 Ibid., para. 688.
60 Ibid.
61 Ibid., para. 598. The catalogued discriminatory grounds included national, ethnic, political, racial, or religious grounds.
62 Ibid., para. 706.
63 Ibid., para. 731.
64 Ibid.
65 Ibid.
66 Ibid., para. 732. For more discussion of the *Akayesu* definition of rape, see chapter 2, as well as MacKinnon, "Defining Rape Internationally"; Rebecca L. Haffajee, "Prosecuting Crimes of Rape and Sexual Violence at the ICTR: The Application of Joint Enterprise Theory," *Harvard Journal of Law and Gender* 29(1) (2006): 201–222; Obote-Odora, "Rape and Sexual Violence in International Law"; Magalini Karagiannakis, "Case Analysis: The Definition of Rape and Its Characterization as an Act of Genocide—A Review of the Jurisprudence of the International Criminal Tribunal for Rwanda and the Former Yugoslavia," *Leiden Journal of International Law* 12(2) (1999): 479–490.
67 See *Prosecutor v. Akayesu* decision, para. 30.
68 Ibid., para. 31.
69 Ibid., para. 32, which goes on to observe: "The Chamber notes the Accused's emphatic denial of facts which are not entirely within his knowledge"—in other words, the trial chamber discredited the accused's claim not to have been involved in the sexual violence *because* he issued a blanket claim that no such sexual violence occurred.
70 Mibenge, *Sex and International Tribunals.*
71 Which they decided in para. 126 in the affirmative (see Mibenge, *Sex and International Tribunals*)
72 I read this from the amount of time spent analyzing rape, particularly justifying the inclusion of the charge and the ability to convict someone of rape on a superior responsibility theory. For an example of the case being treated controversially, see Chile Eboe-Osuji, "Rape as Genocide: Some Questions Arising," *Journal of Genocide Research* 9(2) (2007): 251–273.
73 See *Prosecutor v. Akayesu* decision, paras. 10A, 429, 447, 686, 688; MacKinnon, "Defining Rape Internationally"; Askin, "Gender Crimes Jurisprudence."

74 *Prosecutor v. Akayesu* decision, count 12, paras. 487–488; Ilias Bantekas, "The Contemporary Law of Superior Responsibility," *American Journal of International Law* 93(3) (1999): 573–595; Nicole Laviolette, "Commanding Rape: Sexual Violence, Command Responsibility, and the Prosecution of Superiors by the International Criminal Tribunals for the Former Yugoslavia and Rwanda," *Canadian Yearbook of International Law* 36 (1998): 93–150.

75 See, e.g., Suzanne Chenault, "And since *Akayesu*—the Development of ICTR Jurisprudence on Gender Crimes: A Comparison of *Akayesu* and *Muhimana*," *New England Journal of International and Comparative Law* 14(2) (2008): 221–238; Allison T. C. Milne, "Prosecuting Cases of Gender Violence in the International Criminal Tribunal for Rwanda," *Buffalo Human Rights Law Review* 11 (2005): 107–128.

76 *Prosecutor v. Akayesu* decision, para. 431.

77 Ibid., paras. 36, 445.

78 See, e.g., African Rights, *Rwanda—Not So Innocent*; Sharlach, "Rape as Genocide"; Jones, "Gender and Genocide in Rwanda."

79 *Prosecutor v. Akayesu* decision, paras. 36, 273, 387, 389, 437–438, 732.

80 See, e.g., general discussions in Nira Yuval-Davis, "Women and the Biological Reproduction of 'the Nation'" *Women's Studies International Forum* 19(1) (1996): 17–24; Snyder et al., "On the Battleground of Women's Bodies"; Sjoberg and Peet, "A(nother) Dark Side." Referring specifically to Rwanda, see, e.g., Alison, "Wartime Sexual Violence"; Christopher W. Mullins, "'He Would Kill Me with His Penis': Genocidal Rape in Rwanda as a State Crime," *Critical Criminology* 17(1) (2009): 15–33.

81 See, e.g., discussion in Sjoberg and Peet, "A(nother) Dark Side."

82 *Prosecutor v. Akayesu* decision, paras. 597, 599, 687, 688; for a theoretical expansion of this concept, see Sjoberg, "Gender/Violence."

83 See, e.g., discussions in *Prosecutor v. Akayesu* decision, paras. 225, 226, 392, 507, and especially 423, 430, 431.

84 Ibid., para. 423.

85 Ibid.

86 Ibid., para. 421.

87 Ibid., para. 423.

88 Ibid., para. 430.

89 Ibid.

90 Ibid., para. 431.

91 Ibid., para. 421, where sex is a noun for sex organ.

92 Ibid.

93 See, e.g., discussion in Nicola Henry, "Witness to Rape: The Limits and Potential of International War Crimes Trials for Victims of Wartime Sexual Violence," *International Journal of Transitional Justice* 3(1) (2009): 114–134.

94 Discussed in Baaz and Stern, *Sexual Violence as a Weapon of War?*, ch.2.

95 Ibid.

96 For example, I find more than 100,000 pages of testimony and motions in the *Nyiramasuhuko* case, more than 24,000 scholarly articles addressing the case directly, and more than 12,000 results on a normal Google search. For the *Akayesu* case, I find thousands of pages of court proceedings, more than 26,000 Google results, and almost 2,000 scholarly articles addressing the case directly.

97 By inserting the word "internationalized" here, I mean to highlight that most of the court proceedings about the Rwandan genocide happened in Rwanda, both in traditional courts and in various different structures that have been constructed over the years. See, e.g., discussion in Carla J. Ferstman, "Domestic Trials for Genocide and Crimes against Humanity: The Example of Rwanda," *African Journal of International and Comparative Law* 9(4) (1997): 857–877; Phil Clark, *The Gacaca Courts, Post-Genocide Justice and Reconciliation in Rwanda: Justice without Lawyers* (Cambridge, UK: Cambridge University Press, 2010).

98 See, for example, the discussion of Croatian vicims in Zarkov, "The Body of the Other Man."

99 See, as an exemplar, Russell-Brown, "Rape as an Act of Genocide."

100 See, e.g., discussion in Sjoberg and Gentry, *Mothers, Monsters, Whores*; for different perspectives, see, e.g., Buss, "Rethinking 'Rape as a Weapon of War'"; Irina Anderson, "Gender, Shame, and Sexual Violence: The Voices of Witnesses and Court Members and War Crimes Tribunals," *Journal of Sexual Aggression* 20(2) (2014): 250–252. Here, by "hypervisibility," I mean a combination of overcoverage/overattention and sensationalization.

101 See, e.g., discussion of the Democratic Republic of Congo conflict in chapter 3.

INDEX

ABOUT THE AUTHOR

Laura Sjoberg is Associate Professor of Political Science at the University of Florida. She is the author of several books, including *Gendering Global Conflict* and, with Caron Gentry, *Beyond Mothers, Monsters, and Whores.*

Lightning Source UK Ltd.
Milton Keynes UK
UKOW01f2234080117

291595UK00006B/131/P